Network and Communication Technology Innovations for Web and IT Advancement

Ghazi I. Alkhatib
Princess Sumaya University for Technology, Jordan

Information Science
REFERENCE

Managing Director:	Lindsay Johnston
Editorial Director:	Joel Gamon
Book Production Manager:	Jennifer Yoder
Publishing Systems Analyst:	Adrienne Freeland
Assistant Acquisitions Editor:	Kayla Wolfe
Typesetter:	Alyson Zerbe
Cover Design:	Nick Newcomer

Published in the United States of America by
Information Science Reference (an imprint of IGI Global)
701 E. Chocolate Avenue
Hershey PA 17033
Tel: 717-533-8845
Fax: 717-533-8661
E-mail: cust@igi-global.com
Web site: http://www.igi-global.com

Library of Congress Cataloging-in-Publication Data

Network and communication technology innovations for web and IT advancement / Ghazi I. Alkhatib, editor.
    pages cm
  Includes bibliographical references and index.
  Summary: "This book presents studies on trends, developments, and methods on information technology advancements through network and communication technology, bringing together integrated approaches for communication technology and usage for web and IT advancements"-- Provided by publisher.
  ISBN 978-1-4666-2157-2 (hardcover) -- ISBN 978-1-4666-2159-6 (print & perpetual access) -- ISBN 978-1-4666-2158-9 (ebook) (print) 1. Computer networks. I. Alkhatib, Ghazi, 1947-
  TK5105.5.N4646 2013
  621.39'81--dc23
                                    2012019628

British Cataloguing in Publication Data
A Cataloguing in Publication record for this book is available from the British Library.

The views expressed in this book are those of the authors, but not necessarily of the publisher.

Table of Contents

Section 2
Searching and Mining of Web Information

Section 3
Web-Based Applications

Section 4
Web Engineering Network and Communication Platforms

Detailed Table of Contents

Section 1
Ontology, Semantics, and Web Services

Chapter 1

Linda Anticoli, Università di Udine, Italy
Elio Toppano, Università di Udine, Italy

This article addresses the issue of cultural influence in ontology design and reuse. The main assumption is that an ontology is not only a socio-technical artefact but also a cultural artefact. It contains embedded assumptions, core values, points of view, beliefs, thought patterns, etc. Based on results already found in several design fields the authors formulate some preliminary hypotheses about the possible relationships existing between culture and features of design process and produced ontology. A critical and qualitative analysis of six collaborative design systems has been performed to test some of the hypotheses, confirming some of the findings. The authors argue that a "culture aware" attitude may be of great importance for supporting the processes of cross cultural collaborative ontology design and the internalization and localization of these kinds of artefacts.

Chapter 2

Mohammad Ali H. Eljinini, Isra University, Jordan

In this paper, the need for the right information for patients with chronic diseases is elaborated, followed by some scenarios of how the semantic web can be utilised to retrieve useful and precise information by stakeholders. In previous work, the author has demonstrated the automation of knowledge acquisition from the current web is becoming an important step towards this goal. The aim was twofold; first to learn what types of information exist in chronic disease-related websites, and secondly how to extract and structure such information into machine understandable form. It has been shown that these websites exhibit many common concepts which resulted in the construction of the ontology to guide in extracting information for new unseen websites. Also, the study has resulted in the development of a platform for information extraction that utilises the ontology. Continuous work has opened many issues which are disussed in this paper. While further work is still needed, the experiments to date have shown encouraging results.

Chapter 3

Mariam Abed Mostafa Abed, German University in Cairo, Egypt

This paper tests the ability of the Web Service Modeling Ontology (WSMO) and the Web Service Modeling eXecution environment (WSMX) to support the Semantic Web Services technology, and automate the process of web service discovery, selection and invocation. First, it introduced web services and their limitations that were overcome in the vision of the Semantic Web Services technology. Then a Semantic Web Service (SWS) was built on top of WSMO to access the publications of the German University in Cairo (GUC), and was registered to WSMX. To test the validity to the claim, a service request to access the publications of the GUC was sent to WSMX and the process followed by WSMX was investigated. Furthermore, the discussion added a suggestion that would enhance the transparency between the Semantic Web and WSMO-WSMX initiatives.

Chapter 4

Wan Nurhayati Wan Ab. Rahman, Universiti Putra Malaysia, Malaysia
Farid Meziane, University of Salford, UK

The development, registration, discovery, and invocation of quality Web services are vital for the successful implementation of applications using Web services. Considerable research focuses on quality for Web services. Unfortunately, current research on Quality of Service (QoS) for Web services is concentrated on service users and the implementation stage. This research highlights the importance of incorporating QoS at the design and development stages; the authors propose the introduction of QoS at the same time as functional requirements. However, Web Service Description Language (WSDL) describes the functional elements of a Web service, and QoS is significant for this description. Therefore, the authors propose an extension to the WSDL through a generic QoS metamodel, incorporating QoS specifications into the functionalities. This paper begins by defining the required QoS specifications for the development of quality Web services and explores the potential of the Unified Modeling Language as a technique and notation to specify QoS. To properly integrate QoS in the design, the authors propose extensions to the existing UML QoS profile. The paper concludes with the evaluation of the proposed framework and summarises its advantages.

Chapter 5

Bassam Al-Shargabi, Al-Isra University, Jordan
Osama Al-haj Hassan, Al-Isra University, Jordan
Alia Sabri, Applied Science University, Jordan
Asim El Sheikh, Arab Academy for Banking and Financial Sciences, Jordan

Software is gradually becoming more built by composing web services to support enterprise applications integration; thus, making the process of composing web services a significant topic. The Quality of Service (QoS) in web service composition plays a crucial role. As such, it is important to guarantee, monitor, and enforce QoS and ability to handle failures during execution. Therefore, an urgent need exists for a dynamic Web Service Composition and Execution (WSCE) framework based on QoS constraints. A WSCE broker is designed to maintain the following function: intelligent web service selection decisions based on local QoS for individual web service or global QoS based selection for composed web services, execution tracking, and adaptation. A QoS certifier controlled by the UDDI registry is proposed to verify the claimed QoS attributes. The authors evaluate the composition plan along with performance time analysis.

Section 2
Searching and Mining of Web Information

Chapter 6

This paper proposes probabilistic models for social media mining based on the multiple attributes of social media content, bloggers, and links. The authors present a unique social media classification framework that computes the normalized document-topic matrix. After comparing the results for social media classification on real-world data, the authors find that the model outperforms the other techniques in terms of overall precision and recall. The results demonstrate that additional information contained in social media attributes can improve classification and retrieval results.

Chapter 7

A traditional crawler picks up a URL, retrieves the corresponding page and extracts various links, adding them to the queue. A deep Web crawler, after adding links to the queue, checks for forms. If forms are present, it processes them and retrieves the required information. Various techniques have been proposed for crawling deep Web information, but much remains undiscovered. In this paper, the authors analyze and compare important deep Web information crawling techniques to find their relative limitations and advantages. To minimize limitations of existing deep Web crawlers, a novel architecture is proposed based on QIIIEP specifications (Sharma & Sharma, 2009). The proposed architecture is cost effective and has features of privatized search and general search for deep Web data hidden behind html forms.

Chapter 8

This article introduces intelligent watermarking scheme to protect Web images from attackers who try to counterfeit the copyright to damage the rightful ownership. Using secret signs and logos that are embedded within the digital images, the technique can investigate technically the ownership claim. Also, the nature of each individual image is taken into consideration which gives more reliable results. The colour channel used was chosen depending on the value of its standard deviation to compromise between robustness and invisibility of the watermarks. Several types of test images, logos, attacks and evaluation metrics were used to examine the performance of the techniques used. Subjective and objective tests were used to check visually and mathematically the solidity and weakness of the used scheme.

Chapter 9

Faisal Alkhateeb, Yarmouk University, Jordan

Amal Alzubi, Yarmouk University, Jordan

Iyad Abu Doush, Yarmouk University, Jordan

Shadi Aljawarneh, Isra University, Jordan

Eslam Al Maghayreh, Yarmouk University, Jordan

In this paper, the authors propose a novel approach to search and retrieve authoring information from online authoring databases. The proposed approach combines keywords and semantic-based methods. In this approach, the user can retrieve such information considering some specified keywords and ignore how the internal semantic search is being processed. The keywords entered by the user are internally converted by the system to a semantic query that will be used to search the requested information. The authors then use (X)HTML-based templates for the automatic construction of BibTeX elements from the query results.

Chapter 10

Petr Aksenov, Hasselt University, Belgium

Kris Luyten, Hasselt University, Belgium

Karin Coninx, Hasselt University, Belgium

Localisation is a standard feature in many mobile applications today, and there are numerous techniques for determining a user's location both indoors and outdoors. The provided location information is often organised in a format tailored to a particular localisation system's needs and restrictions, making the use of several systems in one application cumbersome. The presented approach models the details of localisation systems and uses this model to create a unified view on localisation in which special attention is paid to uncertainty coming from different localisation conditions and to its presentation to the user. The work discusses technical considerations, challenges and issues of the approach, and reports on a user study on the acceptance of a mobile application's behaviour reflecting the approach. The results of the study show the suitability of the approach and reveal users' preference toward automatic and informed changes they experienced while using the application.

Section 3
Web-Based Applications

Chapter 11

Khadhir Bekki, Ibn Khaldoune University, Algeria

Hafida Belachir, Boudiaf University, Algeria

This article proposes a flexible way in business process modeling and managing. Today, business process needs to be more flexible and adaptable. The regulations and policies in organizations, as origins of change, are often expressed in terms of business rules. The ECA (Event-condition-action) rule is a popular way to incorporate flexibility into a process design. To raise the flexibility in the business processes, the authors consider governing any business activity through ECA rules based on business rules. For adaptability, the separation of concerns supports adaptation in several ways. To cope with flexibility and adaptability, the authors propose a new multi concern rule based model. For each concern, each business rule is formalized using their CECAPENETE formalism (Concern -Event-Condition-Action-Post condition- check Execution- Number of check -Else-Trigger-else Event). Then, the rules based process is translated into a graph of rules that is analyzed in terms of relations between concerns, reliably and flexibility.

Chapter 12

Bassam Al-Shargabi, Isra University, Jordan
Fekry Olayah, Isra University, Jordan
Waseem AL-Romimah, University of Science and Technology, Yemen

In this paper, an experimental study was conducted on three techniques for Arabic text classification. These techniques are Support Vector Machine (SVM) with Sequential Minimal Optimization (SMO), Naïve Bayesian (NB), and J48. The paper assesses the accuracy for each classifier and determines which classifier is more accurate for Arabic text classification based on stop words elimination. The accuracy for each classifier is measured by Percentage split method (holdout), and K-fold cross validation methods, along with the time needed to classify Arabic text. The results show that the SMO classifier achieves the highest accuracy and the lowest error rate, and shows that the time needed to build the SMO model is much lower compared to other classification techniques.

Chapter 13

Basel Magableh, Trinity College Dublin, Ireland
Stephen Barrett, Trinity College Dublin, Ireland

Anticipating context changes using a model-based approach requires a formal procedure for analysing and modelling context-dependent functionality and stable description of the architecture which supports dynamic decision-making and architecture evolution. This article demonstrates the capabilities of the context-oriented component-based application model-driven architecture (COCA-MDA) to support the development of self-adaptive applications; the authors describe a state-of-the-art case study and evaluate the development effort involved in adopting the COCA-MDA in constructing the application. An intensive analysis of the application requirements simplified the process of modelling the application's behavioural model; therefore, instead of modelling several variation models, the developers modelled an extra-functionality model. COCA-MDA reduces the development effort because it maintains a clear separation of concerns and employs a decomposition mechanism to produce a context-oriented component model which decouples the applications' core functionality from the context-dependent functionality. Estimating the MDA approach's productivity can help the software developers select the best MDA-based methodology from the available solutions. Thus, counting the source line of code is not adequate for evaluating the development effort of the MDA-based methodology. Quantifying the maintenance adjustment factor of the new, adapted, and reused code is a better estimate of the development effort of the MDA approaches.

Chapter 14

Mayayuki Shinohara, Kanagawa Institute of Technology, Japan

Akira Hattori, Kanagawa Institute of Technology, Japan

Shigenori Ioroi, Kanagawa Institute of Technology, Japan

Hiroshi Tanaka, Kanagawa Institute of Technology, Japan

Haruo Hayami, Kanagawa Institute of Technology, Japan

Hidekazu Fujioka, Morinosato 4-Chrome Association in Atsugi City, Japan

Yuichi Harada, Morinosato 4-Chrome Association in Atsugi City, Japan

This paper presents a hazard/crime incident information sharing system using cell phones. Cell phone penetration is nearly 100% among adults in Japan, and they function as a telecommunication tool as well as a Global Positioning System (GPS) and camera. Open source software (Apache, Postfix, and MySQL) is installed on a system server, and together with the information service provided by Google Maps, are used to satisfy system requirements for the local community. Conventional systems deliver information to all people registered in the same block, even if an incident occurred far from their house. The key feature of the proposed system is that the distribution range of the hazard notification e-mail messages is determined by the geometrical distance from the incident location to the residence of each registered member. The proposed system applies not only to conventional cell phones but also smart phones, which are rapidly becoming popular in Japan. The new system functionality has been confirmed by a trial using members of the local community. System operation began after the successful trial and a training meeting for the local residents. System design, verification results, and operating status are described in this paper.

Section 4
Web Engineering Network and Communication Platforms

Chapter 15

Wael Toghuj, Isra University, Jordan

Ghazi Alkhatib, Princess Sumaya University for Technology, Jordan

Digital communication systems are an important part of modern society, and they rely on computers and networks to achieve critical tasks. Critical tasks require systems with a high level of reliability that can provide continuous correct operations. This paper presents a new algorithm for data encoding and decoding using a two-dimensional code that can be implemented in digital communication systems, electronic memories (DRAMs and SRAMs), and web engineering. The developed algorithms correct three errors in codeword and detect four, reaching an acceptable performance level. The program that is based on these algorithms enables the modeling of error detection and correction processes, optimizes the redundancy of the code, monitors the decoding procedures, and defines the speed of execution. The performance of the derived code improves error detection and correction over the classical code and with less complexity. Several extensible applications of the algorithms are also given.

Chapter 16

Maytham Safar, Kuwait University, Kuwait

Hasan Al-Hamadi, Kuwait National Petroleum Company, Kuwait

Dariush Ebrahimi, Kuwait University, Kuwait

Wireless sensor networks (WSN) have emerged in many applications as a platform to collect data and monitor a specified area with minimal human intervention. The initial deployment of WSN sensors forms a network that consists of randomly distributed devices/nodes in a known space. Advancements have been made in low-power micro-electronic circuits, which have allowed WSN to be a feasible platform for many applications. However, there are two major concerns that govern the efficiency, availability, and functionality of the network—power consumption and fault tolerance. This paper introduces a new algorithm called Power Efficient Cluster Algorithm (PECA). The proposed algorithm reduces the power consumption required to setup the network. This is accomplished by effectively reducing the total number of radio transmission required in the network setup (deployment) phase. As a fault tolerance approach, the algorithm stores information about each node for easier recovery of the network should any node fail. The proposed algorithm is compared with the Self Organizing Sensor (SOS) algorithm; results show that PECA consumes significantly less power than SOS.

Chapter 17

Lu Ge, Loughborough University, UK

Gaojie J. Chen, Loughborough University, UK

Jonathon. A. Chambers, Loughborough University, UK

The implementation of cooperative diversity with relays has advantages over point-to-point multiple-input multiple-output (MIMO) systems, in particular, overcoming correlated paths due to small inter-element spacing. A simple transmitter with one antenna may exploit cooperative diversity or space time coding gain through distributed relays. In this paper, similar distributed transmission is considered with the golden code, and the authors propose a new strategy for relay selection, called the maximum-mean selection policy, for distributed transmission with the full maximum likelihood (ML) decoding and sphere decoding (SD) based on a wireless relay network. This strategy performs a channel strength tradeoff at every relay node to select the best two relays for transmission. It improves on the established one-sided selection strategy of maximum-minimum policy. Simulation results comparing the bit error rate (BER) based on different detectors and a scheme without relay selection, with the maximum-minimum and maximum-mean selection schemes confirm the performance advantage of relay selection. The proposed strategy yields the best performance of the three methods.

Chapter 18

Michał Wódczak, Telcordia Technologies, Poland

The current efforts across industry and academia are to develop new paradigms that enable ubiquitous on-demand service provision. This aim may be achievable because of the envisaged deployment of cutting-edge technologies such as cooperative transmission. However, a real advancement is only attainable when autonomic system design principles are taken into account. Looking at the concept of the Relay Enhanced Cell, one may come across commonalities with Mobile Ad-hoc Networks. Especially in Local Area scenarios, Base Stations seem to resemble advanced Access Points, while fixed and movable

Relay Nodes might be replaced by powerful mobile User Terminals. On top of it, Generic Autonomic Network Architecture would help accommodate the fact that network devices may expose autonomic cooperative behaviors, allowing them to play certain roles. Finally, such a network must interact with Operations Support System deployed by the network operator for uninterrupted, continued operation.

In this paper, the authors present a description of a new Web search engine model, the compressed index-query (CIQ) Web search engine model. This model incorporates two bit-level compression layers implemented at the back-end processor (server) side, one layer resides after the indexer acting as a second compression layer to generate a double compressed index (index compressor), and the second layer resides after the query parser for query compression (query compressor) to enable bit-level compressed index-query search. The data compression algorithm used in this model is the Hamming codes-based data compression (HCDC) algorithm, which is an asymmetric, lossless, bit-level algorithm permits CIQ search. The different components of the new Web model are implemented in a prototype CIQ test tool (CIQTT), which is used as a test bench to validate the accuracy and integrity of the retrieved data and evaluate the performance of the proposed model. The test results demonstrate that the proposed CIQ model reduces disk space requirements and searching time by more than 24%, and attains a 100% agreement when compared with an uncompressed model.

Preface

INTRODUCTION

This is the sixth book of the series entitled Advances in Information Technology and Web Engineering containing updated articles published in volume VI (2011) of the *International Journal of Information Technology and Web Engineering*, with the title of "Network and Communication Technology Innovations for Web and IT Advancement." This preface reports on current and future trends in information technology and Web engineering pertaining in particular to emerging technology platforms that facilitate networking and communication between organizations and enterprises. These include mainly network and data virtualization and its emerging platform of cloud computing, Internet operation system (OS), security issues, and data transfer quality issues. Finally, the preface provides a discussion on current vendors supporting these new emerging information technologies. In addition, several suggestions on application scenarios, challenges, and research directions are interspersed throughout the preface based on these emerging trends.

Virtualization allows isolated and disparate physical resources, such as servers, operating systems, applications, or storage devices to be integrated and seen as multiple virtual logical resources; or vice versa treats multiple physical resources as a single virtual logical resource. It hides the physical characteristics of these computing resources, which in turn simplifies access and interactions among these resources and users. The new multicore systems allow virtualization at the desktop reducing organizations' cost of ownership, and increasing operations' reliability and flexibility. On the hand, network and data virtualization are made possible by cloud computing environment. As an indication of the future virtualization deployment, a survey reports that respondents ranked virtualization technologies as follows: server, storage, application, desktop, network, and I/O virtualizations (McTigue, 2012).

As data and information access had moved from GUI-Window based to Internet browsers, enhancing functionality of browsers became a necessity, thus the development of the term Internet OS. Implementing these new technologies to link enterprise resources raised two issues: security and data quality transfer. The preface provides current discussions and some future suggested solutions to these two issues.

VIRTUALIZATION

Here are some basic definitions before starting the discussion on virtualization (Waters, 2012):

- **Hypervisor:** The most basic virtualization component. It's the software that decouples the operating system and applications from their physical resources. A hypervisor has its own kernel and it's installed directly on the hardware, or "bare metal." It is, almost literally, inserted between the hardware and the OS.
- **Virtual Machine (VM):** A self-contained operating environment—software that works with, but is independent of, a host operating system. In other words, it's a platform-independent software implementation of a CPU that runs compiled code. A Java virtual machine, for example, will run any Java-based program (more or less). The VMs must be written specifically for the OSes on which they run. Virtualization technologies are sometimes called dynamic virtual machine software.
- **Paravirtualization:** A type of virtualization in which the entire OS runs on top of the hypervisor and communicates with it directly, typically resulting in better performance. The kernels of both the OS and the hypervisor must be modified, however, to accommodate this close interaction. A paravirtualized Linux operating system, for example, is specifically optimized to run in a virtual environment. *Full virtualization*, in contrast, presents an abstract layer that intercepts all calls to physical resources.
  Paravirtualization relies on a virtualized subset of the x86 architecture. Recent chip enhancement developments by both Intel and AMD are helping to support virtualization schemes that do not require modified operating systems. Intel's "Vanderpool" chip-level virtualization technology was one of the first of these innovations. AMD's "Pacifica" extension provides additional virtualization support. Both are designed to allow simpler virtualization code, and the potential for better performance of fully virtualized environments.

Gartner Group defines Virtualization as "the abstraction of IT resources that masks the physical nature and boundaries of those resources from resource users. An IT resource can be a server, a client, storage, networks, applications or OSs. Essentially, any IT building block can potentially be abstracted from resource users. Abstraction enables better flexibility in how different parts of an IT stack are delivered, thus enabling better efficiency (through consolidation or variable usage) and mobility (shifting which resources are used behind the abstraction interface), and even alternative sourcing (shifting the service provider behind the abstraction interface, such as in cloud computing). A key to virtualization is being able to effectively describe what is required from the resource in an independent, abstracted, and standardized method. In essence, cloud computing is about abstracting service implementation away from the consumers of the services by using service-based interfaces (i.e., the interface for cloud-computing services is about virtualization—an abstraction interface). To a provider, virtualization creates the flexibility to deliver resources to meet service needs in very flexible, elastic, and rapidly changing manner. The tools that make that happen could be virtual machines, virtual LANs (VLANs), or grid/parallel programming." (gartner.com, 2012)

Others provide eight definitions for virtualization (Murphy, 2012). The preface classifies these definitions into internal, external virtualization, and hybrid strategies.

Internal Virtualization

Hardware Virtualization

Hardware virtualization is very similar in concept to OS/Platform virtualization, and to some degree is required for OS virtualization to occur. Hardware virtualization breaks up pieces and locations of physical hardware into independent segments and manages those segments as separate, individual components. Although they fall into different classifications, both symmetric and asymmetric multiprocessing are examples of hardware virtualization. In both instances, the process requesting CPU time isn't aware which processor it's going to run on; it just requests CPU time from the OS scheduler and the scheduler takes the responsibility of allocating processor time. Another example of hardware virtualization is "slicing": isolating specific portions of the system to run in a "walled garden," such as allocating a fixed 25% of CPU resources to bulk encryption. If there are no processes that need to crunch numbers on the CPU for block encryption, then that 25% of the CPU will go unutilized. If too many processes need mathematical computations at once and require more than 25%, they will be queued and run as a FIFO buffer because the CPU isn't allowed to give out more than 25% of its resources to encryption. Asymmetric multiprocessing is a form of pre-allocation virtualization where certain tasks are only run on certain CPUs. In contrast, symmetric multiprocessing is a form of dynamic allocation, where CPUs are interchangeable and used as needed by any part of the management system. Pre-allocation virtualization is perfect for very specific hardware tasks, such as offloading functions to a highly optimized, single-purpose chip. However, pre-allocation of commodity hardware can cause artificial resource shortages if the allocated chunk is underutilized. Dynamic allocation virtualization is a more standard approach and typically offers greater benefit when compared to pre-allocation. For true virtual service provisioning, dynamic resource allocation is important because it allows complete hardware management and control for resources as needed; virtual resources can be allocated as long as hardware resources are still available. The negative side of dynamic allocation implementations is that they typically do not provide full control over the dynamicity, leading to processes which can consume all available resources.

Operating System Virtualization

The most prevalent form of virtualization today, virtual operating systems (or virtual machines), is quickly becoming a core component of the IT infrastructure. Virtual machines are typically full implementations of standard operating systems, such as Windows Vista or RedHat Enterprise Linux, running simultaneously on the same physical hardware. Virtual Machine Managers (VMMs) manage each virtual machine individually; each OS instance is unaware that 1) it's virtual and 2) that other virtual operating systems are (or may be) running at the same time. Companies like Microsoft, VMware, Intel, and AMD are leading the way in breaking the physical relationship between an operating system and its native hardware, extending this paradigm into the data center. As the primary driving force, data center consolidation is bringing the benefits of virtual machines to the mainstream market, allowing enterprises to reduce the number of physical machines in their data centers without reducing the number of underlying applications. This trend ultimately saves enterprises money on hardware, co-location fees, rack space, power, and cable management.

Storage Virtualization

Storage virtualization can be broken up into two general classes: block virtualization and file virtualization. Block virtualization is best summed up by Storage Area Network (SAN) and Network Attached Storage (NAS) technologies: distributed storage networks that appear to be single physical devices. Under the hood, SAN devices themselves typically implement another form of Storage Virtualization: RAID. iSCSI is another very common and specific virtual implementation of block virtualization, allowing an operating system or application to map a virtual block device, such as a mounted drive, to a local network adapter (software or hardware) instead of a physical drive controller. File virtualization moves the virtual layer up into the more human-view file and directory structure level. Most file virtualization technologies appear in front of storage networks and monitors which files and directories reside on which storage devices, maintaining global mappings of file locations. When a request is made to read a file, the user may think this file is statically located on their personal remote drive; however, the file virtualization machine knows that the file is actually located on a server in a data center across the globe at a different website location. File-level virtualization obscures the static virtual location pointer of a file from the physical location, allowing the back-end network to remain dynamic. If the IP address for the server has to change, or the connection needs to be re-routed to another data center entirely, only the virtual machine's location map needs to be updated, not every user that wants to access their physical drive.

External Virtualization

Application Server Virtualization

Application Server Virtualization has been around since the first load balancer, which explains why "application virtualization" is often used as a synonym for advanced load balancing. The core concept of application server virtualization is best seen with a reverse proxy load balancer: an appliance or service that provides access to many different application services transparently. In a typical deployment, a reverse proxy will host a virtual interface accessible to the end user on the "front end." On the "back end," the reverse proxy will load balance a number of different servers and applications such as a web server. The virtual interface—often referred to as a Virtual IP or VIP—is exposed to the outside world, represents itself as the actual web server, and manages the connections to and from the web server as needed. This enables the load balancer to manage multiple web servers or applications as a single instance, providing a more secure and robust topology than one allowing users direct access to individual web servers. This is a one:many (one-to-many) virtualization representation: one server is presented to the world, hiding the availability of multiple servers behind a reverse proxy appliance. Application Server Virtualization can be applied to any (and all) types of application deployments and architectures, from front-ending application logic servers to distributing the load between multiple web server platforms, and even to the back-end operations in the data center to the data and storage tiers with database virtualization.

Application Virtualization

While they may sound very similar, Application Server and Application Virtualization are two completely different concepts. The technology is exactly the same, only the name has changed to make it more IT-PC. Softgrid by Microsoft is an excellent example of deploying application virtualization. Although you may be running Microsoft Word 2007 locally on your laptop, the binaries, personal information, and running state are all stored on, managed, and delivered by Softgrid. Your local laptop provides the CPU and RAM required to run the software, but nothing is installed locally on your own machine. Other types of Application Virtualization include Microsoft Terminal Services and browser-based applications. All of these implementations depend on the virtual application running locally and the management and application logic running remotely.

Management (Security) Virtualization

If you implement separate passwords for your root/administrator accounts between your mail and web servers, and your mail administrators don't know the password to the web server and vise versa, then you've deployed management virtualization in its most basic form. The paradigm can be extended down to segmented administration roles on one platform or box, which is where segmented administration becomes "virtual." User and group policies in Microsoft Windows XP, 2003, and Vista are an excellent example of virtualized administration rights as this scenario describes: Alice may be in the backup group for the 2003 Active Directory server, but not in the admin group. She has read access to all the files she needs to back up, but she doesn't have rights to install new files or software. Although she is logging into the same sever that the true administrator is logs into, her user experience differs from the administrator. Management virtualization is also a key concept in overall data center management. It's critical that the network administrators have full access to all the infrastructure gear, such as core routers and switches, but that they not have admin-level access to servers.

Network Virtualization

Network virtualization may be the most ambiguous, specific definition of virtualization. For brevity, the scope of this discussion is relegated to what amounts to virtual IP management and segmentation. A simple example of IP virtualization is a VLAN: a single Ethernet port may support multiple virtual connections from multiple IP addresses and networks, but they are virtually segmented using VLAN tags. Each virtual IP connection over this single physical port is independent and unaware of others' existence, but the switch is aware of each unique connection and manages each one independently. Another example is virtual routing tables: typically, a routing table and an IP network port share a 1:1 relationship, even though that single port may host multiple virtual interfaces (such as VLANs or the "eth0:1" virtual network adapters supported by Linux). The single routing table will contain multiple routes for each virtual connection, but they are still managed in a single table. Virtual routing tables change that paradigm into a one:many relationship, where any single physical interface can maintain multiple routing tables, each with multiple entries. This provides the interface with the ability to bring up (and tear down) routing services on the fly for one network without interrupting other services and routing tables on that same interface.

Hybrid Virtualization

Service Virtualization

Finally, the macro definition of virtualization: service virtualization or *enterprise virtualization*. Service virtualization is consolidation of all of the above definitions into one catch-all catchphrase. Service virtualization connects all of the components utilized in delivering an application over the network, and includes the process of making all pieces of an application work together regardless of where those pieces physically reside. This is why service virtualization is typically used as an enabler for application availability. For example, a web application typically has many parts: the user-facing HTML; the application server that processes user input; the SOA gears that coordinate service and data availability between each component; the database back-end for user, application, and SOA data; the network that delivers the application components; and the storage network that stores the application code and data. Service virtualization allows each one of the pieces to function independently and be "called up" as needed for the entire application to function properly. When we look deeper into these individual application components, we may see that the web server is load-balanced between 15 virtual machine operating systems, the SOA requests are pushed through any number of XML gateways on the wire, the database servers may be located in one of five global data centers, and so on. Service virtualization combines these independent pieces and presents them together to the user as a single, complete application. While Service virtualization may encompass all the current definitions of virtualization, it's by no means where IT will stop defining the term. With the pervasive and varied use of the word (as well as the technologies it refers to), a "final" definition for virtualization may never materialize.

Among the eight definitions presented above, the following deemed appropriate to this preface: application server virtualization, application virtualization, administrative virtualization, network virtualization, and storage virtualization. Finally, service virtualization is a hybrid approach of connecting one or more of the above definitions.

The preface provides a schematic view of the relationships between the eight definitions, as shown in Figure 1.

Figure 1. Classification of virtualization definitions

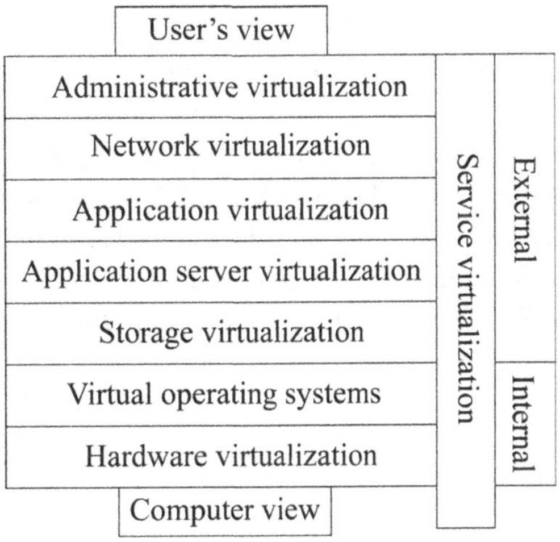

Internet OS

A clear definition of Internet OS could not be found. This preface reports on one view as presented in (O'Reilly, 2010).

Internet Operating System is an Information Operating System. Among many other functions, a traditional operating system coordinates access by applications to the underlying resources of the machine – things like the CPU, memory, disk storage, keyboard and screen. The operating system kernel schedules processes, allocates memory, manages interrupts from devices, handles exceptions, and generally makes it possible for multiple applications to share the same hardware.

As a result, it's easy to jump to the conclusion that "cloud computing" platforms like Amazon Web Services, Google App Engine, or Microsoft Azure, which provide developers with access to storage and computation, are the heart of the emerging Internet Operating System.

The underlying services accessed by applications today are not just device components and operating system features, but *data subsystems*: locations, social networks, indexes of web sites, speech recognition, image recognition, automated translation. It's easy to think that it's the sensors in your device – the touch screen, the microphone, the GPS, the magnetometer, the accelerometer – that are enabling their cool new functionality. But actually, these sensors are just inputs to massive data subsystems living in the cloud.

Increasingly, application developers don't do low-level image recognition, speech recognition, location lookup, social network management, and friend connect. They place high level function calls to data-rich platforms that provide these services.

The following sections provide a discussion on what new subsystems a "modern" Internet Operating System might contain.

Search

Because the volume of data to be managed is so large, because it is constantly changing, and because it is distributed across millions of networked systems, search proved to be the first great challenge of the Internet OS era. Cracking the search problem requires massive, ongoing crawling of the network, the construction of massive indexes, and complex algorithmic retrieval schemes to find the most appropriate results for a user query. Because of the complexity, only a few vendors have succeeded with web search, most notably Google and Microsoft. In addition to web search, there are many specialized types of media search. For example, any time you put a music CD into an internet-connected drive, it immediately looks up the track names in CDDB using a kind of fingerprint produced by the length and sequence of each of the tracks on the CD. Other types of music search, like the one used by cell phone applications like Shazam, look up songs by matching their actual acoustic fingerprint. Many of the search techniques developed for web pages depends on the rich implied semantics of linking, in which every link is a vote, and votes from authoritative sources are ranked more highly than others. This is an implicit user-contributed metadata that is not present when searching other types of content, such as digitized books. One can expect significant breakthroughs in search techniques for books, video, images, and sound to be a feature of the future evolution of the Internet OS.

Media Access

Just as a PC-era operating system has the capability to manage user-level constructs like files and directories as well as lower-level constructs like physical disk volumes and blocks, an Internet-era operating system must provide access to various types of media, such as web pages, music, videos, photos, e-books, office documents, presentations, downloadable applications, and more. Each of these media types requires some common technology infrastructure beyond specialized search:

- **Access Control:** Since not all information is freely available, managing access control – providing snippets rather than full sources, providing streaming but not downloads, recognizing authorized users and giving them a different result from unauthorized users – is a crucial feature of the Internet OS.
- **Caching:** Large media files benefit from being closer to their destination. A whole class of companies exist to provide Content Delivery Networks; these may survive as independent companies, or these services may ultimately be rolled up into the leading Internet OS companies similar to what Microsoft did when acquired or "embraced and extended" various technologies resulting in making Windows the dominant OS of the PC era.
- **Instrumentation and Analytics:** Because of the amount of investment at stake, an entire industry has grown up around web analytics and search engine optimization. At the same time, one can expect a similar wave of companies that instrument social media and mobile applications, as well as particular media types.

Communications

The internet is a communications network using, for example, email and chat. Now, with the widespread availability of VoIP, and mobile phone joining the "network of networks," voice and video communications are an increasingly important part of the communications subsystem.

Payment

Payment is another key subsystem of the Internet Operating System. Companies like Apple that have 150 million credit cards on file and a huge population of users accustomed to using their phones to buy songs, videos, applications, and now ebooks, are going to be in a prime position to turn today's phone into tomorrow's wallet.

Examples are PayPal and Google Checkout. PayPal obviously plays an important role as an internet payment subsystem that's already in wide use by developers. Their recent developer conference had over 2000 attendees. Their challenge is to make the transition from the web to mobile. On the other hand, Google Checkout has been a distant also-ran in web payments, but the Android Market has given it new prominence in mobile, and will eventually make it a major internet payment subsystem.

Advertising

Advertising has been the most successful business model on the web. While there are signs that e-commerce – buying everything from virtual goods to a lunchtime burrito – may be the bigger opportunity in mobile (and perhaps even in social media), there's no question that advertising will play a significant role.

Location

Location is the indispensible component of mobile apps. When a phone knows where its owner is, it can find your friends, find services nearby, and even better authenticate a transaction.

Maps and directions on the phone are intrinsically cloud services – unlike with dedicated GPS devices, there's not enough local storage to keep all the relevant maps on hand. But when turned into a cloud application, maps and directions can include other data, such as real-time traffic (indeed, traffic data collected from the very applications that are requesting traffic updates – a classic example of "collective intelligence" at work.)

Time

Time is an important dimension of data driven services – at least as important as location, but as yet less fully exploited. Calendars are one obvious application, but activity streams are also organized as timelines; stock charts link up news stories with raise or drops in price. Time stamps can also be used as a filter for other data types (as Google measures frequency of update in calculating search results, or as RSS feed or social activity stream)

Image and Speech Recognition

The Web as Platform is going to be dominated by data services built by network is effected by user-contributed data, is that increasingly; the data is contributed by sensors.

Government Data

Long before recent initiatives like <a href=http://data.govdata.gov, governments have been a key supplier of data for internet applications. Everything from weather, maps, satellite imagery, GPS positioning, and SEC filings to crime reports have played an important role in successful internet applications. Now, government is also a recipient of crowd sourced data from citizens. For example, FixMyStreet and SeeClickFix submit 311 reports to local governments – potholes that need filling, graffiti that needs repainting, streetlights that are out.

The Future of the Browser

While the claims that the browser itself is the new operating system are as misguided as the idea that it can be found solely in cloud infrastructure services, it is important to recognize that control over front end interfaces is at least as important as back-end services. Companies like Apple and Google that have substantial cloud services and a credible mobile platform play are in prime front seat in the platform wars of the next decade. But the browser, and with it control of the PC user experience, is also critical.

Security Issues

The National Institute of Standards and Technology (NIST) has issued the final version of its recommendations for securely configuring and using full computing virtualization technologies. The security recommendations are contained in the *Guide to Security for Full Virtualization Technologies* (NIST Special Publication (SP) 800-125). The draft report was issued for public comment in July 2010.

Virtualization adds a low-level software layer that allows multiple, even different operating systems and applications to run simultaneously on a host. "Full virtualization" provides a complete simulation of underlying computer hardware, enabling software to run without any modification. Because it helps maximize the use and flexibility of computing resources—multiple operating systems can run simultaneously on the same hardware—full virtualization is considered a key technology for cloud computing, but it introduces new issues for IT security.

For cloud computing systems in particular, full virtualization can increase operational efficiency because it can optimize computer workloads and adjust the number of servers in use to match demand, thereby conserving energy and information technology resources. The guide describes security concerns associated with full virtualization technologies for server and desktop virtualization and provides recommendations for addressing these concerns. Most existing recommended security practices also apply in virtual environments and the practices described in this document build on and assume the implementation of practices described in other NIST computer security publications.

The guide is intended for system administrators, security program managers, security engineers and anyone else involved in designing, deploying or maintaining full virtualization technologies. NIST SP 800-125 recommends organizations:

- Secure all elements of a full virtualization solution and maintain their security.
- Restrict and protect administrator access to the virtualization solution.
- Ensure that the hypervisor, the central program that runs the virtual environment, is properly secured.
- Carefully plan the security for a full virtualization solution before installing, configuring and deploying it.

However, full virtualization, where one or more OSs and the applications they contain are run on top of virtual hardware, has some negative security implications. Virtualization adds layers of technology, which can increase the security management burden by requiring additional security mechanisms. Also, combining many systems onto a single physical computer can cause a larger impact if a security compromise occurs. In addition, some virtualization systems allow ease of share of information between virtually integrated systems; this convenience can lead to the possibility of an attack vector if it is not carefully managed. In some cases, virtualized environments are quite dynamic, which makes creating and maintaining the necessary security boundaries more complex. Further issues may include the need to develop policies for backup, recovery, redundancy, change and configuration management, separation of duties, and least privilege.

Others security benefits to virtualization may include seamless business continuity and disaster recovery, single points of control over multiple virtualized systems, role-based access which facilitate the implementation of discretional access control and mandatory access control mechanisms, and additional auditing and logging capabilities for large infrastructures that would allow audit trails to be establish in association of a central repository of access logs.

In (Marko, 2012a), the author reported that in the 2012 *InformationWeek* "State of the Data Center Survey" shows that half of 256 respondents will have at least 50% of their production servers virtualized by the end of next year; 26% will have 75% or more. In response to budget allocation of maintenance vs innovation percentages in data center operation, one third of the budget is allocated to innovation (Marka, 2012b).

Major vendors of virtualization are VMware (VMware.com), Cisco (Cisco.com), and Juniper (juniper.net) with all offering their respective unique products.

Data Transfer Quality Issues

Cloud computing (CC) is becoming an important platform for providing computing services through data virtualization and other services. This issue is motivated by the frequent need to transfer and reconcile large data sets in virtualized and cloud environments. In CC environments, data is transferred as follows: back and forth between the enterprise and the cloud, intra-clouds, and inter-clouds. By using error correction code (ECC) schemes or algorithms, data is coded at the sending end and errors, if any, must be discovered and corrected at the recipient end in order to restore original data transferred. The research area compares different algorithm used in CC environment, such as Biff codes generation from invertible Bloom lookup tables (IBLTs), Reed Solomon, and Layer Interleaving. One other approach for ECC is based on an algorithm for data encoding and decoding using a two-dimensional code that can be implemented in digital communication systems (Toghuj & Alkhatib, 2011). To measure performance of ECC algorithms, the purported research uses parameters, such as setup for error rate, timing, thresholds, failure probabilities, and complexity level. The research should develop requirements engineering (RE) for the use of the new algorithm in different CC and virtualization environments. In the first stage, RE for deploying the algorithm in private clouds is needed. The algorithm will be packaged and deployed in the cloud to be downloaded by enterprises using private or hybrid cloud computing environments. In the second stage, intra-cloud computing environment RE should be developed. Finally, RE for inter-cloud computing data transfer should be specified. Private cloud is selected as the proposed implementation of CC platform for security purposes, while data virtualization is used as an information-as-a-service (IaaS) application for its handling of data virtualization features and functionality, such as real-time integration, data quality, transformation, caching, and modeling. This research paradigm is the ground breaking research for future research involving the development of a prototype in a private/hybrid CC environment using data virtualization applications.

Vendors

Major vendors for virtualization include large enterprise software vendors such as IBM, Sun, BEA Systems, HP, BMC, and CA; in addition to many standalone vendors.

Also ERP vendors are providing services for migrating ERP systems from tradition processing environment to the virtual environment, such as SAP OS/DB migration of SAP from HP-UX to VCE Vblock Systems running x86/Red Hat Linux.

In the next list, the top 10 vendors are exposed (Hess, 2010).

1. **VMware:** VMware dominates the server virtualization market. Its domination doesn't stop with its commercial product, vSphere. VMware also dominates the desktop-level virtualization market and perhaps even the free server virtualization market with its VMware Server product. VMware remains in the dominant spot due to its innovations, strategic partnerships and rock-solid products.

2. **Citrix:** Citrix was once the lone wolf of application virtualization, but now it also owns the world's most-used cloud vendor software: Xen (the basis for its commercial XenServer). Amazon uses Xen for its Elastic Compute Cloud (EC2) services. So do Rackspace, Carpathia, SoftLayer and 1and1 for their cloud offerings. On the corporate side, it includes Bechtel, SAP and TESCO.

3. **Oracle:** Oracle acquisition of Sun Microsystems now makes it an impressive virtualization player. Additionally, Oracle owns an operating system (Sun Solaris), multiple virtualization software solutions (Solaris Zones, LDoms and xVM) and server hardware (SPARC).

4. **Microsoft:** Microsoft came up with the only non-Linux hypervisor, Hyper-V, to compete in a tight server virtualization market that VMware currently dominates. Not easily outdone in the data center space, Microsoft offers attractive licensing for its Hyper-V product and the operating systems that live on it. For all Microsoft shops, Hyper-V is a competitive solution. And, for those who have used Microsoft's Virtual PC product, virtual machines migrate to Hyper-V quite nicely.

5. **Red Hat:** For the past 15 years, everyone has recognized Red Hat as an industry leader and open source champion. Hailed as the most successful open source company, Red Hat entered the world of virtualization in 2008 when it purchased Qumranet and with it, its own virtual solution: KVM and SPICE (Simple Protocol for Independent Computing Environment). Red Hat released the SPICE protocol as open source in December 2009.

6. **Amazon:** Amazon's Elastic Compute Cloud (EC2) is the industry standard virtualization platform. Ubuntu's Cloud Server supports seamless integration with Amazon's EC2 services. EngineYard's Ruby application services leverage Amazon's cloud as well.

7. **Google:** When you think of Google, virtualization might not make the top of the list of things that come to mind, but its Google Apps, AppEngine and extensive Business Services list demonstrates how it has embraced cloud-oriented services.

8. **Virtual Bridges:** Virtual Bridges is the company that invented what's now known as virtual desktop infrastructure or VDI. Its VERDE product allows companies to deploy Windows and Linux Desktops from any 32-bit or 64-bit Linux server infrastructure running kernel 2.6 or above.

9. **Proxmox:** Proxmox is a free, open source server virtualization product with a unique feature: It provides two virtualization solutions. It provides a full virtualization solution with Kernel-based Virtual Machine (KVM) and a container-based solution, OpenVZ.

10. **Parallels:** Parallels uses its open source OpenVZ project, mentioned above, for its commercial hosting product for Linux virtual private servers. High density and low cost are the two keywords you'll hear when experiencing a Parallels-based hosting solution. These are the two main reasons why the world's largest hosting companies choose Parallels. Parallels have also developed a containerized Windows platform to maximize the number of Windows hosts for a given amount of hardware.

Virtualization Case Studies

VMWare website contains a comprehensive list of cases which include companies, such as Revlon, Sage group, Southwest airlines, SAP, and IBM. In another view, the list contains many application areas, such as educational institutions both school districts and universities, medical companies, financial institutions, and many other industries. It also lists both US national cases as well as international cases from Germany, France, Japan, and China. (vmware.com, 2012)

Challenges of Achieving Virtualization

Several challenges face enterprises attempting to realize virtualization:

- Selection applications to be migrated to virtualization on private, public, and or hybrid clouds.
- Selection and evaluation of tools based on features. These may include comparisons between major vendors and smaller stand alone vendors.
- Managing the migration process to virtualization, whether single, multiple, or hybrid.
- Perhaps wait for Gartner Group to issue its standard Magic Quadrants of virtualization vendors.

With these technologies in mind for the evolving network enterprise, it is hoped that future research will address several issues related to the adaptation of these technologies.

This sixth summation book include articles published in volume VI of the IJOTWE. The articles are reclassified and organized into four sections titled, respectively: Ontology, Semantics, and Web Services; Searching and Mining of Web Information; Web-based Applications; and Web Engineering Network and Communication Platforms. The first section includes two articles on the QofS of Web service applications, and two applications: Medical semantic and culture effect on ontology design. The last article evaluates the effect of related standard on semantic Web services. The next section include two major article on emerging areas of search and mining of information: social media mining, deep Web crawler. Next is articles are on watermarking of Web images, generating authoring information, ubiquitous localization of mobile users. The application section III contains modeling business processes, language classification algorithms, software model driven architecture, and cell phone hazard information sharing subsystem. The last section presents articles on the IT side of Web engineering: network and communication innovations. One article developed an improve error correction algorithm that has potential effect on emerging innovative applications to improve data quality transfer, such as cloud computing, virtualization both internal and external, global position systems (GPS), and geographical information systems (GIS). A second article exposes the design of new novel compressed search engine, that when combined with the previous article could improve performance and efficiency of data location and retrieval. Two article in this section exploit the wireless network platform to improve network operation.

Ghazi I. Alkhatib
Princess Sumaya University for Technology, Jordan

REFERENCES

Brown, E. (2011). NIST issues final version of full virtualization security guidelines. Retrieved February 2, 2011, from http://www.nist.gov/itl/csd/virtual-020111.cfm

Gartner.com. (2012). *IT glossary: Virtualization.* Retrieved October 10, 2012, from gartner.com/it-glossary/virtualization

Hess, K. (2010). Top 10 virtualization technology companies. Retrieved April 20, 2010, from http://www.serverwatch.com/trends/article.php/3877576/Top-10-Virtualization-Technology-Companies.htm

Marko, K. (2012a, June 22). Virtualization security: Where's the innovation? *InformationWeek*. Retrieved from http://www.informationweek.com/security/management/virtualization-security-wheres-the-innov/240002016

Marko, K. (2012b, June). 2012 state of the data center. *InformationWeek reports*.

McTigue, J. (2012, June). Anywhere, anytime application delivery. *InformationWeek reports*.

Murphy, A. (2012). *Virtualization defined*. (f5 White paper). Retrieved October 10, 2012, from f5.com/pdf/white-papers/virtualization-defined-wp.pdf

O'Reilly, T. (2010, March 29). *The state of the internet operating system*. Retrieved from http://radar.oreilly.com/2010/03/state-of-internet-operating-system.html

Scarfone, K., Souppaya, M., & Hoffman, P. (2011). Guide to security for full virtualization technologies. NIST Special Publication 800-125, *Recommendations of the National Institute of Standards and Technology*, January, 2011.

Toghuj, W., & Alkhatib, G. (2011). Improved algorithm for error correction. *International Journal of Information Technology and Web Engineering*, *6*(1), 1–12. doi:10.4018/jitwe.2011010101

VMWare. (2012). *Customer case studies*. Retrieved October 13, 2012, from vmware.com/a/customers/product

Waters, J. (2012). *Virtualization definition and solutions*. Retrieved from http://www.cio.com/article/40701/Virtualization_Definition_and_Solutions?page=3&taxonomyId=3112

Williams, A. (2011, April 19). *A comparison of 5 virtualization vendors*. Retrieved from http://www.serverwatch.com/trends/article.php/3877576/Top-10-Virtualization-Technology-Companies.htm

Section 1
Ontology, Semantics, and Web Services

Chapter 1
How Culture May Influence Ontology Co-Design:
A Qualitative Study

Linda Anticoli
Università di Udine, Italy

Elio Toppano
Università di Udine, Italy

ABSTRACT

This article addresses the issue of cultural influence in ontology design and reuse. The main assumption is that an ontology is not only a socio-technical artefact but also a cultural artefact. It contains embedded assumptions, core values, points of view, beliefs, thought patterns, etc. Based on results already found in several design fields the authors formulate some preliminary hypotheses about the possible relationships existing between culture and features of design process and produced ontology. A critical and qualitative analysis of six collaborative design systems has been performed to test some of the hypotheses, confirming some of the findings. The authors argue that a "culture aware" attitude may be of great importance for supporting the processes of cross cultural collaborative ontology design and the internalization and localization of these kinds of artefacts.

INTRODUCTION

Ontology engineering has been traditionally viewed as a purely technical activity. As a consequence the social, communicative and rhetorical aspects that are at the base of collaborative ontology design and reuse are usually filtered out or not adequately tackled (Toppano et al., 2008). The main assumption we make is that an ontol-

ogy is not only a socio-technical artefact but also a cultural artefact (Toppano, 2010). It embodies assumptions, deep values, points of view, beliefs, etc. of the community that developed it. The (re) use of an ontology - either when it is used as a metamodel for an entire application (or for a part of it) or when it is used to annotate and support reasoning about specific web resources - informs the perception, interpretation, and action in the

DOI: 10.4018/978-1-4666-2157-2.ch001

world. Ontology designers, instead of simply making an "object," are actually creating a persuasive argument that is embodied within the artefact and that comes to life whenever a user uses the ontology as a means to some end (Buchanan, 1985). In this study we intend to explore how culture may influence collaborative ontology design. Recently several research efforts have been devoted to study the role of culture in design. These efforts mainly concentrate in the field of interface design (Marcus & Gould, 2000; Ford & Kotzé, 2005), (Kersten et al., 2002), and web design (Wurtz, 2005; Callahan, 2005; Pfeil et al., 2006). This interest is strictly related to the internalization and localization processes of these products. Despite the importance of cultural factors, at present we do not know studies that have tackled this problem in the field of ontology engineering. We argue instead that a "culture-aware" approach may be of great importance for the development of systems (e.g., web services) that more or less implicitly adopt ontologies and for supporting the processes of intercultural collaborative design. This study is a preliminary investigation. We have reviewed relevant literature on cross-cultural design and tried to distil some findings that could be useful in our application domain. We are aware of the fact that such findings might be specific to the inquiry context in which they were discovered (i.e., that people may exhibit different cultural characteristics when assessed in different contexts). However, we think that such an effort can be used as a starting point for future more focused and rigorous work. The paper is organized as follows. We start with a brief discussion of the concept of culture, dimensions of cultural variation and the role culture has on thought. Next we summarize some perspectives about technology that we deem relevant to understand the different orientations of researchers about the nature of ontology and its development. Thirdly, some hypotheses about how culture may influence the concept of ontology adopted by researchers, the structure of the ontology conceptualisation and the

design process are formulated. Finally, a critical analysis of six systems is presented in order to test some of the hypotheses, followed by conclusions and future work.

THEORETICAL BACKGROUND

What is Culture?

According to Hofstede (1991, 2003) culture is a "collective programming of the mind which distinguishes the members of one group from another" and consists of "common characteristics", that influence a groups' response to its environment. Schein (1999) asserts that culture is a "set of basic assumptions - shared solutions to universal problems of external adaptation (how to survive) and internal integration (how to stay together) - which have evolved over time and are handed down from one generation to the next." Other scholars (Hall, 1990; Geertz, 1973) adopted a communication related definition of culture and focus on shared meanings. They suggest that culture consists of patterned ways of thinking that are shared across people in a society; they are based on a set of taken-for-granted assumptions and core values that influence individuals' mental models, cognition, attitudes, behaviours and are embodied in physical and symbolic artefacts. Thus, understanding the assumptions grounding a culture is needed to distinguish among cultures and discover coherence and meanings within them. In distributed collaborative ontology development we distinguish among different types of cultures: 1) national or regional ones; 2) ethnic cultures spanning national geographic boundaries such as Arab or Latin Americans cultures; 3) corporate cultures based on shared practices, 4) professional cultures such as those emerging when a cross functional team develops an ontology. In many cases, discriminating the cultures is not a clear-cut task, which complicates the job of ontology design usually belonging to several cultures simultaneously. For example, differences in specific professional cultures are apparent when experts use their own views to conceptualise a domain. National cultures emerge during ontology negotiations: some people are concerned with the way things are done (i.e., process-oriented), others with the outcomes of decisions (i.e., result-oriented); some people are more normative and prefer tight control (e.g., formal rules and policies) others are more pragmatic and prefer loose control, etc.

Dimensions of Culture

Researchers attempted to find observable indicators providing a framework for cross-cultural comparisons. Important work has been undertaken by Hall (1990), Hofstede (2003), and Trompenaars (1997) among the others. Hofstede identified the following cultural dimensions:

1. Individualism/Collectivism
2. Power Distance
3. Uncertainty Avoidance
4. Masculinity/Femininity
5. Long Term Orientation

Hofstede's dimensions were often criticized for their close association with national culture. Nevertheless, or because of this simplification, his dimensions have been widely used to analyze cross-cultural communication between organizations or to explain differences in web interfaces or learning styles. In order to better support our analysis we have added two further dimensions proposed by Hall, namely, Time Perception and Contextuality. Table 1 illustrates the complete set of dimensions used in the present study.

Time orientation is linked to contextuality. High context cultures tend to be polychronic which means that people are involved in many different activities with different people at the same time. Additionally this time perspective stresses high involvement of people which produces a greater degree of context and completion of transactions rather than adherence to a predetermined schedule and deadlines (Kersten et al., 2002).

Table 1. Cultural dimensions used in the study

Dimensions	Description
I: Individualism-Collectivism	Reflects the way members emphasize their own needs over the group's needs; the degree to which one's self identity is defined according to individual characteristics or by the characteristics of the group to which (s)he belongs to
PD: Power Distance	The extent that large differentials of power and, therefore, inequality are accepted in a given culture; high PD cultures are characterized by a strong sense of hierarchy, a preference for differentiated status and restricted communication between members belonging to different levels of the hierarchy
MA: Masculinity-Femininity	Reflects the degree to which either masculine norms such as achievement, and material orientation or feminine norms like relationship, people orientation and quality of life are important in a culture
UA: Uncertainty Avoidance	The level of risk accepted by a culture, which can be gleaned from the emphasis on rule obedience, ritual behaviour, and labour mobility
LTO: Long Term Orientation	Degree to which a society takes a long-term versus a short term orientation in life; high LTO means more concern to social norms, "saving face" and time along a continuum including past, present, and future; low LTO means more task oriented and more likely to view ethical obligations as constraints
TP: Time Perception	The ability to attend to single events (monochronic time) or multiple events (polychronic time) simultaneously
CX: Contextuality	The importance of contextual factors in communication processes; in low context cultures people expect each other to express information clearly, whereas people belonging to high context cultures usually put as much weight towards the context of a communication as to the communication itself

Culture and Thought

Nisbett et al. (2001) point out the differences between the analytic thought and the holistic thought which are characteristic of the Westerns and the East Asians respectively. We briefly review some results of their study which are relevant for the following:

- **Features of Analytic Thought:** The world is made by objects which are understood as individuals or particulars and which have properties (discreteness); detachment of the objects from the context; tendency to focus on the attributes of the objects and to assign objects to categories; preference for using rules about categories to explain and predict the object behaviour; preference for formal models of the natural world and abstract logic; avoidance of contradiction; focus on scientific theories and investigation.
- **Features of Holistic Thought:** The world is a collection of overlapping substances (focus on continuity and relationships); orientation to the context or field as a whole, including attention to relationships between the focal object and the field, and a preference for explaining and predicting events on the basis of such relationships; preference for associative thought, for intuition and empiricism. Orientals have not a concept of nature distinct from human or spiritual entities; genius for practicality and experience-based knowledge; preference for dialectic that involves reconciling, transcending, and accepting apparent contradictions; emphasis on change, on the need for multiple perspectives and a search for the middle way between opposing propositions.

The above differences are based on distinct characteristics of the ancient Greek and Chinese societies that are considered foundation of the Western and Oriental Cultures. Greeks located the power in the individual, had a sense of personal freedom together with a tradition of debate and argumentation, they had the presumption that the world could be understood by the discovery of rules. On the other hand, Chinese had a greater sense of reciprocal social obligation or collective agency; the sense that the behaviour of the individual should be guided by the expectations of the group; in-group harmony was preferred to confrontation such as debate. In short, the Greek society was more object and individual-centred while the Chinese one was more context and social-centred. Later we shall try to exploit the consequences of these thought differences in the design of conceptual structure of ontologies.

TECHNOLOGY ORIENTATION

Technology can be defined as the set of artefacts and the set of cultural beliefs, practices, and texts surrounding the production, use, distribution, and conceptualizations of those artefacts, designed to produce some cultural condition. The relationship between culture, society and technology has been studied within the philosophy of technology. Three perspectives on technology have been proposed (Kersten et al., 2002):

- **Instrumental Perspective:** Argues that technology is neutral and indifferent to the variety of ends towards which it can be employed.
- **Substantive Perspective:** Argues that technology constitutes a new type of cultural system that restructures the entire social world as an object of control.
- **Critical Perspective:** Suggests that technology is a rational process of development that is neutral *per se* but becomes value- and ideology-laden in the design, implementation and use of technical systems.

We can observe that each of the three theories of technology leads to different perspectives on the design and development of software technology. Instrumental perspective posits that system design and development can be done in isolation from the users and their situation. Substantive perspective posits that system design and development can be done for the betterment of the users leading to new social and cultural values and systems. Critical perspective posits that system design and development is never neutral and can be used to propagate and infirm social and cultural values and systems. Also relevant is the concept of *technological mediation* (Verbeek, 2006). Things-in-use can be understood as mediators of human-world relationships. When a technological artefact is used, it facilitates people involvement with reality, and in doing so, it co-shapes how humans can be present in their world (i.e., their action, praxis) and their world for them (i.e., their perception and interpretation). In other words, technological artefacts play an active role in the relationship between humans and their world: they transform what we perceive; when mediating our praxis they translate (e.g., invite or inhibit) actions and behaviours. The concept introduced by Latour and Akrich to describe the influence of artefacts on human actions is "script" (Akrich, 1992; Verbeek, 2006). Like the script of a movie or a theatre play, artefacts prescribe their users how to act when they use them. The scripts of artefacts suggest specific actions and discourage others. The adoption of a particular perspective about technology has cultural basis. People adopting an instrumental perspective, for example, are more likely to belong to cultures with a higher uncertainty avoidance orientation than people adopting a substantive or critical perspective.

HOW CULTURE INFLUENCES ONTOLOGY DESIGN AND REUSE

In studying the relationships between culture and ontology development it is possible to adopt several perspectives (Figure 1). One perspective (a) is to study the culture embedded in an ontology as the result of the cultural programming of its human creators or as a reflection of the organizational cultures of design teams. We call these aspects the "Culture *in* the Ontology." One research question relevant to this perspective is: How do different cultures interact during cross-cultural collaborative design? Another perspective (b) is developing "Ontologies for Cultures." This is strictly related to the processes of software internationalization and localization. The main assumption is that when we use an ontology as a metamodel or as a domain model for an application it directly affects the core (the mechanics) of the application which becomes culture dependent like the interface. So the main research question is: How to localize ontologies? Finally reuse (c). We have adopted a communication based approach to design according to which designers delegate the ontology to represent themselves and their culture in the operational context of the user. In this way the ontology becomes a *mediator* (Toppano, 2010). According to the critical orientation, the (re)use of the ontology by a community affects the user experience and entails the potential adoption of the culture that is embodied within it. In the following we mainly focus on the culture in ontology.

Culture in Ontology

A central problem is to understand which aspects of an ontology may be influenced by a culture. We organize our analysis into three parts: 1) the role of technology orientation in the definition of ontology; 2) the conceptual structure of the ontology; and 3) the process of collaborative design.

Figure 1. Perspectives in studying the relationships between culture and ontology development: a) culture in ontology, b) ontologies for cultures and c) ontology reuse

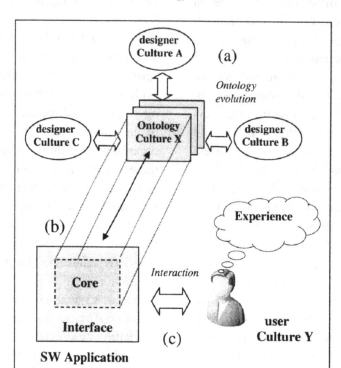

Technology Orientation and the Concept of Ontology

If we compare the various definitions of ontology proposed in the literature at least two points of view emerge. Some scholars focus on (meta) modelling and consider an ontology as "an explicit and formal specification of a conceptualization" or "a formal specification of a vocabulary" that describes a domain and can be used as a basis for the development of a knowledge base (Perez & Benjamins, 1999). Others include in the definition social aspects and consider an ontology as "an explicit and formal specification of a *shared* conceptualization" or "a formal and *consensual* specification of a conceptualization providing a *shared understanding* of a domain that can be communicated across people and application systems" (Fensel, 2001) or again "a *treaty* - a social agreement - among people with some common

motive in sharing " (Gruber, 2004). Of course, differences in the definitions have profound consequences on the development process: requiring that the ontology meaning is shared among designers entails the adoption of some form of discussion process which could be omitted if we ignore this aspect. We argue that differences in the definition of Ontology have cultural basis and depend on the technological orientation of researchers. For example, from the observation of the different definitions of "ontology (computer science) settled in Wikipedia, translated from many languages, emerges that some countries are more likely to provide a formal definition, while others prefer (in particular Asian countries) a more social-oriented one. Therefore, the following hypothesis is advanced:

H0: Culture influences first and foremost the adopted concept of Ontology. More specifically, those who follow an instrumental perspective are more likely to ignore contextual and social aspects in favour of the more objective and individualistic ones. The reverse is true for those who adhere to the substantive or critical perspective.

By abstracting an ontology from its context of development and viewing it as an "object" we do not take into account some important issues such as the unstable, dynamic and approximate nature of conceptualizations, or the role of technological mediation that an ontology plays when it is embedded within an Information System and thus the ethical responsibility of the designers.

Conceptual Structure of the Ontology

The central point here is the identification of possible mismatches among ontologies and the association of these differences to cultural effects. We distinguish between the conceptual content of an ontology (the knowledge level) and its terminological realization (the symbolic level). In this study we focus on conceptualization mismatches; they arise whenever we encounter differences in the concepts identified in the domain and the way in which those concepts are related. Formally, a conceptualization may be described by a conceptual schema i.e. a tuple $<E,R,A/D>$ where: i) $E=\{Ei\}$ is a set of entity types, ii) $R=\{R_j^k(E_{j1},..E_{jk})\}$ is a set of relation types; iii) $A/D=\{Ai/Dj\}$ is a set of attributes representing general properties of entities or relation types with associated domains of values. Figure 2 shows a minimal conceptualization (top left) and possible variations. More specifically we assume that two conceptualizations represent:

1. The same relations, attributes and domains but have different entities. For example two conceptualizations distinguish the same entity (class) Ei but divide the class into

Figure 2. Differences between conceptualisations

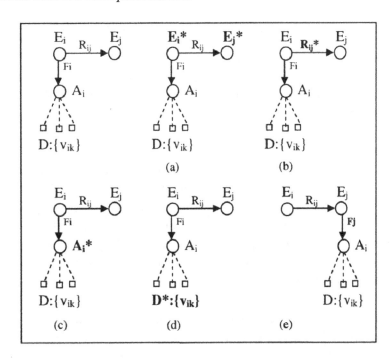

different subclasses Ej*. This happens when we use different categorization criteria, different specialization or aggregation levels.

2. The same entities, attributes and domains but have different relations. For example one conceptualization uses a *part-whole* relation between Ei and Ej while another uses an *individual-collection* relation.
3. The same entities and relations but different attributes.
4. The same entities, relations and attributes but different domains of values.
5. The same entities, relations, attributes and domains but a different assignment of attributes to entities.
6. Different entities, relations, attributes and domains or a combination of the previous cases.

The main question is: Is it possible to link conceptual differences to cultural dimensions? More specifically: What is the effect of analytic and holistic thought in the design of a conceptualization?

We hypothesize that:

H1: Designers characterized by analytic thought prefer conceptualizations: i) with few entities with many attributes and attribute values; ii) organized into few tall hierarchies; mainly type-of (i.e., taxonomic) hierarchies; iii) with few etherarchical relations (e.g., associative relations); iv) expressing a single point of view (or a limited number of points of view)

On the other hand:

H2: Designers animated by holistic thought prefer conceptualizations: i) with many entities with few attributes and attribute values; ii) organized into many shallow hierarchies; either type-of (i.e., taxonomic) or part_of (i.e., mereological) hierarchies; iii) with many etherarchical relations (e.g., asso-

ciative relations); iv) expressing different points of view.

The above hypotheses can be justified on the base of the different orientation of the analytic and the holistic thought with respect to the context, the capacity to discriminate objects in a field and the attitude to preserve differences among points of view and use associations. If these hypotheses are valid we expect different conceptual architectures: single monolithic structures with a tall hierarchical organization (analytic thought), etherarchical or mixed structures such as a constellation of shallow hierarchical taxonomies connected by associative relationships (holistic thought).

The Process of Collaborative Design

We have organized the discussion according to the following issues:

- The design methodology and the model of collaboration.
- The kind of contribution (operations) allowed.
- The model of negotiation including mechanisms to achieve consensus.

We argue that culture influences the choice of design methodology. Cultures with a high degree of uncertainty avoidance are expected to prefer formal and systematic methods inspired to software engineering. These methods are prescriptive and result from abstracting design experiences. They respond to people's discomfort with uncertainty and ambiguity and preference for predictability and control. Cultures with a low degree of uncertainty avoidance are likely to prefer more flexible and situated methods to take into accounts complex aspects of the development and usage contexts such as, for example, potential conflicts arising from the various stakeholders (including the final users) involved in design, the processes of collaborative modelling, meaning construction and sharing, the specific characteristics of ontology deployment. The collaborative construction of a shared conceptualization can be regarded as a kind of collaborative knowledge construction process involving people with different background knowledge and perspectives about the domain, different values and interests, etc. We distinguish among different forms of "collaboration" according to the degree or reciprocal engagement:

- **Multi-Perspectival:** Participants join together to work on a common design problem; they operate separately on the whole problem or on parts of the problem without interacting; then split apart unchanged when work is done. Effort is additive but not integrative.
- **Inter-Perspectival:** Participants join to work on a common design problem; the interaction among them may forge a new conceptualization by linking or merging individual solutions. Effort is integrative but not constructive.
- **Trans-Perspectival:** Participants joint together to *define* and solve the design problem in the context of application; the process is dynamic, flexible, transient, generative, reflective and social. Effort is constructive (i.e., new knowledge is produced).

The transition from one form to the next one entails the adoption of a richer and richer model of collaboration i.e. from a simple co-operation process based on work division to a complex activity of co-design and the introduction of several contextual aspects. According to the above observations we expect that:

H3: Designers belonging to cultures characterized by high power distance, high uncertainty avoidance and analytic thought are likely to prefer formal, general and systematic design methods. More specifically:

H3.1: A multi-perspectival form of collaboration is likely to be preferred by individualistic and low context cultures;
H3.2: An inter-perspectival form of collaboration is likely to be preferred by cultures with a medium/low index of individualism and medium/high context;
H3.3: A trans-perspectival form of collaboration is likely to be preferred by cultures with a high index of collectivism and high context.

In collaborative design, people can contribute in various ways. At the operational level they may propose changes to the conceptualization under construction. At the problem and reflective levels, they may participate to the definition, clarification and reformulation of the current design problem as well as to the justification, discussion, evaluation and selection of ontology change proposals. Solution and design problems coevolve. The need to share the meaning of the designed ontology - as emphasized by some definitions of ontology - introduces a further level of collaboration concerning the construction of a common understanding as discussed in Toppano (2010). Modification may be of three types: adding new elements (i.e., entity types, relations, attributes/values), deleting and correcting existing ones. We argue that culture has an effect on both the contributions each participant produces and on the type and frequency of specific modification actions (Pfeil et al., 2006). Thus we hypothesize that:

H4: Designers belonging to cultures with a high index of power distance are likely to produce few deleting and correcting actions.

In high power distance cultures people are used to accept authority and have a strong sense of hierarchy. Deleting and correcting actions are powerful actions because a person using them enforces his or her opinion and declares the opinion of others wrong. Thus it is expected that people feel reluctant to delete or correct somebody else's work.

H5: Designers belonging to cultures with a high index of individualism and masculinity are likely to produce many corrective actions.

Corrective actions stress the opinion of the individual who corrects or changes a version written by another member of the design team. By correcting another member the individual opinion prevails over the group consensus. Furthermore, it is likely that the number of adding actions decreases because the individual is more interested in the achievement of personal goals than of those of the group. Masculinity stresses the importance of success and progress; thus we expect a positive correlation between masculinity and corrective actions.

H6: Designers belonging to cultures with a high index of uncertainty avoidance are likely to produce few contributions on any kind.

Every edit is in a way an unpredictable action connected to a possibility of error; people will feel a constant insecurity and anxiety and thus will make fewer total contributions.

Finally we consider negotiation. We argue that culture influences negotiation with respect to the following aspects: 1) the expectations of designers regarding the outcomes, the efficiency of the process and the quality of the final solution; 2) the "atmosphere" surrounding the process including negotiation strategy and perceived attractiveness (Kersten et al., 2002) and 3) the negotiation process itself, more specifically the consensus mechanisms and argumentation model adopted.

We hypothesize that:

H7: Designers belonging to cultures with a high index of individualism and masculinity are likely to have higher expectation levels

concerning the outcomes and are expected to exhibit more contending behaviour (i.e., a competitive approach, leading to win/lose agreements) and less problem solving attitude than designers from a more collectivistic orientation who consider the negotiation as a way for solving a common problem to the satisfaction of all participants (i.e., a integrative approach, leading to a win-win agreement).

People from holistic cultures are more interested in maintaining the harmony within the group than entering in a conflicting situation even at the detriment of personal positions. Analytic thought can influence expectations, the attitude for perspective making and negotiation, the will to complete the task and to reach a consensus at any cost even with compromises. Concerning the consensus mechanisms and the argumentation model we hypothesize that:

H8: Designers from high context cultures will use more discussion (e g., attach more text messages with proposals) than designers from low context cultures.
H9: Designers from higher individualistic cultures and analytic thought will prefer decision-based negotiation rather than argumentation based negotiation.
H10: Designer from higher feminine cultures and holistic thought will prefer low structured argumentation based negotiation

Ontology (Re)use

What are the cultural effects of ontology reuse? By adopting a critical perspective we assume that the use of application Xa - embodying ontology Oa developed by A - by user B, set up values and norms of the culture associated to Oa in the operational context and practices of user B and potentially in the culture of B. An ontology is like a pair of glasses: it mediates what we can perceive by providing a set of concept types and relations through which we interpret reality. At the same time, it invites to answer specific questions about the modelled reality: those (i.e., the competence questions) that can be specified and reasoned about with the given conceptualization. Therefore, the ontology affects both interpretation and praxis. Ontologies and practices are strongly interrelated: a change in the practice produces a modification of the associated ontology and vice versa. This fact has profound consequences:

- If the use of an application in a given operational context produces cultural effects we can ask ourselves if these effects are consistent or in conflict with the culture of that context. Besides a syntactical, semantic and pragmatic interoperability we need a cultural interoperability too, which is based on the assumptions, values, norms, etc. implicitly embodied within applications. This aspect is particularly important when we need to reconcile (i.e., link, integrate, merge) ontologies developed by different design teams.

- The critical perspective assigns the designer an ethic responsibility. By designing an ontology the designer potentially affects the future way of interpreting, reasoning and acting of the people who will use it. Therefore, we claim that it is necessary to explicitly represent the basic assumptions and values embodied within an ontology in order to let potential users to understand the social implications of the ontology use and let them evaluate, select an ontology not only on the base of functional and technical aspects but also on cultural ones. These means a "cultural aware" approach to the development of ontologies and ontology-based information systems.

A CASE STUDY

In order to test the acceptability of proposed hypotheses we started a critical effort devoted to the analysis and comparison of some well known systems supporting a distributed or collaborative ontology development. The study is limited to those aspects of the systems under consideration that are related to the design process. Therefore, only a subset of the hypotheses will be taken into account. The aim is to infer the culture embedded within a system through the analysis of some features that are deemed to be relevant to Hofstede's dimensions and compare the inferred culture with the national culture of the design team in order to verify if they are consistent. To this end we exploited the findings about national cultures described in Marcus and Gould (2000) and Hofstede (1991). The systems selected for the analysis are: Knowledge Mediation (Aschoff et al., 2004); Diligent (Pinto et al., 2004); Hcome (Kotis et al., 2005); the Awake Project (Novak et al., 2004); Consensus Building (Karapiperis & Apostolou, 2006); and the YI-Ontology Project (Good et al., 2006). Some of these systems were developed by heterogeneous design teams (i.e., designers belong to different national cultures), others are homogeneous and represent the same or different cultures (Table 4). In the sequel we briefly review some features of the considered systems that are relevant for the analysis. In Knowledge Mediation a facilitator assists participants during discussion in order to support the activities of concept clarification and perspective taking. Discussion is focused on shared meaning and employs techniques from conflict mediation theory to resolve mismatches among points of view. In Diligent there exists an expert board which is in charge to receive the proposals of ontology changes from the participants together with associated justifications and to decide which proposals have to be accepted and applied and which rejected. The use of an expert board introduces a hierarchical structure which is absent in Knowledge Mediation. As explicitly stated in the article (Aschoff et al., 2004) the aim of the discussion is not sharing meaning but to convince others about the goodness of accepted solutions. An interesting feature of the system is the use of RST (Rhetorical Structure Theory) for analysing argumentations proposed by participants and speed up the process of consensus achievement. Hcome employs a well structured conversational model (inspired to IBIS) which is embodied in the system; discussion is based on a limited set of general primitives (e.g., position, argument, issue...) which do not have the expressive power of RST's relationships. Furthermore, the use of a lexicon consultation tool contributes to making the system more structured and predictable. The Awake Project uses Concept Maps and Context Maps to reify the conceptualizations arising within a community of practice and the Reconciler tool to support the reconciliation of multiple perspectives among different communities. Differing from the other systems that try to avoid or limit the emergence of different points of view or to mediate between them, this system tries to preserve conceptual differences and considers them as an added value. The Awake Project is similar to Knowledge Mediation with which it shares several features such as the emphasis on perspective making and taking. However, it seems to be oriented toward a clearer trans-perspectival approach as indicated by the frequent recall to mutual learning. Consensus Building views the process of ontology development as a collaborative problem solving task; it focuses on the achievement of a mutually acceptable solution (which does not necessarily means that the solution has a shared meaning). The process of consensus building is intended as a form of collaborative decision making in which every member of the design team is freely and equally consulted; (s)he can vote and eventually accept the final decision. Voting is done with the Nominal Group Technique. The system employs a facilitator with the aim of encouraging participation and explaining ambiguous proposals; discussion about

the meaning of ontology changes is not supported. The Delphi method is proposed to eliminate all aspects concerning social context; the approach is very structured and rational. In the YI Ontology Project participants contribute to the process of ontology development by proposing terms and relations and evaluating the terms introduced by others by assigning them a score; only the terms whose global score exceeded a given threshold are maintained. Participation is supported by the promise of mystery prizes to the most prolific contributors which indicates a clear "determination to win". No discussion or argumentation processes are allowed; there is no distinction between terms and concepts; it is supposed that the meaning of terms is unique and shared among participants and that it reflects a common point of view about the modelled domain.

Qualitative Analysis and Results

The following main features have been considered for the analysis:

- **Kind of Collaboration (KoC):** Multi-perspectival, inter-perspectival, trans-perspectival.
- **Negotiation Model (NM):** Integrative (win-win), distributive (win-lose), mixed.
- **Consensus Mechanism (CM):** Decision based (e.g., based on voting), argumentation based, mixed.
- **Argumentation Model (AM):** Structured/logical vs. unstructured/dialectical.
- **Distribution of Control (DoC):** Peer-to-peer, mediated (e.g., through a facilitator), hierarchical.

Other features such as, for example, participation (e.g., open community vs. selected group of people), object of design (e.g., vocabulary or conceptualization vs. shared meaning), design level (e.g., individual, social, organisational) have been used to better discriminate between systems when the main features were not sufficient. We assumed the existence of the following relationships among cultural dimensions and system features: 1) Uncertainty Avoidance is linked to Argumentation Model and Consensus Mechanism (the more structured and decision based is the system the less tolerant it is with respect to ambiguity; 2) Contextuality is related to Kind of Collaboration and Consensus Mechanism (it increases by passing from multi-perspectival, decision based systems to trans-perspectival, argumentation based ones; 3) Power Distance is linked to Distribution of Control (e.g., the presence of hierarchical structures); 4) Masculinity is strictly related to Negotiation Model (it is greater for win/lose models than for win/win ones) and 5) Individualism is from this point of view related to masculinity but can be modulated by contextuality. The proposed relationships are supported by intuition without the ambition of scientific rigor.

At this point it is possible to exploit the relationships to evaluate each system and assign a qualitative value (e.g., High, Low) to cultural dimensions. As an instance Table 2 shows the result of this analysis for Knowledge Mediation. Columns represent system features, rows cultural dimensions. We use the italic style to indicate the values of the system features assumed by the system.

Looking at uncertainty avoidance (first row of the table), we assign a low value to this dimension because Knowledge Mediation employs an argumentation based consensus mechanism and uses an unstructured/dialectical argumentation model and these features are considered inversely correlated with uncertainty avoidance. Analo-

Table 2. Example of evaluation of cultural dimensions as a function of system features for knowledge mediation

		Kind of Collaboration	Negotiation Model	Consensus Mechanism	Argumentation Model	Distribution of Control
Uncertainty Avoidance	H			decision-based	structured/logical	
				mixed		
	L			*argumentation-based*	*unstructured/dialectical*	
Contextuality	H	*trans-perspectival*		argumentation-based		
		inter-perspectival		mixed		
	L	multi-perspectival		decision-based		
Power Distance	H					hierarchical
						mediated
	L					*peer-to-peer*
Masculinity	H		Distributive (win-lose)			
			mixed			
	L		*integrative (win-win)*			
Individualism	H	multi-perspectival	distributive (win-lose)	decision-based		
		interperspectival	mixed	mixed		
	L	*transperspectival*	*integrative (win-win)*	*argumentation-based*		

gously for the other dimensions. Table 3 shows the results of the analysis for all considered systems while Table 4 shows the values of the Hofstede's dimensions relative to the national cultures of the researchers involved in the realization of the six systems considered in this study. Data are based on findings discussed in Marcus and Gould (2000) and Hofstede (2003).

In order to compare expected and current values of the dimensions we have subdivided the range of quantitative values (i.e., 0-120) used by Marcus and Hofstede into three subspaces namely [0-40], (40, 80) and [80-120] which are mapped into the qualitative values - L (low), M (medium) and H (high) respectively - used in our qualitative analysis.

The comparison provides evidence that the considered systems reflect some cultural traits of the national culture of their designers. More specifically we can make the following observations:

- Hcome and Consensus Building, which were developed by different teams belonging to the same culture- show similar expected values. Indeed both reflect low PD and I values, high UA and an intermediate MA value.

- There is a good correspondence of all dimensions' values for the YI Ontology Project, Hcome, Consensus Building, Knowledge Mediation and the Awake Project. As an instance Figure 3 shows the

Table 3. The expected values (l:low, h:high) of Hofstede's dimensions with respect to the considered system's features

System	KoC	NM	CM	AM	DoC	Expected
Knowledge Mediation	trans	win-win	argumentation	unstructured; dialectical	peer to peer; facilitator	UA: l CX: h PD: l MA:l IN: l
Diligent	inter	win-lose	mixed	more structured; logical	hierarchical; expert board	UA: h/l CX: h/l PD: h MA:h IN: l
Hcome	inter	mixed	argumentation	structured (IBIS) logical	peer to peer;	UA: h CX: h/l PD: l MA:h/l IN: l
Awake Project	trans	win-win	argumentation	unstructured, dialectical	peer to peer; facilitator	UA: l CX: h PD: l MA:l IN: l
Consensus-Building	mult	win-lose	mixed	structured, logical	peer to peer; facilitator	UA: h CX: l/h PD: l MA:h IN: h/l
YI-Ontology Project	mult	win-lose	decision		peer to peer	UA: l CX: l PD: l MA:h IN: h

Table 4. The actual values of Hofstede's dimensions for the national cultures of design teams

	Authors' Nationality	Dimensions' Values
KMediation: Aschoff, Schmalhofer, van Elst	Germany	PD (35), I (67), MA(66), UA(65)
DILIGENT: Sofia Pinto, Staab, Tempich	Portugal Germany	Portugal: PD (63), I (27), MA (31), UA(104)
Hcome: Kotis, Vouros, Alonso **Consensus Building** Karapiperis, Apostolou	Greece	PD(60), I(35), MA (57), UA(112)
Awake Project: Novak, Cuel, Sarini, Wurst	Germany Italy	Italy: PD (50), I (76), MA (70), UA (75)
YI Ontology Project: Good et al.	Canada	PD (39), I (80), MA(52), UA(48)

results of the comparison relating to YI Ontology Project, developed by a Canadian team. It is possible to see that the estimated values are consistent (they reflect the ordering) with the actual values. In the case of Awake, developed by a project team formed by German and Italian researchers, the estimated values are coherent with the actual ones associated to the considered cultures, although they appear a little underestimated. This is probably related to the choice of the qualitative range used. Less good results are found for Diligent, developed by a cross-cultural team formed by German and Portuguese researchers. The expected values reflect only some of the characteristics of the Portuguese culture as low I value and medium/high PD value, but not others like low MA value and a very high UA value. These last two values seem to be more adherent to the same values belonging to the German culture. It is possible that there exists some predominance of one culture upon the other. For example, in the case of UA seems that the

medium value of German culture predominates upon the higher Portuguese value.

- If we consider the relative position of the considered systems with respect to each single dimension then we find a very good correspondence of expected and actual values for uncertainty avoidance, and a good result for power distance and individuality. Less good results are found for masculinity which shows an inverted order of values. We have no explanation at present for these observed values.

CONCLUSION

In this paper we address the issue of cultural influence in collaborative ontology design. Based on results already found in several design fields, we formulate some preliminary hypotheses about the possible relationships existing between cultural dimensions and features of design process and produced ontology. As we do not have a sufficiently large and heterogeneous set of ontologies we focussed on the design process. A critical

Figure 3. Comparison between the expected and current values of cultural dimensions for the YI ontology project

Canada:

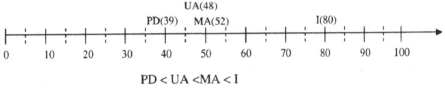

PD < UA < MA < I

YI Ontlogy Project:

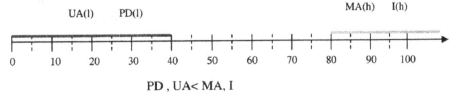

PD , UA< MA, I

analysis of six existing systems supporting collaborative design has been performed in order to test some of the hypotheses. Also in this case it would be interesting to have a set of examples wider and more heterogeneous. The considered systems have been proposed by western researchers (European and North American). There is a lack of examples of methods proposed by Middle Eastern, Asian or South American researchers (i.e., a comparison with a Chinese or an Indian methodology) that surely would have permitted a more complete analysis. Are there examples of Eastern methodologies or is the concept of "method" typically a Western concept (as seems to emerge from Nisbett's studies)?

The analysis strengthens the hypothesis that the considered methods embody aspects of the culture of the developers. This result raises some questions about both the (re) usability of a method and the (re) usability of the products: Can a design method developed by culture A be effectively used by another culture B? Is it necessary to think about localization processes for methods as well as for products? Moreover, which kind of relation exists between culture built into a method and the culture built into the final product? In other words: Do ontologies developed with a given method reflect the culture embedded in the method? And finally, if ontologies incorporate aspects belonging to the cultures in which they were developed, how do we take them into account in the processes of reconciliation of ontologies (for example in the processes of merging, aligning, integrating ontologies) built by others?

As far as the analysis is concerned we highlight the following points. The evaluation is qualitative in nature, and mostly based on intuition. We had not the ambition to provide precise and quantitative results that we think are very difficult to obtain for different reasons i.e.:

1. The difficulty to identify the attributes of a system/product that could effectively reflect cultural aspects (i.e., cultural markers) and could be simply linked to the cultural dimensions.

2. The difficulty of measuring the factors: do binary measurements (e.g., High vs. Low) adequately reflect the underlying continua?

3. It is difficult to characterize the culture of a group since it is generally a mix of different individual sub-cultures (national, professional, organizational,..) whose relative importance is likely context dependent. The risk is always to mistake individual personality for culture. Moreover, the adoption of stereotypes should be done with care.

4. In this study we use past findings about national cultures that we are not sure they are valid today.

The analysis confirms some hypotheses. However, further investigations are needed. We argue that only a real experiment of cross cultural collaborative ontology design might provide data for evaluating all the hypotheses including those concerning the structure of conceptualization and the type of design contribution. This could be an objective of future research work. However we think that this study can be considered as a possible source of insights. If it can help to at least raise the consciousness of the need for progress in this domain, it will fulfill its purpose.

Finally, a general consideration is given. If one adheres to the substantive or the critical perspectives about technology, than ontologies are not culturally neutral. In particular, the phenomenon of technological mediation makes ontology engineering an inherently ethical activity. Ethics, after all, is about the question of how to act, and technologies appear to give material answers to this question.

REFERENCES

Akrich, M. (1992). The description of technical objects. In Bijker, W. E., & Law, J. (Eds.), *Shaping technology/building society: Studies in sociotechnical change* (pp. 205–224). Cambridge, MA: MIT Press.

Aschoff, F., Schmalhofer, F., & van Elst, L. (2004). Knowledge mediation: A procedure for the cooperative construction of domain ontologies. In *Proceedings of the ECAI Workshop on Agent-Mediated Knowledge Management*, Valencia, Spain (pp. 29-38).

Buchanan, R. (1985). Declaration by design: Rhetoric, argument and demonstration in design practice. *Design Issues*, *2*(1), 4–22. doi:10.2307/1511524

Callahan, E. (2005). Cultural similarities and differences in the design of University Websites. *Journal of Computer-Mediated Communication*, *11*(1), 239–273. doi:10.1111/j.1083-6101.2006.tb00312.x

Fensel, D. (2001). Ontologies: Dynamic networks of formally represented meaning. In *Proceedings of the 1st Semantic Web Working Symposium*, Stanford, CA.

Ford, G., & Kotzé, P. (2005). Designing usable interfaces with cultural dimensions. In M. F. Costabile & F. Paternò (Eds.), *Proceedings of the IFIP TC13 International Conference on Human-Computer Interaction*, Rome, Italy (LNCS 3585, pp. 713-726).

Geertz, C. (1973). *The interpretation of cultures*. New York, NY: Basic Books.

Good, B. M., Tranfield, E. M., Tan, P. C., Sheata Singhera, G. K., Gosselik, J., Okon, E. B., & Wilkinson, M. D. (2006). Fast, cheap and out of control: A zero curation model for Ontology development. In *Proceedings of the Pacific Symposium on Biocomputing* (pp. 128-139).

Gruber, T. (2004). Every ontology is a treaty - a social agreement-among people with some common motive in sharing. *Official Bulletin of AIS Special Interest Group on Semantic Web and Information Systems, 1*(3).

Hall, E., & Hall, M. R. (1990). *Understanding cultural differences*. Yarmouth, ME: Intercultural Press.

Hofstede, G. (1991). *Cultures and organizations: Software of the mind*. New York, NY: McGraw-Hill.

Hofstede, G. (2003). *Culture's consequences: Comparing values, behaviours and organizations across nations*. Thousand Oaks, CA: Sage.

Karapiperis, S., & Apostolou, D. (2006). Consensus building in collaborative ontology engineering process. *Journal of Universal Knowledge Management, 1*(3), 199–216.

Kersten, G. E., Kersten, M. A., & Rakowski, W. M. (2002). Software and culture: Beyond the internazionalization of the interface. *Journal of Global Information Management, 10*(4), 86–101. doi:10.4018/jgim.2002100105

Kersten, G. E., Koszegi, S. T., & Vetschera, R. (2002). The effect of culture in anonymous negotiations: Experiment in four countries. In *Proceedings of the 35th Hawaii International Conference on System Sciences*.

Kotis, K., Vouros, G. A., & Alonso, J. P. (2005). HCOME: A tool supported methodology for engineering living ontologies. In C. Bussler, V. Tannen, & I. Fundulaki (Eds.), *Proceedings of the Second International Workshop on Semantic Web and Databases* (LNCS 3372, pp. 155-166).

Marcus, A., & Gould, E. W. (2000). Cultural dimensions and global Web user-interface design: What? So what? Now what? In *Proceedings of the 6th Conference on Human Factors and the Web*, Austin, TX (pp. 1-15).

Nisbett, R. E., Peng, K., Choi, I., & Norenzayan, A. (2001). Culture and systems of thought: Holistic versus analytic cognition. *Psychological Review, 108*(2), 291–309. doi:10.1037/0033-295X.108.2.291

Novak, J., Cuel, R., Sarini, M., & Wurst, M. (2004). A tool for supporting knowledge creation and exchange in knowledge intensive organisations. In *Proceedings of the I-KNOW Conference*, Graz, Austria (pp. 311-319).

Perez, A. G., & Benjamins, V. R. (1999). Overview of knowledge sharing and reuse components: ontologies and problem solving methods. In *Proceedings of the IJCAI Workshop on Ontologies and Problem Solving Methods*, Stockholm, Sweden (pp. 1-15).

Pfeil, U., Zaphiris, P., & Ang, C. S. (2006). Cultural differences in collaborative authoring of Wikipedia. *Journal of Computer-Mediated Communication, 12*(1), 88–113. doi:10.1111/j.1083-6101.2006.00316.x

Pinto, H. S., Staab, S., & Tempich, C. (2004). DILIGENT: Towards a fine-grained methodology for distributed, loosely-controlled and evolving engineering of ontologies. In *Proceedings of the 16th European Conference on Artificial Intelligence*, Valencia, Spain (pp. 393-397).

Schein, E. H. (1999). *The corporate culture survival guide: Sense and nonsense about culture.* San Francisco, CA: Jossey-Bass.

Toppano, E. (2010). A communication-based model of ontology design and (re)use. In *Proceedings of the Intelligent Semantic Web Services and Applications Conference* (pp. 38-44).

Toppano, E., Roberto, V., Giuffrida, R., & Buora, G. B. (2008). Ontology engineering: Reuse and integration. *International Journal of Metadata. Semantics and Ontologies, 3*(3), 233–247. doi:10.1504/IJMSO.2008.023571

Trompenaars, F., & Hampden-Turner, C. (1997). *Riding the waves of culture: Understanding cultural diversity in business.* London, UK: Nicholas Brealey Publishing.

Verbeek, P. (2006). Materializing morality: Design ethics and technological mediation. *Science, Technology & Human Values, 31*(3), 361–380. doi:10.1177/0162243905285847

Wurtz, E. (2005). A cross-cultural analysis of websites from high-context cultures and low context cultures. *Journal of Computer-Mediated Communication, 11*(1), 274–299. doi:10.1111/j.1083-6101.2006.tb00313.x

This work was previously published in the International Journal of Information Technology and Web Engineering (IJITWE), Volume 6, Issue 2, edited by Ghazi I. Alkhatib and Ernesto Damiani, pp. 1-17, copyright 2011 by IGI Publishing (an imprint of IGI Global).

Chapter 2
The Medical Semantic Web:
Opportunities and Issues

Mohammad Ali H. Eljinini
Isra University, Jordan

ABSTRACT

In this paper, the need for the right information for patients with chronic diseases is elaborated, followed by some scenarios of how the semantic web can be utilised to retrieve useful and precise information by stakeholders. In previous work, the author has demonstrated the automation of knowledge acquisition from the current web is becoming an important step towards this goal. The aim was twofold; first to learn what types of information exist in chronic disease-related websites, and secondly how to extract and structure such information into machine understandable form. It has been shown that these websites exhibit many common concepts which resulted in the construction of the ontology to guide in extracting information for new unseen websites. Also, the study has resulted in the development of a platform for information extraction that utilises the ontology. Continuous work has opened many issues which are disussed in this paper. While further work is still needed, the experiments to date have shown encouraging results.

INTRODUCTION

The prolonged course of illness from chronic diseases such as diabetes, hypertension, and asthma results in decreased quality of life for many people around the world. Chronic diseases also impose a huge burden on governments in terms of human resources and costs. Many patients have turned to the Internet to learn more about their chronic diseases, to buy products such as medical devices and medicine, to seek online consulta-

tion, to subscribe to newsletters, and even get information about classes, workshops and other activities, related to their conditions, that are close by. Chronic disease-related websites offer many valuable resources that can aid patients with their life-long management of their illness, but many patients may be unaware of such services. Most patients looking for information on the Internet turn to search engines normally with simple one- or two-keyword queries. After that they are faced with hundreds of thousands of HTML pages to

DOI: 10.4018/978-1-4666-2157-2.ch002

browse. Many people end up just collecting the first few websites and may not obtain adequate results as expected. Most information is still buried or hidden away from casual users or patients.

The semantic web (Berners-Lee et al., 2001), once fully developed, will allow users, for example, to ask questions and obtain precise answers to questions such as the following:

- Where can I find an insulin pump with a capacity larger than 200 units and a weight of less than 120 grams?
- I need the cheapest book about Asthma with a chapter on alternative medicine.
- Is there any workshop on diabetes management in London next month that is intended for pharmacists?
- I need to know the types of food that lower blood pressure and contain low amounts of sugar.
- Where is the closest centre that provides asthma therapy for children?

A special software called Web Agent will interpret such questions into machine understandable queries that work like querying a database using the powerful SQL language. For example, the first question might be interpreted as follows: "SELECT insulin_pump WHERE capacity >200 AND weight <120 FROM some_table". Some queries may not be so obvious such as the last one in the list above! In this case the web agent software must have some information saved about the user such as her/his address, age, browsing habits, etc. so agents can be personalised to adapt to users' needs (Frkovic et al., 2008). These agents will certainly need to work with some form of search engines that traverse the semantic web collecting knowledge into a knowledge base or a database. This is also referred to as parsing and processing ontologies[1]. There has been some limited research in this direction. Probably the most prominent example in this area was Google's version for a search engine for the semantic web which they

called "Swoogle" (Li et al., 2004). In general, such issues are still open for more research.

The possibilities and the different ways of utilising the web with meaningful information being made available to machines become endless, and is also a fertile ground for further research. Patients with any type of disease can benefit from such a future web; however patients with chronic diseases will benefit the most, since most chronic diseases require life-long management. The current web does a great job in linking pieces of related information, displaying images, sounds, etc., in human-understandable ways. Of course, websites having good, understandable design enable information to be easily found and hyperlinks are easy to follow. Such a website does very well in relation to what it is intended to do, and that is to display information for users to read, listen to, or watch. However, since HTML tags are only meant for rendering information on the screen, machines can do very little with such meaningless symbols.

COMMON STRUCTURES: HYPOTHESIS AND ANALYSIS

It has been hypothesised that related websites exhibit common structures. To the author's knowledge, such a hypothesis has never been addressed nor proved before. Based on the analysis made on the collection of chronic disease-related websites, it is suggested that related websites do exhibit common structures (Eljinini et al., 2006). This has been articulated clearly in Figures 1, 2, and 3 taken from Eljinini et al. (2006) where three sets of chronic disease related websites have been extracted and studied in depth.

An ontology has been built firstly for the domain of diabetes websites and then it has been edited to cover the asthma and hypertension-related websites. The methodology used in building the ontology is based on well-defined principles that have been presented by well-known research-

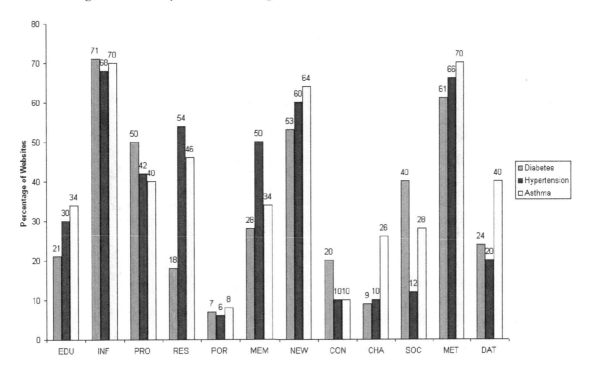

Figure 1. Comparisons of features among the three sets. EDU= Education, INF=Information, PRO=Products, RES=Research, POR=Portal, MEM=Membership, NEW=News, CON=Consultation, CHA=Chatting, SOC=Society, MET=Meta tag, DAT=Date

Figure 2. Comparisons of features related to products. Pub = Publications, Med = medications, MD= Medical Devices, NH = Nutrition and Herbals.

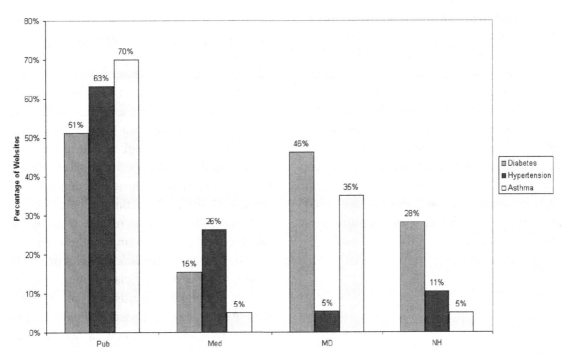

Figure 3. Comparisons of features related to education among the three sets. ACT= Activities, PUB=Publications, CLS=Classes, SPG=Support Groups, PRF=Professionals, PTS=Patients, MEM=Memberships, RES=Research.

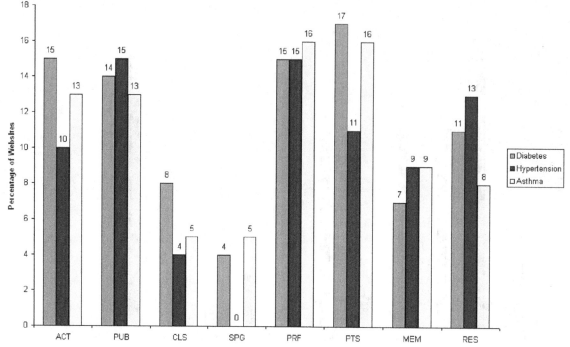

ers in the field. This methodology has been discussed in detail in Eljinini and Sarhan (2007).

The IE system that has being developed during the research work started as a java program used in the analysis of the collected websites. Some special excel spreadsheets have also been designed and prepared to enter the collected data. Once the data were entered into the spreadsheets, they were plotted and analysed, the results are shown in the figures. To ensure high accuracy of the collected data, a sample from the same set of websites has been reselected several months later and the data have been recollected again and then compared with the previously collected ones. The differences between the two were insignificantly small.

METHODOLOGICAL ISSUES AND RELATED WORK

Most web pages on the Internet are in the form of free text. Besides the semantic web, extracting and restructuring information found on the web has become an important task in many fields such as information retrieval and web content mining (Mathias & Jean-Pierre, 2001; Muller et al., 2004). Search engines that utilise the extraction and structuring of information can gain capabilities far beyond those with simple keyword search techniques. Extracting attribute-value pairs allows search engines to resolve word meaning ambiguities. A simple example is the word "bank" which could mean the bank of a river or a bank of money. This is done by classifying terms based on the surrounding words or topic identification. Also, it has been used in the development of domain-specific and focused search engines.

Some researchers are working on mining web content (Rebholz-Schuhmann et al., 2007, 2008; Krallinger & Valencia, 2005). For example, there is the mining of text from the medical literature with an aim of finding association between biomedical concepts (Tsuruoka et al., 2008). The field of data mining, a more mature field, requires that data are prepared in structured format before processing (Witten & Frank, 2000). This implies that to apply normal data mining techniques successfully on web content, first it should be extracted and then transformed into structured format. Information Extraction (IE) has started as an NLP task that is concerned with extracting relevant information from natural text. The two main ingredients for any IE system are a set of extraction rules and a specific template to be filled (Soderland, 1999). The extraction rules are used to find the value for each slot in the template. The end product is actually a set of attribute-value pairs. Today, state-of-the-art approaches in IE are based on machine learning, where the extraction rules are mined from training samples. The training samples are normally tagged instances with labels to be learnt

from, thus these approaches are called supervised. They eliminate the need to write extraction rules manually. However, they require training samples to be supplied and also carry the cost of a decrease in efficiency. This means that the manually created extraction rules perform better. The main problems with these rule-based systems are: first they are expensive and time-consuming to build, and second they are very domain specific, and could not be easily adapted to new domains. Both approaches require a predefined template to be filled by the system. A challenging task that was tackled in our work was to adapt and enhance IE technologies to meet the requirements set for this research work. The resultant system is not completely adaptable to any specific task. However, it is meant to be used with the most common tasks based on the results of the study that was made on the sets of the chronic disease-related websites. Also, since it is object based, it should be easy to customise it and extend it to work with some more specific tasks. Figure 4 shows the system model which is described in more details in Eljinini et al. (2006) and Eljinini (2011).

Figure 4. Overview of the IE framework showing the main components

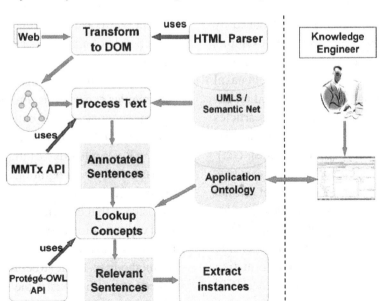

It should be emphasised that one of the objectives has been to determine the most efficient and shortest possible ways to populate the semantic web with the most common and most needed knowledge that should fulfill stakeholder needs. To fulfill this aim the following issues have been addressed.

Providing Common Set of Concepts and Extraction Rules

The first is the development of sets of object–based data structures that cover the most common categories as specified by the ontology for the chronic disease-related websites. According to the earlier study that was made on the three sets of chronic disease-related websites, the two most common and general concepts found were products and services. Other concepts have been categorised under these two concepts, thus forming hierarchies of concepts. The study has shown that 50% of chronic disease-related websites provide products. Every product has a set of attributes such as brand name and price. Attributes for each product type has been determined. These form the slots to be filled when extracting information from a new unseen webpage. Earlier IE systems that have been developed were very task-specific and based on themes that had been planned by DARPA for the MUC conferences. For example, the first and second MUC were about extracting specific information from messages about naval operations. MUC-3 and MUC-4 focused on extracting specific information from news articles about terrorism (i.e. extracting terrorist names, targeted locations, dates, victims' names, etc.). MUC-6 and MUC-7 focused on business events that had been extracted from Wall Street Journal text. Other systems were developed later for other tasks. For example, Soderland et al. (1995) extracted information about hospital discharge reports, Fukuda (1998) extracted information about gene and protein names, Craven (1999) extracted information about molecular interac-

tions, and Rzhetsky (2003) extracted information about molecular pathway data. Some of the early systems that were influenced by MUC adopted the same topics that were chosen by DARPA and were of interest to the agency. To the author's knowledge, no research work has been devoted to find common knowledge in any domain that can be of great benefit to many stakeholders as explained previously. The ontology that was constructed provides an efficient method for organising concepts, their attributes, and the relationship between these concepts.

It has been found that many concepts share the same or some attributes. It should be noted, however, that some of these attributes are also concepts. For example, Figure 5 shows the most common attributes and the percentage of each occurring in other concepts.

For example, the most common attribute for any product is its price. Many IE systems that have been reviewed use regular expressions to extract entities like dates, prices, emails, etc. In this work the nature of these entities has been studied well, and each entity has been encapsulated inside an object along with their own properties and methods. Normally, such methods are used to set and get the values stored in each of the entity's properties. Each entity contains a method that consists of regular expressions for extraction. Not all entities can be extracted with regular expressions. For example, personal names and locations are strings that cannot be extracted with regular expressions. Probably, the simplest way to recognise named entities is by searching a database that contained previously known examples. Researchers have turned to other methods for named entity recognition, which is an active research field. Today there are many algorithms in existence that benefit from some hints such as word capitalisation and other grammatical structures. Other researchers have used machine learning methods to learn structures for discovering named entities that exist in their documents. Some researchers have studied the nature of medical

Figure 5. Most common attributes and their percentage of occurrence in other concepts

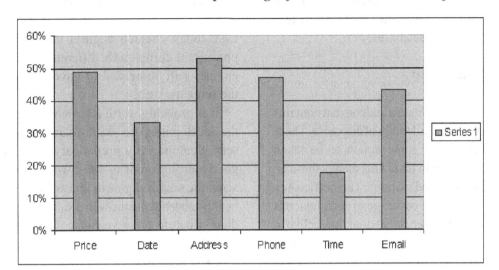

text where some medical terms exhibit a special format that can benefit from special treatment. The problem in this research work has been minimised because the medical terms have been processed by MMTx and classified highly correctly. Most medical terms that were encountered on chronic disease-related websites are terms like the names of medical devices, medicines, special foods such as herbs, vitamins, etc. Because of this, the error rate has been very small when experimenting with web pages that contain products, and conversely very high when experimenting with web pages that contain events. Many phrases that belong to events which contain personal names and locations (i.e. addresses) have been classified "Unknown Phrases." This is an issue which has been left for future work.

Object Oriented Modelling for Information

Programming in an object-oriented language such as Java provides a more natural paradigm for modelling real world objects. Concepts saved in the ontology have been mapped to Java classes and most importantly their attributes and relationships have been preserved as well. Classes in java are

blueprints that describe real word entities such as products and services. Once they are instantiated they become objects, where the attributes are usually populated with their values. Hence, it is exactly like filling the slot of a frame. Viewing the data model for an information extraction system from this perspective simplifies many aspects of the implementation of such a system. It is exactly a divide-and-conquer approach; an object of type price[2] has all the related attributes such as the value, the currency type, a vocabulary control number that links it to its semantic type, and also all related methods. Other entities, such as email and date, have been designed in the same way. Adapting the object-oriented paradigm in the design and implementation of this project has greatly influenced the handling of many issues, such as the output. For the semantic web, OWL has become the standard language for representing knowledge. To comply with the standards, a method named "toOWL" has been implemented in every class of the data model. This method transforms objects into an OWL format that can be displayed on the screen, written to disk, or sent to another process in the same computer or across the globe. At the time when many of the early IE systems were developed, the semantic web was unknown. Their primary interest was only to extract information into some type of structure such as a record in a database.

Concept Matching

Many IE systems facilitate a lexicon that contains terms that represent the domain of discourse. These terms usually trigger some action to be taken once they are found in text. This means these IE systems are term-based systems. Their efficiency depends vitally on the coverage of such lexicons and dictionaries. For very large domains, or like in the case of this research work where the domain(s) is products and services found on chronic disease-related websites, it become impossible to cover all terms. To overcome this problem a novel approach has been developed which is based on concept matching instead of term matching. This method has been presented in Eljinini (2007) and is illustrated in the following example.

ID: BPH2
Name: Blood Pressure Monitor
Description: Easy to Use... press Start - in seconds, your blood pressure and pulse are displayed.
Price: $99.98

The paragraph is first processed by MMTx and some terms are tagged with their semantic concepts. For example, the phrase "Blood Pressure Monitor" is mapped to the concept "Medical Device" and the value "$99.98" is mapped to "Price"[3]. The ontology is then queried to determine the category based on the given concepts. In the above example these concepts are matched with the category "Product". A needed improvement is the requirement to refine the set of rules to return what type of product and instantiate the correct type. Currently, only a few attributes have been tested. More work is needed in this area.

Semantic Search Engines

Like today's search engines that traverse and process the current web, different types of search engines will be needed to traverse and process the semantic web.

It is probably worth researching methods for the development of a health-related semantic web search engine. As a preliminary study, it may a good starting point to use Swoogle or another semantic search engine to find and collect a set of health-related semantic web documents, then study their structure and investigate methods to query such documents in a way that closely parallels the scenarios that were presented early in this paper.

Work in Other Languages

A concept is a concept, no matter what language it is expressed in. However, extracting information in languages other than English is different because IE depends on NLP which is language dependent. For example, the first step in information extraction is tokenisation or term zoning. In some languages, especially those of Asia, this can be a problem where some words are literary connected together to form another entity with a richer meaning. During the process of collecting chronic disease-related websites, some websites written in other European languages, such as Spanish and German, have been discarded. The number of non-English websites is increasing. Investigating IE in other languages at some point will become essential. Or is it best just to translate the text into English and then proceed with English IE? Would this achieve the same results? Does a non English health-related website differ from an English one in terms of the treatment of health-related terms? Are there any standard vocabularies that have been established and used? Etc.

Semantic Data Mining

A more mature field than information extraction is the field of data mining, which has achieved great success during the past decade. Data mining is the process of discovering new knowledge in databases, i.e. in already structured data. Since the semantic web is an extended version of the current web and a structured one, this means that a new field, that we may call "Semantic Web Mining," must emerge that is to apply current data mining methodologies and maybe research new techniques to harvest the semantic web for new knowledge. This would also apply for medical knowledge which should benefit very greatly from such a research.

Work on Other Domains

One of the main objectives of this work was to find common structure in chronic related websites. It is therefore worth looking at other domains in more depth and especially those of a medical nature to see if there are any commonalities that can be discovered. Such examination may benefit other domains.

Semantic Web Tools

The current web has revolutionised the information world in so many ways. During the past decade many tools have been developed for the web in so many different domains. What would be the status and function of such tools with the existence of the semantic web? What added value can the semantic web bring to these tools?

One potential benefit from this project includes the development of tools based on this work that would aid the webmaster in adding a semantic layer to their websites and thereby accelerating the semantic web. An example would be an interactive development environment that could intelligently supervise the webmaster in the process of constructing semantic web documents based on their HTML documents.

Current Search Engines

The current web will not go away with the evolution of the semantic web because the semantic web is another layer(s) that will coexist with the current web. In other words, other files with different extensions live in the same space with the current web. These files hold semantic information about the current web. In this case the current search engines will not go away either. However, they may access these other files to gain some added value. Today, there are many domain-specific search engines and some of them are for the medical domain. How and what is the best way for these types to gain more efficiency?

The E-Worlds in the New Era

During the last few years the world has witnessed the birth of many new concepts. One of these is the e-world, including the likes of e-commerce, e-health, e-government, e-learning, etc. Many issues will rise concerning each one of them with the evolution of the semantic web. In other words, how can each one benefit from the semantic web? Would the addition of a web with meaning have a great impact, such as for example, enhancing the current process that is done today?

Working with Images

Another issue worth looking at is the processing of web content other than text, most importantly processing images. In particular, there is the need to find suitable structures for the management and retrieval of images that reside on chronic disease websites. A picture is worth a thousand words, but how can we give a meaning to pictures residing on the semantic web? Today, image processing on the web is one of the hot research topics that attract many researchers.

CONCLUSION

Looking into the crystal ball one can see that the current web could indeed be brought to its full potential in so many ways. The possibilities become seemingly endless with the new technologies. The acceleration of the development of the semantic web becomes vital to its success and more research is needed to bring the semantic web up to the level where these things start to happen and results are felt.

This research work is directed towards this goal of moving the world faster into the semantic web and to accelerate the process. In the worst case scenario whereby the semantic web should fail, such a system would at least represent added value to existing search engines. The semantic web aims to extend the web into machine understandable form. Therefore, the automation of knowledge acquisition from the current web is becoming an important step towards this goal. The aim of this work was twofold; first to learn what types of information exist in chronic disease-related websites, and secondly how to extract and structure such information into machine understandable form. It has been shown that these websites exhibit many common concepts which resulted in the construction of the ontology to guide in extracting information for new unseen websites. Also, the study has resulted in the development of a platform for information extraction that utilises the ontology. While further work is still needed in this part, the experiments to date have shown encouraging results.

REFERENCES

Berners-Lee, T., Hendler, J., & Lassila, O. (2001). The semantic web. *Scientific American, 284*(5), 28–37. doi:10.1038/scientificamerican0501-34

Craven, M., & Kumlien, J. (1999). Constructing biological knowledge bases by extracting information from text sources. In *Proceedings of the 7th International Conference on Intelligent Systems for Molecular Biology* (pp. 77-86).

Eljinini, M.A. (2011). Health-related information structuring for the semantic web. In *Proceedings of the International Conference on Intelligent Semantic Web-Services and Applications* (p. 6).

Eljinini, M. A., & Sarhan, N. A. (2007). An ontology for extracting information from the World Wide Web. In *Proceedings of the Second Scientific Conference on Administrative and Strategic Thinking in Changing World*, Amman, Jordan.

Eljinini, M. A., Sarhan, N. A., & Carson, E. R. (2006). Towards the semantic web: Extracting common concepts from chronic disease - related websites. In *Proceedings of the International Medical Informatics and Biomedical Engineering Conference*, Amman, Jordan (pp. 118-123).

Frkovic, F., Podobnik, V., Trzec, K., & Jezic, G. (2008). Agent-based user personalization using context-aware semantic reasoning. In I. Lovrek, R. J. Howlett, & L. C. Jain (Eds.), *Proceedings of the 12th International Conference on Knowledge-Based Intelligent Information and Engineering Systems* (LNCS 5177, pp. 166-173).

Fukuda, K., Tsunoda, T., Tamura, A., & Takagi, T. (1998). Toward information extraction: Identifying protein names from biological papers. In *Proceedings of the Pacific Symposium on Biocomputing*, Maui, HI (pp. 707-718).

Krallinger, M., & Valencia, A. (2005). Text-mining and information-retrieval services for molecular biology. *Genome Biology, 6*(7), 224. doi:10.1186/gb-2005-6-7-224

Li, D., Finin, T., Joshi, A., Pan, R., Cost, R., Peng, Y., et al. (2004). Swoogle: A search and metadata engine for the semantic web. In *Proceedings of the Thirteenth ACM Conference on Information and Knowledge Management* (pp. 652-659).

Mathias, G., & Jean-Pierre, C. (2001). Toward a structured information retrieval system on the web: Automatic structure extraction of web pages. In *Proceedings of the International Workshop on Web Dynamics*, London, UK.

Müller, H. M., Kenny, E. E., & Sternberg, P. W. (2004). Textpresso: An ontology-based information retrieval and extraction system for biological literature. *Public Library of Science Biology, 2*(11), 309.

Rebholz-Schuhmann, D., Arregui, M., Gaudan, S., Kirsch, H., & Jimeno, A. (2008). Text processing through Web services: Calling Whatizit. *Bioinformatics (Oxford, England), 24*(2), 296–298. doi:10.1093/bioinformatics/btm557

Rebholz-Schuhmann, D., Kirsch, H., Arregui, M., Gaudan, S., Riethoven, M., & Stoehr, P. (2007). EBIMed—text crunching to gather facts for proteins from Medline. *Bioinformatics (Oxford, England), 23*(2), 237–244. doi:10.1093/bioinformatics/btl302

Rzhetsky, A., Iossifov, I., Koike, T., Krauthammer, M., Kra, P. B., & Morris, M. (2003). GeneWays: A system for extracting, analyzing, visualizing, and integrating molecular pathway data. *Journal of Biomedical Informatics, 37*(1), 43–53. doi:10.1016/j.jbi.2003.10.001

Soderland, S. (1999). Learning information extraction rules for semi-structured and free text. *Machine Learning, 34*, 233–272. doi:10.1023/A:1007562322031

Soderland, S., Fisher, D., Aseltine, J., & Lehnert, W. (1995). CRYSTAL: Inducing a conceptual dictionary. In *Proceedings of the 14th International Joint Conference on Artificial Intelligence* (pp. 1314-1319).

Tsuruoka, Y., Tsujii, J., & Ananiadou, S. (2008). FACTA: A text search engine for finding associated biomedical concepts. *Bioinformatics (Oxford, England), 24*(21), 2559–2560. doi:10.1093/bioinformatics/btn469

Witten, I., & Frank, E. (2000). *Data mining: Practical learning tools and techniques with java implementation.* New York, NY: Academic Press.

ENDNOTES

[1]   One of the definitions of the semantic web is a globally distributed collection of ontologies.

[2]   Note that while price is an attribute of product, it is also a concept on its own.

[3]   Prices are matched using regular expressions during the preprocessing phase since MMTx does not handle numerical values.

This work was previously published in the International Journal of Information Technology and Web Engineering (IJITWE), Volume 6, Issue 2, edited by Ghazi I. Alkhatib and Ernesto Damiani, pp. 18-28, copyright 2011 by IGI Publishing (an imprint of IGI Global).

Chapter 3
WSMO and WSMX Support to the Semantic Web Services Technology

Mariam Abed Mostafa Abed
German University in Cairo, Egypt

ABSTRACT

This paper tests the ability of the Web Service Modeling Ontology (WSMO) and the Web Service Modeling eXecution environment (WSMX) to support the Semantic Web Services technology, and automate the process of web service discovery, selection and invocation. First, it introduced web services and their limitations that were overcome in the vision of the Semantic Web Services technology. Then a Semantic Web Service (SWS) was built on top of WSMO to access the publications of the German University in Cairo (GUC), and was registered to WSMX. To test the validity to the claim, a service request to access the publications of the GUC was sent to WSMX and the process followed by WSMX was investigated. Furthermore, the discussion added a suggestion that would enhance the transparency between the Semantic Web and WSMO-WSMX initiatives.

INTRODUCTION

Specialization was proven to be of direct relationship with increased return especially when the number of people increases. Thus nowadays entities, being them individuals or enterprises, are preferring to specialize in providing a set of services or products and depend on other entities to satisfy the rest of their needs (Romer, 1987). In the world of computer science and software engineering, this is referred to as "Separation of Concerns." The Service Oriented Architecture is an architecture that supports such Separation of Concern, where entities offer their services by encapsulating them, publishing them on the web and allowing their access by service requesters through the Web Services (He, 2003).

Web Services succeeded in enhancing interdependence between entities by supporting software interoperability that allows the automation of applications making use of heterogeneous components across different organizations (Chung,

DOI: 10.4018/978-1-4666-2157-2.ch003

Lin, & Mathieu, 2003). Nevertheless, the Web Services technology had some limitations such as requiring human involvement in choosing the web service most matching his needs, and adapting his application to the specifications of the chosen web service. Hence, the need emerged for web services that can be automatically discovered, selected and invoked.

At the same time, there exists the semantic web technology that promises adding meaning to the web-data and making it machine readable. The combination between the web services technology and the semantic web technology was a solution for the normal web services limitations. Such a combination is the Semantic Web Services technology that suggested adding meaning to web services descriptions and making it machine readable (Stollberg, Shafiq, Domingue, & Cabral, 2006; McIlraith, Son, & Zeng, 2001). That would enable machines to understand the service provided by a web service and the way of its invocation; and consequently be able to perform the whole process of web service discovery, selection and invocation without any need for human intervention.

The Semantic Web Services technology needed extra support like some new standards for meaningful web services descriptions and an execution environment that is aware of these new standards. WSMO and WSMX are two initiatives claiming to be providing the enough support for the new technology. WSMO claims to offer sufficient standards for meaningful web services description, and WSMX is an execution environment that is aware of the WSMO standards (Moran, Zaremba, Mocan, & Bussler, 2004; Kerrigan, 2005).

The validity of this claim is the main focus of this paper. The paper examines the initiatives' ability to meet the promises by developing an SWS on top of WSMO, and invoking a request to test WSMX's ability to automatically discover, select and invoke the appropriate web service. The developed SWS is a search web service that is used to access the publications of the GUC.

It was tested by invoking a service request that searches publications by title.

The paper's flow is as follows: it first introduces the model and technologies used by normal Web Services and discusses their limitations, then it presents the vision of the Semantic Web Services technology and the extra support it needs. After that, it takes a look at the initiatives WSMO and WSMX, and then it presents the developed SWS components and its test results. Finally the paper discusses the results, compares them with the initial vision and then concludes.

WEB SERVICES

Web services are core elements for building distributed systems. They allow different applications to remotely access and utilize their services by sticking to some Internet standards. This interoperability between applications and web services creates the opportunity for developers to build applications utilizing services provided by different departments in different enterprises in different areas all over the world (Lewis, Morris, O'Brien, Smith, & Wrage, 2005; Papazoglou, 2008).

Model and Technologies

Web services technology follows a model called "The Publish-Find-Bind model" that uses the Web Services Description Language (WSDL), the Universal Description, Discovery and Integration (UDDI) standards, and the Simple Object Access Protocol (SOAP) technologies (Papazoglou, 2008; Brown, Johnston, & Kelly, 2002).

The Publish-Find-Bind is a model that consists of the three steps appearing in its name. Starting by Publish, it is the step done by the service provider where the web service is described and then registered to the Web Services Registry (i.e. storing its description) so that it can be reachable by service requesters. Find is the process of discovering candidate web services and selecting an appropriate one that best matches the requester's needs. Finally, Bind is the step where the actual invocation of the selected web service takes place (Papazoglou, 2008; Mahmood, 2007).

Chappell and Jewell (2002) and Srirama and Jarke (2008) explained the technologies used by the model in details; from their explanation, briefly it can be said that:

WSDL is an XML syntax that is used to describe web services by describing the messages exchanged by it and providing sufficient information that helps in its communication with other web service. Chappell and Jewell (2002) used the code in Figure 1 to show the major elements that may appear in a WSDL document (pp. 73-74).

WSDL uses <message> elements to define messages exchanged during the communication with the web service, and <operation> elements

Figure 1. WSDL main elements, adapted from Chappell and Jewell (2002, pp. 73-74)

```
<definitions>
    <import>*
    <types>
        <schema></schema>*
    </types>
    <message>*
        <part></part>*
    </message>
    <PortType>*
        <operation>*
            <input></input>
            <output></output>
            <fault></fault>*
        </operation>
    </PortType>

    <binding>*
        <operation>*
            <input></input>
            <output></output>
        </operation>
    </binding>
    <service>*
        <port></port>*
    </service>
</definitions>
```

to model operations (i.e. services) supported by the web service, and specifies input and output messages for each operation (Chappell & Jewell, 2002).

UDDI is the framework where the web services are published by service providers and then discovered by service requesters. This framework provides standards for describing web services, and discovering them. A web service is described in three categories; these three categories are represented in UDDI as follows:

1. **White Pages:** Business information is provided.
2. **Yellow Pages:** Service information is provided.
3. **Green Pages:** Technical information about a web service is provided.

SOAP is the protocol used in the communication between the web service and the client (i.e. service requester). A SOAP message is basically an XML message that follows the format presented by Newcomer (2002) in Figure 2 (p. 113).

The Envelop element is the container of the message, the Header element is optional and is used to store information about the application, and finally the Body contains the actual data that is to be exchanged between the web service and the client (Chappell & Jewell, 2002; Newcomer, 2002).

This clarifies that WSDL is an XML grammar used to describe web services that are then published to a searchable directory following the UDDI standards, and when found by the client, they exchange messages using SOAP.

Technologies' Limitations

WSDL and SOAP are very Syntacs oriented as they are XML grammers describing formats. This syntacticity of WSDL and SOAP is considered the main limitation of the Web Services technology.

Figure 2. SOAP message format (Newcomer, 2002, p. 113)

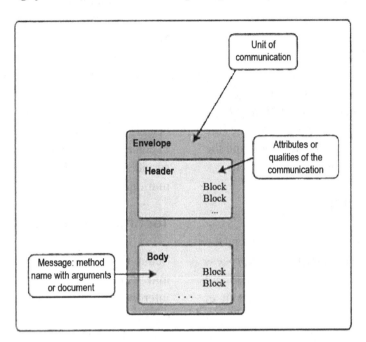

WSDL and Syntactic Interoperability

WSDL supports syntactic descriptions of web services, but fails to recognize the semantic ones. It focuses on defining the structure of the messages being exchanged, and ignores the semantics of these messages creating the so called Syntactic Interoperability (Medjahed, Bouguettaya, & Elmagarmid, 2003; Sycara, Paolucci, Ankolekar, & Srinivasan, 2003). Syntactic interoperability succeeds in allowing the composition of a complex web service from a combination of available simple ones, but fails to automate this process (Sycara et al., 2003; Paolucci, Kawamura, Payne, & Sycara, 2002). This failure is due to the process of locating appropriate web services being a semantic one, as it requires understanding the provided service while considering different ways of its representation (Paolucci et al., 2002).

SOAP and Syntactic Messages

Currently, the syntax of a SOAP message is standardized, but again, no semantics are attached to a SOAP request or response. Consequently, for two web services in order to be able to integrate, they need to agree upon some XML schema to be followed (Zhao, 2004). Obviously this decreases the flexibility of integration. In addition, the preciseness of the exchanged messages is questioned. This can be simply clarified by the following date example: "06/11/2010"; it can either be interpreted as the 6th of November or the 11th of June, depending on the date format used by the application. This creates information ambiguity that adds to the complexity of integration (Zhao, 2004).

The limitations initiated a new vision of a technology that would utilize the Semantic web technology that aims at adding meaning to data across the web, and the Web services technology that is concerned about interoperability;

this technology was the Semantic Web Services technology.

Semantic Web Services

The Semantic Web Services technology was introduced to overcome the limitations of the normal web services. This section introduces the new technology's vision and challenges, and the extra support it needs to achieve this vision.

Vision and Challenges

The Semantic Web Services vision is to extend the dynamicity of the web by automating the process of service discovery, selection, composition and execution (Stollberg et al., 2006; McIlraith et al., 2001).

Fensel and Bussler (2002) portrayed this vision by an example of an application having a task to achieve a certain result; this application should be able to search for candidate web services offering the intended service. After that, the application should be able to choose the service that best matches its needs, taking into consideration that these services may require payment, and the application should then search for the cheapest web service. After the application finds the most appropriate web service, it should be able to perform some mediations so as to resolve any interoperability issues that may appear, and finally invoke the web service without any human intervention.

Achieving such a vision requires addressing two main challenges that were introduced before as the limitations of current web services.

The first challenge, introduced by Sycara et al. (2003), is Semantic descriptions of Web services that open the room for Semantic Interoperability. In other words, the challenge is about adding meaning to web services' descriptions that would allow:

- Meaningful representation of the services provided by a certain web service.

- Explanation of the order of the messages being exchanged and their meaning
- Explanation of the preconditions that need to be satisfied to invoke the service, and the effect of this service invocation.

The second challenge, introduced by Zhao (2004), is reserving the meanings of the messages exchanged between the service requester and the service provider. This can be done adding semantic markup to the exchanged SOAP messages.

Technology Support Needed

Semantic Web Services are different from normal web services as they support automated interoperability and machine readable messages; consequently they need more support than that needed by normal web services.

To illustrate the extra support needed by the technology, Moran et al. (2004) presented an example of a client who needs to find and use a web service booking tickets of flights to Germany or Austria. This client will try first to search for the web service in the Web Services Registry using different keywords like "Train Ticket Reservation," "Book Train Tickets" or "*Fahrschein Reservierung*." The client will have to check the services' descriptions to point out services that meet his requirements. After the client is satisfied with one of the available web services, he will check the associated WSDL document to know how to invoke the web service. Finally the client will have to adjust his application to match the web service description. In this scenario, human intervention was needed in the selection of the web service and understanding the prerequisites of its invocation. To avoid this need for human intervention, descriptions of web services can be formalized and a requester should bind to this formalization when describing the web service he is searching for. Nevertheless, it cannot be assumed that all the requesters and providers would agree on certain data types to use while describing the web services, therefore there should be some mappings between data types used by requesters and providers. Moreover, there should be a framework that is aware of such standards and is able to utilize it so as to compensate for human absence. This framework would perform activities like service discovery and selection, mediation between requester and provider, and the actual service invocation (Moran et al., 2004).

WSMO/WSMX Initiatives

WSMO and WSMX are two initiatives claiming their ability of providing such support for Semantic Web Services. According to Moran et al. (2004) and Kerrigan (2005), WSMO provides the formalization needed for describing web services and the mappings between data types, or in other words, the mappings between Ontologies[1]. On the other hand, WSMX is the environment that allows service requesters to describe services they need in a formal way, and based on these descriptions, the environment selects the appropriate web service, performs the necessary mediations and invokes the web service. Finally, there should be a language following the WSMO standards, and

understood by WSMX, to describe the wed services. This language is the Web Service Modeling Language (WSML). WSML is the formalization for WSMO that gives birth to its standards. It provides the proper syntax and semantics for forming the WSMO elements. This section will visit the WSMO and WSMX initiatives and clarify some concepts related to them.

WSMO

For the formalization of web services descriptions, the WSMO was introduced to act as the ontology for describing aspects needed for discovering a web service and its invocation (Moran et al., 2004; Kerrigan, 2005).

As shown in Figure 3, adapted from de Bruijn et al. (2006), WSMO has four main elements, those are: the Ontology, the Service, the Goal, and the Mediator (p. 35).

Ontologies are representations of "real-world semantics" that are created by some communities and agreed upon by others. They perform such semantics' representation by defining some concepts and the relations between them. These ontologies are then used in describing the services and the goals (de Bruijn et al., 2006, p. 11).

Figure 3. Main WSMO elements, adapted from de Bruijn et al. (2006, p. 35)

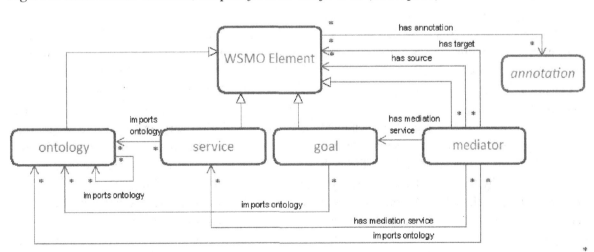

The Service represents the description of the web service, that when invoked achieves a certain service requester's goal. The service is described by defining its capabilities, interface and some non-functional properties. A service's Capability defines the functionality of a web service in terms of Preconditions, Postconditions, Assumptions and Effects. As explained by de Bruijn et al. (2006), Preconditions and Postconditions are "the information space of the Web service before" and "after its execution", and Assumptions and Effects are "the state of the world before" and "after the execution of the Web service" (p. 19). The Interface describes how the web service can be invoked to achieve its specified capabilities. In the interface, the service Choreography and Orchestration are defined. The service Choreography is for the web service's user, be him a human being or another web service, to know how to communicate with the web service. On the other hand, the service Orchestration is about how the web service collaborates with other web services to achieve its capabilities (Stollberg et al., 2006; Fensel & Stollberg, 2005). The non-functional properties are properties that have nothing to do with the execution specifications of a web service. There are no restrictions on nonfunctional properties; however, for the sake of interoperability, some properties are recommended by WSMO, those are "accuracy, financial, networkRelatedQoS, performance, reliability, robustness, scalability, security, transactional, trust" (de Bruijn et al., 2006, pp. 17-18). Moreover, in some cases, the Non-functional properties help in the process of matching service requesters and providers (Herold, 2008b).

The Goal is the objective needs to be achieved by invoking a web service. The goal description can be perceived as the description of the web service required by the requester (Moran et al., 2004; de Bruijn et al., 2006). Accordingly, goal elements are those elements used in the service description.

The Mediator. As mentioned before, it cannot be assumed that all requesters and providers would agree on a set of ontologies to use, and therefore a sort of mapping between concepts and ontologies defined by different users is needed. Mediators provide such a transformation between data described in two different conceptual models (Moran et al., 2004).

WSMX

WSMX is a framework that follows WSMO standards to allow dynamic selection and invocation of web services offering services required by requesters (Moran et al., 2004; Kerrigan, 2005). As explained by Moran et al. (2004) and Herold (2008b), the following steps model the process followed by WSMX to invoke an appropriate web service providing a service required by a goal. Refer to Figure 4 that shows WSMX architecture with the components mentioned in the process underlined

1. The process starts from the communication manager as it serves as the system's entry point.
2. The Message parser validates the received messages and saves them in-memory in a WSMX representation.
3. The Discovery component then starts to match the capabilities required by the goal, with the capabilities of the web services already registered in WSMX. This matching can be held using different criteria that are further discussed by Herold (2008b). The default matching criteria are the Keyword-based discovery and the LightWeight discovery. The former relies on matching the Non-Functional properties defined by the webService and the goal, while the latter compares the Postconditions and the Effects specified in the two interfaces.
4. The Service Discovery component refines the suggested web services resulted from

Figure 4. WSMX architecture, adapted from Herold (2008b, p. 50)

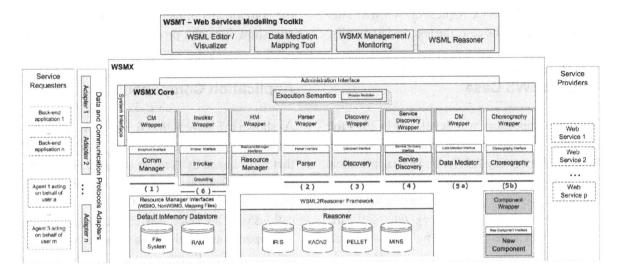

the discovery and chooses the most appropriate web service based on the requester's preferences. Some user preferences can be specified using Non-Functional properties; this is further explained by Herold (2008a).

5. After the web service is chosen and the service requester and provider are specified, appears the need for some mediation activities to resolve the heterogeneity that may exist between the webService and the goal. Two types of mediations take place; those are the *Process Mediation* and the *Data Mediation*. The *Process Mediation*, performed by the Choreography component, resolves the conflicts occurring due to the difference in how the requester and the provider are handling the process. For example the service requester may provide a service with a bulk of data and waits for a response, and at the same time, the provider is expecting the requester to send the data in a certain order so as to perform several service invocations to come up with the intended outcome. On the other hand, *Data Mediation* uses the mediators, already stored in WSMX, to transform the ontologies used by the goal to those used by the webService

in order to possiblize its invocation. It is used another time at the end to convert the ontologies returned from the webService to those used and understood by the goal.

6. Finally WSMX invokes the web service, but before the actual invocation takes place, WSMX needs to transform the instances it has, that are defined in WSML, to SOAP messages that are used by the normal Web Services. This is done by Invoker component using some "Groundings" that are defined by the service provider to convert WSML to XML and vice versa.

After having an overview on what is needed for supporting the Semantic Web Services technology and how WSMX and WSMO claim to be offering this support, next section examines the actual performance of the initiatives.

WSMX/WSMO INITIATIVES TEST

To examine the initiatives' actual capability of supporting the Semantic Web Services technology, the GUC Research Repository-Search Semantic Web Service (GUCrr-sSWS) was developed, following the WSMO standards, and tested by invoking a web service request on WSMX. This section discusses the case, the test, and its results.

Introduction to the GUCrr-sSWS Case

A research repository was developed in 2009 for the GUC by a group of its students. The GUC Research Repository (GUCrr) is a web application that allows browsing, searching and retrieving publications by the GUC through a graphical user interface (i.e. human interface), thus software agents cannot access the GUC publications since the interface does not support machine readability. Addressing this limitation by developing of an SWS for searching the repository was a good opportunity for examining the WSMO and WSMX initiatives. This web service was called the GUCrr-sSWS.

The Developed Software

The GUCrr-sSWS is a very simple web service handling only two use scenarios; those are "Search by Title" and "Search by Author name." Both use scenarios input a single search string and output one matching publication.

According to WSMO, to develop an SWS, the actual web service should be implemented, a WSMO webService should be created describing the web service and the necessary ontologies used by the webService should be defined. Then, to test it, a goal needs to be created, that is representing a request to WSMX, and the ontologies used by it. In addition, the appropriate mediators between the ontologies used by the webService and those used by the goal should be defined. For the sake of simplicity, one ontology for both the webService and the goal was used, and consequently there were no need for mediators. Finally, as mentioned before, WSMX needs some groundings to know how to convert from WSML

to XML and vice versa. This section will discuss the components implemented in the application and show how the process is expected to flow using these components.

Application Components

As shown in Figure 5, the GUCrr is already defining an Application Programming Interface (API) that can be used by the web service to access the GUC's publications. The actual web service was created using this API and the interface IPublicationsSearchService was created to model the two operations of the web service; those are: "titleSearch" and "authorSearch." A WSMO webService, written in WSML, was created to describe the actual webService, and was called AccessPublicationWS. As for the Ontologies, according to the selected use scenarios, the output can be modeled by a 'Publication' concept, and the input can be modeled by a "titleSearch" and an "authorSearch" concepts. All the concepts were created in one ontology called Library that is visualized in Figure 6. A Goal to test the webService was created and called AccessPublicationsGoal. Finally two Groundings were created to help WSMX perform the appropriate conversions between WSML and XML. The first is the Lowering grounding that is used to convert WSML to XML, and the second is the Lifting grounding that is also used to convert XML to WSML. For a better understanding of the application's components, Figure 7 simply illustrates how the process is expected to flow.

Expected Process Flow Expected Process Flow

Figure 7 shows how the process is expected to flow, and considering the search by title use scenario, the following should apply:

Step 1: AccessPublicationGoal should contain the description of the required webSer-

Figure 5. GUCrr-sSWS components

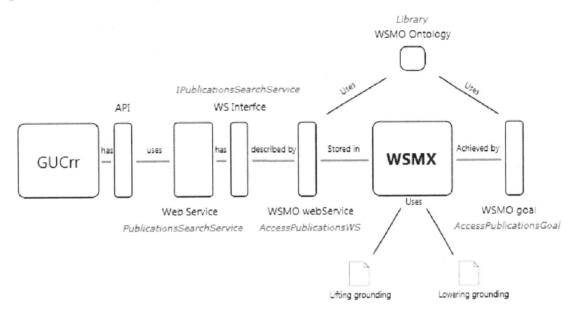

Figure 6. Visualization for the library ontology

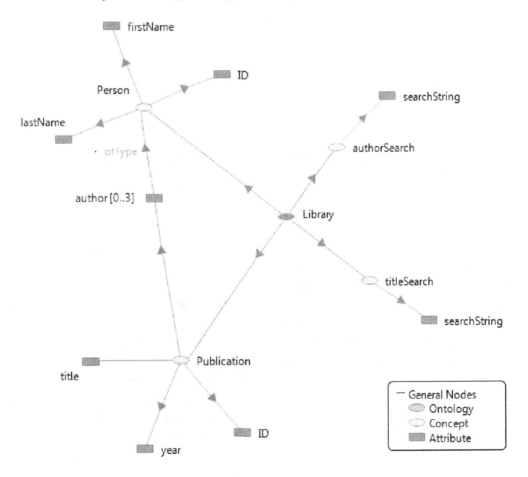

Figure 7. Request to achieve the AccessPublicationsGoal – process flow

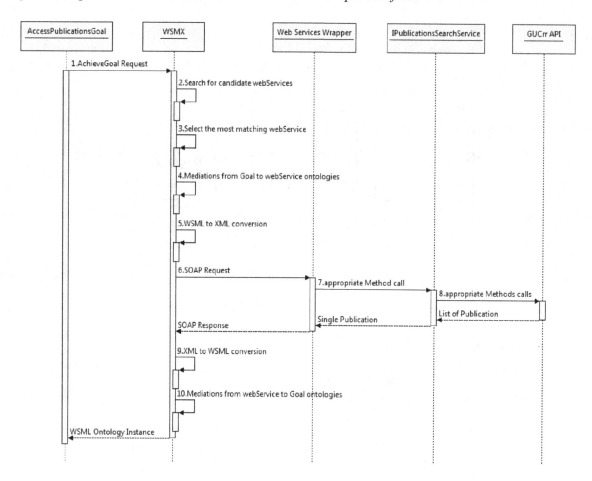

vice, to help in the appropriate webService discovery, and an instance of the concept "titleSearch" that is representing the request.

Step 2: AccessPublicationsWS should be one of a list of discovered candidate matches.

Step 3: AccessPublicationsWS should be selected.

Steps 4 and 10: Do not apply, since the same ontology is used by the webService and the goal.

Steps 5 and 9: The Lowering and the Lifting groundings should be used respectively.

Finally: A Publication instance should be returned to the goal.

The WebService Test

The testing in this paper is concerned with the automation of the selection and invocation processes of the webService. This section will show the results of searching publications by title using the keyword "Constraint Programming."

Service Discovery and Selection

As shown in Figure 8, thirty four webServices were loaded to the WSMX server, only five of them were discovered using the Keyword discovery, *AccessPublicationsWS* was the only webService discovered using the LightWeight discovery and it was the selected one.

Figure 8. WebService Discovery and selection

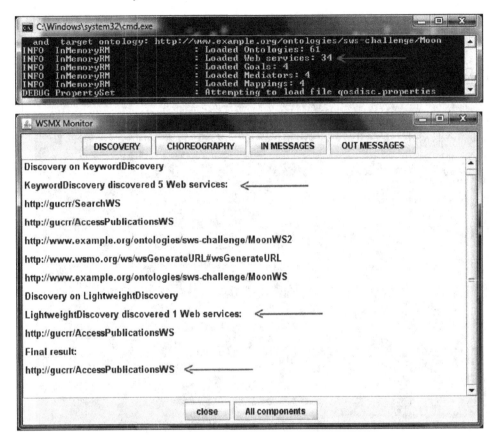

WebService Invocation

The webService was automatically invoked using an appropriate SOAP message that calls the title search with "Constraint Programming" as a search string. After that, the invoked webService replied with a SOAP message containing information about the publication resulted from the search and its authors. Figure 9 shows the exchanged SOAP messages.

WebService Response

Finally, as shown in Figures 10 and 11, the SOAP message is converted to its corresponding WSML representation, and is sent back to the goal in the form of a Publication instance with its two authors.

DISCUSSION

To well interpret the GUCrr-sSWS case and its results presented in the previous section, the expected process flow, presented previously and shown in Figure 7, will be referred to and compared to the actual results.

The process started by an AchieveGoal request, followed by a search for Candidate services, then selecting the most matching service, after that the conversion of the ontology instance to XML then sending the SOAP request, and appropriate methods calls from the web service and the *GUCrr API*, then a SOAP response to WSMX and finally the response conversion to WSML and a *Publication* instance returned to the goal. The steps between sending and receiving SOAP messages will not be discussed since it is out of this paper's scope.

Figure 9. The exchanged SOAP messages

Figure 10. WSML representation for the SOAP response

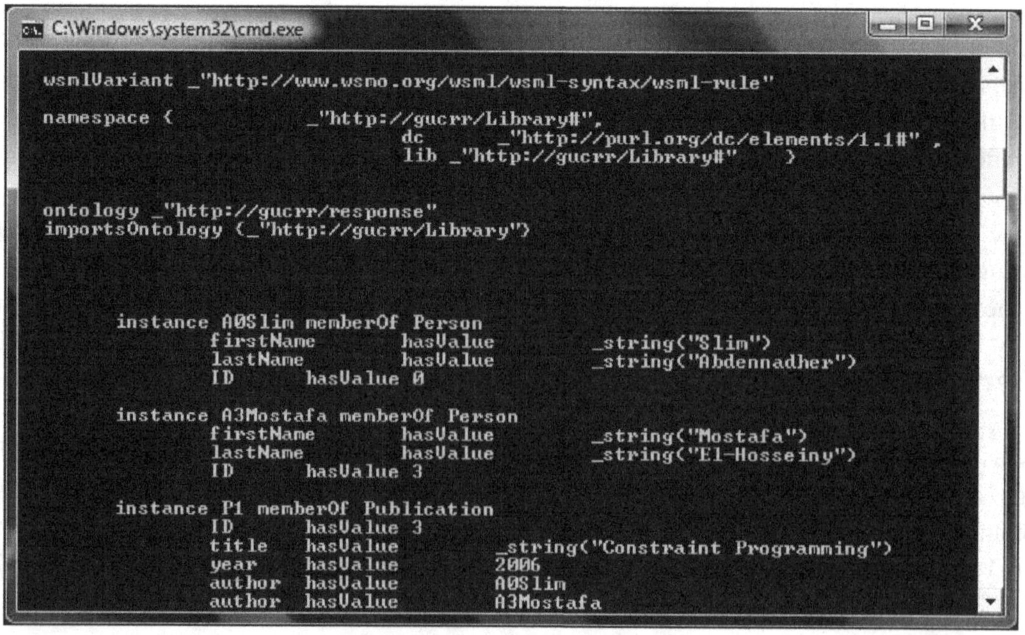

Figure 11. The final response - A publication instance with two authors

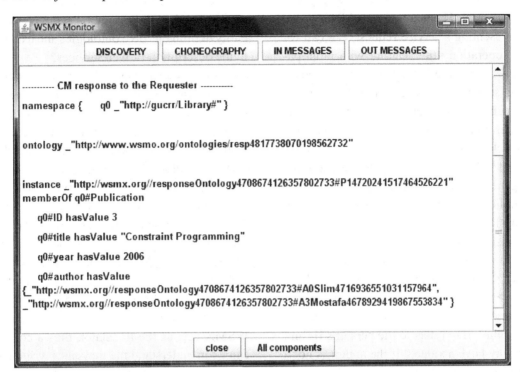

Step 1: AchieveGoal Request. The goal used a titleSearch instance with the searchString "Constraint Programming" to test the first use scenario.

Step 2: Search for candidate webServices. The results showed five discovered webServices from thirty four already loaded to WSMX; this can be explained by the default discovery criteria presented previously. The Keyword discovery that performs a matching between the NFPs discovered the five webServices that had the NFP dc#language hasValue "en- US". On the other hand, the Lightweight discovery which compares the postconditions only discovered the webService AccessPublicationsWS as it is the only web service with the postcondition member of Publication. Obviously the AccessPublicationsWS was in the list of the candidate webServices and this is what was expected in this step.

Step 3: Select the most matching webService. The AccessPublicationsWS was discovered using the two methods, so it was the most matching webService and the results show that it was selected and this complies with the expectations.

(As mentioned before, Steps 4 and 9 do not apply since one ontology is used by the goal and the webService, so there is no need for mediation.)

Step 5: WSML to XML conversion. After service selection and before the invocation, the titleSearch instance is converted to it corresponding XML using the lowering grounding. Figure 9 shows the outgoing SOAP message which is the result of such a conversion.

Step 6: SOAP Request and Response. The generated SOAP message is then used to invoke the actual web service, and the results showed the web service response in Figure 9. The Outgoing SOAP message, representing a service request, is a call for the operation <titleSearch> with input parameter <SearchCriteria> and containing the searchString representing the <title> which is "Constraint Programming". On the other hand, the incoming SOAP message, which is the service response, contains an <out> element presenting the output of the operation titleSearch, which is basically a publication. The returned publication had an <ID> with value 3, a <title> with value Constrain Programming, a <publicatioYear> with value 2006 and two authors resented in two <Author> elements each having <ID>, <fn> and <ln>. The <fn> refers to the First Name, the <ln> refers to the Last Name, and the <ID> refers to the person's ID and it may have a value 0 if the author is not a registered user (i.e. his name is saved as a string). The two authors of the returned publication are: Slim Abdennadher who is an unregistered author, and Mostafa El-Hosseiny with the ID 3.

Step 9: XML to WSML conversion. The lifting grounding is used to convert the returned SOAP message to its corresponding WSML representation shown in Figure 10. Finally, a Publication instance represented by the WSML in Figure 10 is returned to the goal as show in Figure 11.

The steps showed that the expected process has been successfully followed and the service was dynamically discovered, selected and invoked.

Recalling the Semantic Web Services vision that was to enhance interoperability by automating the process of service discovery, selection, composition, and execution. The results showed that WSMO standards and its execution environment, WSMX, were able to achieve such a vision. It also showed that the two limitations of the normal web services were overcome as no human

intervention was needed and the ambiguity of the exchanged SOAP messages is resolved by every entity defining its own ontologies and using them in the description of webServices.

As for the challenges, the first is actually met by WSMO as it requires a definition for the service capability in which the preconditions and the post-conditions of a service invocation are specified. In addition, it requires a webService interface definition that explains how to communicate with the webService and how the webService collaborates with other webServies to offer its functionality. As for adding semantic mark-up to the SOAP messages, this does not seem to be adding in this context since WSMX communicate with both the webService and the goal using their ontologies. In other words, the requester and the provider are using their own languages to communicate, and WSMX acts as the translator, thus a communicator can understand the messages written in his own language with no need to adding semantic mark-up to them. *Nevertheless, adding semantic mark-up to the WSMO ontologies is suggested* so that WSMX may perform its mediation activities depending on the semantics attached to the ontologies and by referring to the semantic web. This would create a transparency between the semantic web and WSMX, and decrease the effort exerted by developers in defining mediators between ontologies.

CONCLUSION

In conclusion, the paper's aim was to test WSMX and WSMO's capability of supporting automatic selection and invocation of a web service. It first introduced the normal web services and technologies used by the Publish-Find-Bind model; those are WSML, UDDI, and SOAP. Then it discussed the necessity of human interference in the process of selecting and invoking the most matching web service as being a limitation of the web services technology. It also added to its limitations the ambiguity of the exchanged SOAP messages between the service requester and the service provider.

Semantic web services were then suggested as a technology that promises overcoming these limitations and automating the process of web service discovery, selection and invocation. The technology suggested describing the web services in a meaningful way that would explain the services it offer, the order of the messages exchanged by the web service, and the preconditions needed for invoking the web service. As for the ambiguity of the exchanged SOAP messages, a suggestion was to add semantic mark-up to the exchanged SOAP messages that would add meaning to the attached data.

The paper explained that Semantic web services need extra support to be able to meet the expectations; this support was a standardization for the web services description, a language that formalizes these standards, and an execution environment that is able to process the service requests based on understanding such standards and language. WSMO, WSML, and WSMX were initiatives claiming to provide the needed support and the paper's aim was to examine the validity of such a claim.

The paper had an overview on WSMO main elements and the process followed by WSMX to respond to a service request. The webService, the goal, the ontology and the mediator were the four main elements of WSMO. The WSMO webService is the semantic description of a certain web service, the goal represents a request for a service, the ontology is used to model the real-world entities recognized by the webService and the goal and the relations between them, and finally the mediator is a sort of mapping between ontologies to model different representations of the same entity. WSMX receives a request to achieve a goal, it starts searching for candidate webServices based on the description provided in the goal then it selects the most matching web-Service according to the user preferences. After that WSMX starts some mediation activities to resolve the heterogeneity between the goal and the selected webService, be it because of different ontologies used or different processes followed. After the mediation is done successfully, WSMX has the request in terms of an ontology instance that is used and understood by the webService. It converts the instance to the corresponding SAOP message, invokes the actual web service, receives a SOAP response, and converts it back to an ontology instance used by the webService. Again WSMX uses the mediators to transform the response represented in an ontology instance used by the webService to an ontology instance used and understood by the goal, and finally sends it as a response to the goal.

The Semantic Web Service discussed in this paper was for accessing the publications of the GUC. It was built on top of an already existing research repository that provides an API for performing a search on the publications available on the repository. The webService implementation only handled searching the publications by author and by title to return the first outputted publication.

The webService was tested by attempting to achieve a goal that needs to search publications by title. The results and the discussion sections showed how the previously mentioned process was followed by WSMX to automatically discover, select and invoke the webService without requiring any human intervention, which was the vision of the Semantic Web Services technology. This shows that the claim by WSMO and WSMX of supporting the Semantic Web Services technology vision is valid, and the initiatives are capable of automating the process of web service discovery, selection and invocation.

The discussion also showed how the idea of describing the webService in a meaningful way was followed by WSMO; while on the other hand, adding semantic mark-up to SOAP messages was of no use in this context since WSMX acts as a translator between the webService and the goal that ends up with each of them using its own language.

Finally, adding semantic mark-up to the ontologies was suggested to enhance the transparency between semantic web services and the semantic web, and to act instead of the mediators.

ACKNOWLEDGMENT

Firstly, I would like to thank my family for providing me with all what is necessary to live, work, and succeed. Thanks to Prof. Dr. Ralf Klischewski for being a very helpful and supportive supervisor. Special thanks to my friend and colleague Nancy Galal for her participation in understanding the WSMO/WSMX technologies and the creation of the SWS, and for her hard work throughout the project. Thanks to the researcher Omair Shafiq for taking time to answer our questions and providing us with the necessary material to understand the technology. Also, thanks to Aya Saad for her help and feedback on the paper. Thanks to Karim El-Sayed and Tasbeeh Othman for being helpful members from the GUCrr team. Finally and firstly and always, thanks to Allah for always being there for everyone.

REFERENCES

Brown, A., Johnston, S., & Kelly, K. (2002). *Using service-oriented architecture and component-based development to build web service applications.* Retrieved from http://citeseerx.ist.psu.edu/viewdoc/download?doi=10.1.1.86.510-&rep=rep1&type=pdf

Chappell, D., & Jewell, T. (2002). *Java web services.* Sebastopol, CA: O'Reilly Media.

Chung, J. Y., Lin, K. J., & Mathieu, R. G. (2003). Web services computing: Advancing software interoperability. *IEEE Computer*, *36*(10), 35–57.

de Bruijn, J., Bussler, C., Domingue, J., Fensel, D., & Hepp, M. Kifer, et al. (2006). *Web service modeling ontology (WSMO).* Retrieved from http://www.wsmo.org/TR/d2/v1.3/D2v1-3_20061021.pdf

Fensel, D., & Bussler, C. (2002). The web service modeling framework WSMF. *Electronic Commerce Research and Applications*, *1*(2), 1–33. doi:10.1016/S1567-4223(02)00015-7

Fensel, D., & Stollberg, M. (2005). *Ontology-based choreography and orchestration of WSMO services.* Retrieved from http://www.wsmo.org/TR/d14/v0.1/d14v01_20050301.pdf

He, H. (2003). *What is service-oriented architecture.* Retrieved from http://www.xml.com/pub/a/ws/2003/09/30/soa.html

Herold, M. (2008a). *WSMX documentation.* Retrieved from http://www.wsmx.org/papers/documentation/WSMXDocumentation.pdf

Herold, M. (2008b). *Evaluation and advancement in context of a tourist information system.* Retrieved from http://www.fh-wedel.de/fileadmin/mitarbeiter/iw/Abschlussarbeiten/MasterarbeitHerold.pdf

Horrocks, I., Patel-Schneider, P. F., & van Harmelen, F. (2003). From SHIQ and RDF to OWL: The making of a web ontology language. *Journal of Web Semantics*, *1*(1), 7–26. doi:10.1016/j.websem.2003.07.001

Kerrigan, M. (2005, June). The WSML editor plug-in to the web services modeling toolkit. In *Proceedings of the 2nd WSMO Implementation Workshop*, Innsbruck, Austria.

Lewis, G., Morris, E., O'Brien, L., Smith, D., & Wrage, L. (2005). *SMART: The service-oriented migration and reuse technique.* Retrieved from http://citeseerx.ist.psu.edu/viewdoc/download?doi=10.1.1.87.6762-&rep=rep1&type=pdf

Mahmood, Z. (2007). Service oriented architecture: Tools and technologies. In *Proceedings of the 11th WSEAS International Conference on Computers*, Crete Island, Greece.

McIlraith, S. A., Son, T. C., & Zeng, H. (2001). Semantic web services. *IEEE Intelligent Systems*, *16*(2), 46–53. doi:10.1109/5254.920599

Medjahed, B., Bouguettaya, A., & Elmagarmid, A. K. (2003). Composing web services on the semantic web. *Very Large Data Bases Journal*, *12*(4), 333–351. doi:10.1007/s00778-003-0101-5

Moran, M., Zaremba, M., Mocan, A., & Bussler, C. (2004, September). Using wsmx to bind requester and provider at runtime when executing semantic web services. In *Proceedings of the 1st WSMO Implementation Workshop*, Frankfurt, Germany.

Newcomer, E. (2002). *Understanding web services: XML, WSDL, SOAP, and UDDI*. Reading, MA: Addison-Wesley.

Paolucci, M., Kawamura, T., Payne, T. R., & Sycara, K. P. (2002). Importing the semantic web in UDDI. *Revised Papers from the International Workshop on Web Services, E-Business, and the Semantic Web*, *2512*, 225-236.

Papazoglou, M. P. (2008). *Web services: Principles and technology*. Upper Saddle River, NJ: Prentice Hall.

Romer, P. M. (1987). Growth based on increasing returns due to specialization. *American Economic Association*, *77*(2), 56–62.

Srirama, S. N., & Jarke, M. (2009). Mobile hosts in enterprise service integration. *International Journal of Web Engineering and Technology*, *5*(2), 187–213. doi:10.1504/IJWET.2009.028620

Stollberg, M., Shafiq, O., Domingue, J., & Cabral, L. (2006, September). Semantic web services: State of affairs. In *Proceedings of the First Asian Semantic Web Conference*, Beijing, China.

Sycara, K., Paolucci, M., Ankolekar, A., & Srinivasan, N. (2003). Automated discovery, interaction and composition of semantic web services. *Web Semantics*, *1*(1), 27–46. doi:10.1016/j.websem.2003.07.002

Zhao, Y. (2004). Combining RDF and OWL with SOAP for semantic web services. In *Proceedings of the 3rd Annual Nordic Conference on Web Services*, Linköping, Sweden.

ENDNOTES

[1]   In this context, the context of the Semantic Web, a data type is represented by an Ontology that is used to represent a real world entity and its relations with other entities (Horrocks, Patel-Schneider, & van Harmelen, 2003).

This work was previously published in the International Journal of Information Technology and Web Engineering (IJITWE), Volume 6, Issue 2, edited by Ghazi I. Alkhatib and Ernesto Damiani, pp. 40-56, copyright 2011 by IGI Publishing (an imprint of IGI Global).

Chapter 4
A Generic QoS Model for Web Services Design

Wan Nurhayati Wan Ab. Rahman
Universiti Putra Malaysia, Malaysia

Farid Meziane
University of Salford, UK

ABSTRACT

The development, registration, discovery, and invocation of quality Web services are vital for the successful implementation of applications using Web services. Considerable research focuses on quality for Web services. Unfortunately, current research on Quality of Service (QoS) for Web services is concentrated on service users and the implementation stage. This research highlights the importance of incorporating QoS at the design and development stages; the authors propose the introduction of QoS at the same time as functional requirements. However, Web Service Description Language (WSDL) describes the functional elements of a Web service, and QoS is significant for this description. Therefore, the authors propose an extension to the WSDL through a generic QoS metamodel, incorporating QoS specifications into the functionalities. This paper begins by defining the required QoS specifications for the development of quality Web services and explores the potential of the Unified Modeling Language as a technique and notation to specify QoS. To properly integrate QoS in the design, the authors propose extensions to the existing UML QoS profile. The paper concludes with the evaluation of the proposed framework and summarises its advantages.

1. INTRODUCTION

Web services have been advocated as the solution to the limitations of previous Web technologies and infrastructures. Their development is based on XML to facilitate interoperability between various services and infrastructures by using a small set of common protocols. Furthermore, Web services develop a uniform representation of network applications that are accessible using multiple communication protocols (Curbera et al., 2001). They are also widely accepted as a clear medium for interoperability between service providers and requesters. Service providers can develop

DOI: 10.4018/978-1-4666-2157-2.ch004

their Web applications by implementing Web services as the underlying platform to distribute information, sell products and provide services to customers. On the other hand, users or potential clients can search for and invoke services hence, providing seamless integration between Internet clients and servers where communications and interoperability are possible even when operating systems and programming languages are different. As stated by Chung et al. (2003) "Web services interoperability allows businesses to dynamically publish, discover and aggregate a range of Web services through the Internet to more easily create innovative products, business processes and value chains." Web services also allow reusable Web component to be integrated over the Internet to ease the development process (Mathijssen, 2005).

There are many available Web services and some of these are very similar in the kind of functionality they provide. Functionality is a service or task for a Web service to offer to users, for example product selling. Even though they are designed for the same purpose, their qualities may differ. Quality of Service (QoS) could make a Web service better than another Web service. Therefore, service providers should consider incorporating QoS when designing and developing their Web services. QoS specification is a non-functional requirement that could improve the functionality and overall quality performance of a Web service. In order to do that, they need to know QoS specifications that are relevant to their Web services. In other words, they need to be aware of providing the necessary quality for their Web services by knowing the factors, characteristics and dimensions that could contribute to develop and provide quality Web services. Moreover, it is essential for service providers, including designers and developers to identify the QoS specifications for their Web services as early as possible in the development life cycle. We believe that QoS specifications could assist people in Web service projects to better understand what

quality represents and to ease service providers in determining it.

Even though QoS focuses mainly on non-functional requirements of Web services, it does affect the overall functionality of Web services. This is because QoS improves Web services' functionality, assists interoperability and communication between service providers and requesters, and provides reliable, relevant and fast services. QoS can be referred to as a description of how well a Web service does, but not what it does. A better understanding of QoS could assist service providers in offering better Web services to users, and the users should be able to get exactly what they want with better quality services. Therefore, users will be able to make the right decisions by choosing high quality Web services to fulfill their needs (Taher et al., 2005). In addition, QoS is very important to ensure that Service-Oriented Architecture (SOA) is effective for enterprise systems (Wang et al., 2004; Menasce et al., 2007) and contributes to the successful implementation of transaction-oriented applications (Pallickara et al., 2006) such as e-commerce applications (Bhatti et al., 2000; Cardellini et al., 2001) as users would expect more in terms of fast service from commercially successful companies (Weller, 2002).

The aim of this research is to define a framework to encourage the inclusion of QoS in the early stage of Web services development. For this purpose, a set of QoS specifications are indentified and then incorporated in a metamodel that can be used as the basis for the development of Web services. We also investigate the usability of Unified Modeling Language (UML) to specify these QoS specifications and its potential to be extended as a technique to model QoS specifications for Web services. Subsequently, the motivation for the research is the need for a QoS metamodel to guide service providers to design and develop quality Web services and help service providers to incorporate QoS specifications into Web service design at the initial development process. We will introduce a lightweight extension to the WSDL to include the QoS specifications through the QoS metamodel. By developing the QoS metamodel, this research will overcome the shortcomings of the quality specification for Web services as reported in the literature. In addition, the paper provides a comprehensive review and description of the QoS specifications that comprise some already existing factors contributing to the QoS and some newly proposed ones.

The QoS metamodel illustrates what functionalities and how they can be extended with the proposed QoS specifications. The basic WSDL specification consists of a definition element as the root, and other elements that include types, message, portType, binding, service and import. All of these elements describe the functionality of a Web service. This research sees the possibility of extending the WSDL specification to include a set of QoS specification to describe the non-functionality of a Web service. These QoS specifications are vital as an augmentation to the existing WSDL specification to assure quality Web services development and implementation. The QoS metamodel could be referred to incorporate QoS specifications into WSDL. Besides, the description of QoS specifications and the QoS metamodel can be used as a reference model for service providers, designers, developers and users to provide, use and select good quality Web services. The QoS metamodel is meant to be general and flexible. Therefore, it is not meant to restrict specific service providers or the use of a certain technique, language or implementation approach. The remaining of this paper is organized as follows. Section 2 highlights the requirements for the QoS metamodel and uses existing literature to select a set of QoS specifications. We investigate the use of UML for the QoS specifications that need to be incorporated into Web services designs in Section 3. Section 4 summarises the work done so far in the development of our QoS metamodel. We demonstrate and validate the practical use of the QoS metamodel to design and develop qual-

ity Web services in Sections 5 and 6. Finally, we give our conclusions in Section 7.

2. REQUIREMENTS FOR THE QUALITY OF SERVICE METAMODEL

In order to form a base of QoS specification, we developed a definition of the QoS for Web services based on our understanding of what QoS is and what it should provide as: "QoS for Web services is the ability of their services to provide added value to the best solution for users' enquiries, taking into account their specific requirements" (WanAbRahman, 2008). QoS refers to the added value that a Web service should provide to improve its quality performance. It tells how Web services should perform and achieve wide acceptance and satisfaction from users. The best solution from the definition refers to the most suitable high quality service that could give exactly what users want. In general, the quality of Web services is not only specified by their functionality, but also their QoS or non-functional requirement (WanAbRahman, 2010).

Previous works from the literature review have considered non-functionality as the main requirement for QoS. Early researchers have emphasized on the importance of QoS from various aspects and scopes, and from users and providers perspectives. In this way, users could contribute to the development of Web services by providing feedback based on their experiences in using Web services. Besides, the QoS for Web services can also be evaluated from the service providers' perspective, and the QoS can be described as a combination of several qualities or properties of a service (Menasce, 2002). Ran (2003) has organized different aspects of QoS into QoS categories and grouped these categories into different types including runtime related QoS, transaction support related QoS, configuration management and cost related QoS, and security related QoS. QoS is also crucial for Web service composition

(Papazoglou & Georgakopoulos, 2003; Milanovic & Malek, 2004). The following are the most used QoS specifications:

- **Service Time:** The length of time taken by services to respond to users' requests (Jin et al., 2002; Chen et al., 2003; Cardoso et al., 2004; Agarwal et al., 2005).
- **Reliability:** The capability of maintaining the service and service quality. For example, perform operation as client wishes via safe network connections (Ran, 2003; Silver et al., 2003; Day & Deters, 2004; Sivashanmugam et al., 2005).
- **Execution Price:** The cost a service requester has to pay for executing an operation (Sahai et al., 2001; Al-Ali et al., 2002; Zeng et al., 2003; Mathijssen, 2005).
- **Availability** refers to the presence of a Web service for a client to connect to it (Al-Ali et al., 2002; Papazoglou & Georgakopoulos, 2003; Zeng et al., 2003; Mathijssen, 2005).
- **Performance:** Measured by throughput and latency. Throughput is the number of Web service requests served at a given time period. Latency is the round-trip time between sending a request and receiving the response. Both are affected by factors like processor speed, code efficiency and network transfer time. Performance can also be determined by response time to guarantee maximum time required to complete a service request (Mani & Nagarajan, 2002; Looker et al., 2004; D'Ambrogio, 2007).
- **Security:** The existence and type of authentication mechanisms, messages encryption and access control that the service offers, confidentiality for any exchanged messages, non-repudiation for requests or messages transferred and resilience to denial-of-service attacks (Looker et al., 2004; D'Ambrogio, 2007).

Other QoS characteristics have been considered by other researchers. These can be summarised as follows:

- **Accessibility:** The capability of satisfying a Web service request (Ouzzani, 2003; Looker et al., 2004; Mathijssen, 2005).
- **Transaction:** The integrity of data operation that is performing by a transaction. It relates to ACID property, which contains the following characteristics (Menasce, 2002; Schmit & Dudstar; 2005; Papazoglou & Kratz, 2006):
  - **Atomicity:** Executes entire transactions or not at all.
  - **Consistency:** Maintains data integrity and consistency in updated transactions.
  - **Isolation:** Individual transactions run as if no other transactions are present.
  - **Durability:** The persistence of results.
- **Capacity:** The maximum number of concurrent requests a server can process to guarantee performance or the number of concurrent connections that is permitted by the service (Al-Ali et al., 2002; Ran, 2003; Mathijssen, 2005).
- **Integrity:** The maintaining of correct and consistent interaction to the source (Mani & Nagarajan, 2002; Looker et al., 2004).
- **Regulatory:** The conformance and compliance to the rules, laws, standards and specifications. This can have effects on availability, performance and reliability through service level agreements (Mani & Nagarajan, 2002; Ran, 2003)
- **Reputation:** Measures the service trustworthiness based on end user's experiences of using the service (Zeng et al., 2003).

Based on existing research, we identified 12 QoS specifications that have been used in existing research related to QoS for Web services. The

QoS specifications are the baseline characteristics that good quality Web services must possess and service providers should consider when developing their Web services. In this research, we choose seven QoS specifications, which are incorporated in our generic QoS metamodel, as illustrated in bold in Figure 1. The remaining five QoS specifications were not chosen because they are unsuitable for our approach that also aims at extending WSDL. Besides, most of them have been used for the implementation, for example, to compare and select the best available services, to find and discover the best services, to distribute information and application, and to provide new and relevant information for requesters.

Table 1 shows the summary of these QoS specifications and their frequency in the reviewed literature and provide a comprehensive description of QoS specifications in Table 2 to be used as a checking list by service providers and designers. In addition to the 12 existing QoS specifications, we propose some relevant QoS dimensions and attributes that could be applied to the QoS specifications (WanAbRahman, 2010). Our contribution towards providing the QoS description is necessary as it consists of a comprehensive QoS specification that could be referred to by service designers, developers and users.

3. UML POTENTIAL TO MODEL QOS AND EXTENSIONS

The main purpose of UML is to model systems such as information systems, technical systems, embedded real-time systems, distributed systems, system software and business systems (Eriksson & Penker, 1998; Bennett et al., 2006). In addition, the main use of UML is to document functional requirements, scope and interaction between users and systems (Kratochvil & McGibbon, 2003; Rumbaugh et al., 2005). Moreover, UML also can be used to model non-functional requirements and systems usability (Jezequel et al., 2002). However, there are very limited works that have applied UML for describing non-functional requirements (Miguel, 2003). Research on the use of UML to model Web services quality is still ongoing and pursued by many researchers. According to OMG, "UML is OMG's most-used specification, and the way the world models not only application structure, behaviour and architecture, but also business process and data structure" (OMG, 2009). Furthermore, "UML can also be used as a metamodelling language, where UML diagrams are used to formalize the abstract syntax of another modelling language" (Sheng & Benatallah, 2005). In this section, we review some related work that

Figure 1. 12 QoS specifications

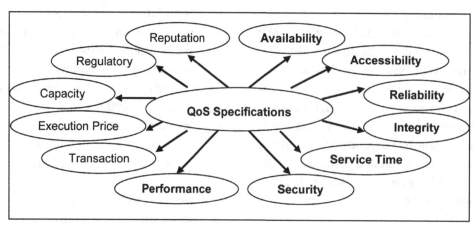

Table 1. The frequency of QoS specifications (WanAbRahman, 2010)

QoS Specification	Percentage (%)
Service time	57.69
Reliability	57.69
Execution price	53.85
Availability	50.00
Performance	34.62
Security	34.62
Accessibility	19.23
Transaction	15.38
Capacity	11.54
Integrity	11.54
Regulatory	11.54
Reputation	3.85

have used UML as a modelling language for non-functional requirements.

The Object Management Group (OMG) has provided QoS specification for modelling QoS and Fault Tolerance (FT) characteristics and mechanisms in UML profile. OMG has introduced a set of general QoS categories, characteristics and dimensions and outlined more relationships between QoS characteristics, constraints and levels with their metamodels (OMG, 2008). However, these QoS characteristics are limited and cannot be used to represent all existing QoS specifications.

Gronmo and Jaeger (2005) proposed a model-driven methodology for building new Web service compositions that optimize QoS using UML. The approach is a control-flow pattern for the automatic selection of services and computation of overall QoS values. Their control flow patterns could enhance the local approach by giving similar results in almost the same QoS to global approach but with shorter computation time. Most of the steps in their methodology are however manual.

Gronmo et al. (2004) converted Web service descriptions in WSDL to UML. Their UML models are integrated to form composite Web services, and the new Web service descriptions are then exported. WSDL-independent UML models are better for understanding what a Web service does and it is adequate for forward and/or reverse engineering Web services. Their two-way transformations from WSDL to UML and vice versa could make the development process more complicated.

Chan and Poernomo (2007) implemented a Model Driven Architecture based framework for the runtime monitoring of QoS properties. They have incorporated UML2 superstructure and UML profile for QoS to provide abstract descriptions of component-and-connector system. Their approach is compliant with OMG and Distributed Management Taskforce technologies that ensure easier integration with other tools and methodologies that comply with similar standards. However, the approach provides a level of trust through the means to verify whether QoS requirements are being met in the deployed system rather than formally prove that requirements are met.

D'Ambrogio (2006) introduced a WSDL metamodel from the WSDL XML schema, and then transforms it into a Q-WSDL metamodel. She focused on QoS for service selection to satisfy service consumers and consider QoS prediction for service providers. The Q-WSDL metamodel is meant to be general and flexible and it can be used for both service providers and requesters. The proposed metamodel is only capable of describing limited QoS characteristics from OMG.

D'Ambrogio and Brocciarelli (2007) introduced a model-driven approach to integrate performance prediction into service composition processes. The foundation of their approach is the P-WSDL that is a lightweight WSDL extension for the description of performance characteristics of a Web service. Their method can be applied for both static (at design time) and dynamic (at execution time) Web services composition. However, their approach only supports static service composition.

Generally, UML has also been used to specify QoS and FT characteristics (Chan & Poernomo, 2007; Miguel, 2003). Previous research has ap-

Table 2. A comprehensive list of QoS specifications with their definitions, descriptions and dimensions

QoS Specifications
1. Availability To ensure the existence of a Web service and its readiness to perform its functionality. The Web service should be available and easy to be discovered at anytime, anywhere. Can be specified by determining the available time/duration of the Web service. TimeToRepair (TTR) and TimeBetweenFailure (TBF) can be applied to measure availability.
2. Accessibility The Web service is accessible and ready to be invoked by users. The Web service is capable of processing users' requests. The MaxNumberOfResponse and the NumberOfCorrectResponse can be used to measure it. High accessibility should provide optimum correct response to service requesters.
3. Reliability It assures for the complete delivery of messages between requesters and service providers and the completeness of transactions. The Web service is stable and can be trusted whatever/whenever unpredictable situations occur. Service providers should provide exception handling for their services to handle errors and faults. Service providers should provide back up for their transactions during hostile situation.
4. Integrity A Web service transaction should be executed properly to provide the correctness of the interaction. A transaction is a sequence of activities that should be completed as a single unit to ensure the success of the transaction. If the transaction is incomplete, all the changes made are rolled back. It guarantees that every message that is sent and received between requester and server arrived is unaltered.
5. Service Time It must be the fastest that the service can be delivered to requesters. Service providers must respond as soon as they receive enquiries from requesters. Deliver fast and correct services are crucial from the users' perspective. It can be specified by the time the Web service receives request and send response.
6. Security Confidentiality assures for data privacy through the verification of the users' identities. Authentication is implemented to identify the right users with correct/approved identities. Authorization is applied to validate only the authorize users can access and invoke the service. Service providers should also record transactions including data, time, users' id and transaction made.
7. Performance Measured by throughput and latency. Good performance of Web services refers to higher throughput and lower latency values. Throughput is the number of Web service requests served at a given time period. Latency is the round-trip time between sending a request and receiving the response. Both affected by factors like processor speed, code efficiency and network transfer time. Performance can be determined by response time to guarantee maximum time required to complete a service request.
8. Transaction: Relates to ACID property The integrity of data operation that is performing by a transaction. Atomicity - executes entire transactions or not at all. Consistency – maintains the data integrity and consistency in update transaction. Isolation – individual transactions run as if no other transactions are present. Durability – is the persistence of results.
9. Execution Price The execution price can be a cost for both, service provider and requester. The cost for service provider includes resources and personnel payment to maintain and update the services. It also refers to an amount of money that service requester has to pay for executing an operation that include charges fee. It can be a compensation rate that is the refund from service provider for not committing to service and/or delivery of goods. It can also be a penalty rate that is the payment from service requesters to cancel the committed service or order commodity after the time out period for transaction to roll back was expired.

continued on following page

Table 2. Continued

QoS Specifications
10. Capacity Is the maximum number of concurrent request that server can process to guarantee performance. Refers to the number of concurrent connections that is permitted by the service. Is applied to determine the capability of Web server to process responses to various requesters. A good Web server should be able to give quick response even though in overload condition.
11. Regulatory Refers to the conformance and compliance to the rules, laws, standards and specifications. Can be achieved through service level agreement (SLA) between service provider and requester. Shows how well services can align with certain regulations. Could effect on availability, performance and reliability.
12. Reputation It is measured through the service trustworthiness based on end user's experience of using the service. Users play important role to rank services based on their familiarity to the services by giving their feedbacks. Different users may give different opinions for the same Web service; various results may arise for one Web service. It is used to compare and select the best available services and to manage the services composition. It is also very useful for the services ranking purpose.

plied UML for quantitative prediction for software and only few for Web services. They used UML to describe WSDL that take into account QoS (Castro, Marcos, & Vela, 2008; D'Ambrogio, 2006; D'Ambrogio & Bocciarelli, 2007; Gronmo et al., 2004; Gronmo & Jaeger, 2005). In conclusion, UML is not only a technique to model functional requirements but also relevant to describe QoS. However, very little research on QoS has used UML for this purpose. This is a new challenge for UML that we want to explore in the development and specification of this QoS metamodel.

4. THE WSDL LIGHTWEIGHT EXTENSION

OMG has introduced quantifiable QoS characteristics in the UML profile, which can be applied for Web services. Some of these existing QoS characteristics and categories are relevant to our QoS specifications and they can be used in the new QoS metamodel. However, the UML profile for QoS is quite limited and therefore could not be applied to represent other QoS specifications, which are not included in the profile. For this reason, the UML capability needs to be extended

and other QoS specifications and dimensions will be introduced to existing UML QoS profiles. Table 3 shows a comparison between the proposed QoS specifications and the existing OMG UML QoS profile.

OMG has considered resource-consuming component (RCC) for the QoS application architectures and QoS-aware specification functions

Table 3. List of the proposed QoS specifications compares to the OMG QoS UML profile

Proposed QoS Specification	OMG UML QoS Profile
Availability	Availability
Accessibility	None
Reliability (delivery messages)	Reliability, recoverability, maturity
Integrity	Integrity
Service time	Efficiency
Security	Security
Performance	Latency, throughput
Transaction	None
Execution price	Scalability
Capacity	Scalability
Regulatory	None
Reputation	None

(QASF) for the QoS application analysis as the basic functional elements of a QoS model. The following subsections show the core concepts of the QoS characteristic in UML:

1. **QoS Characteristic:** Represents an independent unit of quantifiable characteristics of services such as availability, reliability and so forth.
2. **QoS Category:** Classifies QoS characteristics that have relation between one and another into a group to represent them as a bigger component like security.
3. **QoS Dimension:** Represents a dimension to specify and/or measure QoS characteristics for example absolute values, maximum and minimum values and statistical values.
4. **QoS Parameter:** Represents a value that specifies characteristics for example values for username, password, security code and so forth.
5. **QoS Context:** Differentiates the context of quality expression in multiple QoS characteristics and model elements.

We propose two new core concepts related to the QoS characteristic in UML which are:

6. **QoS Rule:** Determines the specification and/or measurement to specific value of QoS dimension whether it is objective or subjective.
    a. **Objective:** Quantitative QoS characteristics that can be measured using certain mathematical formula.
    b. **Subjective:** Qualitative QoS characteristics that can be specified through certain method.
7. **QoS Source:** The foundation to verify from which resources and perspectives that QoS is specified and/or measured internally and/or externally.

a. **Internal:** Inner factors like software and hardware capability that could contribute to QoS.
b. **External:** Outer factors including service users' and service providers' expectation that could contribute to QoS.

We add two new relations that are (i) between QoSCharacteristics (type) and QoSRule (specifies) and (ii) between QoSCharacteristic (type) and QoSSource (verifies) as summarised in Figure 2.

The existing WSDL specification represented in UML is shown in Figure 3 (D'Ambrogio, 2006) and its elements are described as follows (Bequet et al., 2002; Miguel, 2003).

1. **Definition Element:** The root of every WSDL document.
2. **Types Element:** Allows extending the data types provided by XML schemas.
3. **Message Element:** Gives information about the data that travels from one endpoint to another.
4. **Operation Element:** Defines an interaction (resulting in exchange of one or more messages that refer to input, output and fault) between a service consumer and a service in the abstract.
5. **PortType Element:** Describes and defines the operations/methods supported by the Web service.
6. **Binding Element:** Brings the discussion to a more practical level by describing how the operations defined in a *portType* are transmitted over the network.
7. **Port Element:** Locates information about the actual IP address and port of the Web service.
8. **Service Element:** Specifies where to find the Web service.
9. **Import Element:** Allows organizing WSDL documents better.

Figure 2. Proposed metamodel of the core concepts in the QoS characteristic

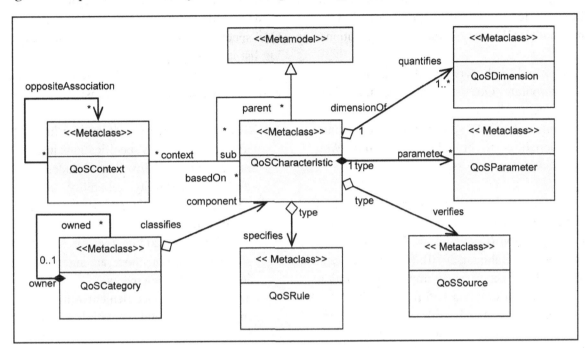

Figure 3. Existing WSDL specification (adapted from D'Ambrogio, 2006)

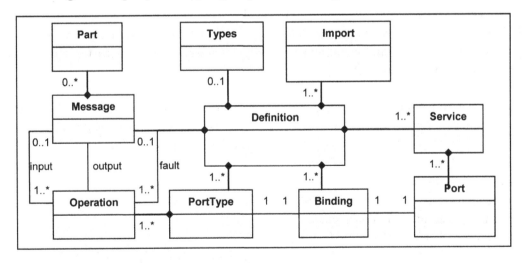

10. **Document Element:** Provides human-readable documentation that can be included inside any other WSDL element.

Different QoS specifications for Web services development and implementation would fit into different usage scenarios. Therefore, our QoS metamodel is meant to be general so that service providers could refer to it as a reference to incorporate a set of selected QoS specifications into their Web services designs. In addition, the QoS metamodel could benefit both Web services and their applications in improving their quality. The following items explain the importance of the QoS metamodel to Web services and their applications:

- Extend Web services description to incorporate QoS specifications into their functionalities.
- Integrate QoS specifications into functionalities to provide high quality Web services.

WSDL service description consists of two parts, the abstract interface and the concrete implementation (Bequet et al., 2002; Yu et al., 2008; WanAbRahman, 2010). However, there is no such classification for this important separation of a service description before. Therefore, this research proposes that it is relevant and necessary to classify those elements in the WSDL specification because they belong to different important categories, which are:

- **Interface:** Describes the availability of Web services including what they are (data type, message and operation), and how to transmit the services (binding).
- **Implementation:** Describes the actual transmission of the services including how to get there (import and service).

Figure 4 illustrates the design of a QoS metamodel to describe both functionality and QoS specification in the WSDL. The basic WSDL specification consists of definition element as the root, and other elements that include types, message, portType, binding, service and import. All of these elements describe the functionality of a Web service. This research sees the possibility of extending the WSDL specification to include the set of QoS specification to describe the non-functionality of a Web service. These QoS specifications are vital as an accomplishment to the existing WSDL specification to assure for high quality Web services development and

implementation. The QoS metamodel could be used to realize the incorporation of those selected QoS specifications into the WSDL. The following list items explain the significant of the QoS metamodel to the WSDL specification that include new classification and QoS extension:

1. To extend a Web service description in WSDL to incorporate QoS specifications into Web service functionality that includes availability, accessibility, reliability, integrity, service time, security and performance.
2. To classify elements in the Web service description by adding two classes to the service definition those are interface and implementation elements.
3. To extend the service element by incorporating availability and accessibility specifications that will ensure its existence and usefulness, and security specification that will guarantee for verification, access-control and time-stamp.
4. To extend the message and the binding elements by incorporating reliability specification that will guarantee for complete delivery of messaging.
5. To extend the operation element by incorporating service time, throughput and latency specifications that should improve the processing time.
6. To extend the port element by incorporating accuracy specification for the Web service integrity.

5. IMPLEMENTATION OF THE METAMODEL USING A CASE STUDY

This section discusses the implementation of the QoS metamodel as the basis towards designing and developing high quality Web services. In our approach, the generic QoS metamodel does not restricted designers and developers to integrate the QoS specifications into their Web services,

Figure 4. QoS metamodel as an extension to WSDL specification

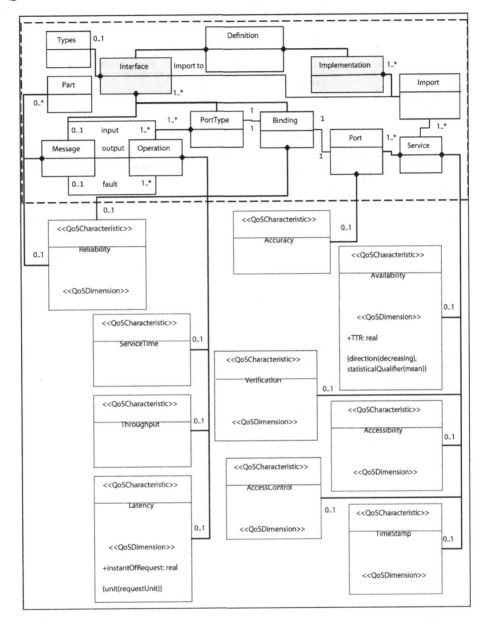

for example, choosing relevant QoS specifications for their Web services, deciding familiar techniques and approaches to incorporate the QoS specifications. The WSDL extension is possible and practical to be applied by Web services providers as Web services functionalities can be improved by extending them to include suitable QoS specifications. This section will elaborate on how to extend the WSDL to add the chosen QoS specifications. We have developed a Web service based project as a case study to implement the QoS specifications and the QoS metamodel. Figure 5 shows the sample implementation of one of our Web services, ItemStockService, Describing a catalogue item for an e-commerce application which includes the item identifier

Figure 5. QoS model as WSDL specifications for the case study

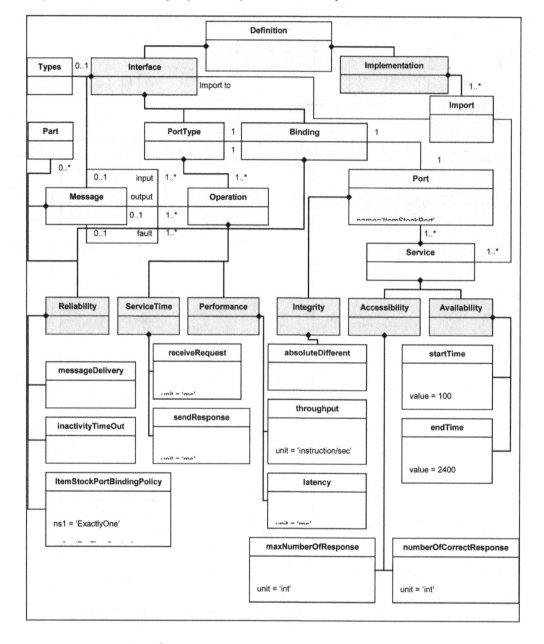

(itemID), description and price with the suitable QoS specifications.

The QoS metamodel is not rigid and can be applied to different ways of WSDL extensions to suit the QoS specifications of Web services. It is up to service providers to decide on how or what techniques they want to use to extend the WSDL. For example, the NetBeans IDE development tool supports adding QoS into Web services However, NetBeans is only capable of including secure services, reliable message delivery and optimizing the transfer of binary data. On the other hand, WSDL specifications could be manually modified to incorporate the QoS specifications. We also include the sample of the manual WSDL extension by providing the QoS through java files and XML schemas. Figure 5 shows the WSDL for Item-StockService with the added QoS specifications that include reliability, availability, accessibility, accuracy, service time and performance.

We have applied two approaches for extending WSDL. The first approach is by editing the Web services' attributes to include QoS from NetBeans 6.5.1 available feature. This feature supports reliability to ensure messages are being transferred as a whole package from service provider to requester. The second approach is by manually incorporating the rest of the QoS specifications into the Web service. In order to do this, we need to create Java files, for example Availability. java, Accuracy.java, Service.Time.java, Latency. java and Throughput.java to represent each of the QoS specifications. Then, we have to import the generated Java files into ItemStockService. By doing this, we only concentrate on Java programming and this will give benefit to Java programmers. Besides, developers who are using other programming languages also should be able to concentrate on their programming languages rather than spending more time to learn XML. This is because many Web services development IDEs and tools support automation generation of WSDL. In other words, developers do not have to generate the WSDL manually. In addition, we can automatically obtain the XML schema from the WSDL specification.

We have chosen those QoS specifications because they are critical to the Web service. E-commerce applications like in the case study require continuous availability where the applications should be always available. The availability is to ensure the existence of Web services and this can be specified by their start and end times. The accessibility should be returned as a percentage *((numOfCorrectResponse/maxNumOfResponse) * 100)* of the correct responses from the Web services. The integrity refers to the accuracy that should give the difference between the results that is expected and provided by the Web services *(expectedResult – providedResult)*. The service time

should return the length of time from receiving a request to sending a response *(receiveRequest + sendResponse)*. The performance is measured by latency through TurnAround value *(instantOfResult - instantOfRequest)* and throughput (instruction / second). As an example, the portion of WSDL interface description for the functionality of the ItemStockService and its implementation are given in Figures 6 and 7, respectively.

In summary, we have developed a Web service application project to incorporate the most important QoS specifications suitable for Web services. Based on the QoS metamodel, we come out with a QoS model specifically designed for the ItemStockService in the case study. Besides, our approach is generic and thus does not restricted the way we apply the QoS metamodel just to one method or technique. This is true as the case study has demonstrated that we have applied different ways to integrate those QoS specifications into the Web services. Furthermore, the QoS metamodel guides service providers to provide high quality Web services by incorporating the chosen QoS specifications into their functionalities as soon as the design and development processes begin. Moreover, this will give good experience for users when using the Web services with the added values being integrated to them without any manual intervention or agreement.

6. VALIDATION OF THE METAMODEL

In this section, we describe the validation processes that we have conducted as four controlled experiments in order to get quantitative data regarding the effectiveness of the QoS metamodel. The validation processes involved two groups of users, novice and experienced software developers. The first experiment intended to expose novice users to Web services and issues related to them. The second experiment was similar to the first one and involved novice users but they were introduced to

Figure 6. WSDL interface description for ItemStockService

```
<?xml version="1.0" encoding="UTF-8" ?>
<definitions xmlns:wsu="http://docs.oasis-open.org/wss/2004/01/oasis-200401-wss-
wssecurity-utility-1.0.xsd" xmlns:soap="http://schemas.xmlsoap.org/wsdl/soap/"
xmlns:tns="http://core/" xmlns:xsd="http://www.w3.org/2001/XMLSchema"
xmlns="http://schemas.xmlsoap.org/wsdl/" targetNamespace="http://core/"
name="ItemStockService">
<ns1:Policy xmlns:ns1="http://schemas.xmlsoap.org/ws/2004/09/policy"
wsu:Id="ItemStockPortBindingPolicy">
<ns1:ExactlyOne>
<ns1:All>
<ns2:RmFlowControl xmlns:ns2="http://schemas.microsoft.com/net/2005/02/rm/policy" />
<ns3:RMAssertion xmlns:ns3="http://schemas.xmlsoap.org/ws/2005/02/rm/policy" />
<ns4:Ordered xmlns:ns4="http://sun.com/2006/03/rm" />
<ns5:UsingAddressing xmlns:ns5="http://www.w3.org/2006/05/addressing/wsdl"
ns1:Optional="true" />
</ns1:All>
</ns1:ExactlyOne>
</ns1:Policy>
<types>
<xsd:schema>
<xsd:import namespace="http://core/"
schemaLocation="http://localhost:8080/FunProductClient/ItemStockService?xsd=1" />
</xsd:schema>
</types>
<message name="getDescription">
<part name="parameters" element="tns:getDescription" />
</message>
<message name="getDescriptionResponse">
<part name="parameters" element="tns:getDescriptionResponse" />
</message>
<message name="getServiceTime">
<part name="parameters" element="tns:getServiceTime" />
</message>
<message name="getServiceTimeResponse">
<part name="parameters" element="tns:getServiceTimeResponse" />
</message>
<message name="getThroughput">
<part name="parameters" element="tns:getThroughput" />
</message>
<message name="getThroughputResponse">
<part name="parameters" element="tns:getThroughputResponse" />
</message>
```

the QoS metamodel. The aim was to guide them to consider QoS specifications when designing their Web services based on the metamodel. The third experiment was for experienced users and the approach was the same as the first experiment. The fourth experiment was as the second experiment but involved experienced users.

We evaluate the results from the validation processes. The evaluation is important as a proof of concept for the practical use of the QoS metamodel for service providers in designing high quality Web services by considering relevant QoS specifications to be integrated into their Web services. In addition, high quality refers to the proposed extension of the WSDL to add in QoS specifications into Web services' functionalities. Each experiment and the results are described in the following sections.

Validation with Novice Users

Novice users are bachelor (Software Engineering) students from the Department of Information System, Faculty of Computer Science and IT, Universiti Putra Malaysia (UPM). We have decided to choose this group of students as our

Figure 7. WSDL implementation description for ItemStockService

```
- <binding name="ItemStockPortBinding" type="tns:ItemStock">
  <ns6:PolicyReference xmlns:ns6="http://schemas.xmlsoap.org/ws/2004/09/policy"
URI="#ItemStockPortBindingPolicy" />
  <soap:binding transport="http://schemas.xmlsoap.org/soap/http" style="document" />
- <operation name="getDescription">
  <soap:operation soapAction="" />
- <input>
  <soap:body use="literal" />
  </input>
- <output>
  <soap:body use="literal" />
  </output>
  </operation>
- <operation name="getServiceTime">
  <soap:operation soapAction="" />
- <input>
  <soap:body use="literal" />
  </input>
- <output>
  <soap:body use="literal" />
  </output>
  </operation>
- <operation name="getThroughput">
  <soap:operation soapAction="" />
- <input>
  <soap:body use="literal" />
  </input>
- <output>
  <soap:body use="literal" />
  </output>
  </operation>
```

validation subject after considering some factors and reasons. The factors include the subjects are from Software Engineering or Computer Science and IT background, they have knowledge on UML (theory and practice) and experience in software development. These factors are used to select only those users that able to provide good and unbiased results, and they are suitable to be involved in the validation. The Head of Department and selected lecturers from UPM were involved in the selection of the subjects.

Experiment 1

The objective of this experiment is to test whether Web service designers who have been exposed to Web services and their issues including functionality and non-functionality can think of QoS specifications to improve Web services quality. These students were given a two-hour workshop session on Web services. The first one hour focused on the introduction to Web services, standard Web technologies for Web services, service oriented architecture, the current WSDL and UDDI, and issues related to the development and implementation of Web services. Then, in the second half, they were asked to design three Web services based on a case study to develop a Web service based application. They need to come out with use cases, collaboration diagram and class diagrams for each of the Web services using UML notations. Even though this experiment focused on Web services' functionalities, this group has been informed about the critical issues regarding poor quality and impact to the development and implementation of Web services.

Experiment 2

The objective of the experiment is to validate the effectiveness of the QoS metamodel to contribute in designing Web services that consider the QoS specifications. This group involved the other half of students from the same class and course as in the Experiment 1. The tasks given were the same as in the Experiment 1 to test their knowledge, understanding and to give practical experience in designing Web services. The contents of the workshop was similar to the previous session but with additional information including QoS, description of the QoS specification, proposed core concept in the QoS characteristic, proposed extension to the existing UML QoS profile and the QoS metamodel development as the WSDL extension. In other words, this group has been introduced to the QoS metamodel to let them know that Web service designers should also consider QoS specifications in order to enhance their Web services quality. The rest of the design process was left to the students to deliver, whether they use the QoS metamodel as guidelines for them to incorporate relevant QoS specification to their WSDL or not. The results for both experiments are described in the following subsections.

Data Analysis, Results, and Evaluation from the Experiments

We took six deliverables from Experiment 1 to be equally compared to another six samples from Experiment 2. All students can deliver good use cases to fulfill the modelling of the functionalities for the Web service based application. From the first experiment, two students got full marks (20%), three of them got 18% and one student got 15%. This means that these students can model the functionalities after they understood the client requirements. Besides, we can consider their application architectures or collaboration diagrams as good. For the development of collaboration diagrams, four students obtained 10% or above

and only, two of them got 5%. However, none of the students has thought of improving the quality of the Web services by introducing QoS requirements. From the results, we can see that without guidance to enhance the quality, the designers only thought about the functionalities of Web services and their applications. This is because they were not aware of the QoS specifications that are also necessary and could improve their Web services. Therefore, the awareness of the QoS specifications and their incorporation into the functionalities are important to service providers. In general, the students can design the application and Web services but they did not consider any QoS specifications even though they knew what is expected from the issues related to Web services. The overall marks for all of the students were less than 70%. We can conclude that functionality alone is not sufficient to design and develop high quality Web services.

Even though six students had submitted their tasks in Experiment 2, the examiner could not open one of the files. This group also delivered very good use cases where four of them got full marks (20%) and one student got 18%. However, almost all students only got 10%, which is half the mark for the collaboration diagrams. This might be because they did not get the big picture of the whole application architecture. On the other hand, these students provided excellent WSDL for their Web services. They managed to get the full mark (20%) for each of the class diagrams for describing the Web services using WSDL. Two students only designed a class diagram that was for one of the Web services. This may be because they did not understand or forgot to provide one class diagram for each of the Web services. The most important point here is that they considered QoS specifications to extend the Web services' functionalities. Obviously, the QoS metamodel has made them think and consider the inclusion of the QoS specifications that are suitable to their Web services functionalities. In general, the QoS metamodel is crucial and necessary for the Web service designers to come out with better Web services that take into account the functionalities and QoS specifications. Those who had incorporated the QoS specifications into their Web services' functionalities and delivered all of the diagrams scored more than 85%. These are very good scores compared to those obtained in the previous experiment.

Figure 8 illustrates the comparison between the overall marks of designing good Web service based applications achieved by subjects from experiments 1 and 2 using a column chart.

In addition, we evaluated the results to prove the good influence and the importance of our comprehensive list of QoS specifications and the QoS metamodel. Table 4 shows the quantitative figures (percentage) of the data that have been analysed. All (100%) designers (subjects from experiments 1 and 2) were informed about the issues related to Web services. These issues include limited guidelines to incorporate QoS specification, ad hoc development, discovery difficulties, unreliable and insecure services, unpredictable performance and slow response time, and irrelevant services. The comprehensive list of QoS specifications is also important as it gives information regarding QoS specifications' definitions, descriptions and dimensions. It has been proved that without having this kind of knowledge, the designers could not even think of any QoS specifications as crucial elements that can be

added to enhance their Web services' capabilities. This fact is true as the Web services designers from Experiment 1 did not have the knowledge and they did not take into account any QoS specifications for their Web services. Besides, the exposure to the QoS metamodel was crucial to them.

They used the QoS metamodel as guidelines to know about what functionalities could be extended, what QoS specifications could be added, what QoS dimensions could be used, how to extend the WSDL and so forth. The awareness of the QoS specifications and the revelation of the QoS metamodel led them to consider and incorporate the relevant QoS specifications into their Web services' functionalities. As a result, 73% of

Table 4. Affect of the QoS metamodel in designing high quality web services

	Experiment 1	Experiment 2
Alert of Web Services Issues	100%	100%
Aware of QoS Specifications	None	100%
Expose to Qos Metamodel	None	100%
Consider to Include QoS	None	73%
Incorporate QoS	None	73%
Design Good Web Services	None	60%

Figure 8. Overall marks of designing good web service based applications

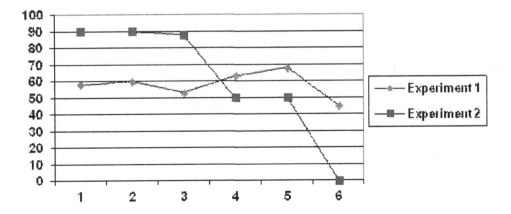

the designers considered including the QoS specifications for their Web services. Moreover, 73% have incorporated the chosen QoS specifications as the extensions to the WSDL. It is encouraging that 60% of the deliverables consisted of good Web services designs. The effectiveness of the QoS metamodel to the designers has encouraged them towards designing good Web services. However, these overall figures are quite low because two designers only delivered two out of six class diagrams for the WSDL and three files from one designer could not be opened.

Experiment 2 has proved that the comprehensive list of QoS specification and the QoS metamodel are important and necessary in designing Web services. The designers referred to the list to get information on QoS specifications, for example, the available QoS specifications that can be chosen from, the description of QoS specifications, their characteristics and dimensions, and so forth. Then, they used the QoS metamodel to get to know which Web services' functionalities can be extended, relevant QoS specifications can be applied, sample of QoS dimensions and parameters can be used and so on. From there, they chose QoS specifications for their Web services and extended the WSDL. Almost none of the designers had any difficulty in understanding and using the QoS metamodel during the experiment. They managed to design Web services with the added value by incorporating the chosen QoS specifications into the functionalities. They agreed and accepted the QoS metamodel as necessary and practical for designing good quality Web services. The QoS metamodel also has eased the designing process. Besides, from the results it shows that every student from Experiment 2 has considered QoS specifications for their Web services' functionalities. In addition, from the designers' performance in Experiment 2, we summarize the benefits regarding the ease of use and the practicality of the QoS metamodel as in the following:

1. A compact and simple generic metamodel comprise of comprehensive information regarding QoS specifications that could be extended in the WSDL.
2. It is very useful to give a clear guidance for designers to take into account the QoS specifications for their Web services.
3. The designers spent less time to learn, understand and use the QoS metamodel as a reference to implement the QoS specifications.
4. It is practical to be applied as the designers have decided to incorporate the chosen QoS specifications into Web services' functionalities.
5. The designers have succeeded in designing high quality Web services that consist of both functionalities and QoS specifications.

Validation with Experienced Users

Experienced users are master students from the Faculty of Computer Science and IT, UPM. The sample chosen took into account their suitability based on their experience on software analysis and design and knowledge on Web services, background, knowledge and experience. The subjects come from different background related to Software Engineering and Computer Science and IT. Some of them working as software developers, IT managers, lecturers and other field related to Software Engineering, Computer Science and IT. Some of them hold a bachelor degree in Software Engineering and the other in Computer Science and IT, from different universities including local and overseas students. They have knowledge of UML (theory and practice) and experience in software development. The Head of Department and selected lecturers from UPM were involved in the selection of the sample.

Experiment 3

The experiment aimed to expose Web services and issues related to it to experienced users. The approach was similar to Experiment 1 but Experiment 3 took shorter time and students were allowed to do their tasks at home. This group was smaller than the bachelor group and was composed of 9 subjects.

Experiment 4

The experiment was similar to Experiment 2 but the targeted users are from the same class as in Experiment 3. However, because of time constraint, they agreed to take, read and do the tasks at home. Only five students took the extra handouts regarding the QoS for Web services. The QoS specifications and the QoS metamodel are new information for them and they agreed to consider the QoS as an approach to improve their Web services.

Evaluation Based on Oral Session with the Subjects

Subjects from Experiment 3 were given information regarding Web services and subjects from Experiment 4 were exposed to the Web services and additional information concerning QoS. Based on the oral session with the subjects from Experiment 3, we conclude that although they knew about Web services' issues but without the awareness of QoS specifications and the QoS metamodel they had no idea and could not think about QoS as the important elements that could enhance the Web services' functionalities. In addition, they could not relate the functionalities with the QoS even though almost the entire Web services issues are concerned with the non-functionalities that refer to QoS. Therefore, they did not consider including QoS in their Web services. However, we have different scenario with subjects from Experiment 4. They agreed to consider including

QoS specifications for their Web services, as they understood that QoS could improve Web services quality. Besides, this solution also could contribute in solving some problems regarding Web services' issues. Table 5 shows quantitative percentage of this evaluation based on the informal oral session with the subjects from both experiments.

From the data in Table 5, we highlight the significance of both QoS specifications and the metamodel for the subjects (experiments 3 and 4) in making their decision to include QoS in their Web services. This data illustrates the importance of the awareness of QoS specifications and the exposure to the QoS metamodel towards considering QoS for Web services. In general, Web service providers need to be alert of Web services issues to know the latest developments in the research field. In addition, the issues indirectly give information regarding factors affecting quality for Web services. Besides, the QoS specifications give information on the existing QoS that could be chosen to suit their Web services' need. Furthermore, the QoS metamodel is necessary for them as a reference on the functionalities that could be extended, QoS specifications and dimensions could be chosen and so forth. The fact that the QoS specifications and the QoS metamodel are important has been emphasized from the quantitative data. We can conclude that these QoS specifications and metamodel are complimentary towards considering QoS for Web services' functionalities.

Table 5. Evaluation of considering QoS for web services with the subjects from experiments 3 and 4

	Experiment 3	Experiment 4
Alert of Web Services Issues	100%	100%
Aware of QoS Specifications	None	100%
Expose to Qos Metamodel	None	100%
Consider to Include QoS	None	100%

Analysis of the Effectiveness of the QoS Metamodel

Even though different background in terms of academic qualification, working experience, mode of study, nationality and age, both novice and experienced users have shown similar results in the controlled experiments as illustrated in Figure 9. For example, bachelor students in Experiment 1 and master students in Experiment 3, and similar to Experiments 2 and 4.

In overall, the results of Experiments 1 and 3 have proved that without the awareness of QoS specifications from the exposure of QoS metamodel could not contribute in providing quality web services. Furthermore, the results of Experiments 2 and 4 have confirmed the effectiveness in terms of the practicality of the QoS metamodel. These include the ease of use, even bachelor students in Experiment 2 have referred to and applied the

QoS metamodel after attending a short session on QoS metamodel; efficient, where both categories of students from Experiments 2 and 4 have considered QoS for their web services; and successful, when the results from Experiment 2 verified the QoS metamodel is the reference for service providers to incorporate QoS specifications into their web services' functionalities and come out with good web service designs. Moreover, we have improved the design process by encouraging them to include the QoS specifications. We have demonstrated in the case study of our approaches by using different technique and tool to incorporate QoS specifications into web services' functionalities based on the QoS metamodel. By doing these, we have contributed to provide very useful references to design and develop high quality web services. More information about the samples characteristics in the four controlled experiments is shown in Table 6.

Figure 9. Effect of the QoS metamodel in designing high quality web services

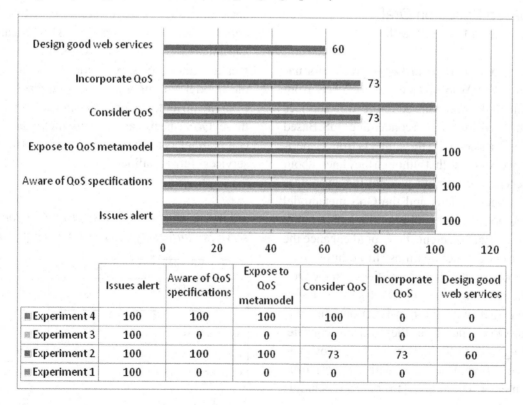

	Issues alert	Aware of QoS specifications	Expose to QoS metamodel	Consider QoS	Incorporate QoS	Design good web services
Experiment 4	100	100	100	100	0	0
Experiment 3	100	0	0	0	0	0
Experiment 2	100	100	100	73	73	60
Experiment 1	100	0	0	0	0	0

Table 6. More details about the group of users' characteristics in the controlled experiments

	Novice Users	Experienced Users
Academic Qualification	Bachelor	Master
Working Experience	None	Yes
Mode of Study	Full-time	Part-time
Nationality	Local	International
Gender	Both Male and Female	Both Male and Female
Age	Between 19 and 24	Between 25 and 45

The Evaluation Method

We have discussed the results as the validation from the evaluation method through the controlled experiments. Controlled experiments are actually an alternative evaluation method after considering few factors and reasons as described in the following:

1. **Limited Factors (Time, Sources and Technical):** Time constraints, inadequate sources and technical problems are the main factors for this limitation. We have been given a quite limited time to complete the research which is impossible for us to come out with a complete e-commerce application. In addition, this will need many sources such as supporting back-end system including e-banking system, third party to process and validate e-payment and so forth. We also face with technical problem to provide a real e-commerce application as this is not a real project to conduct business online.

2. **Could Not Monitor QoS:** As a result, we could not evaluate the Web services based application through monitoring the QoS as this required a full implementation of Web services project and a heavy traffic.

Therefore, we failed to collect data regarding Web services overall performance and this is the reason for seeking another evaluation method.

3. **Users and Implementation Not Main Focus:** The full implementation will lead us to focus more on Web service users whereas monitoring and selecting the best Web services is not the main purpose of this research.

4. **Main Intentions are Design and Development Phases:** Our main intention is to support the initial phases of design and development of good quality Web services that incorporate the selected QoS specifications from the provided comprehensive description and extending their functionalities through WSDL.

5. **Give Hands-On Experience:** The controlled experiments are important to expose Web services designers to the actual process of designing the Web services including understanding a user requirements for the whole Web services application, describing Web services through WSDL and extending the Web services' functionalities to incorporate the chosen QoS specifications using UML.

7. CONCLUSION

In conclusion, the research contribution is very important as it provided a comprehensive description of the identified QoS specifications as the critical quality factors for good Web services and their applications. The comprehensive list of QoS specifications gives very useful information regarding QoS descriptions, their dimensions and attributes. Besides, we have investigated UML QoS profile and proposed another two core specifications for QoS characteristics, which are QoS Rule and QoS Source. In addition, the research has contributed towards the UML QoS extension by introducing other QoS characteristics and their dimensions. Furthermore, this research has discovered that UML is capable to be applied as a metalanguage to model non-functional requirements for Web services through the proposed QoS metamodel.

We have chosen a set of QoS specifications that are practical to be incorporated into Web services' functionalities. The QoS metamodel consists of a framework that model the suggested QoS characteristics and dimensions into WSDL. The QoS metamodel is essential and necessary for service providers to refer as a guideline particularly the chosen QoS specifications that can be incorporated into Web services' functionalities. More to the point, service providers are now alert of the QoS specifications that could be chose and added, get to know that the Web services functionalities could be extended and they can think about QoS attributes as suitable parameters for the relevant QoS specifications to their Web services. Service providers can provide better designs for their Web services by considering suitable QoS specifications to enhance the functionalities.

REFERENCES

Agarwal, V., Dasgupta, K., Karnik, N., Kumar, A., Kundu, A., Mittal, S., & Srivastava, B. (2005). A service creation environment based on end to end composition of web services. In *Proceedings of the 14th International World Wide Web Conference*, Japan (pp. 128-137). New York, NY: ACM.

Akkiraju, R., Flaxer, D., Chang, H., Chao, T., Zhang, L. J., Wu, F., & Jeng, J. J. (2001). A framework for facilitating dynamic e-business via web services. In *Proceedings of the OOPSLA Workshop on Object-Oriented Web Services*, Tampa, FL.

Al-Ali, R. J., Rana, O. F., Walker, D. W., Jha, S., & Sohail, S. (2002). G-QoSM: Grid service discovery using QoS properties. *Computing and Informatics Journal*, *21*, 363–382.

Bennett, S., McRobb, S., & Farmer, R. (2006). *Object-oriented systems analysis and design using UML* (3rd ed.). Berkshire, UK: McGraw-Hill.

Bequet, H., Kunnumpurath, M. M., Rhody, S., & Tost, A. (2002). *Beginning Java web services*. Birmingham, UK: Wrox Press.

Bhatti, N., Bouch, A., & Kuchinsky, A. (2000). Integrating user-perceived quality into web server design. *Computer Networks*, *33*, 1–16. doi:10.1016/S1389-1286(00)00087-6

Cardellini, V., Casalicchio, E., Colajanni, M., & Mambelli, M. (2001). Web switch support for differentiated services. *ACM SIGMETRICS Performance Evaluation Review*, *29*(2), 14–19. doi:10.1145/572317.572320

Cardoso, J., Sheth, A., Miller, J., Arnold, J., & Kochut, K. (2004). Quality of service for workflows and web service processes. *Journal of Web Semantics*, *1*(3), 281–308. doi:10.1016/j.websem.2004.03.001

Castro, V. D., Marcos, E., & Vela, B. (2004). *Representing WSDL with Extended UML*. Retrieved from http://caribdis.unab.edu.co/pls/portal/url/ITEM/3F73657A-ABB5616CEO440003BA3D5405

Chan, K., & Poernomo, I. (2007). QoS-aware model driven architecture through the UML and CIM. *Information Systems Frontiers*, *9*(2-3), 209–224. doi:10.1007/s10796-007-9033-8

Chen, Z., Chia, L. T., Silverajan, B., & Lee, B. S. (2003). UX- An architecture providing QoS - aware and federated support for UDDI. In *Proceedings of the First International Conference on Web Services* (pp. 1-6).

Chung, J. Y., Lin, K. J., & Mathieu, R. G. (2003). Web services computing: Advancing software interoperability. *Computer*, *36*(10), 35–37. doi:10.1109/MC.2003.1236469

Curbera, F., Nagy, W. A., & Weerawarana, S. (2001). *Web services: Why and how.* Retrieved from http://nclab.kaist.ac.kr/lecture/cs744_2003_Spring/Webservices-whyandhow.pdf

D'Ambriogio, A., & Bocciarelli, P. (2007). A model-driven approach to describe and predict the performance of composite services. In *Proceedings of the 6th International Workshop on Software and Performance* (pp. 78-89). New York, NY: ACM.

D'Ambrogio, A. (2006). A model-driven WSDL extension for describing the QoS of web services. In *Proceedings of the IEEE International Conference on Web Services* (pp. 789-796). Washington, DC: IEEE Computer Society.

Day, J., & Deters, R. (2004). Selecting the best web service. In *Proceedings of the Conference of the Centre for Advanced Studies on Collaborative Research*, ON, Canada (pp. 293-307).

Eriksson, H. E., & Penker, M. (1998). *UML toolkit.* Chichester, UK: John Wiley & Sons.

Fung, C. K., Hung, P. C. K., Linger, R. C., Wang, G., & Walton, G. H. (2006). A service-oriented composition framework with QoS management. *International Journal of Web Services Research*, *3*(3), 108–132. doi:10.4018/jwsr.2006070105

Gronmo, R., & Jaeger, M. C. (2005). Model-driven methodology for building QoS-optimised web service compositions. In L. Kutvonen & N. Alonistioti (Eds.), *Proceeding of the 5th IFIP International Conference on Distributed Applications and Interoperable Systems* (LNCS 3543, pp. 68-82).

Gronmo, R., Skogan, D., Solheim, I., & Oldevik, J. (2004, March 28-31). Model-driven Web services development. In *Proceedings of the IEEE International Conference on e-Technology, e-Commerce and e-Service* (pp. 42-45). Washington, DC: IEEE Computer Society.

Jezequel, J. M., Hussmann, H., & Cook, S. (Eds.). (2002). *UML 2002 – The Unified Modeling Language: Model Engineering, Concept and Tools: 5th International Conference.* Berlin, Germany: Springer-Verlag.

Jin, L. J., Machiraju, V., & Sahai, A. (2002). *Analysis on service level agreement of web services* (Tech. Rep.). Palo Alto, CA: Hewlett Packard Laboratory. Retrieved from http://athena.union.edu/~hemmendd/Gradseminar/hpl.pdf

Kratochvil, M., & McGibbon, B. (2003). *UML Xtra-Light: How to specify your software requirements.* Cambridge, UK: Cambridge University Press.

Looker, N., Munro, M., & Xu, J. (2004). Simulating errors in web services. *International Journal of Simulation*, *5*(5), 29–37.

Mani, A., & Nagarajan, A. (2002). *Understanding quality of services for web services.* India: IBM. Retrieved from http://www.ibm.com/developerworks/library/ws-quality.html

Martin, J., Arsanjani, A., Tarr, P., & Hailpern, B. (2003). Web services: Promises and compromises. *Queue*, *1*(1), 48–58. doi:10.1145/637958.639315

Mathijssen, S. (2005). A fair model for quality of web services. In *Proceedings of the 3rd Twente Student Conference on IT*, Twente, The Netherlands.

McGovern, J., Tyagi, S., Stevens, M. E., & Mathew, S. (2003). *Java web services architecture.* San Francisco, CA: Morgan Kaufmann.

Menasce, D. A., Ruan, H., & Gomaa, H. (2007). QoS management in service-oriented architectures. *Performance Evaluation*, *64*(7-8), 646–663. doi:10.1016/j.peva.2006.10.001

Miguel, M. A. (2003). General framework for the description of QoS in UML. In *Proceedings of the 6th IEEE International Symposium on Object-Oriented Real-Time Distributed Computing* (pp. 61-68). Washington, DC: IEEE Computer Society.

Milanovic, N., & Malek, M. (2004). Current solutions for web service composition. *IEEE Internet Computing, 8*(6), 51–59. doi:10.1109/MIC.2004.58

OMG. (2006). *UMLTM profile for modeling quality of service and fault tolerance characteristics and mechanisms, OMG available specification, version 1.0.* Retrieved from http://www.omg.org/docs/formal/06-05-02.pdf

OMG. (2008). *UMLTM profile for modeling quality of service and fault tolerance characteristics and mechanisms specification, version 1.1.* Retrieved from http://www.omg.org/docs/formal/08-04-08.pdf

OMG. (2009). *Unified modeling language.* Retrieved from http://www.uml.org/#UMLProfiles

Ouzzani, M. (2003). *Efficient delivery of web services* (Unpublished doctoral dissertation). Virginia Polytechnic Institute and State University, Blacksburg, VA. Retrieved August 26, 2008, from http://208.22.18.79/~mourad/mourad.ouzzani.pdf

Pallickara, S., Fox, G., Aktas, M. S., Gadgil, H., Yildiz, B., & Oh, S. …Yemme, D. (2006). *A retrospective on the development of web service specifications.* Bloomington, IN: Community Grids Lab, Indiana University. Retrieved from http://www.naradabrokering.org/papers/CGL-WebServices-Chapter.pdf

Papazoglou, M. P., & Georgakopoulos, D. (2003). Service-oriented computing. *Communications of the ACM, 46*(10), 25–28.

Papazoglou, M. P., & Kratz, B. (2006). A business-aware web services transaction model. In A. Dan & W. Lamersdorf (Eds.), *Proceedings of the 4th International Conference on Service-Oriented Computing* (LNCS 4294, pp. 352-364).

Ran, S. (2003). A model for web services discovery with QoS. *ACM SIGecom Exchanges, 4*(1), 1–10. doi:10.1145/844357.844360

Rumbaugh, J., Jacobson, I., & Booch, G. (2005). *The unified modeling language reference manual* (2nd ed.). Boston, MA: Pearson Education.

Sahai, A., Machiraju, V., Sayal, M., Jin, L. J., & Casati, F. (2002). *Automated SLA monitoring for web services.* Palo Alto, CA: HP Laboratories. Retrieved from http://www.hwswworld.com/downloads/9_13_05_a_pdfs/HPL-2002-191.pdf

Schmit, B. A., & Dustdar, S. (2005). Model-driven development of web service transactions. *International Journal of Enterprise Modeling and Information Systems, 1*(1), 46–60.

Sheng, Q. Z., & Benatallah, B. (2005). ContextUML: A UML-based modeling language for model driven development of context-aware web services. In *Proceedings of the International Conference on Mobile Business* (pp. 206-212). Washington, DC: IEEE Computer Society.

Silver, G. A., Maduko, A., Jafri, R., Miller, J. A., & Sheth, A. P. (2003). Modeling and simulation of quality of service for composite web services. In *Proceedings of the 7th World Multiconference on Systemics* (pp. 420-425).

Sivashanmugam, K., Miller, J. A., Sheth, A. P., & Verma, K. (2005). Framework for semantic web process composition. *International Journal of Electronic Commerce, 9*(2), 71–106.

Taher, L., Basha, R., & Khatib, H. E. (2005). Establishing association between QoS properties in service oriented architecture. In *Proceedings of the International Conference on Next Generation Web Services Practices* (pp. 6-11). Washington, DC: IEEE Computer Society.

Topley, K. (2003). *Java web services in a nutshell.* Sebastopol, CA: O'Reilly.

WanAbRahman. W. N. (2010). *UML QoS profile exploration for the specifications of a generic QoS metamodel for designing and developing good quality web services* (Unpublished doctoral dissertation). School of Computing, Science and Engineering, University of Salford, Salford, UK.

Wang, G., Chen, A., Wang, C., Fung, C., & Uczekaj, S. (2004). Integrated quality of service management in service-oriented enterprise architectures. In *Proceedings of the 8th IEEE International Enterprise Distributed Object Computing Conference* (pp. 21-32). Washington, DC: IEEE Computer Society.

Weller, S. (2002). *Web services qualification: A recommendation system and feedback mechanism for web services.* Retrieved from http://www.ibm.com/developerworks/Webservices/library/ws-qual/

Yu, Q., Liu, X., Bouguettaya, A., & Medjahed, B. (2008). Deploying and managing web services: Issues, solutions and directions. *The International Journal on Very Large Data Bases, 17*(3), 537–572. doi:10.1007/s00778-006-0020-3

Zeng, L., Benatallah, B., Dumas, M., Kalagnanam, J., & Sheng, Q. Z. (2003). Quality driven web services composition. In *Proceedings of the 12th International Conference on World Wide Web*, Budapest, Hungary (pp. 411-421). New York, NY: ACM.

Zimmermann, O., Tomlinson, M., & Peuser, S. (2003). *Perspectives on web services: Applying SOAP, WSDL and UDDI to real-world projects.* Berlin, Germany: Springer-Verlag Berlin.

This work was previously published in the International Journal of Information Technology and Web Engineering (IJITWE), Volume 6, Issue 3, edited by Ghazi I. Alkhatib and Ernesto Damiani, pp. 15-38, copyright 2011 by IGI Publishing (an imprint of IGI Global).

Chapter 5
Quality–of–Service Based Web Service Composition and Execution Framework

Bassam Al Shargabi
Al-Isra University, Jordan

Osama Al-haj Hassan
Al-Isra University, Jordan

Alia Sabri
Applied Science University, Jordan

Asim El Sheikh
Arab Academy for Banking and Financial Sciences, Jordan

ABSTRACT

Software is gradually becoming more built by composing web services to support enterprise applications integration; thus, making the process of composing web services a significant topic. The Quality of Service (QoS) in web service composition plays a crucial role. As such, it is important to guarantee, monitor, and enforce QoS and ability to handle failures during execution. Therefore, an urgent need exists for a dynamic Web Service Composition and Execution (WSCE) framework based on QoS constraints. A WSCE broker is designed to maintain the following function: intelligent web service selection decisions based on local QoS for individual web service or global QoS based selection for composed web services, execution tracking, and adaptation. A QoS certifier controlled by the UDDI registry is proposed to verify the claimed QoS attributes. The authors evaluate the composition plan along with performance time analysis.

DOI: 10.4018/978-1-4666-2157-2.ch005

INTRODUCTION

Service-Oriented Architecture (SOA) is an approach to construct distributed systems that bring application functionality as services to end-user applications (Booth, Hass, Mccabe, Newcomer, Champion, & Ferris, 2005). The basic idea of SOA is to compose an application as a set of services that are language and platform independent, communicate with each other using standardized messages like XML, Web services is a technology that realize the SOA.

A web service is a software system identified by a URL, whose public interfaces and bindings are defined and described using XML. Its definition can be discovered by other software systems (Booth, Hass, Mccabe, Newcomer, Champion, & Ferris, 2005). As individual web services are limited in their capability, which created the need for composing existing services to create new functionality in the form of composite service. However, the process of creating composite service is achieved by combining existing elementary or complex services, possibly offered by different providers. For example, a travel plan service can be developed by combining several elementary services such as hotel reservation, ticket booking, car rental, sightseeing package, etc. In carrying out this composition task, one should be concerned with the efficiency and the QoS that the composed process will exhibit upon its execution (Chandrasekaran, Miller, Silver, Arpinar, & Sheth, 2003).

Some proposals are being made to enable dynamic composition of web services and execution monitoring frameworks (Al-Shargabi, El Shiekh, & Sabri, 2010). Few of these proposals address user QoS constraints: whether these constraints are locally on every individual web service or globally for the whole composition process according to Al-Shargabi, El Shiekh, and Sabri (2010). These constraints must be addressed to satisfy client requirements, such as price, availability, so it is necessary to represent required QoS in the selected and composed web services. Moreover, Evaluation of composition process: when the composer selects a web service, it is quite common that many web services have the same functionalities. So it is possible that the composer generates more than one composite service fulfilling the requirements. In that case, the composed web services are evaluated by their overall utilities using the information provided from the non-functional attributes. The most commonly used method is utility functions as in WSCE framework. The requester should specify weights to each QoS attribute and the best composite service is the one that is ranked on top. During the execution of composed web service, some web services may update their QoS properties others may become unavailable. A dynamic composition approach is needed, in which runtime changes in the QoS of the component services are taken into account. It is imperative to design a Web Service Composition and Execution (WSCE) framework that adapts to failure of web services or changes in their QoS offerings to satisfy user requirements or constraints, these issues already have been discussed in previous work by Al-Shargabi, El Shiekh, and Sabri (2010).

The remained of paper organized as follows: the proposed WSCE framework is presented. The next section describes WSCE Broker functions. The following section presents domain registries. The QoS certifier is then presented, followed by analysis and validation. Conclusion and future work are found in the last section.

WSCE FRAMEWORK ARCHITECTURE

The WSCE framework is a broker-based framework for the dynamic composition of web services. The main motivation of the proposed framework is to build a WSCE broker to make intelligent service selection decisions for composite service which fits with user constraints in his/her web process. The main functions of WSCE broker include:

- **Execution Tracking:** WSCE broker has a composition history to record all feasible composition plans of composed services it is aware of, which QoS information of these composition plans are optimal or closer to user constraints.
- **Dynamic Service Selection:** This is the key function of WSCE broker, when the WSCE broker selects web services to execute a web process according to the user-defined utility function, and user's QoS requirements.
- **Dynamic Service Adaptation:** In case of individual web service failure during execution of composite service, the WSCE broker either replaces the failed services or replaces the composition plan with an alternative plan.

The WSCE broker either way can create a new composition plan from scratch. In this framework (Figure 1) a QoS certifier is proposed which is controlled by the UDDI registry to verify the claimed QoS attributes for the registration requests of web service provider.

Web Process

The web process is a collection of related, structured activities or tasks that serve a particular goal for a particular customer or customers. Example of web process that is used in this paper, Travel Planner Service process consists of three tasks, flight reservation, hotel reservation, and car rental. The three atomic tasks (which are not composed) will internally execute the travel planning process. Each task of the three tasks will be executed by 3 web services (execution of three services called composite service) in order to meet user QoS requirements.

Figure 1. WSCE framework architecture

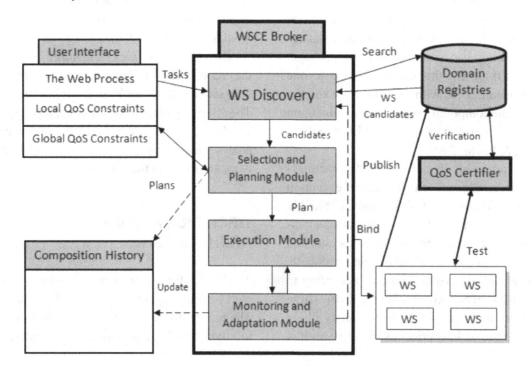

Local QoS Constraints

In local QoS constraints, user can set constraints on each candidate web service to execute individual task, where the execution of service is isolated from other services. This paper only emphasized on five QoS constraints of web service (OMG Specification, 2004), where the user can set constraint values in each individual web service to execute task of web process. Local QoS constraints evaluation criteria of web service and their meanings are as follows (Anbazhagan, & Arun, 2002; O'Sullivan, Edmond, & Hofstede, 2002):

- **Execution Price:** It is the price of executing a web service. The price is usually fixed for each individual web service, but may be changed according to the web service provider's business policy.
- **Execution Duration:** It is the average time expected for executing a web service. Individual execution times upon the requests of the clients vary because the server loads change. Therefore, the average execution time should be updated continuously by the service provider.
- **Availability:** It means the ratio of the time that web service is available for immediate use. It is measured as av= uptime/(uptime+ downtime) and updated by the service provider. The downtime includes the time to repair the web service that has failed.
- **Reputation:** It is the average reputation score of web service evaluated by the clients. The individual reputation scores are likely to be subjective, but the average score becomes trustable as the total number of the usages increases. The reputation score is measured by rep = accumulated score/ total number of usages.
- **Reliability:** The reliability of a web service is the probability that a request is correctly responded to within the maximum expected time frame indicated in the web

service description. Reliability is a measure related to hardware and/or software configuration of web services and the network connections between the service requesters and providers.

Global QoS Constraints

In global QoS constraints, the users can put constraints on the execution of composite service as whole, not on every individual service of the composite service, e.g., price of composite service, and execution duration. The following QoS constraints are used in this framework (Anbazhagan, & Arun, 2002; O'sullivan, Edmond, & Hofstede, 2002):

- **Execution Price:** The execution price of an execution plan of a composite service is the sum of the execution prices of the operations invoked over the services that participate in composite service. In the proposed WSCE framework the user can set a price for the whole composition of Flight, Hotel, and Car rental services. Also the user may wish to get the lowest prices of composed services.
- **Execution Duration:** The execution duration of an execution plan of a composite service is the sum of the execution time of the web services that participates in composite service. In the proposed WSCE framework the user can set the execution duration for the whole composition of Flight, Hotel, and Car rental services. Also the user may wish to get the lowest duration of composed services.
- **Reputation:** The reputation of an execution plan of travel composite service is the average of the reputations of the web services that participate in travel composite service. Reputation constraints should have scaled value between [1-10].
- **Reliability:** The reliability of execution plan of travel composite service is product of aggregated values of reliability for

composed web services that participate in travel composite service.

- **Availability:** The availability of execution plan of travel composite service is product of aggregated values of availability of composed web services that participate in travel composite service.

WSCE BROKER

In WSCE framework, there is a WSCE Broker, which is the mediator between user and public registries and web service providers. WSCE broker is responsible for locating the candidate web service from Universal Description Discovery and Integration (UDDI) registries and returns their Web Service Description Language (WSDL) and URL. The WSCE Broker is provided with an intelligent selection and matching technique to select web services that meet user requirements based on QoS constraints, whether the constraints are local on each individual web service or the whole composition process. The WSCE Broker creates number of composition plans and only one plan will be selected for execution according to user QoS constraints that are set up by user. WSCE Broker controls the execution of the composition plan and monitors the execution of web services and dynamically adapts to any change (e.g., service unavailable) as explained in following subsections.

Web Service Discovery Module

In order to find the right web services, it would be easier if the registries were categorized based on domains as in the proposed WSCE framework, with each registry maintaining only the web services pertaining to that domain, the registries are specialized in certain domain (e.g., Flight domain, Hotel domain, and Car rental domain). That makes it possible to use domain specific ontology. As a result, all the web service definitions pertaining

to that registry may be forced to conform to that ontology and search for services in that domain can be carried out in a relevant registry. The WSCE broker is responsible for web service discovery in public registry according to user requirements. The discovery process will result in a number of candidate web services. The consumer of a web service has a certain functional and QoS requirements, such as "execution duration ≤ 2 ms with execution price $< \$100$." Using the web service discovery module, the WSCE broker searches the UDDI registry for a web service with the required functionality as usual. User can also add constraints to the search operation. One type of constraint is the required QoS. If there were multiple web services in the UDDI registry with similar functionalities, then the QoS requirement would enforce a finer search in WSCE framework. The search would return a web service that offers the required functionality with the desired set of QoS. If there is no web service with these qualities, the WSCE broker sends feedback to user. The user can then reduce their QoS constraints or consider trade-offs between the desired QoS constraints.

The WSCE broker through using web service discovery module conducts a search for candidate web services for each atomic task in the composition process. For this purpose, the following two matching tasks are performed:

1. **Web Service Name Matching:** For each atomic task according to user requirement, the WSCE broker requests the URLs of WSDL documents of candidate web services. For the request, the WSCE broker sends the name of the atomic task to the UDDI. The UDDI will search, and will find group of web services by matching the name of the atomic task with service names in the business services of registered web services, and then returns the URLs of the WSDL documents of candidate web services to the WSCE broker.

2. **Operation Mode and Input/Output Matching:** The inputs and outputs of atomic task should correspond to the input and output messages of WSDL operation. That is, the numbers of input and output messages and the message syntax should be matched between the specification in the atomic process and that in the WSDL documents of the candidate web services. In addition, operation modes of the candidate web services specified in the WSDL documents, such as request-response, and solicit response should be matched with the message transfer type in the corresponding atomic process. This can be done without difficulty by checking the input and output information of the web service specified in the WSDL documents (Myoung, Ouk Kim, & Hyun, 2008).

Selection and Planning Module

The main idea behind this module is to select web services for the composition process, and create number of plans, and select the plan that meet user constraints. First, the goal of the selection is to identify the best assignment of web service candidates to the tasks of the composition. The selection can be performed by either considering or ignoring the arrangement of the tasks. Web service selection based on QoS can be done in two ways; by considering QoS constraints on every individual web service or the whole composition process which is called a global QoS constraints selection.

Web Service Selection Based on Local QoS Constraints

The selection of the web service that will execute a given task of web process is done at the last possible moment and without taking into account the other tasks involved in the web process. When a task actually needs to be executed, the WSEC broker through selection module collects the information about the QoS of each of the web services that can execute this task (namely the candidate web services for this task). After collecting this QoS information, a quality vector (Equation 1) (Zeng, Benatallah, Dumas, Kalagnanam, & Cheng, 2004) is computed for each of the candidate web services, and based on these quality vectors, WSEC broker selects one of the candidate web services by applying a Multiple Criteria Decision Making (MCDM) techniques (Ksalan & Zionts, 2001).

$$q(s,\ t) = \left(q_{pr}\left(s,\ t\right),\ q_{du}\left(s,\ t\right),\ q_{av}\left(s\right),\ q_{re}\left(s\right),\ q_{rep}\left(s\right)\right)$$
$$(1)$$

where s is candidate web service, t is web process task. This selection of web service is based on the weight assigned by the user to each criterion, and a set of user-defined constraints expressed using a simple expression language. Examples of constraints that can be expressed include availability, and price constraints. However, constraints can only be expressed on individual tasks, and not on combinations of tasks. In other words, it is not possible to express the fact that the sum of the durations for two or more tasks should not exceed a given threshold.

To illustrate the local QoS web service selection approach, only 5 quality dimensions used (Anbazhagan, & Arun, 2002), the dimensions are numbered from 1 to 5, with 1=price, 2=duration, 3=availability, 4=reliability, and 5=reputation. Given a task tj in a composite service, there is a set of candidate web services Sj={s1j, s2j,..., snj} that can be used to execute this task. By merging the quality vectors of all these candidate web services, a matrix as in Equation 2, Q=(Qi, j; 1≤i≤n; 1≤j≤5) is built, in which each row Qij corresponds to a Web service sij while each column corresponds to a quality dimension.

$$Q = \begin{pmatrix} Q_{1,1} & Q_{1,2} & \cdots & Q_{1,5} \\ Q_{2,1} & Q_{2,2} & \cdots & Q_{2,5} \\ Q_{n,1} & Q_{n,2} & \cdots & Q_{n,5} \end{pmatrix} \quad (2)$$

A Simple Additive Weighting (SAW) technique is used to select an optimal web service (Zeng, Benatallah, Dumas, Kalagnanam, & Sheng, 2003; Ksalan & Zionts, 2001). There are two phases in applying SAW:

Scaling Phase

Some of the QoS attributes could be negative, i.e., the higher the value, the lower the quality, such as execution duration and execution price. Other QoS attributes are positive, i.e., the higher the value, the higher the quality such as reputation and reliability. For negative QoS attributes, values are scaled according to Equation 3. For positive QoS attributes, values are scaled according to Equation 4.

$$f(x) = \begin{cases} \dfrac{Q_j^{\max} - Q_{i,j}}{Q_j^{\max} - Q_j^{\min}} & if\, Q_j^{\max} - Q_j^{\min} \neq 0 \\ 1 & if\, Q_j^{\max} - Q_j^{\min} = 0 \end{cases}$$

$$(3)$$

$$f(x) = \begin{cases} \dfrac{Q_{i,j} - Q_j^{\min}}{Q_j^{\max} - Q_j^{\min}} & if\, Q_j^{\max} - Q_j^{\min} \neq 0 \\ 1 & if\, Q_j^{\max} - Q_j^{\min} = 0 \end{cases}$$

$$(4)$$

In the above equations, Q_j^{max} is the maximal value of QoS attribute in matrix Q, i.e., $Q_j^{max} = Max(Q_{i,j})$, $1 \leq i \leq n$. While Q_j^{min} is the minimal value of QoS attribute in matrix Q, i.e., $Q_j^{min} = Mi(Q_{i,j})$, $1 \leq i \leq n$. By applying Equations 3 and 4 on Q, QN matrix is obtained QN= (QN i:j; $1 \leq i \leq n; 1 \leq j \leq 5$), in which each row QNj corresponds

to a web service Sij while each column corresponds to a QoS attribute dimension.

Weighting Phase

Equation 5 is used to compute the overall QoS score for each web service:

$$Scor(S_i) = \sum_{j=1}^{5} \left(QN_{i,j} * W_j \right) \quad (5)$$

where Wj $\in$ (0, 1) and

$$\sum_{j=1}^{5} w_j = 1$$

Wj represents the weight of QoS attribute j that is set by user. As stated before, end user express their preference regarding QoS by providing values for the weights Wj. For a given task, the WSCE broker through selection module will choose the web service that has maximum score which satisfies the user constraints for that task. If there are several web services with the same maximum score, one of them is selected randomly. If no web service satisfies the user constraints for a given task, an execution exception will be raised and the WSCE broker will propose to the user to loosen up these constraints.

Web Service Selection Based on Global QoS Constraints

The basic idea of global web service selection based on QoS constraints is that several composition plans are identified and the optimal composition plan is selected that does satisfy user QoS constraints. Assuming that for each task in web process, there is a set of candidate web services

$$S_j = \{S_{1j}, S_{2j}, \ldots\ldots, S_{nj}\}$$

that are available to which task t_j can be assigned. In order to assign a candidate web service S_{ij} to each task t_j in Selection and Planning module: the WSCE broker will generate a set of composition plans P (Equation 7) along with its QoS information according to Equation 6. Table 1 provides aggregation functions for the computation of the QoS of each composition plan, which used by WSCE broker for the computation of QoS attributes of composed web services (CS).

$$(p) = (q_{pr}(p), q_{du}(p), q_{av}(p), q_{re}(p), q_{rep}(p)) \tag{6}$$

$$P = \{p_1, p_2 p_3, \ldots\ldots, p_n\} \tag{7}$$

where P is the composition plans that are generated by the WSCE broker selection and planning module, n is the number of execution plans generated by the WSC Broker.

The WSCE broker needs to select an optimal composition plan. Selection process of composi-

tion plan uses MCDM approach. Once the QoS vector for each composition plan is derived, by accumulating all the composition plans' quality vectors, Q_p matrix is obtained as seen in Equation 8, where each row represents an execution plan's quality vector.

$$Q_p = \begin{pmatrix} Q_{1,1} & Q_{1,2} & \cdots & Q_{1,5} \\ Q_{2,1} & Q_{2,2} & \cdots & Q_{2,5} \\ Q_{n,1} & Q_{n,2} & \cdots & Q_{n,5} \end{pmatrix} \tag{8}$$

The selection of a composition plan relies on applying MCDM approach to the QoS matrix Qp=(Qpi,j; 1≤i≤n; 1≤j≤5) of generated composition plans. In this matrix, each row corresponds to the QoS vector of one possible composition plan for the execution of web process. As in the local QoS based selection approach, a SAW technique is used to select an optimal composition plan. The two phases of applying SAW are scaling and weighting.

Table 1. Aggregation functions for computing the QoS of composition plans (adapted from Zeng, Benatallah, Dumas, Kalagnanam, & Sheng, 2003)

Criteria	Aggregation Function
Price	$CS_{pr}(P) = \sum_{i=1}^{N} Q_{pr}(s_i, t_i)$
Duration	$CS_{du}(p) = \sum_{i=1}^{N} \left(q_{du}(s_1, t_1), \ldots q_{du}(s_N, t_N) \right)$
Reputation	$CS_{rep}(p) = \frac{1}{N} \sum_{i=1}^{N} q_{rep}(s_i)$
Reliability	$CS_{rel}(p) = \prod_{i=1}^{N} (e^{q_{rel}(s_i)*z_i})$
Availability	$CS_{av}(p) = \prod_{i=1}^{N} (e^{q_{av}(s_i)*z_i})$

Scaling Phase

As in the previous section, the needs for scaling the values of each QoS attribute. For negative QoS attribute, values are scaled according to Equation 3. For positive QoS attribute, values are scaled according to Equation 4. Note, the values of Q_j^{max} and Q_j^{min} can be computed without generating all possible composition plans. For example, in order to compute the maximum execution price (i.e., Q_{pr}^{max}) of all the execution plans, we select the most expensive web service for each task and sum up all these execution prices to compute Q_{pr}^{max}. In order to compute the minimum execution duration (i.e., Q_{du}^{min}) of all the composition plans, we select the web service with the shortest execution duration for each task to compute Q_{du}^{min}. The computation cost of Q_j^{max} and Q_j^{min} is thus polynomial. After the scaling phase, the matrix $Q' = (i;j\ ;\ 1 \leq i \leq n;\ 1 \leq j \leq 5)$ is obtained. Q' Represents all composition plans generated by WSCE broker with its QoS attributes in order to be selected to execute web process.

$$Q' = \begin{pmatrix} Q'_{1,1} & Q'_{1,2} & \cdots & Q'_{1,5} \\ Q'_{2,1} & Q'_{2,2} & \cdots & Q'_{2,5} \\ Q'_{n,1} & Q'_{n,2} & \cdots & Q'_{n,5} \end{pmatrix} \quad (9)$$

Weighting Phase

Equation 10 is used to compute the overall QoS score for each composition plan in matrix Q':

$$Scor\left(P_i\right) = \sum_{j=1}^{5}\left(Q'_{i,j} * W_j\right) \quad (10)$$

where Wj $\in$ [0,1] and

$$\sum_{j=1}^{5} w_j = 1$$

Wj represents the weight of QoS attributes. The user can set weights on QoS (i.e., balance the impact of the different QoS attributes) to select a desired composition plan by adjusting the value of Wj. As a final stage, the WSCE broker will choose the composition plan which has the maximum score.

If there is more than one composition plan that has the same score, then the WSCE Broker will select randomly a composition plan to execute the web process. Accordingly, if all composition plans do not meet user expectation or the determined constraints, then the user has to loosen up his QoS constraints or choose one of the available plans that are selected by the WSCE broker, the plans should be optimal or near optimal for user constraints. The selected composition plan is stored in a composition history, which contain the web service included in the composition plan and the QoS information for each web service in a table containing this information. Whatever, the WSCE broker also sends the proceeding composition plan that has the second maximal score just in case if the web services of selected plan failed to deliver or any QoS violation that may occur during execution.

User Constraints

The selection of a composition plan is restricted by the user constraints and their weights, where the selected plan that has maximum score to execute user web process should not exceed the upper limits that are fed by the user according to Equations 11 and 12.

$$q_{pr}\left(p\right) \leq PR \quad (11)$$

$$q_{dr}(p) \leq ED \tag{12}$$

where $q_{pr}(p)$ is the execution price of selected composition plan and $q_{dr}(p)$ is the execution duration of the selected composition plan. The QoS constraints that the user wishes to have upper limits for are the execution price (PR), and execution duration (ED) of web process. Accordingly, the lower limits constraint that is fed by the user for availability, reputation, reliability according to Equations 13, 14, and 15.

$$q_{av}(p) \geq AV \tag{13}$$

$$q_{rel}(p) \geq REL \tag{14}$$

$$q_{rep}(p) \geq REP \tag{15}$$

where $q_{av}(p)$ is the availability of selected composition plan, $q_{rel}(p)$ is the reliability of selected composition plan, and $q_{rep}(p)$ is the reputation of selected composition plan. The QoS constraints that the user wish's to have lower limits for are the availability (AV), reliability (REL), and reputation (REP) of web process.

Accordingly, sometimes the generated composition plans for web process based on the available QoS information of web services does not meet the user QoS constraints but they are close. The selection and planning module of WSCE broker, gives the ability for the user either to select the available composition plan or to change the QoS constraints, where the WSCE broker tries again to find a new optimal composition plan that fits the user new constraints.

Execution Modules

Right after the Selection and Planning, the selected composition plan for web process is sent to the Execution Module, which generates executable BPEL code of composition plan. The WSCE broker orchestrates the included web services to execute composite service. At run time, the WSCE broker monitors the execution of composed web services. If everything goes well, after successful complete executions, the WSCE broker reports the actual recorded QoS to composition history of this composition and put them into the QoS Statistics table.

Monitoring and Adaptation Module

Due to the dynamicity of internet and some of web services may fail or become unavailable. At run-time, during the execution of selected composition plan the WSCE Broker monitor the QoS of composed services for any violations and tries to react if any web service fail to deliver the intended result. If a web service problem occurs during execution, the WSCE broker through monitoring and adaptation module will look up for an alternative web service from the same domain or class in composition history. If there is no alternative web service from the same class which meet the user QoS constraints, the WSCE broker will react to this situation by using the web service discovery module and will look up for new web service that meet the QoS constraints. Either way, the WSCE broker can switch to the backup composition plan to continue execution if all web services on selected composition plan failed to deliver. At the same time, the WSCE broker will adopt the replacement plan for all new web services. The WSCE broker then reports the failure to composition history. The WSCE broker can generate a new composition plan and replacement plan based on the newly deployed web services. The WSCE broker will update the QoS Statistics table (in composition history) of corresponding QoS attribute values (such as reliability, availability, and execution duration.)

QoS Monitoring

The pattern-based aggregation can be applied during the execution of the composition process (Michael, Jaeger, Rojec, & Gero, 2004). With monitoring and adaptation module, the delivered QoS can be captured. If a centralized execution environment in a mediator-based structure executes the composition, the mediator in proposed framework is WSCE Broker. In this framework the monitoring process is performed at run-time by the WSCE broker. It can be seen as history management (El Hadad, Manouvrier, & Rukoz, 2010; Michael, Jaeger, Rojec, & Gero, 2004) for the execution of composed web services as follows.

Recovery

During the execution of selected composition plan the WSCE broker monitors if there is any detected QoS violation during the execution according to the QoS information of the selected composition plan, and notifications or recovery activities can be established. To establish recovery tasks when errors occur during the execution or to check the delivered QoS of individual web services, to analyze the performance of the composition plan, and to predict future characteristics for controlling purposes, the proposed aggregation of QoS values can be performed to deliver a more accurate estimation of the delivered QoS.

QoS Analysis

According to the metrics of the execution of selected composition plan, it is possible to check whether the selected services are delivered with the desired QoS. However, monitoring the QoS only applies to metrics that can be directly derived from the execution, such as execution duration or availability. For example, capturing the execution price during the execution depends on the payment method. Capturing the execution duration of the composition and the execution of individual services can be used to analyze the performance. This information is already verified by the QoS certifier in WSCE framework.

Controlling

Considering composition as realizing of web process (as in use case that used in this paper) as whole or in parts. Controlling execution can benefit from up-to-date information about the progress. It can be determined by WSCE broker thought the aggregation of the QoS attributes of web services selected to execute web process, which can be stored in the composition history and can be used later on for further execution of the same web process.

Dynamic Adaptation during Execution

Due to the dynamicity of internet and some of web service may fail to deliver result or become unavailable, the idea of QoS-based adaption is to keep re-planning in small scope. But there is still many occasions when re-planning is needed, for example, if the failed component web service is the key task on the execution of composed service and there is no other suitable candidate service for this task, the WSCE broker will switch to other composition plan. Therefore, re-planning and how to re-plan are two critical challenges in QoS-based adaptation. Solutions to them are re-planning trigger and re-planning strategies, respectively.

The design of monitoring and adaptation module of the WSCE Broker is tightly bound to the QoS model. The quality values of the specified composition plan of composed service should be used to determine the thresholds. As mentioned, to keep re-planning in limited scope. Therefore, the re-planning should be like a hill climbing process. If only a component web service fails, the WSCE Broker should save the rest of tasks on this composition plan, and check if there are suitable candidate web services for this task. If a suitable component web service is found, the WSCE Broker selects the suitable web service and substitutes the failed web service with the new one. If there is no suitable candidate web service found, the WSCE Broker should abandon the saved to-execute plan and turn to alternative composition plan. In worst case, the re-planning procedure has to start over from scratch.

Composition History

The WSCE broker has a composition history to record all feasible web services it is aware of. The WSCE broker can also build new composition plans or update existing plans based on user requirements and newly discovered web services. Dynamic service adaptation: At run time, the WSCE Broker monitors the execution at every step, such as execution duration of each web service. If everything goes well, after successful complete executions; the WSCE broker reports the actual recorded QoS information to QoS statistics table in composition history. The composition history contains number of composition plans according to pervious processes. The history table includes the following fields (both functional and QoS characteristics about the of web service):

- **ID:** A unique representation of the record.
- **Service Name:** Name of the web service.
- **URL:** Where the web service is located (usually it points to the WSDL file of the service).
- **Namespace URI:** The namespace used for definitions in the service WSDL document. Each web service needs a unique namespace for client applications to distinguish it from other services on the web.
- **Service Class:** Web services belong to different service classes. A Service Class is a group of services that provide similar functionalities with possibly different nonfunctional parameters (QoS).
- **Operation (With Input and Output Parameters):** The actual function provided by web service, e.g., weather report (input: zip code; output: temperature).
- **Description:** Description of the operation.
- **Execution Duration:** The time needed for web service to be executed.
- **Execution Price:** The price of invoking web service.
- **Availability**
- **Reliability**
- **Reputation**
- **Composition Reference:** A web service pointer to which composition plan this web service belongs to.

DOMAIN REGISTRIES

In WSCE framework, the concept of Domain registry is used, where every UDDI registry only contain specific domain of services such as, Hotel booking, Weather forecasting. The structure of UDDI registry is same as the tModel (Blum, 2004; Zhou, Chia, & Lee, 2004) that was used to describe the functional and non-functional information of web services, tModels UDDI registries can be used to provide QoS information on <bindingTemplates>. Using tModel for QoS information for the binding template that represents a web service deployment is generated to represent QoS information. Each QoS metric, such as average response time or average throughput is represented by a <keyedReference> in tModel.

QOS CERTIFIER

The architecture of web services is presented in (Booth, Hass, Mccabe, Newcomer, Champion, & Ferris, 2005), where the web service provider publishes WSDL to UDDI registry. The discovery process is largely unregulated based on UDDI registries. 48% of the production UDDI registries have links that are unusable. These pointers contain missing, broken or inaccurate information (Ran, 2003). Therefore the ability of incorporating quality of service into service discovery and also to make sure all this claimed QoS information by web service provider must be tested and authenticated by the UDDI registry. To overcome these shortcomings the QoS Certifier is introduced in this framework.

The QoS certifier is managed by UDDI registry. The web service provider offers web service by publishing the service into the registry; the registry sends a request to the QoS certifier with the WSDL of web service provider to verify the QoS claims by provider. The QoS certifier verifies the claims of QoS for a web service by a trail invocation of the web service provider. The certifier then reports the recorded QoS information of the provider and compares them to the WSDL of provider. If they match, it sends back to the registry the recorded QoS information of that web service provider, the

register then accepts the request of the provider with both functional description of the service and its associated QoS information.

ANALYSIS AND VALIDATION

Example and Results of Experiments

The web process consists of three tasks: flight reservation, hotel booking, and car rental. The web process can be realized by a new composite service, obtained by coordination of the available component services as follows first it allows the user to buy flight ticket, book a hotel room and to rent a car as illustrated in Figure 2.

The case of Travel Planner Service has three tasks flight booking, booking a Hotel room and Car rental task. Each task needs to be assigned to a web service to be executed. As illustrated in Figure 3 as described in (Al-Masri & Qusay, 2007), there are three different classes of registry, flight booking, hotel reservation, and Car rental class. In each class there are two services discovered by WSCE broker. The WSCE broker generates composition plans for the travel planner process. The composition plan that will be selected to execute composite service is the one that meet user constraints and satisfy his requirements.

Figure 2. Travel planner process

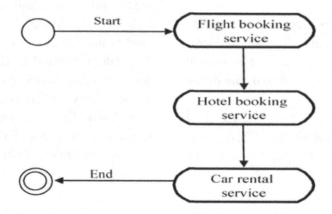

Figure 3. Different classes of web services

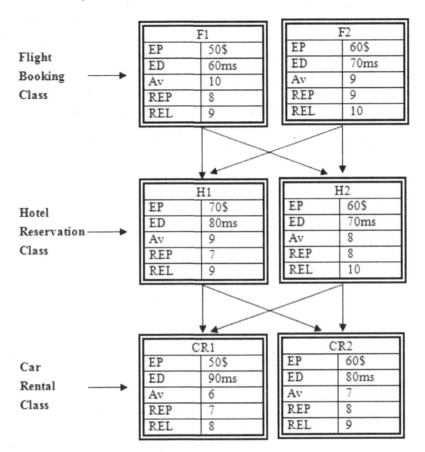

The WSCE broker retrieves the candidate web services for each task as is shown in Figure 3. In the selection module, the WSCE broker generates a number of composition plans for the web process of travel planner service. Each composition plan has its own QoS information aggregated from individual web services (Table 1 contains the aggregation functions for computing the QoS of composition plans) involved in the composition as is shown in Table 2.

Now in order to evaluate the multi-dimensional QoS of each composition plan in Table 2, the WSCE broker uses Simple Additive Weighting (SAW) technique for scaling QoS attributes values to allow a uniform measurement of the multi-dimensional service qualities independent of their

Table 2. Composition plans with their QoS information

ID	QoS Attribute / Composition Plan	EP	ED	AV	REP	REL
1	**F1, H1, CR1**	170	230	540	7.3	648
2	**F1, H1, CR2**	180	220	630	7.6	724
3	**F1, H2, CR1**	160	220	480	7.6	720
4	**F1, H2, CR2**	170	210	560	8	810
5	**F2, H1, CR1**	170	240	486	7.6	720
6	**F2, H1, CR2**	190	230	567	8	810
7	**F2, H2, CR1**	170	230	432	8	800
8	**F2, H2, CR2**	180	220	504	8.3	900

units and ranges. The scaling processes that will be executed by the WSCE broker in selection module, where negative QoS attributes values are scaled according to Equation 3. For positive QoS attributes, values are scaled according to Equation 4, as is shown in Table 3.

Following scaling process is a weighting process (Equation 10) for representing user priorities and preferences for each QoS attribute that matter the most for the user. Lets assumes that the weights for each QoS attribute that represents the user priorities as follows (EP=0.5, ET=0.4, AV=0.0,REP=0.1,REL=0.0}, using Equation 8 To calculate the scores and the weights for each composition plan as it shown in Table 4.

Table 3. Scaling process

ID	QoS Attribute / Composition Plan	EP	ED	AV	REP	REL
1	F1, H1, CR1	0.67	0.33	0.55	0	0
2	F1, H1, CR2	0.33	0.67	1	0.3	0.30
3	F1, H2, CR1	1	0.67	0.24	0.3	0.29
4	F1, H2, CR2	0.67	1	0.65	0.7	0.64
5	F2, H1, CR1	0.67	0	0.27	0.3	0.29
6	F2, H1, CR2	0	0.33	0.68	0.7	0.64
7	F2, H2, CR1	0.67	0.33	0	0.7	0.60
8	F2, H2, CR2	0.33	0.67	0.31	1	1

Table 4. Scores for composition plans

ID	Composition Plan	Score
1	F1, H1, CR1	0.467
2	F1, H1, CR2	0.465
3	**F1, H2, CR1**	**0.800**
4	**F1, H2, CR2**	**0.805**
5	F2, H1, CR1	0.365
6	F2, H1, CR2	0.202
7	F2, H2, CR1	0.537
8	F2, H2, CR2	0.535

According to Table 4, the WSCE broker will choose the composition plan which has the maximal value of score which is the composition plan number 4. If there is more than one composition plan which has the same maximal value of score, then the WSCE Broker will select randomly a composition plan to be executed. Accordingly, the process of selection of a composition plan is restricted by the user constraints, where the selected plan which has maximal score to execute web process should not exceed the upper limits or the lower limits according to Equations 11, 12, 13, 14, and 15 that are fed by the user. As in the example used in this paper, the WSCE broker selects the composition plan 4. The WSCE checks the user constraints (e.g., EP≤170$, ET≤220ms, REP≥8). If composition plan with the higher score meet user constraints, then composition plan 4 meets user constraints which will be selected to execute web process of travel planner service. the selected composition plan along with the composition plan that has the second maximal score will be sent to be stored in composition history with all its recorded QoS values along with WSDL, URI of involved web services of selected the composition plan, which will be used for further execution or used by WSCE broker to monitor the execution of composition plan during execution. The second composition plan is stored in composition history in case of the selected composition plan execution failed to deliver. At run-time, the WSCE broker can either select the second plan 3 to execute user web process or re-plan the whole composition from scratch in case of failure of composition plan 4.

Analytical Hierarchy Process Validation

To validate the selection made by WSCE broker in the proposed framework, Analytical Hierarchy Process (AHP) is used (Belton & Stewart, 2002), which developed by Saaty in 1980. The goal of the

Figure 4. A hierarchy for choice of an optimal composition plan

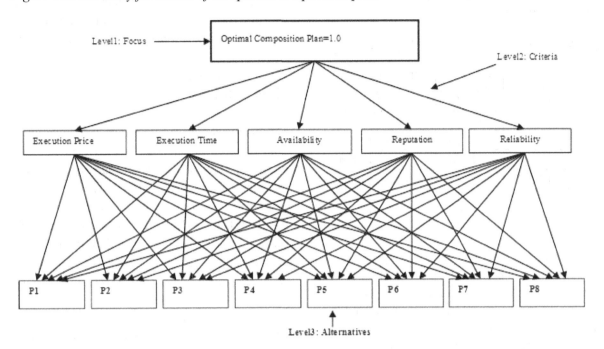

AHP is to enable a decision maker to structure a multi-attribute decision making problem visually in the form of an attribute hierarchy. An attribute hierarchy has at least three levels: the focus or the overall goal of the problem on the top level, multiple criteria that define alternatives in the middle level, and competing alternatives in the bottom level. When criteria are highly abstract, such as, e.g., "well being", subcriteria (or sub-subcriteria) are generated subsequently through a multilevel hierarchy. As in the used example in this paper, at level 1 the focus is to find an optimal composition plan for travel planner service to execute composite service, Level 2 comprises the QoS criteria that contribute to the decision making of which composition plan would be selected according to this criteria: Execution price (EP), Execution time (ET), Availability (AV), Reputation (REP), and Reliability (REL). Level3 consists of the eight possible composition plans: P1, P2, P3, P4, P5, P6, P7, and P8. Figure 4 shows the different levels in a hierarchy structure.

It is obvious that each criterion in level 2 should contribute differently to the focus. As seen in the example, the user sets which of these criteria are more important for him as follows, EP=0.5, ET=0.4, AV=0.0, REP=0.1, and REL=0.0 and these are values are the same values that used by the WSCE broker to select the optimal composition plan.

The next step for the decision maker is to make pair-wise comparisons of the eight alternatives in level 3 with respect to five criteria in level 2, the weight values of pair-wise comparison of eight alternative composition plans with respect to the weights of five criteria in level 2 are taken from Table 3. The results of pair-wise comparison of eight alternatives with 5 QoS criteria are shown in Table 5.

The final stage of the AHP is to compute the contribution of each alternative to the overall goal which is the optimal composition plan by aggregating the resulting weights vertically (table inside Figure 5). The overall priority for each alternative

Table 5. Pair-wise comparison alternatives composition plans and QoS criteria

ID	EP	ED	AV	REP	REL
p1	0.67	0.33	0.55	0	0
p2	0.33	0.67	1	0.3	0.30
p3	1	0.67	0.24	0.3	0.29
p4	0.67	1	0.65	0.7	0.64
p5	0.67	0	0.27	0.3	0.29
p6	0	0.33	0.68	0.7	0.64
p7	0.67	0.33	0	0.7	0.60
p8	0.33	0.67	0.31	1	1
Sum	4.34	4	3.37	4	3.76

is obtained by summing the product of the criteria weight and the contribution of the alternative, with respect to that criterion as illustrated in Figure 5 for the selection of composition plan. Therefore, the decision maker's choice would be plan P4, which has the maximal score among the other alternative composition plans, if the decision was only to be based on these criteria, which is the same composition plan selected by WSCE Broker.

Time Analysis

Time analysis is used to measure the computational time required to select composed web services for web process as in Travel Plan process. Two experiments have been conducted to compute the overall time estimate for the two methods in WSCE framework, local QoS selection of composed web services, and global QoS selection of composed web services. The experiments were performed on a personal computer (Intel Centrino Duo with 1.60 GHz CPU and 1 MB RAM).

Experiment 1 is conducted for the three tasks (flight reservation, hotel booking, and car rental). For each task a different numbers of available candidate web services (5, 10, 15, 20, 25) to be

Figure 5. Priorities for each hierarchal level with scores for composition plans

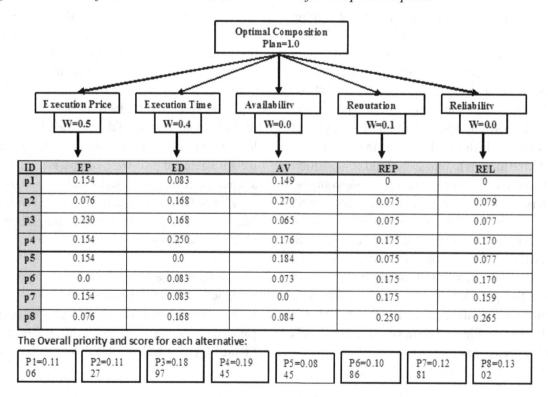

ID	EP	ED	AV	REP	REL
p1	0.154	0.083	0.149	0	0
p2	0.076	0.168	0.270	0.075	0.079
p3	0.230	0.168	0.065	0.075	0.077
p4	0.154	0.250	0.176	0.175	0.170
p5	0.154	0.0	0.184	0.075	0.077
p6	0.0	0.083	0.073	0.175	0.170
p7	0.154	0.083	0.0	0.175	0.159
p8	0.076	0.168	0.084	0.250	0.265

The Overall priority and score for each alternative:

| P1=0.1106 | P2=0.1127 | P3=0.1897 | P4=0.1945 | P5=0.0845 | P6=0.1086 | P7=0.1281 | P8=0.1302 |

composed, and each web service has different QoS properties. The selection in this experiment is based on local QoS of composed web services. Experiment 2 is done for the same three tasks. A different number of available candidate web services (5, 10, 15, 20, 25) to be composed along with different QoS properties. The selection in this experiment is based on global QoS of composed web services. Computational times of the two experiments increased directly as the number of candidate web services increased which is almost

a linear increase as illustrated in Figures 6 and 7. As expected, the computational times for the selection of composed web services based on global QoS constraints are a little bit higher than that of local QoS selection.

As expected, the computational times for the selection of composed web services based on global QoS constraints are a little bit higher than that of local QoS selection. The average of computational times for experiment 1 is 34 ms and 47.6 ms for Experiment 2 compared to (Myoung,

Figure 6. Computational time of selecting composed web services based on local QoS constraints

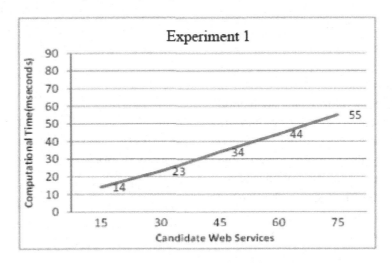

Figure 7. Computational time of selecting composed web services based on global QoS constraints

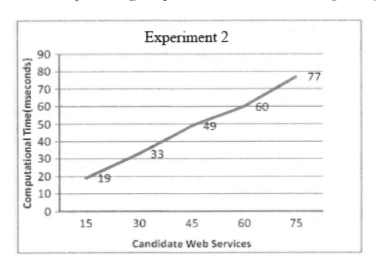

Ouk Kim, & Hyun, 2008), the average of computational times for local QoS based selection of web services is 1.07seconds, and 3.5seconds for global QoS based selection of web services.

CONCLUSION

This paper introduced a web service composition and execution (WSCE) framework based on QoS constraints, the main motivation of WSCE broker to make intelligent web service discovery, service selection decisions based on local QoS for individual web service or global QoS based selection for the whole composed web services with less computational time. Although, during the execution of the composed web services, some web services may update their QoS properties others may become unavailable, the WSCE broker is provided with a QoS monitoring and adaptation for the composed web services during run-time to overcome such issue. QoS certifier controlled by the UDDI registry also proposed to verify the claimed QoS attributes for the registration requests of web service provider. Finally, an evaluation has been conducted to evaluate selection of composition plan using AHP and performance time analysis has been conducted.

The WSCE framework does not support fully-automated web service composition, as a future work would look to make the process of QoS-based web service discovery, selection, composition, execution, and monitoring done automatically. It means that the human factor as a bottleneck is removed and service compositions are made automatically

ACKNOWLEDGMENT

I would like to thank everyone who contributed to the completion of this work.

REFERENCES

Al-Masri, E., & Qusay, H. (2007). QoS-based discovery and ranking of web services. In *Proceedings of the 16th International Conference on Computer Communications and Networks* (pp. 529-534).

Al-Shargabi, B., El Shiekh, A., & Sabri, A. (2010). Web service composition survey: State of the art review. *Recent Patent on Computer science Journal, 3*(2), 91-107.

Anbazhagan, M., & Arun, N. (2002). *Understanding quality of service for Web services*. Retrieved from http://www.ibm.com/developerworks/webservices/library/ws-quality/index.html

Belton, V., & Stewart, T. (2002). *Multi criteria decision analysis – An integrated approach* (pp. 151–159). Boston, MA: Kluwer Academic.

Blum, A. (2004). UDDI as an extended web services registry: Versioning, quality of service, and more. *SOA World Magazine, 4*(6).

Booth, D., Hass, H., Mccabe, F., Newcomer, E., Champion, M., Ferris, C., & Orchard, D. (2005). *Web services architecture*. Retrieved from http://www.w3.org/TR/ws-arch/

Chandrasekaran, S., Miller, J., Silver, G., Arpinar, B., & Sheth, A. (2003). Performance analysis and simulation of composite web services. *International Journal of Electron Commer Bus Media, 13*(2), 18–30.

El Hadad, J., Manouvrier, M., & Rukoz, M. (2010). TQoS: Transactional and QoS-aware selection algorithm for automatic web service composition. *IEEE Transactions on Services Computing, 3*(1), 73–85. doi:10.1109/TSC.2010.5

Ksalan, M., & Zionts, S. (2001). *Multiple criteria decision making in the new millennium*. Berlin, Germany: Springer-Verlag.

Michael, C., Jaeger, G., Rojec, G., & Gero, M. (2004). QoS aggregation for web service composition using workflow patterns. In *Proceeding of the 8th International Enterprise Distributed Object Computing Conference* (pp. 149-159).

Myoung, J., Ouk-Kim, C., & Hyun, I. (2008). Quality-of-service oriented web service composition algorithm and planning. *Journal of Systems and Software, 81*(11), 2079–2090. doi:10.1016/j.jss.2008.04.044

O'Sullivan, J., Edmond, D., & Hofstede, A. T. (2002). What's in a service? *Distributed and Parallel Databases, 12*(23), 117–133. doi:10.1023/A:1016547000822

OMG. (2004). *UML profile for modeling quality of service and fault tolerance characteristics and mechanisms* (Tech. Rep. No. ptc/04-09-012). Retrieved from http://www.omg.org/docs/ptc/04-09-01.pdf

Ran, S. (2003). A model for web services discovery with QoS. *ACM SIGecom Exchanges, 4*(1), 1–10. doi:10.1145/844357.844360

Zeng, L., Benatallah, B., Dumas, M., Kalagnanam, J., & Sheng, Q. (2003). Quality driven web services composition. In *Proceedings of the 12ᵗʰ International Conference on World Wide Web* (pp. 411-421).

Zeng, L., Benatallah, B., Ngu, A. H. H., Dumas, M., Kalagnanam, J., & Chang, H. (2004). QoS-aware middleware for web services composition. *IEEE Transactions on Software Engineering, 30*(5).

Zhou, C., Chia, L., & Lee, B. S. (2004). QoS-aware and federated enhancement for UDDI. *International Journal of Web Services Research, 1*(2), 58–85. doi:10.4018/jwsr.2004040104

This work was previously published in the International Journal of Information Technology and Web Engineering (IJITWE), Volume 6, Issue 3, edited by Ghazi I. Alkhatib and Ernesto Damiani, pp. 57-74, copyright 2011 by IGI Publishing (an imprint of IGI Global).

Section 2
Searching and Mining of Web Information

Chapter 6
Probabilistic Models for Social Media Mining

Flora S. Tsai
Nanyang Technological University, Singapore

ABSTRACT

This paper proposes probabilistic models for social media mining based on the multiple attributes of social media content, bloggers, and links. The authors present a unique social media classification framework that computes the normalized document-topic matrix. After comparing the results for social media classification on real-world data, the authors find that the model outperforms the other techniques in terms of overall precision and recall. The results demonstrate that additional information contained in social media attributes can improve classification and retrieval results.

INTRODUCTION

The rapid growth of technology has led to information overload from online such as blogs (Chen, Tsai, & Chan, 2007), social networks (Tsai, Han, Xu, & Chua, 2009), mobile information (Tsai et al., 2010), and Web services (Tsai et al., 2010). Novelty mining can help solve the problem of information overload by retrieving novel yet relevant information, based on a topic given by the user (Ng, Tsai, & Goh, 2007; Ong, Kwee, & Tsai, 2009), and can be used to solve many business problems, such as in corporate intelligence (Tsai, Chen, & Chan, 2007) and cyber security (Tsai, 2009; Tsai & Chan, 2007). Although users can

retrieve all the novel documents, each document still needs to be read to find the novel sentences within these documents (Tsai & Chan, 2011). Therefore, to serve users better, later studies of novelty mining were performed at the sentence level (Kwee, Tsai, & Tang, 2009; Tang & Tsai, 2009; Tang, Tsai & Chen, 2010; Tsai, Tang, & Chan, 2010; Zhang & Tsai, 2009b). Furthermore, the Web is changing from a datacentric Web into Web of semantic data and Web of services (Yee, Tiong, Tsai, & Kanagasabai, 2009). The use of Web services has significance in the business domain, where they are used as means of communication or exchanging data between businesses and clients (Kwee & Tsai, 2009).

DOI: 10.4018/978-1-4666-2157-2.ch006

Previous studies on social media mining (Tsai, Chen, & Chan, 2008; Liang, Tsai, & Kwee, 2009) use existing Web and text mining techniques without consideration of the additional dimensions present in the social media. Because of this, the techniques are only able to analyze one or two dimensions of the blog data (Tsai & Chan, 2010). In this paper, we propose unsupervised probabilistic models for mining the multiple dimensions present in social media. The models are used in the novel social media classification framework, which categorizes social media according to their most likely topic.

Problem Definition

This paper addresses the problem of multidimensional social media mining, which is a big challenge in the data mining community. Although blogs may share many similarities to Web and text documents, existing techniques need to be reevaluated and adapted for the multidimensional representation of blog data, which exhibit attributes not present in traditional documents. The proposed techniques aim to leverage multiple blog dimensions of authors and links to improve the results of mining information from blog data and to address and solve the problem of mining information from blog data using multiple dimensions of social media.

RELATED WORK

Related work on social media mining include techniques that focus on sentiment or opinion mining, or judging whether a particular blog post is negative, positive, or neutral to a particular object. One of the main tasks in the Text Retrieval Conference (TREC) Blog Track was the Opinion Retrieval Task, which involved finding blog posts that express an opinion about a given topic (Ounis et al., 2006; Macdonald, Ounis, & Soboroff, 2007).

Other studies attempt to filter out spam blogs, or splogs, which can greatly misrepresent any estimations of the number of blogs posted. Previous work in splog detection include splog detection using self-similarity analysis on blog temporal dynamics (Lin et al., 2007) and Support Vector Machines (SVMs) to identify and splogs (Kolari, Finin, & Joshi, 2006).

Other related work in social media mining is topic distillation, which was the second main task in TREC Blog 2007 (Macdonald, Ounis, & Soboroff, 2007). The blog distillation, or feed search, task focuses on blog feeds, which are aggregates of blog posts. Blog distillation task searches for a blog feed with a principle, recurring interest in topic *t*. For a given topic *t*, systems should suggest feeds that are principally devoted to *t* over the timespan of the feed, and would be recommended to subscribe to as an interesting feed about *t* (Macdonald, Ounis, & Soboroff, 2007). This task has direct relevance to the problem of searching for blogs to which a user may wish to subscribe. As many blog posts are inherently noisy, finding the relevant feeds is not a trivial problem.

Other related studies include a joint probabilistic document model (PHITS) (Cohn & Hofmann, 2001) which modeled the contents and inter-connectivity of document collections. A mixed-membership model (Erosheva, Fienberg, & Lafferty, 2004) was developed in which PLSA was replaced by LDA as the generative model. The Topic-Link LDA model (Liu, Niculescu-Mizil, & Gryc, 2009) quantified the effect of topic similarity and community similarity to the formation of a link. The citation-topic (CT) model was proposed in (Guo et al., 2009) for modeling linked documents that explicitly considers the relations among documents.

MODELS FOR SOCIAL MEDIA MINING

Latent Dirichlet Allocation

Latent Dirichlet Allocation (LDA) (Blei, Ng, & Jordan, 2003) is a probabilistic technique which models text documents as mixtures of latent topics, where topics correspond to key concepts presented in the corpus. For example, if observations are words collected into documents, it assumes that each document is a mixture of a small number of topics and that each word is attributable to one of the document's topics. LDA is not as susceptible to overfitting, and is preferred to traditional methods based on Latent Semantic Analysis (LSA) and Probabilistic Latent Semantic Analysis (PLSA), where the number of parameters grows with the number of training documents, making the model prone to overfitting (Tsai & Chan, 2009).

In LDA, each document may be viewed as a mixture of various topics. The topic mixture is drawn from a conjugate Dirichlet prior that is the same for all documents, as opposed to PLSA, where the topic mixture is conditioned on each document Learning the various distributions (the set of topics, their associated word probabilities, the topic of each word, and the particular topic mixture of each blog document) is a problem of Bayesian inference, which can be carried out using variational methods, Markov Chain Monte Carlo methods, or expectation propagation.

Author-Topic (AT) Model

An extension of LDA to probabilistic Author-Topic (AT) modeling (Rosen-Zvi et al., 2004; Steyvers et al., 2004) is proposed for the blogger and topic mining. The AT model is based on Gibbs sampling, a Markov chain Monte Carlo technique, where each author is represented by a probability distribution over topics, and each topic is represented as a probability distribution over terms for that topic (Steyvers et al., 2004).

The AT model has been extended for visualizing blog links and dates. For the Link-Topic (LT) model, each link is represented by a probability distribution over topics, and each topic represented by a probability distribution over terms for that topic. Likewise, for the Date-Topic (DT) model, each date is represented by a probability distribution over topics, and each topic represented by a probability distribution over terms for that topic.

Although the Author-Topic (AT) model has been extended for blog links and dates, the existing techniques based on the AT model are not able to simultaneously analyze the multiple attributes of blog documents. In order to solve the problem of analyzing the multiple attributes of blogs, we propose a new model that can solve the problem of finding the most likely bloggers and links for a given set of topics.

The new model, called the Author-Link-Topic (ALT) model, is motivated by the unique structure and characteristics of blogs that distinguish them from their traditional counterparts (text and Web documents). Figure 1 shows the generative model of the ALT model using plate notation. For each word in the document, an author x is chosen uniformly at random from a. Then, a topic is selected from a distribution over topics, θ, chosen from

Figure 1. Graphical model for the author-link-topic model using plate notation

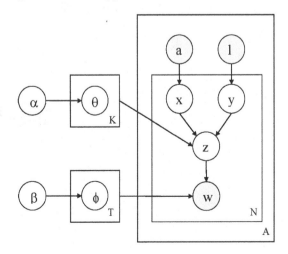

a symmetric Dirichlet (α) prior, and the word is generated from the selected topic. The mixture weights corresponding to the chosen author are used to select a topic z, and a word is generated according to the distribution ϕ corresponding to that topic, drawn from a symmetric Dirichlet(β) prior.

In the Author-Link-Topic (ALT) model, each author and link is represented by a probability distribution over topics, and each topic represented by a probability distribution over terms for that topic.

We have also extended the ALT model for finding the most likely authors and dates for a given set of topics. For the Author-Date-Topic (ADT) model, each author and date is represented by a probability distribution over topics, and each topic represented by a probability distribution over terms for that topic.

The probability is then integrated over ϕ and θ and their Dirichlet distributions and sampled using Markov Chain Monte Carlo methods.

Social Media Classification Framework

A novel blog classification framework is proposed that is able to classify social media into different topics. Figure 2 shows the basic concepts of the classification framework. In this framework, blog documents are processed using stopword removal, stemming, normalization, resulting in the generation of the term-document matrix. Next, different techniques are implemented to create the document-topic matrix. The techniques are described as follows:

From the results of the Author-Link-Topic model, we can obtain a set of document-topic matrices, which can be used to predict the topic given a document. The document-topic matrix (DT_t) based on terms is given by:

$$DT_t = WD' \times WT \tag{1}$$

where WD is the term-document matrix, and WT is the term-topic matrix.

The document-topic matrix (DT_a) based on authors is given by:

$$DT_a = AD' \times AT \tag{2}$$

Figure 2. Social media classification framework

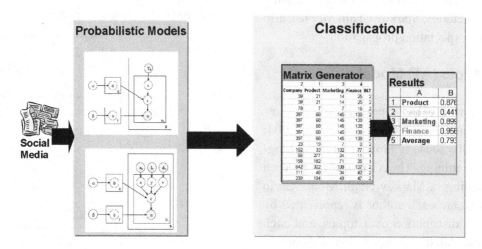

where AD is the author-document matrix, and AT is the author-topic matrix.

Likewise, the document-topic matrix based on links (DT_l) is given by:

$$DT_l = LD' \times LT \qquad (3)$$

where LD is the link-document matrix, and LT is the link-topic matrix. The justification for the equation above is to convert the output of the ALT model LT, which lists the most probably links for each topic, into a list of the most probable documents per topic, DT_l.

The three document-topic matrices were used to create the normalized document-topic matrix (DT_n) given by:

$$DT_n = \frac{DT_t + DT_a + DT_l}{\max\left\|DT_t\right\| + \max\left\|DTa\right\| + \max\left\|DT_l\right\|} \qquad (4)$$

From the document-topic matrix, the classification into different topics can be performed and evaluated against available relevance judgments.

Once we obtain the document-topic matrix, the category corresponding to the highest score for each blog document is used as the predicted category, and compared to the actual blog category. Thus, the corresponding precision and recall can then be calculated.

EXPERIMENTS AND RESULTS

Experiments were conducted on BizBlogs07 (Tsai, Chen, & Chan, 2008), a data corpus of business blogs. BizBlogs07 contains 1,269 business blog entries from various CEOs' blog sites and business blog sites. There are a total of 86 companies represented in the blog entries, and the blogs were classified into four (mutually exclusive) categories based on the contents or the main description of the blog: Product, Company, Marketing, and Finance (Tsai, Chen, & Chan, 2008). Blogs in the Product category describe specific company products, such as reviews, descriptions, and other product-related news. Blogs in the Company category describe news or other information specific to corporations, organizations, or businesses. The Marketing category deals with marketing, sales, and advertising strategies for companies. Finally, blogs in the Finance category relates to financing, loans, credit information (Tsai, Chen, & Chan, 2008).

Author-Link-Topic Results

The Author-Link-Topic (ALT) model is able to find the most probable bloggers and links for a given set of topics. In order to prepare the inputs to the model, we first created a 3159×1269 term-document matrix with term frequency (TF) local term weighting, based on the content of the blogs. In addition, the 118 × 1269 author-document matrix and 75×1269 link-document matrix were also created as inputs to the model, where the links correspond to the respective permalinks.

The author-link-topic distributions were then learned from the blog data in an unsupervised manner. The parameters used in our experiments were the number of topics (t=50) and number of iterations (N=2000). We used symmetric Dirichlet priors in the ALT estimation with α=50/t and β=0.01, which are common settings in the literature (Tsai & Chan, 2009).

The most likely terms and corresponding authors and links from Topic 1 (Product) and Topic 2 (Company) of the entire blog entry collection are listed in Table 1 and Table 2.

As can be seen from the tables, the topics correspond to the four categories of Product, Company, Marketing, and Finance, based on the list of most likely terms. The list of top authors corresponds to the bloggers that are most likely to post in a particular topic. Usually a author with a high probability for a given topic may also post many blogs for that topic. The list of links cor-

Table 1. ALT Topic 1: Product

Term	Probability
mobil	0.01413
devic	0.00918
phone	0.00781
window	0.00768
batteri	0.00688
time	0.00682
servic	0.00652
site	0.00632
run	0.00625
releas	0.00622
Author	
Kevin C. Tofel	0.33943
jk	0.16926
eBAY Developer	0.05434
Jeff	0.05043
Lionel Menchaca	0.02708
FMF	0.02166
Steve Rubel	0.01969
Larry Bodine	0.01810
john dodds	0.01642
Jeff Jaffe	0.01601
Link	
jkontherun.blogs.com	0.52971
ebaydeveloper.typepad.com	0.06591
www.direct2dell.com	0.06406
aws.typepad.com	0.05228
www.freemoneyfinance.com	0.02227
blogs.cisco.com	0.02022
www.autoblog.com	0.01982
pm.typepad.com	0.01899
makemarketinghistory.blogspot.com	0.01681
www.novell.com	0.01638

Table 2. ALT Topic 2: Company

Term	Probability
custom	0.02196
product	0.01667
blog	0.01219
manag	0.01163
world	0.00960
system	0.00925
open	0.00879
dell	0.00872
post	0.00714
brand	0.00690
Author	
Jeff Jaffe	0.08326
FMF	0.08089
john dodds	0.05699
Kevin C. Tofel	0.05439
Diva	0.04812
Bob Langert	0.04402
Manoj Ranaweera	0.03949
Lionel Menchaca	0.03645
jk	0.03032
Jeff	0.02615
Link	
www.direct2dell.com	0.12071
jkontherun.blogs.com	0.08775
www.novell.com	0.08667
www.freemoneyfinance.com	0.08420
makemarketinghistory.blogspot.com	0.05922
www.autoblog.com	0.05233
bloombergmarketing.blogs.com	0.04996
csr.blogs.mcdonalds.com	0.04724
blog.startwithalead.com	0.04679
manojranaweera.wordpress.com	0.04093

responds to the top links for each topic, based on the most likely terms and top authors that post to the topic.

Blog Classification Results

Using the results of the Author-Link-Topic (ALT) model in our blog classification framework, we obtained a set of document-topic matrices, which were used to predict the topic given a blog document. We compared with three other techniques: Author-Date-Topic (ADT), Author-Topic (AT), and Latent Dirichlet Allocation (LDA).

The classification results for precision and recall in each category are shown in Figure 3 and Figure 4. Figure 5 shows the overall results.

As seen from the results, the ALT model was able to obtain better overall precision and recall results than the other techniques. The precision results for the Company category tended to be much lower than the other categories, which could be due to the general nature of the blogs in this category. On the other hand, the precision results for Finance category had the highest accuracy overall, perhaps due to the specialized nature of blogs in this category.

The ALT model was able to improve the overall results of the AT model by taking into consideration the top links. This indicates that additional probability distributions for the top authors and top links help to can improve the classification results.

In contrast, results from the ADT model underperformed the other techniques, due to the inability of the dates to distinguish different categories. This is a reasonable assumption, as dates may be distributed somewhat evenly, and the most likely dates for a given topic may not be useful in blog classification, unless the topic is related to a time-specific event.

DISCUSSION

As seen from the results, the models utilizing links and author information were able to obtain better overall precision and recall results than LDA, which only uses the information on the top terms. The fact that author information increased our

Figure 3. Blog precision results for each category

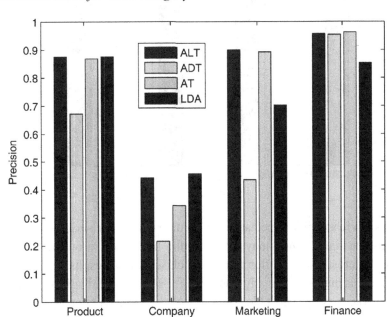

Figure 4. Blog recall results for each category

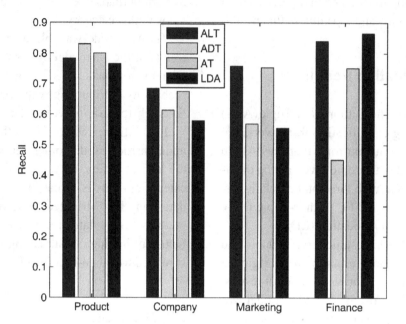

Figure 5. Average precision and recall

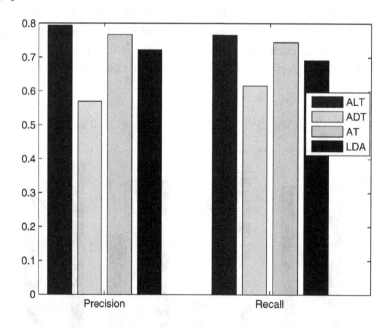

classification results is a reasonable expectation, given the assumption that many authors may post blogs based on their interests, which often may be in the same topics. This may be especially true of business bloggers who may only post blogs in their particular scope of knowledge. Likewise, the links used in our models also increased the classification results, for the similar reasons given for authors. Similar blogs may be posted in links of the same category. For example certain links may contain many blogs related to products, which can have a positive influence on the classification of product blogs.

CONCLUSION AND FUTURE WORK

This paper proposed probabilistic models based on the author-topic model to solve the problem of finding the most likely bloggers and links for a given set of topics. The models allow special attributes of blogs to be exploited for learning a better topic model. We have also extended the model to find the most likely bloggers and dates for a given set of topics. The models have been successfully implemented and evaluated on a real-world collection of business blogs.

A unique social media classification framework that computes the normalized document-topic matrix was applied to different techniques to calculate the classification results. The results for blog classification were compared to the techniques using author-topic, and Latent Dirichlet Allocation. Overall, the results obtained a higher average precision and recall than the other techniques, which indicates that additional blog-specific attributes of authors and links can improve classification results.

We have presented a unique framework of multidimensional social media mining based on the multiple attributes of social media, and shown that additional social media-specific attributes of bloggers and links can be used to improve the classification results. Since the model is unsupervised, it can easily be applied for real-time classification of large numbers of blog documents. Our approach is generic, and may be used for other multidimensional data, such as various types of user-generated content. We hope that our work can spur the development of advanced techniques that exploit multiple characteristics of social media to increase performance across various domains of information retrieval.

REFERENCES

Blei, D. M., Ng, A. Y., & Jordan, M. I. (2003). Latent dirichlet allocation. *Journal of Machine Learning Research*, *3*(1), 993–1022. doi:10.1162/jmlr.2003.3.4-5.993

Chen, Y., Tsai, F. S., & Chan, K. L. (2007). Blog search and mining in the business domain. In *DDDM '07: Proceedings of the 2007 International Workshop on Domain Driven Data Mining* (pp. 55-60).

Chen, Y., Tsai, F. S., & Chan, K. L. (2008). Machine Learning Techniques for Business Blog Search and Mining. *Expert Systems with Applications*, *35*(3), 581–590. doi:10.1016/j.eswa.2007.07.015

Cohn, D., & Hofmann, T. (2001). The missing link – a probabilistic model of document content and hypertext connectivity. *Advances in Neural Information Processing Systems*, *13*, 430–436.

Erosheva, E., Fienberg, S., & Lafferty, J. (2004). Mixed-membership models of scientific publications. *Proceedings of the National Academy of Sciences of the United States of America*, *101*, 5220–5227. doi:10.1073/pnas.0307760101

Guo, Z., Zhu, S., Chi, Y., Zhang, Z., & Gong, Y. (2009). A latent topic model for linked documents. In *SIGIR '09: Proceedings of the 32nd International ACM SIGIR Conference on Research and Development in Information Retrieval* (pp. 720-721).

Kolari, P., Finin, T., & Joshi, A. (2006). SVMs for the Blogosphere: Blog Identification and Splog Detection. In *Proceedings of the AAAI Spring Symposium on Computational Approaches to Analysing Weblogs*.

Kwee, A. T., & Tsai, F. S. (2009). Mobile Novelty Mining. *International Journal of Advanced Pervasive and Ubiquitous Computing*, *1*(4), 43–68. doi:10.4018/japuc.2009100104

Kwee, A. T., Tsai, F. S., & Tang, W. (2009). Sentence-level Novelty Detection in English and Malay. In *Advances in Knowledge Discovery and Data Mining* (LNCS 5476, pp. 40-51).

Liang, H., Tsai, F. S., & Kwee, A. T. (2009). *Detecting Novel Business Blogs*. Paper presented at the 7th International Conference on Information, Communications, and Signal Processing (ICICS).

Lin, Y.-R., Sundaram, H., Chi, Y., Tatemura, J., & Tseng, B. L. (2007). Splog detection using self-similarity analysis on blog temporal dynamics. In *AIRWeb '07: Proceedings of the 3rd International Workshop on Adversarial Information Retrieval on the Web* (pp. 1-8).

Liu, Y., Niculescu-Mizil, A., & Gryc, W. (2009). Topic-link LDA: joint models of topic and author community. In *ICML '09: Proceedings of the 26th Annual International Conference on Machine Learning* (pp. 665-672).

Macdonald, C., Ounis, I., & Soboroff, I. (2007). Overview of the TREC-2007 Blog Track. In *Proceedings of the 16th Text Retrieval Conference (TREC 2007)*.

Ng, K. W., Tsai, F. S., & Goh, K. C. (2007). Novelty Detection for Text Documents Using Named Entity Recognition. In *Proceedings of the 2007 6th International Conference on Information, Communications and Signal Processing* (pp. 1-5).

Ong, C. L., Kwee, A. T., & Tsai, F. S. (2009). *Database Optimization for Novelty Detection*. Paper presented at the 7th International Conference on Information, Communications, and Signal Processing (ICICS).

Ounis, I., de Rijke, M., Macdonald, C., Mishne, G. A., & Soboroff, I. (2006). Overview of the TREC-2006 Blog track. In *Proceedings of TREC 2006: Working Notes* (pp. 15-27).

Rosen-Zvi, M., Griffiths, T., Steyvers, M., & Smyth, P. (2004). The author-topic model for authors and documents. In *AUAI '04: Proceedings of the 20th Conference on Uncertainty in Artificial Intelligence* (pp. 487-494).

Steyvers, M., Smyth, P., Rosen-Zvi, M., & Griffiths, T. (2004). Probabilistic author-topic models for information discovery. In *KDD '04: Proceedings of the 10th ACM SIGKDD International Conference on Knowledge Discovery and Data Mining* (pp. 306-315).

Tang, W., & Tsai, F. S. (2009). Threshold Setting and Performance Monitoring for Novel Text Mining. In *Proceedings in Applied Mathematics: 9th SIAM International Conference on Data Mining 2009* (Vol. 3, pp. 1310-1319).

Tang, W., Tsai, F. S., & Chen, L. (2010). Blended Metrics for Novel Sentence Mining. *Expert Systems with Applications, 37*(7), 5172–5177. doi:10.1016/j.eswa.2009.12.075

Tsai, F. S. (2009). Network intrusion detection using association rules. *International Journal of Recent Trends in Engineering, 2*(1), 202–204.

Tsai, F. S., & Chan, K. L. (2007). Detecting cyber security threats in weblogs using probabilistic models. In *Intelligence and Security Informatics* (LNCS 4430, pp. 46-57).

Tsai, F. S., & Chan, K. L. (2009). Blog Data Mining for Cyber Security Threats. In *Data Mining for Business Applications* (pp. 169-182).

Tsai, F. S., & Chan, K. L. (2010). Redundancy and novelty mining in the business blogosphere. *The Learning Organization, 17*(6), 490–499. doi:10.1108/09696471011082358

Tsai, F. S., & Chan, K. L. (2011). An Intelligent System for Sentence Retrieval and Novelty Mining. *International Journal of Knowledge Engineering and Data Mining, 1*(3), 235–253. doi:10.1504/IJKEDM.2011.037645

Tsai, F. S., Chen, Y., & Chan, K. L. (2007). Probabilistic techniques for corporate blog mining. In *Emerging Technologies in Knowledge Discovery and Data Mining* (LNCS 4819, pp. 35-44).

Tsai, F. S., Etoh, M., Xie, X., Lee, W.-C., & Yang, Q. (2010). Introduction to Mobile Information Retrieval. *IEEE Intelligent Systems*, *25*(1), 11–15. doi:10.1109/MIS.2010.22

Tsai, F. S., Han, W., Xu, J., & Chua, H. C. (2009). Design and Development of a Mobile Peer-to-peer Social Networking Application. *Expert Systems with Applications*, *36*(8), 11077–11087. doi:10.1016/j.eswa.2009.02.093

Tsai, F. S., Kwee, A. T., Tang, W., & Chan, K. L. (2010). Adaptable Services for Novelty Mining. *International Journal of Systems and Service-Oriented Engineering*, *1*(2), 69–85. doi:10.4018/jssoe.2010040105

Tsai, F. S., Tang, W., & Chan, K. L. (2010). Evaluation of Metrics for Sentence-level Novelty Mining. *Information Sciences*, *180*(12), 2359–2374. doi:10.1016/j.ins.2010.02.020

Yee, K. Y., Tiong, A. W., Tsai, F. S., & Kanagasabai, R. (2009). OntoMobiLe: A Generic Ontology-centric Service-Oriented Architecture for Mobile Learning. In *Proceedings of the 2009 10th International Conference on Mobile Data Management (MDM) Workshop on Mobile Media Retrieval (MMR)* (pp. 631-636).

Zhang, Y., & Tsai, F. S. (2009a). Chinese Novelty Mining. In *EMNLP '09: Proceedings of the Conference on Empirical Methods in Natural Language Processing* (pp. 1561-1570).

Zhang, Y., & Tsai, F. S. (2009b). Combining Named Entities and Tags for Novel Sentence Detection. In *ESAIR '09: Proceedings of the WSDM '09 Workshop on Exploiting Semantic Annotations in Information Retrieval* (pp. 30-34).

Zhang, Y., Tsai, F. S., & Kwee, A. T. (in press). Multilingual Sentence Categorization and Novelty Mining. *Information Processing & Management*.

This work was previously published in the International Journal of Information Technology and Web Engineering (IJITWE), Volume 6, Issue 1, edited by Ghazi I. Alkhatib and Ernesto Damiani, pp. 13-24, copyright 2011 by IGI Publishing (an imprint of IGI Global).

Chapter 7
A Novel Architecture for Deep Web Crawler

Dilip Kumar Sharma
Shobhit University, India

A. K. Sharma
YMCA University of Science and Technology, India

ABSTRACT

A traditional crawler picks up a URL, retrieves the corresponding page and extracts various links, adding them to the queue. A deep Web crawler, after adding links to the queue, checks for forms. If forms are present, it processes them and retrieves the required information. Various techniques have been proposed for crawling deep Web information, but much remains undiscovered. In this paper, the authors analyze and compare important deep Web information crawling techniques to find their relative limitations and advantages. To minimize limitations of existing deep Web crawlers, a novel architecture is proposed based on QIIIEP specifications (Sharma & Sharma, 2009). The proposed architecture is cost effective and has features of privatized search and general search for deep Web data hidden behind html forms.

1. INTRODUCTION

Traditional Web crawling techniques have been used to search the contents of the Web that is reachable through the hyperlinks but they ignore the deep Web contents which are hidden because there is no link is available for referring these deep Web contents. The Web contents which are accessible through hyperlinks are termed as

surface Web, while the hidden contents hidden behind the html forms are termed as deep Web. Deep Web sources store their contents in searchable databases that produce results dynamically only in response to a direct request (Bergman, 2001). The deep Web is not completely hidden for crawling. Major traditional search engines can be able to search approximately one-third of the data (He, Patel, Zhang, & Chang, 2007) but in order

DOI: 10.4018/978-1-4666-2157-2.ch007

to utilize the full potential of Web, there is a need to concentrate on deep Web contents since they can provide a large amount of useful information. Hence, there is a need to build efficient deep Web crawlers which can efficiently search the deep Web contents. The deep Web pages cannot be searched efficiently through traditional Web crawler and they can be extracted dynamically as a result of a specific search through a dedicated deep Web crawler (Peisu, Ke, & Qinzhen, 2008; Sharma & Sharma, 2010). This paper finds the advantages and limitations of the current deep Web crawlers in searching the deep Web contents. For this purpose an exhaustive analysis of existing deep Web crawler mechanism is done for searching the deep Web contents. In particular, it concentrates on development of novel architecture for deep Web crawler for extracting contents from the portion of the Web that is hidden behind html search interface in large searchable databases with the following points:

- Analysis of different existing algorithms of deep Web crawlers with their advantages and limitations in large scale crawling of deep Web.
- After profound analysis of existing deep Web crawling process, a novel architecture of deep Web crawling based on QIIIEP (query intensive interface information extraction protocol) specification is proposed (Figure 1).

This paper is organized as follows: In section 2, related work is discussed. Section 3 summarizes the architectures of various deep Web crawlers. Section 4 compares the architectures of various deep Web crawlers. The architecture of the proposed deep Web crawler is presented in section 5. Experimental results are discussed in section 6 and finally, a conclusion is presented in section 7.

2. RELATED WORK

Deep Web stores their data behind the html forms. Traditional Web crawler can efficiently crawl the surface Web but they cannot efficiently crawl the deep Web. For crawling the deep Web contents various specialized deep Web crawlers are proposed in the literature but they have limited capabilities in crawling the deep Web. A large volume of deep Web data is remains to be discovered due to the limitations of deep Web crawler. In this section existing deep Web crawlers are analyzed to find their advantages and limitations with particular reference to their capability to crawl the deep Web contents efficiently.

Application/Task Specific Human Assisted Approach

Various crawlers are proposed in literature to crawl the deep Web. One of the deep Web crawler architecture is proposed by Raghavan and Garcia-

Figure 1. Mechanism of QIIIEP-based deep web crawler

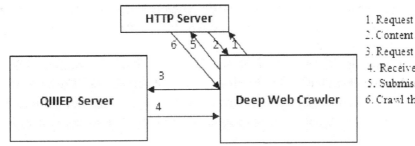

Molina (2001). In this paper, a task-specific, human-assisted approach is used for crawling the hidden Web. Two basic challenges are associated with deep Web search, i.e. the volume of the hidden Web is very large and there is a need of such type of user friendly crawler which can handle search interfaces efficiently. In this paper a model of task specific human assisted Web crawler is designed and realized in HiWE (hidden Web exposure). The HiWE prototype was built at Stanford and it crawls the dynamic pages. HiWE is designed to automatically process, analyze, and submit forms, using an internal model of forms and form submissions. HiWE uses a layout-based information extraction (LITE) technique to process and extract useful information. The advantages of HiWE architecture is that its application/task specific approach allows the crawler to concentrate on relevant pages only and automatic form filling can be done with the human assisted approach. Limitations of this architecture are that, it is not precise in responding to partially filled forms and it is not able to identify and respond to simple dependency between form elements.

Focused Crawling with Automatic Form Filling Based Approach

A focused crawler architecture is proposed by Luciano Barbosa and Juliana Freire (2005). This paper suggests a strategy which deals with the problem of performing a wide search while avoiding the crawling of irrelevant pages. The best way is to use a focused crawler which only crawl pages relevant to a particular topic. It uses three classifiers to focus its search: Page classifier is which classifies pages, belonging to topics, Form classifier is used to filter out useless forms and Link classifiers is used to identify links that are likely to lead to pages that contain searchable form interfaces in one or more steps. Advantages of this architecture are that only topic specific forms are gathered and unproductive searches are avoided

because of application of stopping criteria. A limitation of this architecture is that quality of forms is not ensured since thousands of forms are retrieved at a time. Furthermore scope of improvement in this type of crawler is that focused crawlers can be used for making domain specific crawlers like hidden Web database directory.

Automatic Query Generation for Single Attribute Database Based Approach

A novel technique for downloading textual hidden Web contents is proposed by Ntoulas, Zerfos, and Cho (2005). There are two basic challenges in implementing a hidden Web crawler; firstly the crawler should understand and model a query interface secondly the crawler should generate meaningful queries to issue to the query interface. To address the above mentioned challenges, this paper suggests how a crawler can automatically generate queries so that it can discover and download the hidden Web pages. It mainly focuses on textual databases that support single-attribute keyword queries. An advantage of this technique is that query is generated automatically without any human intervention therefore crawling is efficient and limitation of this technique is that it focuses only on single attribute databases. Further an extension can be made to this work by including multi-attribute databases.

Task Specific and Domain Definition Based Approach

A technique for deep Web crawling based on task-specific approach is proposed by Alvarez, Raposo, Cacheda and Pan (2006). In this approach, a set of domain definition is provided to the crawler. Every domain definition defines a particular data collecting task. The deep Web crawler recognizes the relevant query forms by using domain definition. The functioning of this model is based on a shared list of routes (URLs). The overall crawling process consists of several sub crawling processes which may run on different machines. Each crawling process selects a route from the route list, analyzes it and downloads the relevant documents. The advantage of this algorithm is that results are very effective against the various real words data collecting tasks. Further scope in this regard is to make this algorithm to be capable of automatically generate new queries from the results of the previous ones.

Focused Crawling Based Approach

A focused crawler named DeepBot for accessing hidden Web content is proposed by Alvarez, Raposo, Pan, Cacheda, Bellas, and Carneiro (2007). In this work an algorithm is developed for developing the DeepBot, which is based on focused crawling for extracting the deep Web contents. Challenges behind the crawling of the deep Web contents can be broadly classified into two parts, i.e., crawling the Hidden Web at server-side and crawling the Hidden Web at client-side. Advantages of this DeepBot crawler are that a form may be used in this crawling but it may have some field that do not correspond to any attribute of the domain, Accuracy of DeepBot crawler is high when more than one associated text are present in the field. The context related to the whole form is also considered in the crawling mechanism and DeepBot is fully compatible with java-script sources. A disadvantage of such type of crawling is that all the attributes of the form should be filled completely and precisely. Problem in crawling arises when one uses sources with session mechanisms. As a future work, modification can be done in the DeepBot crawler so that it can be able to generate new quires in automatic fashion.

Sampling Based Approach

An approach to deep Web crawling by sampling based technique is proposed Lu, Wang, Liang, Chen, and Liu (2008). One of the major challenges while crawling the deep Web is the selection of the queries so that most of the data can be retrieved at a low cost. A general method is proposed, which maximize the coverage of the data source, while minimizing the communication cost. The strategy behind this technique is to minimize the number of queries issued, by maximizing the possibility of the unique returns of each query. An advantage of this technique is that it is a low cost technique that can be used in practical applications and limitation of this algorithm is that the efficiency of the crawler reduces when the sample and pool size is very large. As a future work, modification can be done to lower the overlapping rate so that the maximum Webpages can be downloaded.

Domain Specific Search with Relevancy Based Approach

An architectural framework of a crawler for locating deep Web repositories using learning multi-agent systems is proposed by Akilandeswari and Gopalan (2008). This paper uses multi-agent Web mining system to discover pages from the hidden Web. Multi-agents system is used when there are troubles in storing large amount of data in the database indices. The proposed system has variety of information agents interacting with each other to learn about their environment so that they can retrieve desired information effectively. Advantages of this framework are that crawling through this technique is efficient because the searching is concentrated on a specific domain. The crawling technique of this framework extract the relevant Web forms by using the learning multi-agents and it learns effectively which reduces form retrieval time. Limitation of this framework is that it is not easy to maintain multiple agents. In future, this framework can be extended so that genetic algorithms can be implemented in the crawler to perform a broad search to improve the harvest rate.

Domain-Specific Deep Web Sources Discovery Based Approach

A technique of domain-specific deep Web sources discovery is proposed by Wang, Zuo, Peng, and He (2008). It is difficult to find the right sources and then querying over them online in huge collection of useful databases. Hence, this paper presents a new method by importing focused crawling technology to automatically accomplish deep Web sources discovery. Firstly, Websites are located for domain-specific data sources based on focused crawling. Secondly, it is judged where the Website exists in deep Web query interface. Lastly, judgment is done to find whether the deep Web query interface is relevant to a given topic. Implementation of focused crawling technology facilitates the identification of deep Web query interface located in a specific domain and capturing of relevant pages associated with the topic. This method has dramatically reduces the quantity of pages for the crawler to crawl the deep Web. Advantage of this technique is that fewer numbers of pages need to be crawled since it applies focused crawling along with the relevancy search of the obtained results about the topic. Limitation of this technique is that it does not take into account the semantics, i.e., a particular query result could have several meanings. As a future work this technique can be extended to include semantics while querying.

Input Values for Text Search Inputs Based Approach

A technique for surfacing deep Web contents is proposed by Madhavan, Ko, Kot, Ganapathy, Rasmussen, and Halevy (2008). Surfacing the deep Web is a very complex task because html forms can be associated with different languages and different domains. Further large quantities of forms are associated with text inputs which require the submission of valid input values. For this purpose authors have proposed a technique for choosing input values for text search inputs by which keywords can be accepted. Advantage of this technique is that it can efficiently navigate for searching against various possible input combinations. The limitations as well as future work in this regard can be to modify the technique to deal with forms associated with java script and to analyze the dependency between the values in various inputs of a form in more depth.

Label Value Set (LVS) Table Based Approach

A framework of Deep Web Crawler is proposed by Peisu, Ke, and Qinzhen (2008). The proposed framework processes the actual mechanics of crawling of deep Web. This paper deals with the problem of crawling a subset of the currently uncrawled dynamic Web contents. It concentrates on extracting contents from the portion of the Web that is hidden behind search forms in large searchable databases. This proposed framework presents a model of form with form submission facility. One of important characteristics of this proposed crawler is that it uses Label Value Set (LVS) table. Access and additions to the LVS table is done by LVS manager. The LVS manager also works as an interface for different application specific data sources. Advantage of this deep Web crawler is that it uses the additional modules like LVS table which help the crawler to design the model of frame. If the crawler uses the LVS table than the number of successful form submissions increase. Limitations of this framework are that crawler is unable to extract label (E) and the value of domain (D) in LVS is repeated.

Minimum Executing Pattern (MEP) and Adaptive Query Based Approach

A technique for crawling deep Web contents through query forms is proposed by Liu, Wu, Jiang, Zheng, and Liu (2009). The proposed technique of crawling the deep Web content is based on minimum executing pattern (MEP). The query in this technique is processed by deep Web adaptive query method. Query interface is expended from single text box to MEP set by using deep Web adaptive query method. A MEP, associated with keyword vector is selected for producing optimum local query. Advantages of this technique are that it can handle a different Web forms very effectively and its efficiency is very high compared to non prior knowledge methods. Further it also minimizes the problem of "data islands" to some extent. The limitation of this technique is that it does not produce good results in case of the deep Web sites which have limited size of result set. Further Boolean logic operators, such as AND, OR, NOT, cannot be used in queries which can be a part of the future work.

Iterative Self Organizing Data Analysis (ISODATA) Based Approach

A novel automatic technique for classifying deep Web sources is proposed by Zhao (2010). The classification of deep Web sources is a very critical step for integrating the large scale deep Web data. This proposed technique is based on iterative self organizing data analysis (ISODATA) technique. This technique is based on hierarchical clustering method. Advantage of this technique is that it allows the user to browse the relevant and valuable information. Method for extraction of characteristics in Web pages can be further improved to browse the valuable information.

Continuously Update or Refresh the Hidden Web Repository Based Approach

A framework for incremental hidden Web crawler is proposed by Madaan, Dixit, Sharma, and Bhatia (2010). In a world of rapidly changing information, it is a highly required to maintain and extract the up-to-date information. For this, it is required to verify whether a Web page has been changed or not. The time period between two successive revisits needs to be adjusted based on probability of updating of the Web page. In this paper, architecture is proposed that introduces a technique to continuously update or refresh the hidden Web repository. Advantages of this incremental hidden Web crawler is that information fetched is updated even if Web pages change and limitation of this incremental hidden Web crawler is that efficient indexing technique is required to maintain the Web pages in the repository. In future, a modified architecture of a search engine based on incremental hidden Web crawler using some indexing technique can be designed to index the Web pages that stored in the repository.

Reinforcement Learning Based Approach

An efficient deep Web crawling technique using reinforcement learning is proposed by Jiang, Wu, Feng, Liu, and Zheng (2010). In the reinforcement learning technique, the deep Web crawler works as agent and deep Web database plays a role of environment. The deep Web crawler identifies a query to be submitted into a deep Web database, depending upon Q-value. The advantage of this technique is that deep Web crawler itself decides about a crawling technique to be used by using its own experience. Further, it also permits the use of different characteristics of query keywords. Further scope in this technique is that to develop an open source platform can be developed for deep Web crawling.

After going through analysis of deep Web crawlers, it is concluded that each deep Web crawler has certain limitations with reference to their capabilities of efficient crawling of the deep Web contents. Some of the challenges for efficient deep Web crawling are that a crawler should not overload the Web servers. A deep Web crawler must be robust against hazardous situations. It must be fault tolerant so that its performance degrades gracefully. It should be highly configurable. The download rate of a crawler must be adequate so as to process the harvested data. A crawler must be flexible to enable quick adoption to new publishing technologies and formats used on the Web as they become available. The crawler must include the management tools that enable the quick detection of its failure. The deep Web crawler should have a focused way of crawling the information from the deep Web. They should automatically download the pages from the deep Web so that search engine can index them.

3. SUMMARY OF VARIOUS DEEP WEB CRAWLER ARCHITECTURES

By going through the literature analysis of some of the deep Web crawlers, It is concluded that every crawler have some relative advantages and limitations. A tabular summary is given in Table 1, which summarizes the techniques, advantages and limitations of some of important deep Web crawlers.

4. COMPARISON OF THE VARIOUS DEEP WEB CRAWLER ARCHITECTURES

Based on the literature analysis, a comparison of some of various deep Web crawlers architectures is shown in Table 2 and Table 3. Comparison is done on the basis of some parameters such as technique used, need of user support, reflection of change in Web page, automatic query selection; accuracy of data fetched, database sampling and focused crawling.

Table 1. Summary of various deep Web crawler architectures

Authors, Year	Technique	Advantages	Limitations
Raghavan et al., 2001	Extraction is application/task specific.	Extraction of irrelevant pages is minimized.	Crawling is not precise due to possibility of missing of some pages.
Barbosa et al., 2005	Focused crawling with automatic form filling.	Crawling is highly relevant, which saves time and resources.	Quality of forms is not ensured and form verification is a complex task.
Ntoulas et al., 2005	Based on automatic query generation form.	Efficient crawling due to crawler generated query.	Does not involve frequently used multi-attribute database.
Alvarez et al., 2006	Task specific approach. A set of domain definition is provided to the crawler. Every domain definition defines a particular data collecting task. The deep Web crawler recognizes the relevant query forms by using domain definition.	Results are very effective against the various real words data collecting task.	Algorithm can be modified to be able to automatically generate new queries from the results of the previous ones.

continued on following page

Table 1. Continued

Authors, Year	Technique	Advantages	Limitations
Alvarez et al., 2007	Focused crawling for extracting deep Web contents	Accuracy is high with the field having more than one associated text. The context of the whole form is used. Fully compatible with java-script sources	The form should be filled precisely and completely. Difficulty with sources having session mechanism.
Lu et al., 2007	Sampling data from the database.	Low cost, Efficient in practical applications.	Efficiency is less in case of large sample and pool size.
Akilandeswari et al., 2008	Use of multi-agent system on a large database.	Time efficient, fault tolerant and easy handling due to multi-agents.	Cost may be high due to maintenance of multi-agents.
Wang et al., 2008	Focused crawling and results are located in a specific domain.	Crawl fewer numbers of pages due domain specific technique.	Sometimes semantics may be wrong due to crawling of useless pages.
Madhavan et al., 2008	Input values for text search inputs are selected. Identification of inputs for a particular type of values.	It can efficiently navigate for searching against various possible input combinations.	Technique can be modified to deal with forms associated with java script and the dependency between the values in various inputs of a form can be analyzed in more depth.
Peisu et al., 2008	Proposes a model of form. Form submission with four additional modules with LVS table.	Successful form submissions increase with the use of LVS table.	If crawler is unable extract label (E) then the value of domain (D) in LVS is repeated.
Liu et al., 2009	Based on the concept of minimum executable pattern (MEP).	Effective handing of different Web forms. Higher efficiency against non prior knowledge method. Reduces the problem of "data islands".	Results are not good with Websites having limited size of result set. Boolean logic operators (AND,OR,NOT) cannot be used.
Zhao, 2010	Based on iterative self organizing data analysis (ISODATA) technique.	Allows the user to browse the relevant and valuable information.	Extraction method of characteristics in Web pages can be further improved to browse the valuable information.
Madaan et al., 2010	Regularly updates Web repository.	Fetched Web pages are regularly updated.	Indexing of Web page is required.
Jiang et al., 2010	Based on reinforcement learning technique. Deep Web crawler works as agent and deep Web database plays a role of environment. Identify a query to be submitted into a deep Web database, using Q-value.	Deep Web crawler itself decides about a crawling technique to be used by using its own experience. Permits the use of different characteristics of query keywords.	Can be developed as an open source platform for deep Web crawling.

5. PROPOSED WORK

By going through literature analysis with their relative comparison with reference to efficient deep Web crawling, it is observed that each deep Web crawler has limitations in efficient crawling of the deep Web. To fulfill this need, a novel architecture for efficient deep Web crawling is proposed with particular reference to QIIIEP specification. Proposed architecture incorporates all the features of existing deep Web crawlers and tries to minimize the limitations of existing deep Web crawlers. Figure 2 shows the architecture of proposed novel deep Web crawler mechanism.

Table 2. Comparison of the various deep Web crawler architectures

Crawling Technique → Parameter ↓	Crawling the Hidden Web	Searching for Hidden Web Databases	Downloading Textual Hidden Web Contents	Domain Specific Deep Web Sources Discovery	Approach to Deep Web Crawling by Sampling	Framework for Incremental Hidden Web Crawler	Locating Deep Web Repositories Using Multi-Agent Systems
Technique used	Application/task specific human assisted approach.	Focused crawling with automatic form filling.	Automatic query generation for single attribute database.	Domain specific relevancy based search.	Sampling of data from the database.	Frequent updation of Web repository.	Multi-agent system is helpful in locating deep Web contents.
Need of the user's support	Human interface is needed in form filling.	No human interface is needed in form filling.	User monitors the filling process.	It doesn't require user's help.	Not mentioned.	It doesn't require user's help.	Users monitor the process.
Reflection of Web page changes	It doesn't reflect such a change	No concept involved for dealing with it.	It doesn't reflect such a change.	Such changes are not incorporated	It doesn't reflect such a change.	It keeps refreshing the repository for such changes.	It doesn't reflect such a change.
Automatic query selection	Such feature has not been incorporated	Nothing is mentioned about such a feature.	Query selection is automatic.	Nothing is mentioned about such a feature.	Automated query selection is done.	Nothing is mentioned about such feature.	Nothing is mentioned about such feature.
Accuracy of data fetched	Data fetched can be wrong if the Web pages change.	Data fetched can be wrong if the Web pages change.	Data fetched can be wrong if the Web pages change.	Data fetched can be wrong if the Webpages change.	Data fetched can be wrong if the Web pages change.	Data fetched can be wrong if the Webpages change.	Only correct data is obtained since repository is refreshed at regular time interval.
Database sampling	Such feature is not incorporated.	Such feature is not incorporated.	Such feature is not incorporated.	Such feature is not incorporated.	Large database is sampled into smaller units.	Such feature is not incorporated.	Such feature is not incorporated.
Focused crawling	Focused crawling is not involved although it is task specific.	Focused crawling is the basis of this work.	Nothing is mentioned about focused crawling.	Focused crawling is done.	Nothing is mentioned about such concept.	Nothing is mentioned about it.	Nothing is mentioned about it.

Table 3. Comparison of the various deep Web crawler architectures

Crawling Technique → / Parameters ↓	A Framework of Deep Web Crawler	Google's Deep Web Crawl	Efficient Deep Web Crawling Using Reinforcement Learning	Crawling Deep Web Contents through Query Forms	Study of Deep Web Sources Classification Technology	A Task-Specific Approach for Crawling the Deep Web
Technique used	Proposes a model of form with form submission facility with four additional modules with LVS table.	Input values for text search inputs are selected and identification of input for a particular type of values.	Based on reinforcement learning technique. Deep Web crawler works as agent and deep Web database plays a role of environment. Identify a query to be submitted using Q-value.	Minimum executable pattern (MEP) and based adaptive query technique.	Based on iterative self organizing data analysis (ISODATA) technique.	Task specific approach. A set of domain definition is provided to the crawler. Every domain definition defines a particular data collecting task. The deep Web crawler recognizes the relevant query forms by using domain definition.
Need of user's support	Human interaction is not needed for modeling the form.	Human interface is needed in form filling.	Human interaction is required	Need of user support.	No need of user support.	No need of user support.
Reflection of Web page change	No effect of Web page changes in the result.	There is effect of these changes in the result because it is based on the content of the pages.	There is effect of these changes in the result but changes may generate an error.			
Automatic query selection	Yes	No	Yes	Yes	-	No
Accuracy of data fetched	Good	Data can be wrong if the Web pages change.	High	Average	-	Average.
Database sampling	No	Yes	Yes	Yes	-	Yes
Focused crawling	Yes	Yes	Yes	Yes	-	It is task based crawling.

Figure 2. Architecture of proposed deep web crawler mechanism

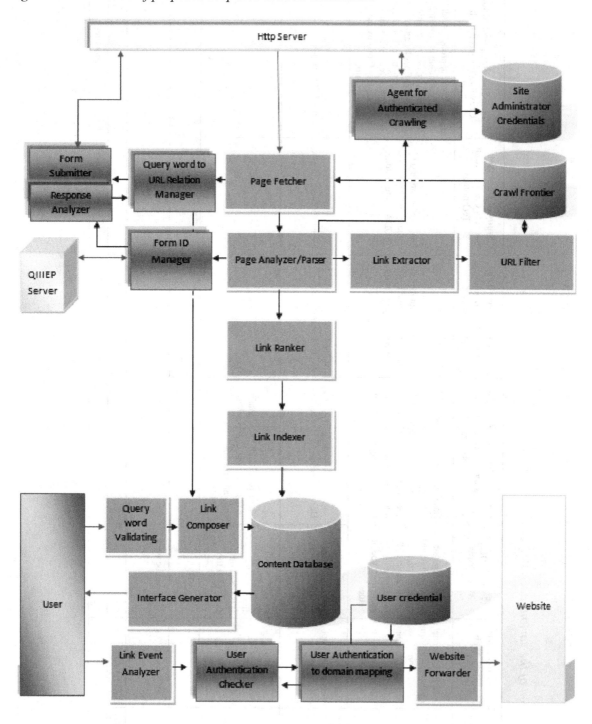

Description of Modules of Proposed Architecture for Deep Web Crawler Mechanism

What follows is a module-wise description of proposed novel architecture of deep Web crawler.

Agent for Authenticated Crawling Module

This module works when the information in a site is hidden behind the authentication form. It stores authentication credentials of every domain in its knowledge base situated at crawler, which is provided by the individual user. At the time of crawling, it automatically authenticates itself on the domain for crawling the hidden Web contents. The crawler extracts and store keywords from contents and makes it available to privatized search service to maintain the privacy issue.

Page Fetcher Module

Page fetcher fetches the pages from the http server and sends them to the page analyzer to check whether it is required appropriate page or not based on the topic of search and the kind of form, the page contains.

Page Analyzer/Parser Module

The page analyzer/parser is used to parse the contents of the Web page. Texts and links are extracted. The extraction of links and text is done on the basis of the concept of page classifier. Form classifier link is used to filter the pages topic wise. It also filters out useless forms and identifies links that are likely to lead to pages that contain searchable form interfaces.

Form ID Generator

This module helps to implement QIIIEP (query intensive interface information extraction protocol) on current architecture of Website. It parses every form of that Web site and merge the form ID with QIIIEP server query word list so that at the time of crawler request the crawler, it identifies the search interface properly for sending the request of keywords to the QIIIEP server.

Form Submitter Module

After filling the form, the form submitter sends again the request to the HTTP server for the further retrieval. This module simply sends the filled form to the http server for further information.

Query Word to URL Relation Manager Module

This module generates meaningful queries to be issued to the query interface. It stores each and every query word associated with specific element of form by creating reference of domain path, so that at the time of link generation, query word can be mapped to provide the contents by sending query word in post request to the domain.

Crawl Frontier

Crawl Frontiers contains all the links which are yet to be fetched from the HTTP server or the links obtained after URL filter. It takes a seed URL to start the procedure and processes that page and retrieves all forms, and adds and rearranges them to the list of URLs. The list of those URLs is called crawl frontier.

Link Extractor Module

Link Extractor extracts the links or the hyper links from the text file for the further retrieval from the HTTP server. The extraction of links is done as per the link identified by the page analyzer/parser that is likely to lead to pages that contain searchable form interfaces in one or more steps. This dramatically reduces the quantity of pages for the crawler to crawl in deep Web. Fewer numbers of pages are needed to be crawled since it applies focused crawling along with searching the relevancy of obtained result to the topic and hence result in limited extraction of relevant links.

Query Intensive Interface Information Extraction Protocol (QIIIEP) Server

QIIIEP (Sharma & Sharma, 2009) is an application-level protocol for semantic otology based query word composition, identification and retrieval systems. It is based on request/response semantics. This specification defines the protocol referred to as QIIIEP 1.0. The QIIIEP server work on this protocol. QIIIEP (Query Intensive Interface Information Extraction Protocol) reduces complexity by using pre-information about the form and its elements from QIIIEP server. The knowledge base is either generated by auto query word extractor or it is provided by site administrator.

Link Ranker Module

This module is responsible for providing the best match query word assignment to the form filling process and reduce the over loading due to less relevant queries to the domain. It is required to rank the link accordingly so the more information is gathered from each link. This is based on link ranking algorithm.

Link Indexer Module

This module plays an important role in the indexing of the generated keywords to the content database. Indexer collects, parses, and stores data to facilitate fast and accurate information retrieval. It maps the keywords to URL for the fast access and retrieval.

Content Database Module

Content Data Base stores all the generated links or keywords in the Content Data Base. When user put any query into the user interface, the index is matched with the corresponding links and information is displayed to the user for further processing.

Searching Agent Module

It provides the searching interface through which user places the query. This involves the searching of keywords and other information stored in the content database which is actually stored in it after the whole process of authenticated crawling.

Link Composer Module

This module takes the reference from the Query word to URL Manager for the form submission.

Interface Generator Module

Interface generator is used to give the view of the contents stored in the content database after the search is completed. For example, the interface generator shows the list of relevant links indexed and ranked by link ranker module and link indexer module respectively.

Link Event Analyzer

Link event analyzer analyzes the link which is activated by the user so that it could forward the request to display the page on the requested URL.

User Authentication to Domain Mapping Module

This module of crawler is responsible for mapping the login credentials provided by users to the crawler with the information provider domain. The main benefit of using this mapper is to overcome the hindrance of information retrieval between result link and information. The crawler uses the mapping information to allow the specific person to receive information contents directly from the domain by automatic login procedure and eliminate the step of separate login for user.

Working Steps of Proposed Architecture for Deep Web Crawler Mechanism

The steps proposed are:

1. Crawler request to the Web server to fetch a page.
2. The second step has three parts:
    a. After the page is fetched it is being analyzed and parsed for the relevant contents (links and text).
    b. The page is sent to the query word to URL relation manager.
    c. If the authentication of administrator credentials is required then the links are sent to the agent for authenticated crawling.
3. After being analyzed by the page analyzer/parser, links are selected and filtered out.
4. Filtered URLs sent to crawl frontier, which again chooses a link and sends it to the page fetcher.
5. Now, crawler analyzes the form to identify the search interface. The form must include the form id.
6. Then the form id is used to send the request to query word to the QIIIEP (query intensive interface information extraction protocol) server, where the extraction takes place to correlate the form fields.
7. Now, the server replies to the crawler about each entry to that form.
8. Crawler sends the filled form by placing the received query words to the HTTP server.
9. Crawler crawl the contents generated by that query word.
10. Finally fetched pages are ranked, indexed and stored in the search engines database.

User interacts with user interface through the following steps:

1. User enters the query about search.
2. The query words validation takes place and link composer fetches the link from the data base according to the query word.
3. Now links are searched from the content database.
4. The content is then provided to the user with the help of interface generator.
5. The link, i.e. chosen by the user, diverts the user for user authentication through domain mapper so that the user can retrieve those authenticated contents without explicit login.
6. Query word, submitted to URL relation manager use the post and get request to generate the specific page.
7. The link opens the Website in a browser.

The algorithm for the simple Web crawler is given below:

Input initial URL = seed.
1. Maintain a queue Q={u}.
2. While(Q!=NULL).
3. Pop a element from Q.(using FIFO).
4. Process that URL and fetch all the relevant URL's.
5. Assign an unique index for each page visited.
6. For each relevant URL's fetched (URL1,URL2,URL3…..).

7. If(URL1 is not indexed && URL1 does not belong to Q).
8. Add URL1 to Q.
9. end.

The algorithm for deep Web data extraction is given below:

1. Extract Web page by using initial seed URL or crawl frontier.
2. Analyze for contents and form.
3. Extract query URL from page and store in crawl frontier after applying filter.
4. If page content form.
5. Request query word for all the elements in form from QIIIEP server.
6. Submit and extract the deep Web contents.
7. Manage query word to URL relation.
8. Rank and index the page and store in content database.
9. Go to step 1.

The algorithm for search and result link generator is given below:

1. User input in the form of query.
2. If this is a valid query then goto step3.
3. Search the content database as follows:
   a. Efficient query is generated.
   b. Check the indexed words and the corresponding links.
   c. IF query words match then.
   Select the appropriate links and go to step 4.
   else:
   goto interface generator & display keywords did not match & stop.
4. If found then Interface generator will display the results.
5. Link event analyzer will take user authentication to domain mapping if site want login.
6. If user's credential found authenticated on Website and open specific page by using query word to URL relation manager.

else:
Display login form of that Web site.
7. If Web site does not want login.
8. Just open the deep Web content by using query word to URL relation manager.

The code for parser, downloader and link repository module is given in Box 1.

Features of the Theoretically Justified Proposed Architecture

These features are given below:

1. This proposed architecture crawl the deep Web if the administrator of that site follows the framework of QIIIEP based on focused crawling.
2. It definitely removes the complex task of query interface identification and values allotment as the huge majority of deep Web query interfaces on the Web are html forms.
3. The program tries to classify deep Web query interface according to different users.
4. Dynamic discovery of deep Web sources are done according to the user's query.
5. Provide input i.e. auto of filling the form of search queries.
6. Auto form ID generation and auto query extraction modules are used by QIIIEP server to extend its knowledge.
7. Privatized search plus general domain search are the two features which are based on the overall protocol.
8. Authenticated crawling is provided for privatized search.
9. Forms are classified with various levels depending on the administrator.
10. Different domains will have their content links and indexes in different databases.
11. Implicit authentication takes place when registered user clicks on a link at domain site.

Box 1. Link repository module

```
void Crawler_book_1() throws IOException,MalformedURLException
  {
        try
         {
        Class.forName("sun.jdbc.odbc.JdbcOdbcDriver");
        Connection con=DriverManager.getConnection("jdbc:odbc:Web");
        Statement stmt=con.createStatement();
        ResultSet rs=stmt.executeQuery("select id from book");
         while(rs.next())
        {
            count=Integer.parseInt(rs.getString(1));
        }
        try{
{

          urlc =new URL(seedurl);
        pageInput = new InputStreamReader(urlc.openStream());
         source = new BufferedReader(pageInput);
}

        }catch(NullPointerException e){}
while ((sourceLine = source.readLine()) != null)
        {
            content += sourceLine ;
        }
tag = Pattern.compile("href=\"(.*?)\"",Pattern.DOTALL);
         mtag = tag.matcher(content);
        while (mtag.find())
        {
          content = mtag.group(1);
          if(content.startsWith("http:"))
          {
              if(!(content.endsWith(".css")||content.endsWith(".xml")))
              {
                  // System.out.println(""+content);
                dsp=""+content;
        ta.append(dsp+"\n");repaint();
                    if(!ar.contains(content))
                    {
                      ar.add(content);
                    }
              }
```

continued on following page

Box 1. Continued

```
        }
    }
  ai=ar.iterator();
  while(ai.hasNext())
  { content1=null;
      runner.sleep(100);
      System.out.println(ai.hasNext());
        o=ai.next();
    urls=new URL(""+o);
    pageInput1 = new InputStreamReader(urls.openStream());
  ta.append(dsp+"\n");repaint();
      source1 = new BufferedReader(pageInput1);
  dsp="link";
  ta.append(dsp+"\n");repaint();
  while ((sourceLine = source1.readLine()) != null)
  {
    (!(content1.contains("under construction")||content1.contains("cannot be dis-
played ")||content1.contains("not available")))
            content1 += sourceLine ;
  }
  tag1= Pattern.compile("<form(.*?)</form>",Pattern.DOTALL);
  mtag1 = tag1.matcher(content1);
dsp="The Forms Link Are:....."+mtag1.find();
  ta.append(dsp+"\n");repaint();
  while ((mtag1.find()))
  {
      content1 = mtag1.group(0);
      dsp=""+content1;
  ta.append(dsp+"\n");repaint();
      tag2= Pattern.compile("book",Pattern.DOTALL);
      mtag2 = tag2.matcher(content1);
      tag3= Pattern.compile("author",Pattern.DOTALL);
      mtag3 = tag3.matcher(content1);
       tag4= Pattern.compile("title",Pattern.DOTALL);
      mtag4 = tag4.matcher(content1);
       tag5= Pattern.compile("isbn",Pattern.DOTALL);
      mtag5 = tag5.matcher(content1);
      if(mtag2.find()||mtag3.find()||mtag4.find()||mtag5.find())
      {
          dsp="Both r found";
  ta.append(dsp+"\n");repaint();
```

continued on following page

Box 1. Continued

```
tag6= Pattern.compile("action=\"(.*?)\"",Pattern.DOTALL);
mtag6 = tag6.matcher(content1);
 System.out.println("tag6"+mtag6.find());
if(!(mtag6.group(1).contains("http")))
{
    //System.out.println("www found");
    dsp="www found";
ta.append(dsp+"\n");repaint();
    content1=mtag6.replaceAll("action="+o+mtag6.group(1));
}
try
{
  count++;
qry="insert into book values('"+count+"','"+o+"')";
        stmt.executeUpdate(qry);
```

12. The final content page opened after link is clicked which was crawled by post or get request.

13. Only the meta data of private area is stored so there is no privacy issue for crawling authenticated private content.

14. There is a huge list of query word generated through cross-site user query submission module but the ranking algorithm choose most appropriate query word for specific query interface to reduce the bandwidth wastage.

Limitations of Existing Deep Web Crawlers Improved through Proposed Architecture

Limitations that are improved by the proposed architecture follow:

1. Crawling is precise and the chances of missing of pages are less. As we are using multithreaded downloading techniques so multiple threads run simultaneously which eliminate the chances of page miss. URL filter module makes the crawling very precise, eliminating the duplicate links.

2. It involves multi-attribute database accessing.

3. Form verification can be done very easily with the help of our form manager which extracts different domains attribute accordingly.

4. The form filling can be done very precisely and the user needs not to fill the complete form.

5. Extraction method that is improved by query word extraction module.

6. Useless pages if crawled cannot affect the semantics.

7. Time and cost is less due to the use of multithreaded downloading technique and automatic form filling by the QIIIEP server.

8. Forms with searchable interfaces are provided directly to the users.

9. Web page forwarding technique that is used while forwarding by submitting the form has no chances of error at all. If the action part is not start with = "http://" then we have attached the relative link part to the Web

site, so if any relative link comes then it is attached with the Web site and is forwarded to related page.

6. EXPERIMENTAL RESULTS

The experiment has conducted on a machine having Intel Core 2 Duo T5870 @ 2.0 GHz with 2 GB of RAM. This machine was running with Windows 7 OS. Tests are performed using WAMP server equipped with php v. 5.2.6 and mysql v. 5.0.51b., Microsoft Visual Basic 2008.net 3.5 and Net beans IDE. All of the tests were performed on Firefox 3.5.4. All tests were performed multiple times to minimize measurement errors. Results of the various modules are shown in Table 4.

Certain performance metric are defined and calculated to judge the overall performance of the deep Web crawler. Objectives of the performance metric are given below.

1. Analytical data based on the number of sites visited which reflects the reach of the crawler.
2. Assessment of the different forms which show the ratio of relevant forms processed.
3. Calculation of the performance ratio to check the overall efficiency of the deep Web crawler.

Performance Metrics are calculated as follows. The various performance criteria are taken to measure the overall efficiency of proposed deep Web crawler architecture and its results are as follows.

Deep Web crawler is implemented based on QIIIEP specification and the corresponding results are analyzed. Three different test domains are used to judge the precision of retrieved contents. Table 5 shows the form identification statistics and Table 6 shows the query words and content extraction statistic.

The graph shown in Figure 3 is plotted between received query words and successful content extraction at different domain. It can be concluded from the graph that contents extraction are close to query words received at a satisfactory level for all three domains. The successful content extraction means relevant page have more than five query words and minimum length of content is four hundred words.

Table 7 shows the default values for some of the parameters that are used for experiments.

Table 4. Results of the various modules

Modules	Results
1. Page Fetcher	The downloaded html content
2. Page Analyzer	Selected pages which contain forms.
3. Form Id Manager	A list of Search Interfaces (forms).
4. QIIIEP SERVER	Provide query word to the forms wherever possible and give result to response analyzer.
5. Form Submitter	Send the filled form to the Http server.
6. Link Extractor	A list of extracted links those are relevant.
7. Link Ranker Module	A list of ranked links.
8. Link Composer Module	Composed list of links by using query word to URL relation manager.
9. Interface Generator	Shows the list of relevant links ranked by rank module & link indexer.
10.Link Filter	Fresh links are shown.

Table 5. Form identification statistics

Domain	Query Forms	Context Identification
Auto	5	5
Book	8	8
Job	12	12

As indicated in Table 7, the crawler encountered 41 forms during crawling of the 12 sites, of which 2 were ignored, because form id manager do not found any associated id corresponding to the sites.

Figure 4 shows the number of links generated for a particular query word search and the overall count of pages indexed with given query words.

The graph shows the number of pages in result for the specific query word. It depends upon the total number of crawled pages. For overall 1508 stored pages the results have good ratio.

Harvest Ratio

To evaluate the performance of the proposed architecture, the "harvest ratio" is adopted as the performance metrics, which is the ratio of relevant Web pages downloaded among all the downloaded Web pages. Here relevant downloaded pages are those which have at least five times repeated query word in overall content. It is defined as follows:

$$HR= (RWPD/AWPD)*100$$

Table 6. Query words and content extraction statistics

Domain	Form ID	Query Words Received	Successful Content Extraction
Auto	55c64ad2fDd6a6ef4388b33c54123890	34	30
Book	eOcftfd062a28403d966261Obe421eOe	56	42
Job	67c76add7110dbe02Obb401a4672565f	131	96

Figure 3. Comparison of success with number of query words at different domain

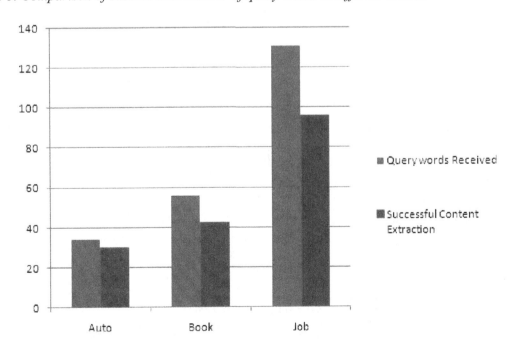

Table 7. Parameters and values statistics

Parameter	Default Value
No. of sites visited	12
No. of links stored	1508
No. of forms encountered	41

where HR= harvest ratio, RWPD= relevant Web pages downloaded and AWPD= all Web pages downloaded.

Table 8 depicts the domains and its relevant Web pages downloaded and all Web pages downloaded statistic.

The harvest ratio for different domain is shown in Table 9.

The result shows very good harvest ratio when considering a focused domain approach which reflects that proposed architecture is significantly improved compared to existing approach. Figures 5 and 6 show screen snapshots from the implementation of the hidden Web crawler system.

Summary of the Results of Proposed Architecture

The features of proposed architecture are improved from the features of the existing crawlers as proposed architecture deals with the overall strategy of hidden query interfaces including the features of both privatized search and general search for the deep Web data that is hidden html forms. Every solution is taken into consideration to make the crawler as efficient as possible including all the features of the existing Web crawlers. Proposed architecture tries to minimize the overall cost and time that are relevant to the deep Web searching. However at some points, time and space complexity are compromised with performance but overall results are as per expectation. Proposed architecture performs better compared to other existing crawlers as reflected from performance metric. For example, the performance of the proposed architecture is better and satisfactory with reference to number of links crawled. Cost

Figure 4. Graph showing number of links generated for a particular query words search

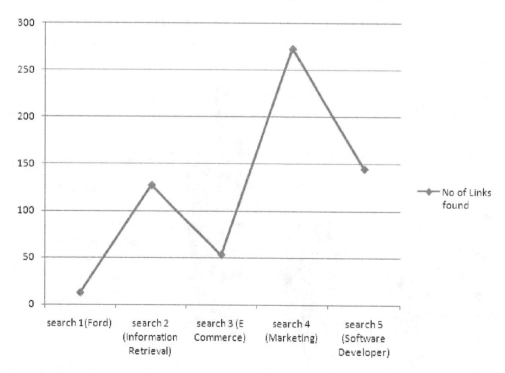

Table 8. Domains and statistics for the relevant Web pages downloaded and all Web pages downloaded

Domain	Job	Book	Auto
RWPD	629	377	93
AWPD	795	531	182

Table 9. Domains and harvest ratio statistics

Domain	Harvest Ratio
Job	79.11%
Book	77.99 %
Auto	51.09 %

Figure 5. Snapshot graphical user interface of hidden web crawler

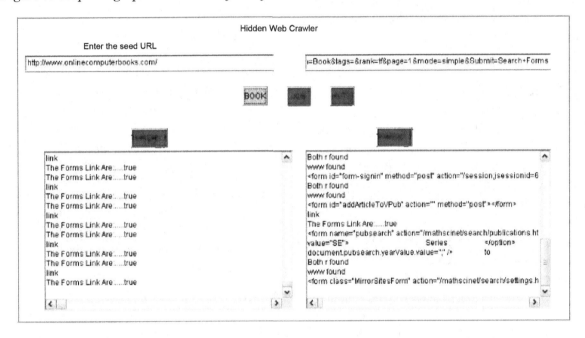

Figure 6. Snapshot of database for hidden web crawler

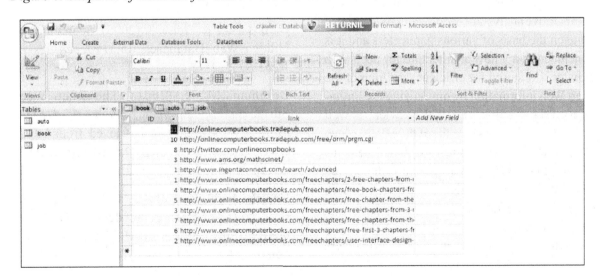

of the deep Web search also reduces through this crawler due to searching with domain specific formula. Initial seed set of links is such that the number of relevant search interfaces and forms are quite effective. Pre determination of the domain context provide effective results with more than 40% effective links with forms extraction on every loop while generating links for the databases. At last performance metric are calculated after the implementing and integrating all the modules and necessary modifications are done to improve the model.

7. CONCLUSION

Deep Web information has a very large volume compared to surface Web and the quantity of deep Web content depends upon underlying domain and crawling mechanism. Extraction of deep Web information can be highly fruitful for a general user or a specific user. Traditional Web crawlers have limitations in crawling the deep Web information so some of the Web crawlers are specially designed for crawling the deep Web information yet a very large amount of deep Web information is yet to be explored due to inefficient crawling of the deep Web. In literature survey, analysis of some of the important deep Web crawlers is done to find their advantages and limitations. A comparative analysis of deep Web crawlers is also done on the basis of various parameters and it is concluded that a new architecture for deep Web crawler is required for efficient searching of the deep Web information by minimizing the limitations of the existing deep Web crawlers as well as incorporating the strengths of the existing deep Web crawlers. The architecture should be compatible to crawl existing deep Web with nominal modification with ongoing infrastructure based on QIIIEP specification. A novel architecture for deep Web crawler is proposed which possesses the all the features of existing deep Web crawlers

but tries to minimize limitations of existing deep Web crawlers. Experiments results reflect that it is efficient both for privatized as well as general search for the deep Web information, which is hidden behind the html forms. The proposed architecture is cost and time effective as search process depends on query interface crawling the contents with ranking of most appropriate keyword against the context of domain.

REFERENCES

Akilandeswari, J., & Gopalan, N. P. (2008). An Architectural Framework of a Crawler for Locating Deep Web Repositories Using Learning Multi-Agent Systems. In *Proceedings of the 2008 3rd International Conference on Internet & Web Applications and Services* (pp. 558-562).

Alvarez, M., Raposo, J., Cacheda, F., & Pan, A. (2006). *A Task-specific Approach for Crawling the Deep Web*. Retrieved from http://www.engineeringletters.com/issues_v13/issue_2/EL_13_2_19.pdf

Alvarez, M., Raposo, J., Pan, A., Cacheda, F., Bellas, F., & Carneiro, V. (2007). A Focused Crawler for Accessing Hidden Web Content. In *Proceedings of DEECS2007* (pp. 18–25). San Diego, CA: DeepBot.

Barbosa, L., & Freire, J. (2005). Searching for Hidden-Web Databases. In. *Proceedings of WebDB, 05*, 1–6.

Bergman, M. K. (2001). The Deep Web: Surfacing Hidden Value. *Journal of Electronic Publishing, 7*(1). Retrieved from http://www.press.umich.edu/jep/07-01/bergman.html. doi:10.3998/3336451.0007.104

He, B., Patel, M., Zhang, Z., & Chang, K. C. (2007). Accessing the deep Web. *Communications of the ACM, 50*(5), 94–101. doi:10.1145/1230819.1241670

Jiang, L., Wu, Z., Feng, Q., Liu, J., & Zheng, Q. (2010). Efficient Deep Web Crawling Using Reinforcement Learning. In *Advances in Knowledge Discovery and Data Mining* (LNCS 6118, pp. 428-439).

Liu, J., Wu, Z., Jiang, L., Zheng, Q., & Liu, X. (2009). Crawling Deep Web Content through Query Forms. In *Proceedings of the 5th International Conference on Web Information Systems and Technologies*, Lisbon, Portugal (pp. 634-642).

Lu, J., Wang, Y., Liang, J., Chen, J., & Liu, J. (2008). An Approach to Deep Web Crawling by Sampling. In *Proceedings of the IEEE/WIC/ACM Web Intelligence Conference*, Sydney, NSW, Australia (pp. 718-724).

Madaan, R., Dixit, A., Sharma, A. K., & Bhatia, K. K. (2010). A Framework for Incremental Hidden Web Crawler. *International Journal on Computer Science and Engineering, 2*(3), 753–758.

Madhavan, J., Ko, D., Kot, L., Ganapathy, V., Rasmussen, A., & Halevy, A. (2008). Google's Deep-Web Crawl. In. *Proceedings of VLDB, 2008*, 1241–1252.

Ntoulas, A., Zerfos, P., & Cho, J. (2005). Downloading Textual Hidden Web Content through Keyword Queries. In *Proceedings of JCDL* (pp. 101-109).

Peisu, X., Ke, T., & Qinzhen, H. (2008). A Framework of Deep Web Crawler. In *Proceedings of the 27th Chinese Control Conference*, Kunming, China.

Raghavan, S., & Garcia-Molina, H. (2001). Crawling the hidden Web. In *Proceedings of the 27th International Conference on Very Large Data Bases*, Rome, Italy.

Sharma, D. K., & Sharma, A. K. (2009). Query Intensive Interface Information Extraction Protocol for Deep Web. In *Proceedings of the IEEE International Conference on Intelligent Agent & Multi-Agent Systems* (pp. 1-5).

Sharma, D. K., & Sharma, A. K. (2010). Deep Web Information Retrieval Process: A Technical Survey. *International Journal of Information Technology and Web Engineering, 5*(1), 1–21. doi:10.4018/jitwe.2010010101

Wang, Y., Zuo, W., Peng, T., & He, F. (2008). Domain-Specific Deep Web Sources Discovery. In *Proceedings of the Fourth International Conference on Natural Computation*.

Zhao, H. (2010). Study of Deep Web Query Interface Determining Technology. In *Proceedings of CESCE 2010* (Vol. 1, pp. 546-548).

This work was previously published in the International Journal of Information Technology and Web Engineering (IJITWE), Volume 6, Issue 1, edited by Ghazi I. Alkhatib and Ernesto Damiani, pp. 25-48, copyright 2011 by IGI Publishing (an imprint of IGI Global).

Chapter 8
Using Watermarking Techniques to Prove Rightful Ownership of Web Images

Abdallah Al-Tahan Al-Nu'aimi
Isra University, Jordan

ABSTRACT

This article introduces intelligent watermarking scheme to protect Web images from attackers who try to counterfeit the copyright to damage the rightful ownership. Using secret signs and logos that are embedded within the digital images, the technique can investigate technically the ownership claim. Also, the nature of each individual image is taken into consideration which gives more reliable results. The colour channel used was chosen depending on the value of its standard deviation to compromise between robustness and invisibility of the watermarks. Several types of test images, logos, attacks and evaluation metrics were used to examine the performance of the techniques used. Subjective and objective tests were used to check visually and mathematically the solidity and weakness of the used scheme.

INTRODUCTION

Digital technologies changed all the perceptual video and audio transmission systems and the world became digital. With the incredible progress in digital transmission systems and the huge amount of information includes data, images, audio and video throughout the world, the need for protection of this multimedia efforts becomes very important (Hartung & Girod, 1997; Lu & Liao, 2001). Among all others types of digital signals, images play an important role in this digital world. The images have a greater impact on human beings than words and sound. So, there is more concentration on protecting images from illegal copying, manipulation and distribution in the last years.

The World Wide Web contains millions of different kinds of digital images. Some of them are freely downloadable and the others are not. Taken into consideration the rightful ownership to access some of them, the others are not. In contrast to analogue images, digital images can be easily copied, manipulated, stored and distributed which lead to a big challenge regarding the protection of copyrights.

DOI: 10.4018/978-1-4666-2157-2.ch008

Many papers tackled the problem of proving the real owner of digital images (Gulstad & Bruvold, 2003; Chen, Horng, & Wang, 2003). Among other technologies, watermarking comes into view as a powerful technology that share in solving this big challenge. Different watermarking algorithms were submitted to literature some of them can be seen in Hyvarinen (1999) and Cox, Kilian, Leighton, and Shamoon (1997).

Watermarking is an intelligent digital technology for embedding certain secret information in multimedia products to preserve the copyright and authentication, and to overcome the problem of theft and tampering (Fu & Au, 2002; Anderson & Petitcolas, 1998). For images, watermarking depends on embedding certain stream of bits or small images within the pixels of the original images to prove who the real owner is (Mohammad, Alhaj, & Shaltaf, 2008). On the contrary to cryptography, which restricts access to the information from the beginning to prevent illegal usage, watermarking gives the evidence of illegal attacking after it has happened. So, the real owner has the ability to prove technically that he is the real owner for that work. The watermarking approach of verifying the identity of the real owner is similar to the crimes investigation approach that is done by law enforcement authorities after the occurrence of unlawful events. The understanding of indictment evidence and conviction serves as a deterrent of the future crimes. Thus, watermarking technology depends on how these cases are prosecuted in copyright protection authorities, besides its dependence on technological factors.

The main idea of watermarking for digital images is putting some secret information that is related to the real owner in his image so he can extract this information later to prove his ownership. This may be done via using the direct spatial domain or the indirect transform domain. Putting the secret information in the spatial domain of certain image means that the numerical values of the image pixels will be directly changed corresponding to the amount and nature of the added secret information. In the other hand, using certain transform domain to change the image to a new case and host the secret information in the resulted coefficients of the new version of the image may give some additional benefits. There are several types of different transforms that are used in literature for such uses. Some of them are Discrete Fourier Transform (Solachidis & Pitas, 2001, 2004), Discrete Cosine Transform (Huang & Guan, 2004) and Discrete Wavelet Transform (Feng & Yang, 2005; Kunder & Hatzinakos, 2004).

From point of view of the human visual perceptual, the digital image watermark may be divided into: visible and invisible. Visible watermarks have a low number of applications, while invisible watermarks have more applications and represent the desired case. The visible watermark can be seen by the human visual system (Chen, Horng, & Wang, 2003), and the human eye sees the watermark within the background of the image like what is found in the backgrounds of television broadcasting stations and what is used in some applied programs like Microsoft Word at the background of its pages to prove originality and authenticity. The most obvious disadvantage of visible watermarks is that they can be filtered, changed and removed. So, the visible watermarks are categorized within fragile watermarks that cannot withstand against the attacks. Invisible watermarks are embedded in the host image and the human eye cannot see them. Thus, the existence of it cannot be determined unless some advanced operations are carried out using professional algorithms (Joseph, Ruanaidh, & Pun, 1998; Lu, Liao, & Kutter, 2002). On the other hand, visible watermarks can be categorized into: fragile which may filtered, changed and removed easily; robust which can withstands against intentional and unintentional attacks (Ganic & Eskicioglu, 2005); and semi fragile which represent intermediate case. Every type of these techniques of different robustness is used in several types of applications. These applications contain, but are not limited to, the following applications:

proof of ownership, labeling, text watermarking, authentication, transactional watermarks, covert communications, executable watermarks, copy and playback control, image and video watermarking, audio watermarking and authentication (Banett & Sytems, 1999; Muharemagic & Furht, 2006; Podilchuk & Delp, 2001).

The watermarks that are used to represent the secret embedded information within the host image can either use a binary bit string or a small image. The binary bit string may be of random numbers, or it may characterize meaningful information like serial number, name, date, etc. while the small image characterize a meaningful shape like a legend, seal or any other visual scene. Sequences of random numbers are mostly used to stamp gray images which represent low level watermarking. In these methods, the payload is low and the invisibility criterion is achieved. But the robustness issue is poor and some types of attacks can remove or damage the secret information embedded in the image as a watermark. In this work, binary logos and small images are used to represent the secret information embedded within the host images. Also, colored images are used for hosting the watermarks instead of gray images that are used mainly in most of the submitted techniques. This represents high level watermarking.

The quality of the watermarked image, which has the secret information, must be still acceptable and the viewer cannot differentiate between it and the original image. The algorithm should be robust regarding putting and re-extraction of the secret information despite the existence of several types of attacks. Furthermore, it must be secure enough to prevent the others from knowing or removing the watermark which will be more advantage if it is large enough to carry useful information. The secret payload that is embedded within the watermarked image depends usually on the nature of the host image and the algorithm used to embed the secret information.

In the watermark detection and extraction process, the watermarking systems may be catego-

rized into two types: blind and non-blind systems (Tzeng, Hwang, & Chern, 2002). The blindness means that the host image is not needed in the detection and extraction part, which makes it more popular and practical (Zeng & Lio, 1999). But, this blindness affects the robustness issue. Non-blind watermarking system is the opposite of the blind type, with better robustness. One may choose between blindness with less robustness or more robustness with non-blind system, which depends on the application.

Any watermarking technique or algorithm must satisfy certain requirements to be considered as successful process. The former of these requirements is that the watermark must be invisible (Kutter & Winkler, 2002). Also, it must not affect the quality of the host image. Moreover, the watermark must be easily extracted in a reliable and convenient way for the legal operations. Furthermore, the watermark must be compatible with the host image. Besides all that, the hiding process of the watermarking must be robust enough to make the watermark has the ability to withstand several types of intentional and unintentional attacks.

One of the major problems related to watermarking technology is how to investigate and validate the success of any proposed algorithm or technique submitted to literature and how to compare every novel work with the previous works in the area. Most of the submitted works use certain image or certain type of images which cannot be generalized to the other types of images. Moreover, mostly just one type of objective test is used to ensure and validate the success of the watermarking technique which is not enough to prove the success.

In this article, several subjective and objective tests are used to ensure and validate the success of the proposed watermarking technique to prove the rightful ownership of the web images.

The following sections are organized as follows: First, the hiding part is explained. The extraction part is shown next. Simulation and results are then discussed and finally, conclusions are seen.

THE HIDING PROCESS

One of the most important issues in watermarking technology is the robustness of the technique that is used to embed the watermark within the host image. Robustness means that always there is an ability to retrieve the watermark from the host image in spite of the possible attacks that may suffer from it. But, this may alter the invisibility of the watermark which is inversely proportional to the robustness. Invisibility means that no one can see the watermark that is hidden in the host image.

Compromise between these two contradictory issues is very important. Besides that, the quality of the host image must be still acceptable after embedding the watermark and no distortion altered the watermarked image quality. The security of how to hide and extract the watermark in a way that is difficult for any attacker to know or guess is another important issue as well.

The proposed algorithm in this paper has succeeded in satisfying all the mentioned requirements. In this algorithm, the watermarks used are binary logos and images that are hidden in coloured images represented by RGB colour format.

The first step in this proposed algorithm is the splitting of the original RGB image to the three main color layers (R, G & B) and computing the standard deviation (SD) for each of them. The color layer that has the median value for the standard deviation is chosen to be the host layer that will carry the watermark. The choice of the layer that has the median standard deviation value ensures a tradeoff between the robustness and the invisibility of the watermark. Then, this layer is divided to blocks of pixels. After that, the watermark itself is divided into pixels. The pixels of the watermark are scrambled using certain key to get a new version of the watermark with lack of understanding of the scene visually. This represents the first level of security. The second level of security is satisfied by scrambling the blocks of the host layer to be watermarked using another key. The number of blocks that resulted

from dividing the chosen layer depends on both the size of the host image and the size of the watermark. In the experiments corresponded to this work, the image size of the watermark relative to the size of the host image is 1:16. Thus, the number of the host blocks is equal to the number of the guest pixels. This means that the value of each individual watermark pixel alter the values of the sixteen corresponding pixels of the host color layer which represents one block of pixels. The complete process for hiding the watermark within the host image is explained in Figure 1.

The pixels of each block are arranged on descending order depending on its values (Lee & Lee, 1999). The embedding process of the watermark within the host color layer depends on changing the pixel values of each block depending on the value of the corresponding pixels of the watermark. If the watermark pixel value is 1, the values of the odd rows pixels are changed and take the maximum value of the corresponding row. The values of the even rows are increased by certain value which depends on the difference between the maximum and the minimum values of the block pixels multiplied by certain small value which controls the condition of the watermarked image quality and adjust the tradeoff between robustness issue and invisibility issue.

If the watermark pixel value is 0, the values of the even rows pixels are changed and take the minimum value of the corresponding row. The values of the odd rows are decreased by certain value which depends on the difference between the maximum and the minimum values of the block pixels multiplied by certain value.

THE EXTRACTION PROCESS

The process of watermark detection and re-extraction from the watermarked image depends on the existence of two security keys, the watermark and the host image. The pixels values of each watermarked block are added to each others to get

Figure 1. Block diagram for the hiding process

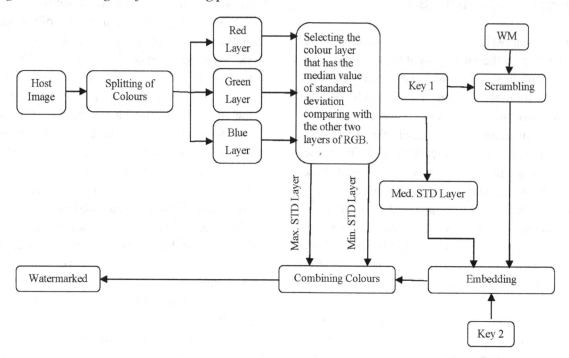

a specific resultant value. This value is compared with the corresponding value for the same block of the original host image before embedding the watermark. If the watermarked block has the bigger value, the re-extracted value for the watermark is 1, otherwise it is 0.

The same process is done for the rest of the blocks. After this process is finished for all blocks, the scrambled watermark achieved. The final step is to get the original watermark using the proper key.

When the watermarked image does not suffer from any attack, the extracted watermark will be identical to the original watermark and all the secret information that is represented by this watermark is identical to the original. In the case of illegal attacks, the extracted watermark will be slightly modified and there are some differences comparing in compared to the original. In spite of that, the extracted watermark and information are still enough to determine the real owner of the image.

SIMULATION AND RESULTS

Most of the previous works in literature use certain images or certain types of images which represents narrow band of test and validation. The images have broad band of features with different objects, shapes, lines, edges, colours, etc, and all these features must be taken into consideration while investigating any algorithm. To validate the success of this work, different kinds of RGB coloured images are used with different kinds of watermarks. Fifty different RGB coloured images of 24 bit depth and of size 512×512 pixels are used as host images. These images are of different nature and features and cover most of images types. Also, twenty different watermarks of size 128×128 pixels are tested in this algorithm.

The imagery results for one sample image called 'Cells' with one sample watermark called 'Copyright' are seen in Figures 2, 3, and 4.

Figure 2 contains the imagery results that represent the hiding part and filtering attacks stage.

Figure 2. Imagery results for sample image 'Cells' for the embedding and filtering attack stage, (a) is the original host image; (b) is 'Copyright' watermark; (c) is the watermarked image; (d) is the difference image between the original image and the watermarked image; (e) is the low passed image and (f) is the median image

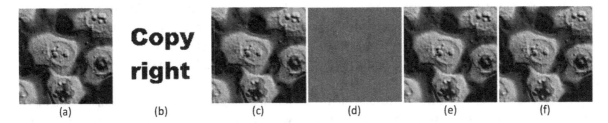

Figure 3. Imagery results for sample image 'Cells' for the attacking stage, (a) is the RGB to gray image; (b) is the scaled image; (c) is the JPEG 50 compressed image; (d) is the JPEG 75 compressed image; (e) is the cropped image and (f) is the rotated image

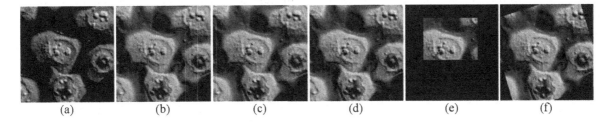

Figure 4. Imagery results for sample image 'Cells' for the extracting stage, (a) watermark after low pass filtering attack; (b) watermark after median filtering attack ; (c) watermark after scaling attack; (d) watermark after JPEG 50 attack; (e) watermark after cropping attack and (f) watermark after rotation attack

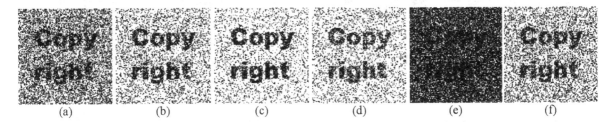

Part (a) represents the original host image which is called 'Cells'; part (b) represents the watermark called 'Copyright'; part (c) represents the resulted watermarked image after embedding the watermark within it; part (d) represents the difference image between the original image and the watermarked image; part (e) represents the re-sulted image after low-pass attack the and part (f) represents the resulted image after median attack.

Figure 3 contains the imagery results that represent the attacking stage. These images represent the resulted watermarked images after they suffer from several types of attacks which try to damage the watermarks. Part (a) represents the resulted watermarked image after RGB to gray image attack; part (b) represents the resulted watermarked image after scaled attack; part (c) represents the resulted watermarked image after JPEG 50 attack; part (d) represents the resulted watermarked image after JPEG 75 attack; part (e) represents the resulted watermarked image after cropping attack and part (f) represents the resulted watermarked image after rotation attack.

Figure 4 contains the imagery results that represent the extraction stage. These images represent the re-extracted watermarks from the watermarked images after they suffer from several types of attacks. Part (a) represents the extracted watermark after low-pass filtering attack; part (b) represents the extracted watermark after median filtering attack; part (c) represents the extracted watermark after scaling attack; part (d) represents the extracted watermark after JPEG 50 attack.

Other imagery results for another sample image called 'Pear' with the same sample watermark

which is called 'Copyright' are seen in Figures 5, 6, and 7.

Figure 5 contains the imagery results that represent the hiding part and filtering attacks stage. Part (a) represents the original host image which is called 'Pear'; part (b) represents the watermark called 'Copyright'; part (c) represents the resulted watermarked image after embedding the watermark within it; part (d) represents the difference image between the original image and the watermarked image; part (e) represents the resulted image after low-pass attack the and part (f) represents the resulted image after median attack.

Figure 6 contains the imagery results that represent the attacking stage. These images represent the resulted watermarked images after they suffer from several types of attacks which try to damage the watermarks.

Part (a) represents the resulted watermarked image after RGB to gray image attack; part (b) represents the resulted watermarked image after

Figure 5. Imagery results for sample image 'Bear' for the embedding and filtering attack stage, (a) original host image; (b) 'Dallah' watermark; (c) watermarked image; (d) difference image between the original image and the watermarked image; (e) low passed image and (f) median image

Figure 6. Imagery results for sample image 'Bear' for the attacking stage, (a) RGB to gray image; (b) scaled image; (c) JPEG 50 compressed image; (d) JPEG 75 compressed image; (e) cropped image and (f) rotated image

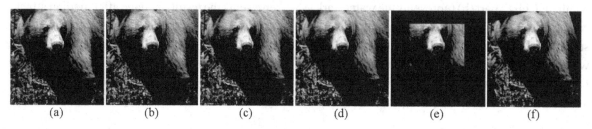

Figure 7. Imagery results for sample image 'Bear' for the extracting stage, (a) watermark after low pass filtering attack; (b) watermark after median filtering attack ; (c) watermark after scaling attack; (d) watermark after JPEG 50 attack; (e) watermark after cropping attack and (f) watermark after rotation attack

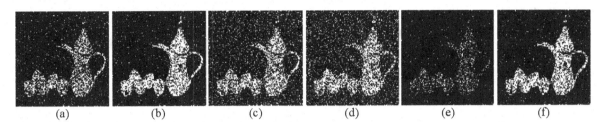

(a)   (b)   (c)   (d)   (e)   (f)

scaled attack; part (c) represents the resulted watermarked image after JPEG 50 attack; part (d) represents the resulted watermarked image after JPEG 75 attack; part (e) represents the resulted watermarked image after cropping attack and part (f) represents the resulted watermarked image after rotation attack.

Figure 7 contains the imagery results that represent the extraction stage. These images represent the re-extracted watermarks from the watermarked images after they suffer from several types of attacks.

Part (a) represents the extracted watermark after low-pass filtering attack; part (b) represents the extracted watermark after median filtering attack; part (c) represents the extracted watermark after scaling attack; part (d) represents the extracted watermark after JPEG 50 attack.

By checking Figure 2(a) and (b), which represent the original host image and the watermarked image respectively, the viewer cannot differentiate between them.

This means that the proposed algorithm had been succeeded in hiding useful secret information within colored images to prove the rightful ownership and the originality of the image.

The human visual system cannot differentiate between the host and the watermarked images. So, the invisibility is ensured and no one can see the watermark. The quality of the watermarked image is still acceptable and there is no distortion in the contents of the image. In spite of the strong attacks that try to damage the watermarks, the extracted watermarks are still recognizable and very similar to the watermarks belongs to the legal owner which prove who is the real owner.

At the extraction stage, the retrieval of the watermarks from the watermarked images is very simple. Despite several types of attacks having taken place, the success of retrieving the embedded watermarks was proved. The retrieved watermarks are clear visually enough to know that to whom these watermarks are belong.

Two objective tests are made to check the results numerically. The peak signal to noise ratio (PSNR) (Al-Tahan Al-Nu'aimi & Qahwaji, 2006), which is a measure of the quality of the watermarked image and gives the evidence to the invisibility criterion, is computed. The PSNR value is computed for the host colour layer using Equation 1.

$$PSNR = 10 \log_{10} \frac{255^2}{MSE} = 20 \log_{10} \frac{255}{\sqrt{MSE}}$$

(1)

where MSE is the mean squared error between the watermarked layer resulted after the hiding process and the original host layer of the image.

The minimum PSNR resulted, after testing 50 samples of host RGB images with 20 different types of watermarks is 27.46 dB. This high value of PSNR ensures invisibility and quality. The complete results for the PSNR values after hiding process is seen in Figure 8.

The similarity measure; SIM, is used to check the similarity between two images. One way of computing SIM is seen in Equation 2.

$$SIM(X_{org}, X_{wat}) = \frac{X_{org}.X_{wat}}{\sqrt{X_{org}.X_{wat}}} \qquad (2)$$

where X_{org} represents the host image pixel value and X_{wat} represents the watermarked image pixel value. A normalized version; SIM_{norm} is calculated using Equation 3.

$$SIM(X_{org}, X_{wat}) = \frac{\frac{X_{org}.X_{wat}}{\sqrt{X_{org}.X_{wat}}}}{\frac{X_{org}.X_{org}}{X_{org}.X_{org}}} \times 100 \qquad (3)$$

The multiplication here is logic operation done on a bit level. Another improved version is the Structural Similarity; SSIM which is a powerful assessment tool to calculate the similarity between images (Wang, Bovic, Sheikh, & Simoncelli, 2004). This tool depends on factors related to

the Human Visual System (HVS), to investigate the similarity between images. Equation 4 below represents this version.

$$SSIM(x,y) = \frac{(2\mu_x\mu_y + c_1)(2\sigma_{xy} + c_2)}{(\mu_x^2 + \mu_y^2 + c_1)(\sigma_x^2 + \sigma_y^2 + c_2)}$$

$$(4)$$

where μ_x and μ_y are the averages of the block values for block x and y respectively, σ_x^2 and σ_y^2 are the variances of the block values for x and y respectively, σ_{xy} is the covariance of x and y, L is the dynamic range and c_1 and c_2 are constants with values directly proportional to L^2. The percentage similarity based on SSIM test is computed for the host and the watermarked images.

The minimum similarity for all the experiments is 92% which is high enough to prove the quality of the watermarked images and ensure the invisibility criterion. This means that the watermarked images are very similar to the original host images.

Subjective experiments are performed as well to test the algorithm. Twenty volunteers were chosen and they sat down in front of the computer screen individually. Three versions of every test image used in the algorithm were displayed on the screen next to each other. The three versions represented two identical copies of the original

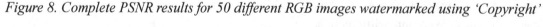

Figure 8. Complete PSNR results for 50 different RGB images watermarked using 'Copyright'

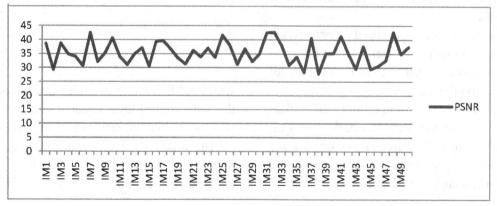

host image and one copy of the watermarked image. The volunteers were asked to determine the image that looked different among the three images. This test was repeated for the main fifty sample images.

The results for all these experiments were the same; no volunteer could differentiate between the three versions of the test images, and they could not decide which version of the three was the watermarked one. This means that the quality of the images is preserved and the watermark is invisible.

Furthermore, the volunteers were asked to view each extracted watermark and decide to which watermark from the twenty different watermarks it is more similar. All the viewers chose the right watermark. This means that in spite of attacking the watermarked images using strong attacks, the watermarks still robust enough to carry its visual information and prove the rightful ownership for the used images.

CONCLUSION

The proposed algorithm has been succeeded in solving the problem of rightful ownership for RGB coloured images that are spreading on Web. Binary logos and small images were used as watermarks that carry user dependent information that may represent his personality, company or trade mark. The algorithm is proved his robustness against several strong attacks. Also, the security of the algorithm is very high with two secret keys. The quality and invisibility criteria were proved. Several subjective and objective tests were done with many types of images, watermarks and attacks. The amount of information that is carried by the watermarks as payloads is big enough to represent valuable information that may be used in additional applications besides protecting the rightful ownership.

REFERENCES

Al-Tahan Al-Nu'aimi, A. S., & Qahwaji, R. S. (2006). Digital coloured images watermarking Using YIQ colour format in discrete transform domain. In *Proceedings of the Fourth Saudi Technical Conference and Exhibition*, Riyadh, Saudi Arabia (pp. 383-388).

Anderson, R. J., & Petitcolas, F. A. (1998). On the limits of steganography. *Journal of Selected Area in Communications*, *16*(4), 474–481. doi:10.1109/49.668971

Banett, R., & Sytems, S. (1999). Digitl watermarking: Applications, techniques and challenges. *Electronics & Communications Engineering Journal*, *11*(4), 173–183. doi:10.1049/ecej:19990401

Chen, T. H., Horng, G., & Wang, S. H. (2003). A robust wavelet-based watermarking scheme using quantization and human visual system model. *Pakistan Journal of Information and Technology*, *2*(3), 213–230.

Cox, I., Kilian, F., Leighton, F., & Shamoon, T. (1997). Secure spread spectrum watermarking for multimedia. *IEEE Transactions on Image Processing*, *6*, 1673–1687. doi:10.1109/83.650120

Feng, X., & Yang, Y. (2005). A new watermarking method based on DWT. In Y. Hao, J. Liu, Y.-P. Wang, Y.-m. Cheung, H. Yin, L. Jiao et al. (Eds.), *Proceedings of the International Conference on Computational Intelligence and Security* (LNCS 3802, pp. 1122-1126).

Fu, M. S., & Au, O. C. (2002). Data hiding watermarking for halftone images. *Transactions on Image Processing*, *11*(4), 477–484. doi:10.1109/TIP.2002.999680

Ganic, E., & Eskicioglu, A. M. (2005). Robust embedding of visual watermarks using DWT-SVD. *Journal of Electronic Imaging*, *14*(4), 4304. doi:10.1117/1.2137650

Gulstad, G., & Bruvold, K. (2003). *Digital image watermarking technique for copyright protection.* Retrieved from http://ucsb.edu/bruvold/ece178/report/repeam6report.html

Hartung, F., & Girod, B. (1997). Copyright protection in video delivery networks by watermarking of precompressed video. In S. Fdida & M. Morganti (Eds.), *Proceedings of the Second European Conference on Multimedia Applications, Services and Techniques* (LNCS 1242, pp. 423-436).

Huang, F., & Guan, Z. H. (2004). A hybrid SVD-DCT watermarking method based on LPSNR. *Pattern Recognition Letters, 25*(15), 1769–1775. doi:10.1016/j.patrec.2004.07.003

Hyvarinen, A. (1999). Sparse code shrinkage: Denoising of nongaussian data by maximum likelihood estimation. *Neural Computation, 11*(7), 1739–1768. doi:10.1162/089976699300016214

Joseph, J. K., Ruanaidh, O., & Pun, T. (1998). Rotation, scale and translation invarient digital image watermarking. *Signal Processing, 66*(3), 303–317. doi:10.1016/S0165-1684(98)00012-7

Kunder, D., & Hatzinakos, D. (2004). Toward robust logo watermarking using multiresolution image fusion principles. *IEEE Transactions on Multimedia, 6*(1), 185–198. doi:10.1109/TMM.2003.819747

Kutter, M., & Winkler, S. (2002). A vision-based masking model for spread-spectrum image watermarking. *IEEE Transactions on Image Processing, 11*(1), 16–25. doi:10.1109/83.977879

Lee, C. H., & Lee, Y. K. (1999). An adaptive digital image watermarking technique for copyright protection. *IEEE Transactions on Consumer Electronics, 45*(4), 1005–1015. doi:10.1109/30.809176

Lu, C. S., & Liao, H. Y. (2001). Multipurpose watermarking for image authentication and protection. *IEEE Transactions on Image Processing, 10*(10), 1579–1592. doi:10.1109/83.951542

Lu, C. S., Liao, H. Y., & Kutter, M. (2002). Denoising and copy attacks resilient watermarking by exploiting prior knowledge at detector. *IEEE Transactions on Image Processing, 11*(3), 280–292. doi:10.1109/83.988961

Mohammad, A. A., Alhaj, A., & Shaltaf, S. (2008). An improved SVD-based watermarking scheme for protecting rightful ownership. *Signal Processing, 88,* 2158–2180. doi:10.1016/j.sigpro.2008.02.015

Muharemagic, E., & Furht, B. (2006). Survey of watermarking techniques and applications. *Multimedia Watermarking Techniques and Applications, 91.*

Podilchuk, C. I., & Delp, E. J. (2001). Digital watermarking: Algorithms and applications. *Signal Processing Magazine, 18*(4), 33–46. doi:10.1109/79.939835

Solachidis, V., & Pitas, I. (2001). Circularly symmetric watermark embedding in 2-D DFT domain. *IEEE Transactions on Image Processing, 10*(11), 1741–1753. doi:10.1109/83.967401

Solachidis, V., & Pitas, I. (2004). Watermarking polygonal lines using fourier descriptors. *Computer Graphics and Applications, 24*(3), 44–51. doi:10.1109/MCG.2004.1297010

Tzeng, J., Hwang, W. L., & Chern, I. L. (2002). Enhancing image watermarking methods with/without reference images by optimization on second-order statistics. *IEEE Transactions on Image Processing, 11*(7), 771–782. doi:10.1109/TIP.2002.800895

Wang, Z., Bovic, A., Sheikh, H., & Simoncelli, E. (2004). Image quality assessment: From error visibility to structural similarity. *IEEE Transactions on Image Processing, 13*(4), 600–612. doi:10.1109/TIP.2003.819861

Zeng, W., & Lio, B. (1999). A statistical watermark detection technique without using original images for resolving rightful ownership of digital images. *IEEE Transactions on Image Processing, 8*, 1534–1548. doi:10.1109/83.799882

This work was previously published in the International Journal of Information Technology and Web Engineering (IJITWE), Volume 6, Issue 2, edited by Ghazi I. Alkhatib and Ernesto Damiani, pp. 29-39, copyright 2011 by IGI Publishing (an imprint of IGI Global).

Chapter 9

Searching and Generating Authoring Information:
A Hybrid Approach

Faisal Alkhateeb
Yarmouk University, Jordan

Iyad Abu Doush
Yarmouk University, Jordan

Amal Alzubi
Yarmouk University, Jordan

Shadi Aljawarneh
Isra University, Jordan

Eslam Al Maghayreh
Yarmouk University, Jordan

ABSTRACT

In this paper, the authors propose a novel approach to search and retrieve authoring information from online authoring databases. The proposed approach combines keywords and semantic-based methods. In this approach, the user can retrieve such information considering some specified keywords and ignore how the internal semantic search is being processed. The keywords entered by the user are internally converted by the system to a semantic query that will be used to search the requested information. The authors then use (X)HTML-based templates for the automatic construction of BibTeX elements from the query results.

1. INTRODUCTION

The World Wide Web (WWW) has become the first source of knowledge for many subjects. It can be seen as an extensive information system that allows exchanging the resources as well as documents. The semantic web is an evolving ex- tension of the web aiming at giving well defined forms and semantics to the web resources (e.g., content of an HTML web page) (Berners-Lee et al., 2001).

Due to the growth of the semantic web, se- mantic search has become an attracting area. The term refers to methods of searching web

DOI: 10.4018/978-1-4666-2157-2.ch009

documents beyond the syntactic level of matching keywords. Exposing metadata is an essential point for a semantic search approach associated with the semantic web. RDF (Resource Description Framework) (Manola & Miller, 2004) is a knowledge representation language dedicated to the annotation of resources within the Semantic web. Currently, many documents are annotated via RDF due to its simple data model and its formal semantics. For example, RDF can be embedded in (X)HTML web pages using the RDFa annotations (Adida & Birbeck, 2008) and in SMIL documents (Bulterman et al., 2005) using RDF/XML (Beckett & McBride, 2004). SPARQL (Prud'hommeaux & Seaborne, 2008) is a W3C recommendation language developed in order to query RDF knowledge bases, e.g., retrieving nodes from RDF graphs. In addition, it can be used to construct RDF graphs from the instantiation of the query result to the graph pattern (i.e., an RDF graph with variables) specified in the CONSTRUCT clause of the query.

Semantic web languages (i.e., RDF and OWL) can be used for knowledge encoding and it can be used by services, tools and applications (Finin & Ding, 2006). The semantic web will not help only human to search web contents, but also machines will be able to process web contents. This can help in creating intelligent services, customized web and can have more powerful search engines (Decker et al., 2000).

The common approach for searching web contents is based on using keywords. More precisely, both queries and documents are typically treated at a word or gram level. The search engine is missing a semantic-level understanding of the query and can only understand the content of a document by picking out documents with the most commonly occurring keywords.

The objective of this paper is to provide a novel approach for retrieving authoring information that combines keyword-based and semantic-based approaches. In this approach, the user is interested only in retrieving authoring information considering some specified keywords and ignores how

the internal semantic search is being processed. In particular, the user is interested in searching authoring information from online authoring information portals (such as DBLP, ACM, IEEE, etc.). For example, show me all documents of the author "faisal alkhateeb" or "jerome euzenat" with a title containing "SPARQL." In the proposed approach, keywords are used for collecting authoring information about the authors, which are then filtered with semantic search (using RDF and SPARQL) based on the semantic relations of the query. After that, the query results are used to generate BibTeX elements using (X)HTML-based templates.

The remainder of the paper is organized as follows: a review of related work is discussed in Section 2. We introduce the research background in Section 3. The proposed approach is presented in Section 4 as well as a case study will be illustrating the proposed approach. Section 5 provides the details on generating BibTeX elements using (X)HTML-based templates. Conclusions drawn from this study are presented in Section 6.

2. RELATED WORK

Traditional search engines use keywords as their search basis. Semantic search applies semantic processing on keywords for a better retrieval search. Hybrid search utilizes the keyword search from regular search along with the ability to use semantic search to query and reason using metadata. Using ontologies, the search engines can find pages that have different syntax but similar semantics (Decker et al., 2000).

The hybrid search provided users with more capabilities for searching and reasoning to obtain enhanced results. According to Bhagdev et al. (2008) there are three types of queries using hybrid search:

- Semantic search using the defined metadata and the relations between instances.

- Regular search using keywords.
- Search for keywords within a specific content.

Kiryakov et al. (2004) proposed a system in which the user can select between keyword based search or ontology based search, but the user cannot merge the two approaches.

Another work by Bhagdev et al. (2008) introduced a search method that combines ontology and keyword search based methods. The research results show that the use of a hybrid search gives a better performance over keyword search or semantic search.

Rocha et al. (2004) combined ontology based information retrieval with regular search. They used spread activation algorithm to obtain activation value of the relevance of search results with keywords. The links in the ontology are given weights according to certain properties. The proposed method does not identify promptly the unique concepts and relations.

In another work, Gilardoni et al. (2005) provided integration of keyword based search with ontology search, but with there is no capability for Boolean queries.

Hybrid search is implemented by some large companies in the industry. Google Product Search is a semantic search service from Google which searches for products by linking between different attributes in the knowledge base to retrieve a product. Sheth et al. (2002) use keyword query to apply multi-domain search by automatically classifying and extracting information along with ontology and meta data information.

Guha et al. (2003) presented a semantic search that combines traditional search and other data from distributed sources to answer the user query in more details. In the reference (Davies & Weeks, 2004), the QuizRDF is introduced. QuizRDF is a system that combines the traditional search method with the ability to query and navigate RDF. The system is shortcoming when there is a chaining in the query.

CE2 is a model for hybrid search (Wang et al., 2008). It integrates databases and Information Retrieval (IR) technologies for large scale querying. Resources to be queried are represented in a form of graphs while queries are represented in some form of conjunctive queries restricted to tree shaped with only one single distinguished variable (i.e., the root of the tree).

A "deep segmentation" technique (Fu et al., 2010) for disambiguating of keyword queries issued against RDF database. GoNTogle is a framework for document annotation and retrieval built on top of Semantic web and IR technologies (Bikakis et al., 2010). The system supports manual and automatic ontology-based annotation for several formats of documents as well as a combination of keyword-based and semantic-based search over documents. Herzig (2011) presents a hybrid search ranking system for structured and unstructured data.

In this research, we have independently developed a framework that combines keyword and semantic-based (using RDF and SPARQL) search for extracting information from online portals and then have presented a structured approach for generating BibTeX elements using (X)HTML-based templates as shown in Section 5. According to the Related Work, none of the proposed systems in the literature deal explicitly with the problem of extracting authoring information and generating BibTeX elements from the extracted information.

3. RESEARCH BACKGROUND

This section provides an overview of the elements that are necessary for presenting the proposed approach namely: BibTeX, RDF, and SPARQL.

3.1. BibTeX

BibTeX (Patashnik, 1988; Fenn, 2006) is a tool and a file format which are used to describe and process lists of references, mostly in conjunction with LaTeX documents. BibTeX makes it easy to cite sources in a consistent manner through separating bibliographic information from the presentation of this information. BibTeX uses a style-independent text-based file format for lists of bibliography items, such as articles, books and thesis. Each bibliography entry contains some subset of standard data entries: author, booktitle, number, organization, pages, title, type, volume, year, institution and others. The types shown in Box 1 are recognized by virtually all BibTeX styles: article, book, booklet, conference, inproceedings, phdthesis, etc.

3.2. RDF

RDF is a language for describing resources. In its abstract syntax, an RDF document is a set of triples of the form <subject, predicate, object>.

As illustrated in Box 2, there exists in-proceedings document, which is a coauthored by two persons named "Faisal Alkhateeb" and "Jerome Euzenat", whose title is "PSPARQL".

An RDF document can be represented by a directed labeled graph, as shown in Figure 1, where the set of nodes is the set of terms appearing as a subject or object in a triple and the set of arcs is the set of predicates (i.e., if <s, p, o> is a triple, then there is an edge from node s labeled with p to the node o).

3.3. SPARQL

SPARQL is the query language developed by the W3C for querying RDF graphs. A simple SPARQL query is expressed using a form resembling the SQL SELECT query:

```
SELECT B FROM u WHERE P
```

where u is the URL of an RDF graph G to be queried, P is a SPARQL graph pattern (i.e., a pattern

Box 1. An instance of a BibTeX element

```
@article{DBLP:AlkhateebBE09,
     author = {Faisal Alkhateeb and Jean-Francois Baget and Jerome Euzenat},
     title = {Extending SPARQL with regular exp-
     ression patterns (for querying RDF)},
     journal = {J. web Sem.},
     volume = {7},
     number = {2},
     year = {2009},
     pages = {57-73}, }
```

Box 2. An assertion of RDF triples

```
{<ex:person1 foaf:name "Faisal Alkhateeb">,
<ex:document1 BibTeX:author ex:person1>,
<ex:document1 rdf:type BibTeX:inproceedings>,
<ex:document1 BibTeX:title "PSPARQL">,
<ex:person1 foaf:knows ex:person2>,
<ex:person2 foaf:name "Jerome Euzenat">,
<ex:document1 BibTeX:author ex:person2>}
```

Figure 1. An RDF graph

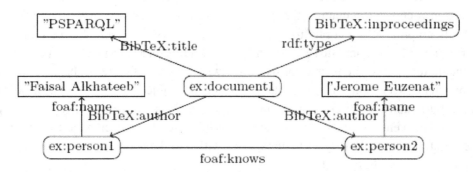

constructed over RDF graphs with variables) and B is a tuple of variables appearing in P. Intuitively, an answer to a SPARQL query is an instantiation of the variables of B by the terms of the RDF graph G such that the substitution of the values to the variables of P yields to a subset of the graph G. When using RDFS semantics (Brickley & Guha, 2004), this intuitive definition is irrelevant and one could apply RDFS reasoning rules to calculate answers over RDFS documents.

This query in Box 3 could be used, when evaluated against the RDF graph of Figure 1, to return the answers in Table 1.

In RDF, there exists a set of reserved words (called RDF Schema or simply RDFS; Brickley & Guha, 2004) that designed to describe the relationships between resources and properties, e.g., classA subClassOf classB. It adds additional constraints to the resources associated to the RDFS

terms, and thus permitting more consequences (reasoning). See Box 4.

SPARQL provides several result forms other than SELECT that can be used for formatting the query results. For example, a CONSTRUCT query can be used for building an RDF graph from the set of answers to the query. For each answer to the query, the variable values are substituted in the RDF graph pattern and the merge of the resulting RDF graphs is computed. This feature can be viewed as rules over RDF permitting to build new relations from the linked data. See Box 5.

This query constructs the RDF graph (containing the coauthor relation) by substituting for each located answer the values of the variables ?author and ?document to have the following graph (as done for SPARQL, we encode the resulting graph in the Turtle language, see Box 6).

Box 3. Consider the RDF graph in Figure 1 representing some possible authoring information. For instance, the existence of the following triples {<document1, rdf:type, BibTeX:inproceeding>, <document1, BibTeX:title, "PSPARQL">} asserts that there exists an inproceeding document whose title is "PSPARQL." This SPARQL query models this information.

```
SELECT *
FROM <Figure1>
WHERE {
        ?document BibTeX:author ?author .
        ?document BibTeX:title "PSPARQL" .
        ?author foaf:name ?name .}
```

Table 1. Answers of the query in Example 3

#	?document	?author	?name
1	ex:document1	ex:person1	"Faisal alkhateeb"
2	ex:document1	ex:person2	"Jereome Euzenat"

4. METHODOLOGY

We have implemented the Extraction of Authoring Information (EAI) system in order to achieve the following:

Given: A user query in the form of textual keywords.

Find: A set of BibTeX elements that are relevant to the query.

The proposed methodology consists of the following major phases: connecting to Google search engine, connecting to DBLP page and extracting BibTeX elements, converting BibTeX to RDF and keywords to SPARQL query, and then evaluate the SPARQL query against the RDF document. The first two phases deal with extracting the author information based on keyword search. The third and fourth phases represent the semantic search. In the following sections, we present the basic work flow of the system as well as its main components.

4.1. System Work Flow

As shown in Figure 2, the system works as follows: (i) the user enters the keywords to be searched such as keywords from author name, title of the paper, year of publication, etc.; (ii) then, Google search engine is used to correct misspelled entered keywords as well as finding the pages for the corrected entered keywords; and (iii) After that, BibTeX elements will be extracted and these.

Box 4. Using the RDF graph presented in Figure 1, we can deduce the following triple <ex:document1 rdf:type BibTeX:proceedings> from the following triples <ex:document1 rdf:type BibTeX:inproceedings> and <BibTeX:inproceedings rdfs:subClassOf BibTeX:publications>. Hence, the following SPARQL query will returns the same set of answers described in Box 1 because the inproceedings is a subclass of publications.

```
:
SELECT *
FROM <Figure1>
WHERE {
?document rdf:type BibTeX:publications .
?document BibTeX:author ?author .
?document BibTeX:title "PSPARQL" .
?author foaf:name ?name . }
```

Box 5. An example of CONSTRUCT query

```
CONSTRUCT {?author BibTeX:coauthorof ?document .}
FROM <Figure1>
WHERE {      ?document BibTeX:author ?author .
             ?document BibTeX:title "PSPARQL" .
             ?author foaf:name ?name . }
```

Box 6. Graph encoded in Turtle language

```
@prefix ex: <http://ex.org/>.
ex:person1 BibTeX:coauthorof ex:document1 .
ex:person2 BibTeX:coauthorof ex:document1 .
```

Figure 2. Basic flow of the system

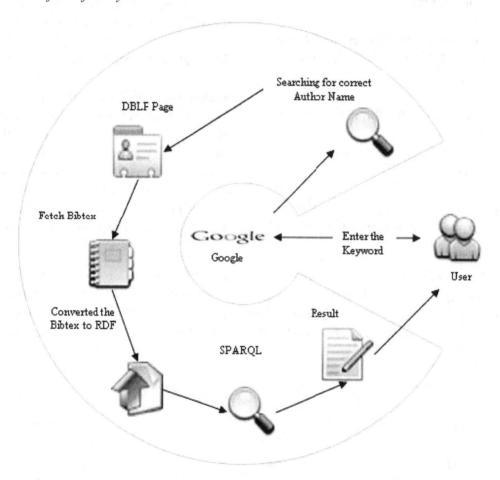

BibTeX elements will be converted into RDF document. The corrected keywords will be transformed to a SPARQL query to be used for querying the RDF document corresponding to the extracted BibTeX elements.

4.2. System Components

The following are the main components of the system:

- **Google Search:** After entering the keywords in the corresponding fields, they will be passed to a component that connects to Google search engine. The magic

URL http://www.google.com/search?hl=ar &=+"searchParameters" of Google search engine will be used to search for the specified keywords. To this end, there could be two cases returned from this search either: correct author name; or misspelled author name. In the second, the new search path "did you mean structure" will be used to reconnect to the Google search engine. This process is repeated until finding the corresponding author page in the specified authoring database (DBLP, ACM, IEEE, etc).

- **BibTeX Extractor:** This component is responsible for extracting the BibTeX elements and saving them in a file. This component contains several methods; each of them is specific to a bibliography database. This is due to the fact that each bibliography database has its own style to include BibTeX elements in the authoring web pages. Therefore, we suggest including BibTeX elements in web pages as an RDFa annotations.

- **BibTeX Parser:** BibTeX elements are then converted to RDF documents using results from the BibTeX parser that we have implemented in the system. Note that if the RDFa is used to annotate BibTeX elements, then there is no need for this parser. In this case, the online RDF distiller could be used to extract RDF documents corresponding to the annotated BibTeX elements from web pages. In addition to the RDF triples that correspond to the BibTeX entries, RDF triples corresponding to RDFS relationships (such as <BibTeX:inproceedings rdfs:subClassOf BibTeX:proceedings> and <BibTeX:booklet rdfs:subClassOf BibTeX:book>) are added to the RDF document. This allows the reasoning for more results.

- **Keywords to SPARQL Query:** The entered keywords are also used to build a SPARQL query. Then, the query is used to filter the results obtained in the search based on keywords. More precisely, when entering keywords, the user selects the type of the data entry to be entered such as "Title", "Author", "Publication", "Pages", and so on. Note that, the user can enter multiple authors. If the keyword begins with underscore "_", this means that the entered keyword is part of the BibTeX data entry. In this case, the "regex" function can be used in the Filter constraint to build the SPARQL query. Otherwise, it is considered to be an exact search for such keyword. The user can specify the relationship between the entered keywords (i.e., "or" or "and"). When building the SPARQL query, these relationships correspond to the "UNION" and "AND" SPARQL query graph patterns.

- **Query Evaluator:** This component is used to evaluate the SPARQL query (i.e., the query obtained from the entered keywords) against the RDF document (i.e., the RDF document obtained from the file containing the BibTeX elements) to find and construct the precise results. Any query evaluator could be used at this stage, but we have used the Jena framework.

- **Generating BibTeX:** The results of the query are then used to generate BibTeX elements using (X)HTML templates (Section 4).

It should be noticed that DBLP provides the capability of searching by allowing users to pose keyword-based queries over only its bibliography dataset. One can pose the query "alkhateeb jerome euzenat" that searches for documents matching the keyword "alkhateeb" or "jerome euzenat".

The search process in DBLP offers good features such as a search is triggered after each keystroke with instant times if the network connection is not lame and case insensitive search (Bast et al., 2008). However, a misspelled keyword such as "alkhateb" has no hits while "alkhateeb" returns five documents. Additionally, the semantic relations are neither fully preserved nor well defined. In particular, one can post the query "alkhateebeuzenat" that provides 79 documents while putting a space after the pipe "alkhateeb euzenat" provides only 2 documents.

4.3. Case Study

Figure 3 shows the main menu of the user interface of the system. The user can select the database to be searched for using in the "Library" combo box. The author name can be entered in the "Author" text area. The "Add" button could be used to

add more options to be searched (Figure 4). The user then clicks on the "Search" button when all values are entered.

Suppose that the user had entered "faisal alkhateb" as an author, "jerome euzenat" as another author, and "_sparql" as the "and" selected DBLP as a search database. The "or" is used to connect the authors and "and" to connect the title. Then the query equation will be as: ((Author or Author)) and Title)= ((faisal alkhateeb or jerome euzenat) and sparql).

The search will be performed in Google to check whether the author name exists in DBLP or not. In this case study, the Google search engine corrects the misspelled author name "faisal alkhateb" and uses "faisal alkhateeb" instead to connect to the DBLP with the correct name. Then the BibTeX elements corresponding to the keywords "faisal alkhateb," "jerome euzenat," and "sparql" are extracted from DBLP (see Box 7).

Figure 3. User Interface of the system

Figure 4. Search result of the user query

Box 7. BibTeX elements extracted from DBLP

```
@article{DBLP:AlkhateebBE09,
author = {Faisal Alkhateeb and Jean-Francois Baget and Jerome Euzenat},
title = {Extending SPARQL with regular expression patterns (for querying RDF)},
journal = {J. web Sem.},
volume = {7},
number = {2},
year = {2009},
pages = {57-73},}
```

The BibTeX elements will be then converted to RDF document. The corrected entered keywords will be used to build the SPARQL query in Box 8 to filter the results.

Note that the keyword "sparql" begins with underscore "_" and so it is considered to be part of the title while other keywords such "`faisal alkhateeb" do not begin with underscore and is considered to be the full author names. The user

can specify a range for the publishing years. For instance, show me the authoring information between "2004" and "2008". In this case, the user can enter "2004-2008" in the year field, which is converted to the following part of a SPARQL query (see Box 9).

The above SPARQL query is evaluated against the obtained RDF document and the matched results of the query is provided to the user in the

Box 8. SPARQL query used for filtering

```
CONSTRUCT{ ?doc BibTeX:author "Faisal Alkhateeb"
?doc BibTeX:author "Jerome Euzenat"
...}
FROM<RDF document corresponds to BibTeX>
WHERE{{{ ?doc BibTeX:author "Faisal Alkhateeb".
?doc BibTeX:title ?title.
?doc BibTeX:year ?year.
?doc BibTeX:pages ?pages. }
Union { ?doc BibTeX:author "Jerome Euzenat".
?doc BibTeX:title ?title.
?doc BibTeX:year ?year.
?doc BibTeX:pages ?pages. }}
{ ?doc BibTeX:title ?title }
FILTER(regex(?title, "^sparql"))}}
```

Box 9. Year field converted to SPARQL query

```
?document BibTeX:hasyear ?year . FILTER ((?year >=2004) && (?year <= 2008))
```

"Search Results" Textbox with the number of results (47 results in this example). Once the results are completely matched, the user will be provided with BibTeX of the results as RDFa+(X) HTML format. The generation of BibTeX will be discussed on the following section.

5. BIBTEX GENERATION

Generating BibTeX elements consists mainly of the following stages, which are discussed in details in the following subsections:

- We represent BibTeX elements as (X) HTML documents, thus preserving the original template of the BibTeX element.

- We propose to annotate BibTeX elements, which are represented as (X)HTML documents, using RDFa.
- We use RDFa+(X)HTML-based templates to permits generating annotated BibTeX elements based on RDF data (representing bibliography information) and SPARQL queries (built automatically from the BibTeX template to be generated).

5.1. RDFa Annotations for BibTeX Elements

With the emergence of the Semantic Web (Berners-Lee et al., 2001), new applications based on semantic and expressive repositories can be developed. The BibTeX elements are encoded in more semantic form using RDF (or even OWL). More precisely, a BibTeX element could be represented by an RDF document by converting each entry to an RDF triple. For instance, the following BibTeX data:

```
author = { Faisal Alkhateeb }
```

could be represented by the following RDF triple:

```
_:bitexElement BibTeX:author "Faisal
Alkhateeb".
```

However, the template of the original BibTeX element is not preserved using such transformation. Another way to represent BibTeX elements is to embed them in (X)HTML documents. Figure 5 presents the displayed page of a (X)HTML document for a particular BibTeX element. In addition to preserving the template of the BibTeX element, such representation allows to annotate the BibTeX elements using RDFa.

As an example, Figure 6 provides an (X)HTML document annotated with RDFa for the BibTeX element of Figure 5. Moreover, semantic-based queries (such as SPARQL-based queries) could be used to search for BibTeX elements based on querying the RDFa annotations. In particular, RDFa annotations can be extracted using RDFa extractors (such as the online RDFa distiller), and then queried the extracted ontology using SPARQL queries. Thus, ad-hoc routines are not necessary to be built for extracting BibTeX elements from online bibliography database web pages for searching particular information.

5.2. BibTeX Templates

A BibTeX template is simply an (X)HTML document (i.e., an XML document) with some variables. These variables represent fields that will be instantiated from the query result. Figure 7 shows an example of such a template for an in-proceedings BibTeX element where variables are elements starting with ?. Note that template variables may also start with $ as in SPARQL. In this template, variables are located in specific tags (e.g., <sparqlmm:var name="?CityNameDeparture">).

Figure 5. (X)HTML web page containing a BibTeX element

```
-------------------------------------------------
@article{DBLP:AlkhateebBE09,
  author     = {Faisal Alkhateeb and Jean-Francois
                  Baget and Jerome Euzenat},
  title      = {Extending SPARQL with regular ex-
pre-
                  ssion patterns (for query-
ing RDF)},
  journal    = {J. Web Sem.},
  volume     = {7},
  number     = {2},
  year       = {2009},
  pages      = {57-73},
  ee         = {http://dx.doi.org/10.1016/j.websem.
                  2009.02.002},
  bibsource = {DBLP,http://dblp.uni-trier.de},}
-------------------------------------------------
```

Figure 6. RDFa annotations in the (X)HTML document for the BibTeX element of Figure 4

```
----------------------------------------------------------
<body>
  <div xmlns:BibTeX="http://purl.oclc.org/NET/
      nknouf/ns/BibTeX#" xmlns:DBLP="http://
      www.pubzone.org/dblp/" typeof="BibTeX:
      article">
    <p>@article{<a property = "BibTeX:haskey">
             http://www.pubzone.org/dblp/ournals/
             ws/AlkhateebBE09</a> .
    <br/>
        author    = {<a rel="BibTeX:hasauthor">Faisal
                     Alkhateeb and Jean-Francois
                     Baget and Jerome Euzenat</a>
                     },<br/>
        title     = {<a property="BibTeX:hastitle">
                     Extending SPARQL with regul-
                     ar expression patterns (for
                     querying RDF) </a>},<br/>
        journal   = {<a property="BibTeX:hasjournal">
                     J. Web Sem.</a>},<br/>
        volume    = {<a property="BibTeX:hasvolume">
                     7</a>},<br/>
        number    = {<a property="BibTeX:hasnumber">
                     2</a>},<br/>
        year      = {<a property="BibTeX:hasyear">
                     2009</a>},<br/>
        pages     = {<a property="BibTeX:haspages">
                     57-73</a>},<br/>
        ee        = {<a property="BibTeX:ee">http://
                     dx.doi.org/10.1016/j.websem.
                     2009.02.002</a>},
    <br/>}
    </p>
  </div>
</body>
----------------------------------------------------------
```

5.3. Constructing BibTeX Elements Using Templates and SPARQL

This section provides a possible approach for constructing BibTeX elements based on BibTeX templates and SPARQL queries.

In this approach, the user fills the information about the BibTeX element to be generated. For example, to generate BibTeX elements of the publications of "faisal alkhateeb" in "2009," she/he needs to enter "faisal alkhateeb" in the author value and "2009" in the year value as shown in Figure 7. This template implicitly forms a SPARQL query that could be generated automatically to give the following one (see Box 10).

When the data entry ends with "$" (such as "faisal alkhateeb$"), then it will be treated as an exact search. Otherwise it will be treated as part of the data entry to be retrieved (such as "sparql"). In the later case, the "regex" function is used in the FILTER constraint in the constructed query.

Then, we substitute the variables by their matched values according to the set of answers of the query. If a variable occurs inside the specific tag sparqlmm:var, the whole tag, including its content, is replaced by the value of that variable. We

Figure 7. RDFa+(X)HTML template for BibTeX elements

```
---------------------------------------------------------------
<body>
  <div xmlns:BibTeX="http://purl.oclc.org/NET/
      nknouf/ns/BibTeX#" xmlns:DBLP="http://
      www.pubzone.org/dblp/" typeof="BibTeX:
      article">
    <p>@article{<a property = "BibTeX:haskey">
          <span><sparqlmm:var name="?key">?key
          </sparqlmm:var></span></a>,
      <br/>
        author    = {<a rel="BibTeX:hasauthor">
          faisal alkhateeb$</a>},<br/>
        title     = {<a property="BibTeX:hastitle">
          sparql</span></a>},<br/>
        journal   = {<a property="BibTeX:hasjournal">
          <span><sparqlmm:var name="?journal">?journal
          </sparqlmm:var></span></a>},<br/>
        volume    = {<a property="BibTeX:hasvolume">
          <span><sparqlmm:var name="?volume">?volume
          </sparqlmm:var></span></a>},<br/>
        number    = {<a property="BibTeX:hasnumber">
          <span><sparqlmm:var name="?number">?number
          </sparqlmm:var></span></a>},<br/>
        year      = {<a property="BibTeX:hasyear">
          2009</a>},<br/>
        pages     = {<a property="BibTeX:haspages">
          <span><sparqlmm:var name="?pages">?pages
          </sparqlmm:var></span></a>},<br/>
        OPTee     = {<a property="BibTeX:ee">
          <span><sparqlmm:var name="?ee">?ee
          </sparqlmm:var></span></a>,
      <br/>}
    </p>
  </div>
</body>
---------------------------------------------------------------
```

Box 10.

```
CONSTRUCT { <BibTeX-template>}
WHERE {
?doc rdf:type BibTeX:inproceedings .
?doc BibTeX:author "faisal alkhateeb" .
?doc BibTeX:title ?title .
?doc BibTeX:year 2009 .
?doc BibTeX:volume ?volume .
...
OPTIONAL { ?doc BibTeX:ee ?ee . }
FILTER (regex (?title, "^sparql"))}
```

repeat the process to obtain (X)HTML documents containing BibTeX elements for each answer of the query. It should be noticed that the BibTeX elements are generated together with RDFa annotations. Moreover, optional data entries can be specified as in BibTeX by prefixing them with "OPT" (as in the case of "OPTee" of Figure 7).

6. CONCLUSION

In this paper, we have presented an approach to search and extract authoring information. The proposed approach is based on keyword and semantic search approaches. In the keyword search part, the keywords entered by the user are used to collect authoring information. In this part, the Google search engine is used to correct the misspelled keywords, in particular the author's name, thus retrieving more results. Moreover, ad-hoc routines are used to extract bibliography elements from online databases. So, we inset BibTeX elements in Web pages as RDFa annotations so that standard methods can be used.

In the semantic part, the SPARQL query obtained from entered keywords is queried against the metadata corresponding to the authoring information, which allows giving more precise results. We have used the Jena framework for storing RDF and evaluating SPARQL queries over RDF data. Additionally, we have used a structured approach for generating BibTeX elements using (X)HTML-based templates. Thus the generated BibTeX elements are annotated using RDFa and can be used by other services. Though the template in our work is restricted for generating BibTeX elements, it can be used for generating any XML document since the templates are based on RDFa+(X)HTML.

REFERENCES

Adida, B., & Birbeck, M. (2008). *RDFa primer – bridging the human and data webs*. Retrieved from http://www.w3.org/TR/xhtml-rdfa-primer/

Beckett, D., & McBride, B. (2004). *RDF/XML syntax specification (revised)*. Retrieved from http://www.w3.org/TR/rdf-syntax-grammar/

Berners-Lee, T., Hendler, J., & Lassila, O. (2001). *The semantic web*. Retrieved from http://www.sciam.com/article.cfm?articleID=00048144-10D2-1C70-84A9809EC%588EF21

Bhagdev, R., Chapman, S., Ciravegna, F., Lanfranchi, V., & Petrelli, D. (2008). Hybrid search: Effectively combining keywords and semantic searches. In *Proceedings of the 5th European Semantic Web Conference on The Semantic Web: Research and Applications* (pp. 554-568).

Bikakis, N., Giannopoulos, G., Dalamagas, T., & Sellis, T. (2010). Integrating keywords and semantics on document annotation and search. In *Proceedings of the International Conference On the Move to Meaningful Internet Systems: Part II* (pp. 921-938).

Brickley, D., & Guha, R. (2004). *RDF vocabulary description language 1.0: RDF schema*. Retrieved from http://www.w3.org/TR/rdf-schema/

Bulterman, D., Grassel, G., Jansen, J., Koivisto, A., Layaida, N., & Michel, T. ...Zucker, D. (2005). *Synchronized Multimedia Integration Language (SMIL 2.1)*. Retrieved from http://www.w3.org/TR/SMIL/

Davies, J., Krohn, U., & Weeks, R. (2002). Quizrdf: Search technology for the semantic web. In *Proceedings of the 11th International WWW Conference Workshop on RDF and Semantic Web Applications*.

Decker, S., Melnik, S., van Harmelen, F., Fensel, D., Klein, M., & Broekstra, J. (2000). The semantic web: the roles of XML and RDF. *IEEE Internet Computing, 15*(3), 63–73. doi:10.1109/4236.877487

Fenn, J. (2006). Managing citations and your bibliography with BibTeX. *The PracnTeX Journal, 4*. Retrieved from http://www.tug.org/pracjourn/2006-4/fenn/

Finin, T., & Ding, L. (2006). Search engines for semantic web knowledge. In *Proceedings of XTech: Building Web 2.0.*

Fu, H., Gao, S., & Anyanwu, K. (2010). Disambiguating keyword queries on RDF databases using "deep" segmentation. In *Proceedings of the IEEE Fourth International Conference on Semantic Computing* (pp. 236-243).

Gilardoni, L., Biasuzzi, C., Ferraro, M., Fonti, R., & Slavazza, P. (2005). Lkms - a legal knowledge management system exploiting semantic web technologies. In *Proceedings of the International Semantic Web Conference* (pp. 872-886).

Guha, R., McCool, R., & Miller, E. (2003). Semantic search. In *Proceedings of the 12ᵗʰ International Conference on World Wide Web* (pp. 700-709).

Herzig, D. M. (2011). Hybrid search ranking for structured and unstructured data. In *Proceedings of the 8ᵗʰ Extended Semantic Web Conference on the Semantic Web: Research and Applications - Part II* (pp. 518-522).

Kiryakov, A., Popov, B., Terziev, I., Manov, D., & Ognyano, D. (2004). Semantic annotation, indexing, and retrieval. *Web Semantics: Science. Services and Agents on the World Wide Web, 2*(1), 49–79. doi:10.1016/j.websem.2004.07.005

Manola, F., & Miller, E. (2004). *RDF primer*. Retrieved from http://www.w3.org/TR/rdf-primer/

Patashnik, O. (1988). *Bibtexing*. Retrieved from http://ftp.ntua.gr/mirror/ctan/biblio/bibtex/contrib/doc/btxdoc.pdf

Prud'hommeaux, E., & Seaborne, A. (2008). *SPARQL query language for RDF*. Retrieved from http://www.w3.org/TR/rdf-sparql-query/

Rocha, C., Schwabe, D., & Aragao, M. P. (2004). A hybrid approach for searching in the semantic web. In *Proceedings of the 13th International Conference on World Wide Web* (pp. 374-383).

Sheth, A., Bertram, C., Avant, D., Hammond, B., Kochut, K., & Warke, Y. (2002). Managing semantic content for the web. *IEEE Internet Computing, 6*(4), 80–87. doi:10.1109/MIC.2002.1020330

Wang, H., Tran, T., & Liu, C. (2008). CE2: towards a large scale hybrid search engine with integrated ranking support. In *Proceedings of the International Conference on Information and Knowledge Management* (pp. 1323-1324).

This work was previously published in the International Journal of Information Technology and Web Engineering (IJITWE), Volume 6, Issue 3, edited by Ghazi I. Alkhatib and Ernesto Damiani, pp. 1-14, copyright 2011 by IGI Publishing (an imprint of IGI Global).

Chapter 10
A Unified Approach to Uncertainty–Aware Ubiquitous Localization of Mobile Users

Petr Aksenov
Hasselt University, Belgium

Kris Luyten
Hasselt University, Belgium

Karin Coninx
Hasselt University, Belgium

ABSTRACT

Localisation is a standard feature in many mobile applications today, and there are numerous techniques for determining a user's location both indoors and outdoors. The provided location information is often organised in a format tailored to a particular localisation system's needs and restrictions, making the use of several systems in one application cumbersome. The presented approach models the details of localisation systems and uses this model to create a unified view on localisation in which special attention is paid to uncertainty coming from different localisation conditions and to its presentation to the user. The work discusses technical considerations, challenges and issues of the approach, and reports on a user study on the acceptance of a mobile application's behaviour reflecting the approach. The results of the study show the suitability of the approach and reveal users' preference toward automatic and informed changes they experienced while using the application.

INTRODUCTION

Location is considered to be among the most important types of context (Varshavsky & Patel, 2009). The success of location-aware applications and location-based services still keeps location being the topic of a good deal of research efforts today (Dey, Hightower, de Lara, & Davies, 2010). Recent advances in technology and research help to refine the existing and develop new approaches to location determination, achieving yet better accuracy and making location sensing available

DOI: 10.4018/978-1-4666-2157-2.ch010

in a greater number of places and situations users are in throughout the day.

However, the resultant ubiquitous availability of the knowledge about location in diverse environments indoors and outdoors brings in its own issues and challenges. As stated by Banerjee, Agarwal, Bahl, Chandra, Wolman, and Corner (2010), there are two major types of location determination techniques: infrastructure-based, such as Ubisense (http://www.ubisense.net) or PlaceLab (LaMarca et al., 2005), and peer-based, such as Virtual Compass (Banerjee et al., 2010) or RELATE (Gellersen, Lukowicz, Beigl, & Riedel, 2010). Each of them initially provides data in its own format (see Figure 1), often different in the level of granularity, frequency of updates, reliability, coverage, means of delivery, etc. This diversity can significantly affect applications that want to make use of different tracking technologies. For example, an existing framework might have little or no support of certain subtle but yet meaningful differences in location data provided

by different localisation systems, or it may just not recognise an available system at all (e.g., due to the incompatibility of the communication channel used to receive the data). Besides, technical limitations and constraints inevitably present in location determination result in uncertainty about location, thus raising further discrepancies in an application's functionality (Girardin, 2007). But from the user viewpoint, changes, which are in our case initiated by run-time localisation, should be handled in a way that would preserve the continuity of this user's interaction with the application (Massink & Faconti, 2002). And in order to integrate the above limitations and changes of location into the application's behaviour, we need a unified view on the data different localisation techniques provide, as well as on the metadata describing the techniques themselves.

This work presents a strategy for handling the diversity of localisation systems and the representation of location data they provide. In particular, we present an approach that models the

Figure 1. Location information provided by a particular localisation system is often organised in a specific format according to this system's needs or restrictions

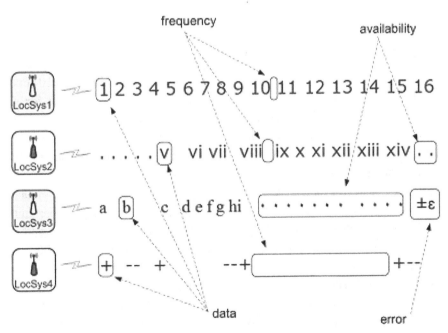

properties of localisation systems and uses this model to build a unified view on localisation throughout a large-scale pervasive environment. Our approach takes into account any localisation system in the environment and only requires that a semantic description of this system's infrastructure and its location data in a specified format has been created at design-time and made available at the moment the system is employed. We explicitly consider uncertain and incomplete information about location in our model and establish its further use in pervasive location-aware applications. We discuss technical considerations, issues and challenges of our approach and also report about a user study conducted on a prototype location-aware application we developed for evaluating the proposed approach. In particular, we investigated users' reaction to knowing about the changes in their localisation at run-time under different conditions of uncertainty about their location. The results of the study showed users' acceptance of automatic changes and revealed their preference for the awareness of the cause of those changes. This finding supports our assumption that users prefer to stay aware of the nature of the uncertainty coming from localisation.

RELATED WORK

An increasing role of pervasive and ubiquitous computing, coupled with the success of location-aware applications, stimulated researchers to tackle problems in which multiple location tracking technologies are involved. For example, Hansen, Wind, Jensen, and Thomsen (2009) presented Streamspin, a platform for the creation and delivery of location-based services, in which they focused on the key aspects of seamless handover between GPS for outdoors and WiFi-based localisation for indoors based on the fact whether either system was detectable. The results of their experiments clearly indicated the need for such kind of support. Aksenov, Luyten, and Coninx

(2009) outline how spatial relationships generated under different location tracking conditions can affect interaction between resources. The reported simulated use-case illustrates how the details of interaction may change under different localisation, thereby indicating that considering multiple localisation systems may be important for the continuity of interaction.

Ranganathan, Al-Muhtadi, Chetan, Campbell, and Mickunas (2004) describe MiddleWhere, a distributed middleware system that treats location information as an independent service separated from the rest of the application. The suggested infrastructure is based on a model of spatial relations and reasoning about location is supported by that separate service. However, the main focus was on fusing location data whenever possible in order to provide more accurate positions. Coronato, Esposito, and Pietro (2009) present a service for locating mobile objects tracked by multiple localisation systems. A localisation system in their model belongs to an ontology of physical locations, which is linked to an ontology of semantic locations by the concept of "Atomic Location," common to both. The service then applies a set of reasoning rules to find out a better location among the available ones and to resolve possible location conflicts. However, location providers are considered as they are, so nothing is said about their finer details or metadata. Finally, Stevenson, Ye, Dobson, and Nixon (2010) introduce LOC8, a programming framework for supporting the use of location by pervasive applications. The framework is based on two ontologies: an ontology of spaces and relationships between them (the space model), and an ontology describing multiple location providers and their metadata in order to incorporate positioning uncertainty, such as the accuracy of measurements and coverage area (the sensing model). A number of presented use cases illustrate how the querying process works, followed by a discussion about the efforts that the creators of location-aware applications should take into account with respect to supporting different positioning systems. This work mainly focuses on the development aspects whereas we place the user in the foreground.

On the other side, the problem of revealing the uncertainty about location sensing to users has also been given attention. In particular, researchers have been investigating how the users of location-aware applications should be informed about it. For example, Dearman, Varshavsky, de Lara, and Truong (2007) found out that showing the error of location helped users in map-based navigational tasks. They modelled the error of a GSM-based localisation system as the radius of a circle drawn around a user's estimated position on a mobile map. The results of their field study reveal that finding an object is perceived to be easier and happens faster when the uncertainty is visualised. Lemelson, King, and Effelsberg (2008) report on a survey that investigated users' preferences for the visualisation of the uncertainty of their indoor position. They showed the participants several ways the error could be visualised and then asked them to choose the best visualisation for each of the four described scenarios. The participants clearly indicated their preference for an in-map visualisation drawn on top of the corresponding area on a map. Benford et al. (2006) discuss the importance of addressing uncertainty about location and propose five strategies of dealing with it – remove it, hide it, manage it, reveal it, and exploit it, where the choice of the appropriate strategy depended on the context of use and application needs. However, it has been concluded in the follow-up research that a good representation of uncertainty remains a challenge (Opperman, Broll, Capra, & Benford, 2006), and Patel, Kientz, and Gupta (2010) point out that finding a suitable representation to use in general-purpose applications for non-experts may be even more challenging.

Thus, the two areas – supporting the diversity of localisation technologies and making users aware of the uncertainty about their location – receive considerable attention from the research community, each playing an essential role in the creation of location-aware applications for pervasive environments. However, their combination still seems to be scarcely presented, so we show how they can be intertwined.

THE SYSTEM

There are three components in our system: a unifying component, a location processing component (LPC), and a visualisation component. The unifying component receives location updates, prepares them for further processing by converting into a common format of location data, and sends them to the location processing component. The location processing component then processes each received update in accordance with the involved reasoning rules and sends the result to the visualisation component that eventually informs the user about the changes.

All information in the environment is exchanged via Web to Peer (W2P), a message-oriented peer-to-peer communication system based on HTTP (Vanderhulst, Luyten, & Coninx, 2007). Since internet-capable mobile devices have become widespread and it is now possible to connect to the web almost everywhere in urban areas, using an HTTP-based communication framework ensures easy and stable delivery of location updates. Furthermore, using a peer-to-peer topology allows us to decentralise access to location tracking provision, which is consistent with our aim to use both local systems (e.g., Ubisense; Virtual Compass, Banerjee et al., 2010) and global services (e.g., Skyhook, http://www.skyhookwireless.com).

The structure of our system is outlined in Figure 2 and is discussed in detail in the three subsections below.

Figure 2. System overview: GSN (II) handles all incoming location data (I) and produces a location update in the unified format (III); the location processing component LPC (IV) processes the update and informs the users who get the new update visualised on their devices (VI); all communication in the environment happens via Vanderhulst et al.'s (2007) W2P protocol (V)

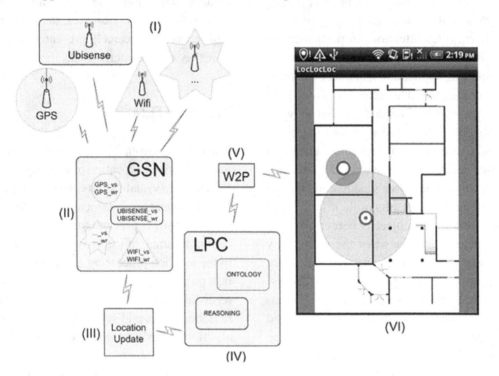

The Unifying Component

In general, a different localisation system has a different set of parameters. For example, it can produce 2D coordinates of an object every 10 seconds or only provide an update if the object is within proximity to a certain sensor so that the time of the next update is unknown (e.g., a passive RFID tag is detected only if it is close enough to an RFID reader). Furthermore, the produced location data may have an arbitrary structure (see Figure 1). Nevertheless, every situation has to be correctly interpreted. To address this diversity, we introduce a software layer that converts different formats of location tracking data into a common, unified format. The layer employs the Global Sensor Network (GSN) (see Figure 2(II)), a middleware for diverse sensor data processing

proposed by Aberer, Hauswirth, and Salehi (2007). GSN supports introducing new location sensing techniques at run time and it has proved to work successfully in multiple occasions. It requires that each localisation system has a so called "virtual sensor," which is an XML description of this system's characteristics and parameters. This parameterisation is then used by a Java-based wrapper, a piece of software code that handles the received location update in accordance with the details specified in the virtual sensor.

The virtual sensor and the corresponding Java-based wrapper are the key elements of the unification process. They need to be created at the design phase of each localisation system and have to be made available when this system is activated in the environment. Although their creation is a one-time activity and, once completed, will cause no harm at run-time, it nevertheless requires some acquaintance with the Java programming language and the XML notation, which may become a barrier to the announcement of a custom localisation system in the environment. To aid in this inclusion, we have implemented a sample wrapper with the W2P communication already established. Using this wrapper, the creation of a particular Java-based wrapper would only require one to specify the data the localisation system in question delivers in the form understood by W2P. Figure 3(b) shows an example of such specification. The virtual sensor can be customised similarly (see Figure 3(a)). Note that if a localisation system does not contain a certain parameter (e.g., no update rate for passive RFID tags) then the corresponding field should be just left empty, and it will be treated appropriately during the location processing stage. Additionally, since the architecture of the GSN framework supports peer-to-peer communication between

multiple GSN nodes in the environment, location data provided by a particular localisation system attached to a remote GSN node are accessible through the network, thus ensuring the required scalability with respect to location processing.

The Location Processing Component

Once location updates have been converted into the unified format (see Figure 2(III)), they are sent to the location processing component (LPC) (see Figure 2(IV)). LPC is a custom application that processes incoming location updates and decides about the positions and the statuses of the tracked objects.

At the core of LPC is an ontology that describes the semantics of localisation systems and of the data they supply. Ontologies have proved to be a powerful means for describing contextual

Figure 3. Customising: (a) extract from a sample virtual sensor required by GSN; (b) extract from a sample Java-based wrapper required by GSN

```
...
...
<processing-class>
        <class-name>gsn.vsensor.w2PVirtualSensorProcessor</class-name>
        <init-params />
        <output-structure>
                <field name="timestamp" type="varchar(13)"/>
                <field name="tag_id" type="varchar(15)"/>
                <field name="locsys_id" type="varchar(8)"/>
                <field name="update_rate" type="Integer"/>
                <field name="xcoord" type="double"/>
                <field name="ycoord" type="double"/>
                <field name="error" type="double"/>
        </output-structure>
</processing-class>
...
...                                                                      (a)
```

```
postStreamElement(
        w2p.getLocationEvent().getTimestamp(),
        w2p.getLocationEvent().getTagId(),
        w2p.getLocationEvent().getLocSysId(),
        w2p.getLocationEvent().getUpdateRate(),
        w2p.getLocationEvent().getX(),
        w2p.getLocationEvent().getY(),
        w2p.getLocationEvent().getError(),
        ...
        ...
);                                                                      (b)
```

information of various origin when one wants to reason about this information (Bouamrane, Luz, & Masoodian, 2008); in particular, about people's location (Niu & Kay, 2008). Besides, ontologies describing different contexts can be combined, thereby extending a pool of reasoning rules and thus offering improved context-aware services (Strobbe et al., in press). Our ontology adheres to the Web Ontology Language (OWL) (http://www. w3.org/2004/OWL/) and consists of two parts: the semantics of a localisation system itself and the location data this system produces. Figure 4 shows an example of our ontology visualised as a graph. This way, the ontology handles the details of various localisation systems and their location updates, and the XML-based virtual sensor defined in GSN acts as a protocol for registering a new localisation system and notifying about its updates. The syntax of OWL is based on XML therefore matching the ontology with the virtual sensor description is convenient.

Within the scope of this work we involved a basic set of parameters from each localisation system, such as its update rate and precision. We then considered the received error and the age of a location update to decide about its validity and appropriateness with respect to a possible handover. The age depended on the update rate so that a location update was considered obsolete when

it became older than the time of the two next scheduled updates or the universal threshold of ten seconds, whichever happened first. This simple approach to comparing location updates was justified by the informative nature of the initial evaluation that aimed at guiding further improvements to the system and identifying parts that would need to be changed. In general, reasoning about the validity and appropriateness of the provided location involves other techniques (e.g., fusion) and parameters, including those from the user model (walking speed), the task model (attending a meeting), the topology of the environment (locations on water are invalid), etc. Therefore, the LPC's reasoning functionality can be extended to include an external ontology handling and reasoning engine. For example, Stevenson et al.'s (2010) LOC8 framework could be integrated when it is released.

The Visualisation Component

Finally, after LPC has processed the update, the corresponding changes must be communicated to the interested client applications. Therefore we also include a visualisation component that informs the user about the changes (see Figure 2(VI)). Benford et al. (2006) suggested that a mobile user can be in one of the following four

Figure 4. Example of an ontology for modelling localisation, with separate concepts for describing the properties of a localisation system and the details of a single location update, i.e., the location data produced by the system

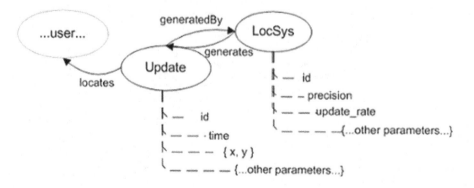

'states of being': connected and tracked, connected but not tracked, tracked but not connected, and neither connected nor tracked. Analogous to this, we address awareness of run-time localisation and propose a classification of statuses of a user's location tracking: (a) a new location update has been received with an initial positioning error (see Figure 5(a)); (b) the uncertainty area is gradually extending (see Figure 5(b)); (c) if the second threshold of the update rate has been exceeded, the marker transforms into a cross and the uncertainty area is no longer highlighted but replaced with a single dashed-line (see Figure 5(c)); and (d) the previous state extends further until the maximum threshold (currently set to 20 metres) is reached (see Figure 5(d)).

We visualise a user's position on a map as a circle of a certain radius. The radius stands for the accuracy of the position measurement, and this visualisation is often used in map-based applications (e.g., Dearman et al., 2007; Google Maps for mobile–http://www.google.com/mobile/maps). In our case, the radius extends with time and the visualisation incorporates the data and metadata that we are interested to know about. In general, other shapes that depend on the nature of the system and take into account the topology of the environment and user preferences may suit better (e.g., Baus & Kray, 2002; Burigat & Chittaro, 2011; Lemelson et al., 2008) but determining the most appropriate visualisation is beyond the scope of the current work. Note that the proposed

Figure 5. Visualisation of status of a user's location tracking distinguishes between four different states of awareness: (a) a regular update is received with an initial error; (b) the precision area extends while the next update is missing; (c) location tracking is possibly unavailable; and (d) location information is outdated (visualisation is static)

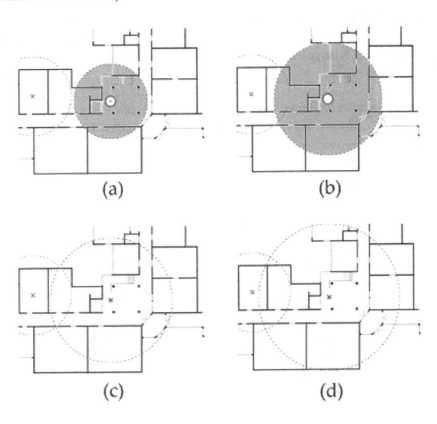

approach to visualisation equally applies to both moving and stationary users. The visualisation changes depending on the system's ability to locate a user, i.e., regardless of this user's movement.

EVALUATION

User Study

Our user study pursued two goals. First, we wanted to evaluate the feasibility of the proposed approach in general and to explore how changes and transition between available localisation systems would be functioning. The second goal was to get users' opinion on whether the awareness of changes influences the understanding and satisfaction from using the application.

We involved three localisation systems in our study: Ubisense, GPS, and a WiFi-based localisation based on a *weighted centroid algorithm* (Cheng, Chawathe, LaMarca, & Krumm, 2005) and the *best candidate set* approach for position error estimation (Lemelson, Kjærgaard, Hansen,

& King, 2009). Each system covered a different area (see Figure 6) and had a different level of accuracy. Overlaps existed only in the Ubisense coverage area (room B in Figure 6) where the WiFi-based localisation produced a location as well but the considerably more accurate Ubisense was always preferred in that room.

The developed application had two modes of awareness regarding the detected location: one mode showed the position alone without any additional information whereas the other mode also displayed the positioning error. Besides, we also introduced two modes of reflecting the change of the active tracking system. In one, the user was notified of a change (a pop-up message was displayed on the screen) whereas no feedback was provided in the other mode. Each mode of awareness of uncertainty about position was then coupled with each mode of notifications about changes in the active tracking. This resulted in four different modes of presenting the information: (A) both uncertainty and notification; (B) only uncertainty; (C) only notification; or (D) none of them. Figure 7 shows the application screenshots in each of the four modes, labelled as above. Us-

Figure 6. A part of the map of area involved in the user study. Positions around zone A are tracked by GPS, around zone B by Ubisense, and the rest of the area is controlled by a WiFi-based localisation. The areas marked with a cross cannot be walked into. Arrows indicate available walking paths.

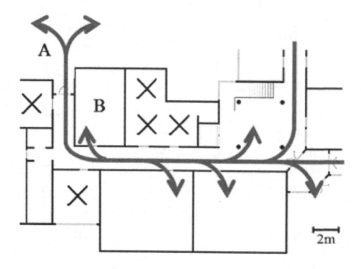

Figure 7. Four different modes of status awareness and changes in one's localisation offered to participants of user study

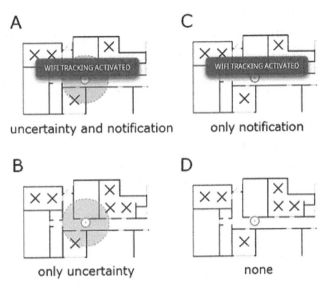

ing these four modes, we wanted to verify the following two statements that we made about the introduced awareness:

S1: Under the same visualisation conditions, users' impressions about being aware of the changes in the active tracking are positive. That is, mode A would be preferred to mode B, and mode C would be preferred to mode D.

S2: Mode A would be ranked as the preferred mode out of the four.

A previous study has shown that users of map-based navigation applications preferred to rotate their mobile device physically when aligning the orientation of the map with their walking direction (Seager & Stanton Fraser, 2007). Therefore we did not implement any automatic or digital rotation functionality and relied on the participants' ability to rotate the device physically, and we informed the participants about this condition. Since we confined the conditions of the study to a maximum of three moving objects on the map at the same time, we used simple colour-based visualisa-

tion. The colours involved were a tint of orange ("F37021" in HEX), a tint of blue ("0084A2" in HEX), and a tint of green ("78BF1C" in HEX). Any of those three colours was assigned to each participant for the duration of the experiment, and there were no remarks about any disadvantages or inconveniences caused by the assigned colour. The application was deployed on an HTC Desire Android smartphone.

We involved eight participants (5m, 3f) in our study. Seven of them had an IT background and one was a graphics designer. They were all employees, visitors or computer science students of the university, but were not involved in our research. Two participants did not wish to disclose their age, and the other six were between 20 and 34 years old (M=26.7, median=27). We asked the participants to rank their experience of 1) using map-based applications for navigation, and 2) working with smartphones, on a five-point Likert-type scale: 0-none, 1-a bit, 2-some, 3-quite a bit, 4-a lot of. The average values were, respectively, 2.1 (median=2) for navigation experience and 2.6 (median=2.5) for smartphone experience.

We used a within-group design, so each participant evaluated all four application modes. The task we asked our participants to do in each mode was the same: carrying a smartphone with our application running in one of the four modes, the participants were instructed to walk throughout the area shown in Figure 6 (the arrows in the figure indicate available walking paths). As they walked, the participants had to observe the presented information available in the currently running mode. There were between 1 and 3 objects tracked at every certain moment. The participant was always one of the objects, and the other two objects were played by experimenters. Upon completing the walking part in each mode, the participants were asked to evaluate their experience of using the application in that mode using the following relevant criteria of the NASA-TLX questionnaire (http://humansystems.arc.nasa.gov/groups/TLX/): mental demand, performance, effort, and frustration. We would like to note here that the suggested task did not have any constraints with respect to time or labour; therefore we did not include the other two criteria, physical demand and temporal demand, present in the original questionnaire, for evaluating them would not have been representative. The participants were also invited to provide additional comments to support the given rankings. In the end of the experiment, we also asked the participants to rank all four modes together. The assignment of the modes was done according to a Latin Square design. Table 1 shows the final assignment per participant. Each participant needed on average 40 minutes to complete the entire experiment.

Results

To verify S1, we compared the TLX scores each participant gave to mode A (uncertainty and notification) with those the same participant gave to mode B (only uncertainty); and the scores given to mode C (only notification) with those given

Table 1. Order of application modes in which each participant received them

Participant	Mode (A)	Mode (B)	Mode (C)	Mode (D)
P1	3	4	1	2
P2	1	2	3	4
P3	2	1	4	3
P4	3	4	1	2
P5	4	3	2	1
P6	4	3	2	1
P7	2	1	4	3
P8	1	2	3	4

to mode D (neither uncertainty nor notification). Overall, the participants provided 128 scores (8-participants x 4-TLX-criteria x 4-modes), which formed 64 pairs of values grouped by mode for comparison as appropriate (i.e., {mode A vs. mode B} and {mode C vs. mode D} for each of the four criteria by each participant). P6 and P8 who evaluated altogether 16 pairs experienced no difference between the two modes within either pair. The other participants evaluated altogether 48 pairs, 19 of which were ranked as giving no change, 27 times the informed case was preferred, and 2 times the mode without notifications was ranked higher, all the facts together confirming our statement S1. Figure 8 compares these numbers in a chart. It is worth noting that the average difference of the preference of the informed mode to its non-informed compartment in terms of the 21 gradations of the TLX-scale was much greater ($M=5.12$, $SD=2.9$) compared to those when the non-informed mode was preferred (the two differences were 1 and 2 gradations, respectively). For example, P7 supported the difference in the scores she gave to the required mental demand in modes C(7) and D(18) with a conclusion that "since no precision information was shown, (I) was thinking which tracking was actually currently active. (I) should be outside of the Ubisense area but still unknown if (I am) tracked by it or not."

Figure 8. An informed switch between location tracking systems (i.e., with an explicit notification) was the preferred option within the same visualisation

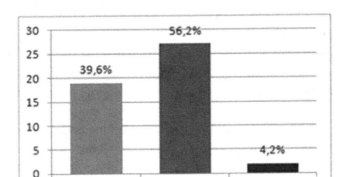

Table 2 shows the scores the participants gave to each mode in the end of the experiment, from 4 (best) to 1 (worst). Six of the eight participants preferred the mode with both uncertainty and notification active during navigation (mode (A)), confirming our statement S2. P4, who preferred mode C to the three others, explained his preference by saying, "The uncertainty circles brought too much information onto the screen, but notification about a change was helpful because it allowed me to know the situation," thus voting for the informed visualisation also. P8, on the contrary, found notification messages unnecessary because, as he stated, "when (I) got notified, (I) started to wonder what the new tracking was about. (I) lost focus and thought of the information that appeared." However, he found the information on the uncertainty quite helpful. It is interesting to note that P8 was the only one who gave the maximal score (4) to his experience with both map-based navigation and smartphones.

DISCUSSION

The main purpose of the study was to evaluate the feasibility of the approach to coping with diverse localisation systems and to collect users' impressions about the additional awareness of this diversity. Besides, we also wanted to identify potential flaws and issues prior to developing further extensions and performing an extended field study when the cost of a delay or an overlooked fact is naturally much higher and repetition is quite problematic and expensive (Consolvo, Harrison, Smith, Chen, Everitt, Froelich, & Landay, 2007). Therefore we performed our initial evaluation on a small scale using a prototype with a set of

Table 2. Scores, from 4 (best) to 1 (worst), that each participant gave to application modes (A), (B), (C), and (D)

Participant	Mode (A)	Mode (B)	Mode (C)	Mode (D)
P1	4	2	2	1
P2	4	3	1	1
P3	4	2	2	1
P4	2	1	4	3
P5	4	3	1	2
P6	4	3	2	1
P7	4	3	2	1
P8	3	4	1	2
Average Score	3.63	2.63	2.25	1.5

basic properties. The feedback we received was generally inspiring.

Prior research results confirmed people's preference for receiving information about their positional uncertainty. In our study we additionally allowed users to know the reasons for this uncertainty. We did not intend to measure the degree of the effect the awareness would have but rather wanted to learn whether there would be any benefit from knowing about it. The obtained results showed that users chose to remain aware of the cause of the changes they experienced.

Our evaluation focused on map-based navigation throughout a building and its immediate vicinity. In general, the amount and type of location information users are willing to share or would like to receive varies considerably. The suitability of collecting and providing such information depends, in particular, on the tasks the users are performing (Reilly, Dearman, Ha, Smith, & Inkpen, 2006).

CONCLUSION

We presented an approach to coping with the diversity of available techniques for location sensing in a pervasive environment. The framework integrated different localisation systems based on their semantic description in the form of an ontology. The key aspect of the approach was the conversion of an arbitrary location update into a unified format. The unified update was then processed by a separate location processing component that especially dealt with uncertainty present in localisation. The means for location gathering and the peer-to-peer network topology we used ensured the applicability of the approach to large-scale environments (e.g., a district of a city). We explicitly revealed the uncertainty about provided locations and changes in that uncertainty to the user. The results of our initial evaluation

showed users' acceptance and preference for automatic and informed changes in their location tracking conditions.

Further improvements in our approach lie in extending the ways localisation systems can be integrated in the framework. Possible solutions include developing mapping components for the currently required Java-based wrapper or accomplishing mappings for the different systems on the ontology level. Ontology mapping allows one to discover similarities and differences between systems automatically using an ontology reasoner such as Pellet (http://clarkparsia.com/pellet). Also, we are working on an extended user study that elaborates on different options of presenting location tracking conditions as well as analyses their influence on user performance in navigation-based tasks.

ACKNOWLEDGMENT

Part of the research at EDM is funded by EFRO (European Fund for Regional Development) and the Flemish Government. Funding for this research was also provided by the Research Foundation – Flanders (F.W.O. Vlaanderen, project CoLaSUE, number G.0439.08N).

REFERENCES

Aberer, K., Hauswirth, M., & Salehi, A. (2007). Infrastructure for data processing in large-scale interconnected sensor networks. In *Proceedings of the 8th International Conference on Mobile Data Management* (pp. 198–205).

Aksenov, P., Luyten, K., & Coninx, K. (2009). Coping with variability of location sensing in large-scale ubicomp environments. In *Proceedings of the International Workshop on Sensing and Acting in Ubiquitous Environments* (pp. 1–5).

Banerjee, N., Agarwal, S., Bahl, P., Chandra, R., Wolman, A., & Corner, M. (2010). Virtual Compass: relative positioning to sense mobile social interactions. In *Proceedings of the 8th International Conference on Pervasive Computing* (pp. 1–21).

Baus, J., & Kray, C. (2002). Frames of reference, positional information and navigational assistance. In S. M. Haller & G. Simmons (Eds.), *Proceedings of the 15th International Florida Artificial Intelligence Research Society Conference* (pp. 461–465). AAAI Press.

Benford, S., Crabtree, A., Flintham, M., Drozd, A., Anastasi, R., & Paxton, M. (2006). Can you see me now? *ACM Transactions on Human-Computer Interaction, 13*(1), 100–133. doi:10.1145/1143518.1143522

Bouamrane, M.-M., Luz, S., & Masoodian, M. (2008). Ontologies in interactive systems. In *Proceedings of the 1st International Workshop on Ontologies in Interactive Systems* (pp. 3–6).

Burigat, S., & Chittaro, L. (2011). Pedestrian navigation with degraded GPS signal: investigating the effects of visualizing position uncertainty. In *Proceedings of the 13th International Conference on Human Computer Interaction with Mobile Devices and Services* (pp. 221–230).

Cheng, Y.-C., Chawathe, Y., LaMarca, A., & Krumm, J. (2005). Accuracy characterization for metropolitan-scale Wi-Fi localization. In *Proceedings of the 3rd International Conference on Mobile Systems, Applications and Services* (pp. 233–245).

Consolvo, S., Harrison, B., Smith, I., Chen, M., Everitt, K., Froelich, J., & Landay, J. (2007). Conducting in situ evaluations for and with ubiquitous computing technologies. *International Journal of Human-Computer Interaction, 22*(1–2), 103–118.

Coronato, A., Esposito, M., & Pietro, G. (2009). A multimodal semantic location service for intelligent environments: an application for smart hospitals. *Personal and Ubiquitous Computing, 13*(7), 527–538. doi:10.1007/s00779-009-0223-x

Dearman, D., Varshavsky, A., de Lara, E., & Truong, K. N. (2007). An exploration of location error estimation. In *Proceedings of the 9th International Conference on Ubiquitous Computing* (pp. 181–198).

Dey, A., Hightower, J., de Lara, E., & Davies, N. (2010). Location-based services. *IEEE Pervasive Computing / IEEE Computer Society [and] IEEE Communications Society, 9*(1), 11–12. doi:10.1109/MPRV.2010.10

Gellersen, H., Lukowicz, P., Beigl, M., & Riedel, T. (2010). Cooperative relative positioning. *IEEE Pervasive Computing / IEEE Computer Society [and] IEEE Communications Society, 9*(4), 78–89. doi:10.1109/MPRV.2010.18

Girardin, F. (2007). Bridging the social-technical gap in location-aware computing. In *Proceedings of the 25th Conference on Human Factors in Computing Systems Extended Abstracts* (pp. 1653–1656).

Hansen, R., Wind, R., Jensen, C. S., & Thomsen, B. (2009). Seamless indoor/outdoor positioning handover for location-based services in Streamspin. In *Proceedings of the 10th International Conference on Mobile Data Management* (pp. 267–272).

LaMarca, A., Chawathe, Y., Consolvo, S., Hightower, J., Smith, I., Scott, J., et al. (2005). Place Lab: device positioning using radio beacons in the wild. In *Proceedings of the 3rd International Conference on Pervasive Computing* (pp. 116–133).

Lemelson, H., King, T., & Effelsberg, W. (2008). A study on user acceptance of error visualization techniques. In *Proceedings of the International Workshop on Human Control of Ubiquitous Systems*.

Lemelson, H., Kjærgaard, M. B., Hansen, R., & King, T. (2009). Error estimation for indoor 802.11 location fingerprinting. In *Proceedings of the 4th International Symposium on Location and Context Awareness* (pp. 138–155).

Massink, M., & Faconti, G. (2002). A reference framework for continuous interaction. *Universal Access in the Information Society, 1*(4), 237–251. doi:10.1007/s10209-002-0027-5

Niu, W., & Kay, J. (2008). Location conflict resolution with an ontology. In *Proceedings of the 6th International Conference on Pervasive Computing* (pp. 162–179).

Opperman, L., Broll, G., Capra, M., & Benford, S. (2006). Extending authorizing tools for location-aware applications with an infrastructure visualization layer. In *Proceedings of the 8th International Conference on Ubiquitous Computing* (pp. 52–68).

Patel, S. N., Kientz, J. A., & Gupta, S. (2010). Studying the use and utility of an indoor location tracking system for non-experts. In *Proceedings of the 8th International Conference on Pervasive Computing* (pp. 228–245).

Ranganathan, A., Al-Muhtadi, J., Chetan, S., Campbell, R., & Mickunas, M. D. (2004). MiddleWhere: a middleware for location-awareness in ubiquitous computing applications. In *Proceedings of the 5th International Conference on Middleware* (pp. 397–416).

Reilly, D., Dearman, D., Ha, V., Smith, I., & Inkpen, K. (2006). "Need to know": examining information need in location discourse. In *Proceedings of the 4th International Conference on Pervasive Computing* (pp. 33–49).

Seager, W., & Stanton Fraser, D. (2007). Comparing physical, automatic and manual map rotation for pedestrian navigation. In *Proceedings of the 25th Conference on Human Factors in Computing Systems* (pp. 767–776).

Stevenson, G., Ye, J., Dobson, S., & Nixon, P. (2010). LOC8: A location model and extensible framework for programming with location. *IEEE Pervasive Computing / IEEE Computer Society [and] IEEE Communications Society, 9*(1), 28–37. doi:10.1109/MPRV.2009.90

Strobbe, M., Van Laere, O., Ongenae, F., Dauwe, S., Dhoedt, B., & De Turck, F., Demeester, P., & Luyten, K (in press). Integrating location and context information for novel personalised applications. *IEEE Pervasive Computing / IEEE Computer Society [and] IEEE Communications Society*.

Vanderhulst, G., Luyten, K., & Coninx, K. (2007). Middleware for ubiquitous service-oriented spaces on the web. In *Proceedings of the 21st International Conference on Advanced Information Networking and Applications Workshops* (pp. 1001–1006).

Varshavsky, A., & Patel, S. (2009). Location in ubiquitous computing. In Krumm, J. (Ed.), *Ubiquitous computing fundamentals* (pp. 285–320). Boca Raton, FL: Chapman and Hall/CRC.

This work was previously published in the International Journal of Information Technology and Web Engineering (IJITWE), Volume 6, Issue 4, edited by Ghazi I. Alkhatib and Ernesto Damiani, pp. 20-34, copyright 2011 by IGI Publishing (an imprint of IGI Global).

Section 3
Web-Based Applications

Chapter 11
Towards a Flexible and Adaptable Modeling of Business Processes

Khadhir Bekki
Ibn Khaldoune University, Algeria

Hafida Belachir
Boudiaf University, Algeria

ABSTRACT

This article proposes a flexible way in business process modeling and managing. Today, business process needs to be more flexible and adaptable. The regulations and policies in organizations, as origins of change, are often expressed in terms of business rules. The ECA (Event-condition-action) rule is a popular way to incorporate flexibility into a process design. To raise the flexibility in the business processes, the authors consider governing any business activity through ECA rules based on business rules. For adaptability, the separation of concerns supports adaptation in several ways. To cope with flexibility and adaptability, the authors propose a new multi concern rule based model. For each concern, each business rule is formalized using their CECAPENETE formalism (Concern -Event-Condition-Action-Post condition- check Execution- Number of check -Else-Trigger-else Event). Then, the rules based process is translated into a graph of rules that is analyzed in terms of relations between concerns, reliably and flexibility.

INTRODUCTION

Service-oriented architecture (SOA) with its enabling Web Services is currently offering best technological solutions to distributed and loosely-coupled cross-organizational business applications (Papazoglou, 2007). Web-services are explicit computational units, which can through their interfaces be universally described, published and more importantly (dynamically) composed using XML-based standards (e.g., WSDL, UDDI, BPEL4WS, WS-CDL) (Alonso, 2004). As these standards are maturing, more and more world-wide cross-organizations are opting for service

DOI: 10.4018/978-1-4666-2157-2.ch011

oriented solutions. Consequently, all capabilities and limitations of this new paradigm are being at proof towards developing realistic service-driven applications. Adaptability and correctness, besides knowledge-intensiveness belong to the most challenging issues (Papazoglou, 2008). Indeed, whereas WSDL and BPEL are inherently static and manual, but realistic services are deemed to be highly adaptive and evolving.

The BPEL language does not provide any support for the specification of either authorization policies or authorization constraints on the execution of activities composing a business process (Bertino, 2006). It is important that such an authorization model be high-level and expressed in terms of entities that are relevant from the organizational perspective (Bertino, 2006).

The regulations and policies in organizations are often expressed in terms of business rules that are sometimes defined as high-level structured statements that constrain, control, and influence the business logic (Business Rules Group, 2005). Business Rules Group (2005) defines the business rules that are "the set of policies for regulating the whole business within and out-side an organization." They represent main driving force for adaptability and competitiveness.

The ECA pattern has been widely adopted for business rules (Wan-Kadir, 2003). They are an interest way to incorporate flexibility into a process design. And, they are a popular approach to catch unanticipated events and adapt to exceptions (Ahn, 2000).

Separation of concerns provides a way to separate development of the functionality and the crosscutting concerns (e.g., quality of service, security). This principle has become one of the cornerstone principles in software engineering, and has lead to a wide spread of aspect-oriented programming (AOP) approach (Kazhamiakin, 2010).

The advantages in addressing each concern separately are transparency, evolution, understandability and scalability. More, it is necessary

to bring them together to understand which global system properties emerge at any given activity (Aoumeur, 2009).

In order to incorporate flexibility and adaptability into a business process design, and benefit of the advantages of separation of two concerns: security and interaction in business process modeling, we propose, in this paper, a new rule-based model that wants to improve the flexibility, adaptability and verification of business process.

For each concern (security or interaction), we govern any business activity through our CECAP-ENETE formalism (Concern -Event-Condition-Action-Post condition- check Execution- Number of check -Else-Trigger-else Event) based on business rules. We study the relationships between the rules of the same concern and between the rules of the different concerns. Based on these relationships, we translate the rules based process into a graph of rules. The analysis of this graph allows managing the change on the rules, to identify risks of exceptions at verification step and managing these exceptions at execution step.

The work in reference (Boukhebouze, 2010) provides a useful inspiration for our work, but it doesn't support the multi concerns. It governs the business rules on one view and doesn't discuss risks of security concern like deny of service. It also does not support the intervention of designer to mark some risks of exceptions in modeling step which it is necessary, in some cases, to perform the execution of business process.

The rest of this paper is organized as follows. In the second section, we present our new multi-concern rules based model. The third section explains the management of flexibility in process multi-concern modeling. In the fourth section, we discuss the healing of exceptions in the rules based process. We give a related work and finally, wrap up by some concluding remarks and further required extensions of this work.

MULTI CONCERN RULES BASED MODELING OF BUSINESS PROCESS

Definition

Business rules are considered policies, laws and know-how for doing business in any cross-organizations. The Business process is defined as set of rules and their sequence describe the behavior of the process.

Governing the business rules as ECA rules with separation of concerns have many benefits including (Aoumeur, 2009) (1) the inherent ability of adapting any concern rules before imposing them on running services or components; (2) the promotion of understandability of each concern in isolation and then the study of the coherent composition.

To cope with flexibility, adaptability and separation of the concerns: interaction and security, we propose the formalism CECAPENETE to govern business rules as follows:

TYPE	Concern
On	Event
IF	Condition
DO	Action
CHECK	Post Condition
POINT	Execution check
NB	Number of action repetition
Else	Else action
Post Event	Trigger
Else event	else Event

Its semantics is: for each concern (C) when the event (E) occurs, the activated rule evaluates the condition (C). The condition is either a Boolean expression or a SQL query on the database. If the condition is satisfied, the action (A) is executed. If not, the Else action (E) is executed. Action is either a database operation or an arbitrary application program that is executed. The validation of the

rule depends of the Post condition (P). The rule is validated only if the post condition is true. If this condition is false, the action may be repeated until NB (N) times, if the post condition still false. If after NB(N) times, the post condition still false, so the Else action will executed. The events triggered (T) (post events, else Events) design the set of events raised after the execution of the actions (Action, Else action).

Example

In order to give an intuitive idea about our approach, let us consider the following scenario, inspired from Boukhebouze (2010). Upon receipt of customer order, the calculation of the initial price of the order and shipper selection is done simultaneously. When both tasks are complete, a purchase order is sent to the costumer. In case of acceptance, a bill is sent back to the customer. Finally, the bill is registered. Four constraints exist in this scenario: 03 security constraints and 01 interaction constraint. The security constraints are: 1) the client must be authenticated in the company system to control purchases. 2) The client must be authenticated in bank system to do banking. 3) If the amount of the bill exceeds some value m, the client must have an authorization to pay bill. The interaction constraint is that the bill payments must be made 15 days before the delivery date. Figure 1 shows the modeling of this example.

This model represents the business process of the purchase order process as set of CECAPENETE rules. The business rules are governed separately on two views or concerns. The security view and the interaction view. The separation of concerns promotes the understandability of each concern in isolation. For example, the rules R2, R9, R12, R13, and R14 are of security concerns that govern security constraints. These rules may be modeled and handled by a security expert designer, independently of other concerns. The rest of rules may be modeled and handled by an interaction expert designer. The three rules R2

Figure 1. CECAPENETE rules set of purchase order process

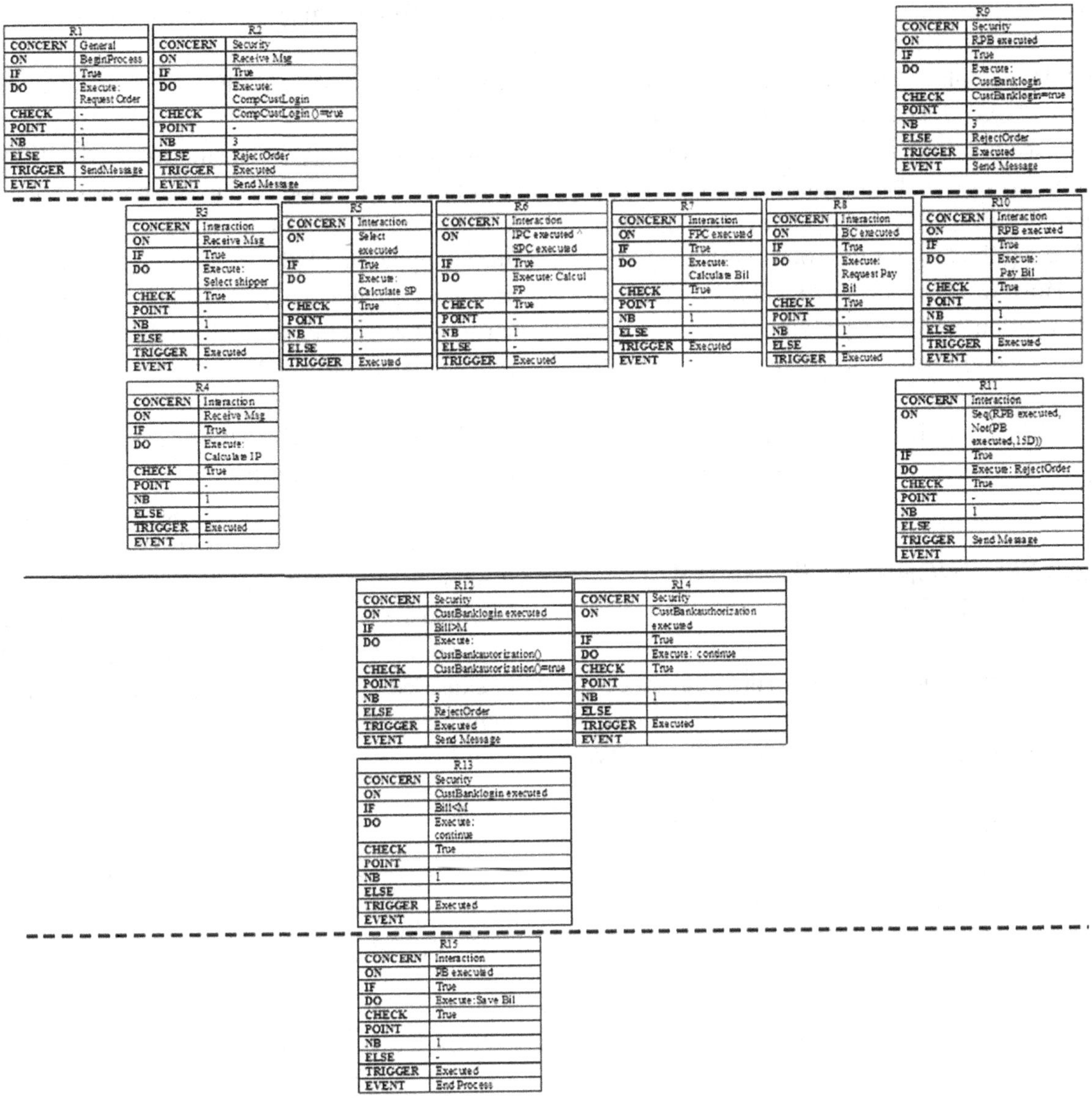

R1

CONCERN	General
ON	BeginProcess
IF	True
DO	Execute: Request Order
CHECK POINT	-
NB	1
ELSE	-
TRIGGER	SendMessage
EVENT	-

R2

CONCERN	Security
ON	Receive Msg
IF	True
DO	Execute: CompCustLogin
CHECK POINT	CompCustLogin ()=true
NB	3
ELSE	RejectOrder
TRIGGER	Executed
EVENT	Send Message

R9

CONCERN	Security
ON	RPB executed
IF	True
DO	Execute: CustBanklogin
CHECK POINT	CustBanklogin=true
NB	3
ELSE	RejectOrder
TRIGGER	Executed
EVENT	Send Message

R3

CONCERN	Interaction
ON	Receive Msg executed
IF	True
DO	Execute: Select shipper
CHECK POINT	True
NB	1
ELSE	-
TRIGGER	Executed
EVENT	-

R5

CONCERN	Interaction
ON	Select executed
IF	True
DO	Execute: Calculate SP
CHECK POINT	True
NB	1
ELSE	-
TRIGGER	Executed

R6

CONCERN	Interaction
ON	IPC executed ^ SPC executed
IF	True
DO	Execute: Calcul FP
CHECK POINT	True
NB	1
ELSE	-
TRIGGER	Executed

R7

CONCERN	Interaction
ON	FPC executed
IF	True
DO	Execute: Calculate Bil
CHECK POINT	True
NB	1
ELSE	-
TRIGGER	Executed
EVENT	-

R8

CONCERN	Interaction
ON	BC executed
IF	True
DO	Execute: Request Pay Bil
CHECK POINT	True
NB	1
ELSE	-
TRIGGER	Executed

R10

CONCERN	Interaction
ON	RPB executed
IF	True
DO	Execute: Pay Bil
CHECK POINT	True
NB	1
ELSE	-
TRIGGER	Executed
EVENT	-

R4

CONCERN	Interaction
ON	Receive Msg
IF	True
DO	Execute: Calculate IP
CHECK POINT	True
NB	1
ELSE	-
TRIGGER	Executed
EVENT	-

R11

CONCERN	Interaction
ON	Seq(RPB executed, Not(PB executed,15D))
IF	True
DO	Execute: RejectOrder
CHECK POINT	True
NB	1
ELSE	-
TRIGGER	Send Message
EVENT	

R12

CONCERN	Security
ON	CustBanklogin executed
IF	Bill>M
DO	Execute: CustBankautorization()
CHECK POINT	CustBankautorization()=true
NB	3
ELSE	RejectOrder
TRIGGER	Executed
EVENT	Send Message

R14

CONCERN	Security
ON	CustBankautorization executed
IF	True
DO	Execute: continue
CHECK POINT	True
NB	1
ELSE	
TRIGGER	Executed
EVENT	

R13

CONCERN	Security
ON	CustBanklogin executed
IF	Bill<M
DO	Execute: continue
CHECK POINT	True
NB	1
ELSE	
TRIGGER	Executed
EVENT	

R15

CONCERN	Interaction
ON	PB executed
IF	True
DO	Execute: Save Bil
CHECK POINT	True
NB	1
ELSE	-
TRIGGER	Executed
EVENT	End Process

(policy of Company customer login) R3 (policy of initial price calculation), R4 (policy of shipper selection) have the same event to be activated. It is "begin process" event that represents customer order (it may be, for example, clicking on the button "Place an order"). However, they can't be activated at the same time, because they are of two different concerns. The security concern has more priority. In result, the rule R2 is activated before the rules R3 and R4. More, the rules R3 and R4 cannot be activated if the R2 is not activated successfully or not validated. In other words, the condition and post condition of the R2 must be satisfied. If not, the order will be rejected, so, it will be useless to activate the rules R3 and R4. In a positive case, R3 and R4 will be activated in the same time, because they are of the same concern. In turn, the execution of these rules actions actives another rules. And so on, until the end of process rules set.

So, the business process of the purchase order in this example is governed in a flexible way as a set of ECAPNETE rules divided on two concerns: security concern and interaction concern. A flexibility way mean that we can implement changes in some rules (parts of a business process) without affecting the rest of rules (other parts).

How to manage this flexibility? What are the relationships between the rules of the same concern, and the rules of different concerns? How to recognize and heal the functional exceptions in rules based process? Some answers for these questions are given in the next sections.

MULTI CONCERN FLEXIBILITY MANAGEMENT

To automate the management of the multi concern rules based modeling of business process; we need to study the relationships between the rules. We study the relationships between rules of the same concern and between rules of different concerns.

Relationships between Rules of the Same Concern

Based on Boukhebouze (2010), we identify three relationships between business rules of the same concern.

Inclusion Relationship

It means that a rule (base rule) includes the functionality of another rule (inclusion rule). In other words, the completion of the base rule's action requires the completion of the inclusion rule's action.

For instance, in our example, on interaction concern, the shipping price must be calculated before to calculate the final price. On security concern, to have authorization of bank to pay a bill greater than an amount M, customer bank authentication is required. See Figure 2.

Extension Relationship

It means that a rule (extension rule) extends the functionality of another rule (base rule). So, the completion of the extend rule's action achieves the completion of the base rule's action. For instance, on interaction concern, a loyal bank customer can withdraw with credit, if he has not enough to pay the bill. So, a new credit rule R16 is added. As a consequence, there is an extension relationship between R10 (pay bill) and R16 (rule of withdrawal with credit).

On security concern, we suppose that if a consumer has forgotten his password and he cannot login in the company system, so he will be asked to give secret information. As result, the new rule R17 (verification forgetting password) is extended by the rule R2 (company customer login). See Figure 3.

Figure 2. Inclusion relationships

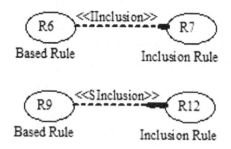

Figure 3. Extension relationship

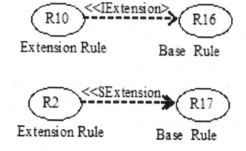

Cause/Effect Relationship

It means that a rule (cause rule) activates another rule (effect rule). So, the execution of the cause rule will activate the effect rule. For example, on interaction concern, the rule R1 (begin of process) activates the rule R3 (select shipper). On security concern, the rule R9 (customer bank login) activate the rule R12 (customer bank authorization)

The I-cause/effect relationship is between tow interaction rules. And, the cause/effect relationship is between two security rules. For an example see Figure 4.

Relationships between Rules of Different Concerns

In this topic, there is only the cause/effect relationship between rules. We distinguish two kinds of this relation.

The IS cause/effect relationship that Interaction rule activates a security rule. For an example see Figure 5.

The SI Cause/effect relationship is that a Security rule activates an interaction rule.

If an interaction rule has an I-cause/effect relation with an interaction effect rules and have a IS cause/effect with a security effect rule, so the security one has a SI Cause/effect with these effect interaction rules, if the action executed of the security rule is executed successfully(or execute continue action). If not, the security rules activated (directly or by transitivity) by this security rule and their action executed is "continue", have SI Cause/effect relation with these interaction effect rules.

In other words, these interaction effect rules cannot be activated if there is not "continue" action executed by the security effect rules. For an example see Figure 6.

Based on Boukhebouze (2010), we define a graph rule of the business process in order to formalize the flexibility management of a process model and its influence on the process model.

The vertices of this graph represent the business rules, and arcs represent the relationships between the various rules. We define the graph of rules formally as follows:

Figure 6. SI cause/effect relationship

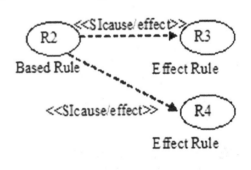

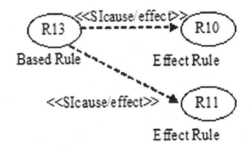

Figure 4. Cause/effect relationship

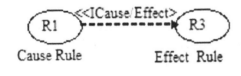

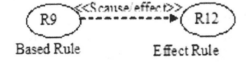

Figure 5. Extension relationship

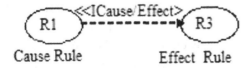

Definition 1: A graph of rules is a directed graph Gr (R, Y) with:

- R is a set of vertices that represent business rules.
- Y is a set of arcs that represent three kinds of relationships.
- Y_i is a sub set of Y such that if y_i (r_i, r_j) then r_i is included in r_j and both r_i, r_j are of the same concern.
- Y_e is a sub set of Y such that if y_e (r_i, r_j) then r_i extend r_j and both r_i, r_j are of the same concern.
- Y_{sc} is a sub set of Y such that if y_{sc} (r_i, r_j) then r_i activate r_j and both r_i, r_j are of the security concern.
- Y_{isc} is a sub set of Y such that if y_{isc} (r_i, r_j) then r_i activate r_j (SI cause relationship) and r_i is of interaction concern and r_j is of the security concern.
- Y_{sic} is a sub set of Y such that if y_{sic} (r_i, r_j) then r_i activate r_j (SI cause relationship) and r_i is of security concern and r_j is of the interaction concern.
- Y_{ic} is a sub set of Y such that if y_{ic} (r_i, r_j) then r_i activate r_j (I-cause relationship) and both r_i, r_j are of interaction concern, but it doesn't exist $y_{isc}(r_i, r_k)$ witch r_k is of security concern.

The graph of rules aims to determine which rules are impacted by the change of such a rule. A cause/effect graph is given in the next section.

EXCEPTIONS HEALING OF BUSINESS PROCESS

The exceptions healing of the business process means that detecting the functional errors on the process and the risks on changing rules. These risks may be exceptions raised at runtime, like infinite loop, process non-termination, and services deny.

In order to ensure the reliability of a business process through exceptions healing, we try to recognize the exceptions at modeling time and after modeling time. The detecting of errors early is useful for designers to verify their modeling at high level. However, the identification of functional errors should have a process data state and an execution scenario. But, it is often difficult to have such information at the modeling time (Boukhebouze, 2010).

To verify functioning of the business process after modeling step, we use a cause/effect sub-graph of rules graph (Boukhebouze, 2010), this sub graph is selected because it represents how the process rules set is activated, and formalize the process functioning.

To determine an error as infinite loop, for example, which puts a process in an endless state, we search a circuit in this sub-graph.

If rule R12 of security concern, in the previous example, is modified to allow customers to change their order if they have not the bank authorization (Figure 1), then the new rule R9 will rerun the process by activating rule R2. So, the new the cause/effect sub-graph resembles Figure 7.

This cause/effect sub-graph contains two circuits (R2, R3, R5, R6, R7, R8, R9, R12) and (R2, R4, R6, R7, R8, R9, R12). Each circuit represents a loop in the process and it may be infinite. We note that we can't determine whether circuit can be terminated, because we haven't a data state in modeling step (Boukhebouze, 2010). But, each circuit represents a risk of infinite loop to verify in the execution step.

Boukhebouze (2010) uses automatic exceptions recognition in order to assure the self healing of business process. But, in this paper, we use both manual and automatic exceptions recognition. We argue that in the manual one the modeler can help to identify or determine some risks of exceptions on the business process. For example, R2 and R9 are two rules of authentication. R2 is the rule to login on the company system; R9 is the rule to login on the bank system. The risk of services deny can occur on the two systems. This may be detected at run time, if there is lot of suc-

Figure 7. Extension relationship

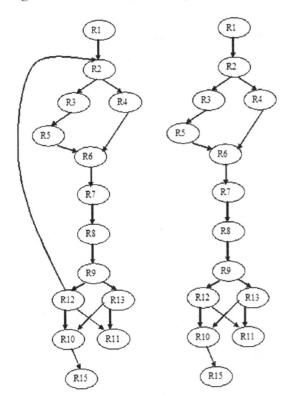

cessive logins failed. But, it can't be detected in automatic exception handling step. For business process performance requirements, the modeler can help to determine the login rules which represent the most risk of service deny. For example, the modeler can recognize that the bank system represent the risk of service deny more then the company system.

The exception handling is done to handle the risks of exceptions detected on previous step. The aim of exception handling step is to monitor the business process at run time on the parts which can eventually cause such exceptions, in order to avoid unstable situation and how to react to compensate them. We adopt the exception handling given in Boukhebouze (2010) but with some main differences.

In Boukhebouze (2010), the exception handling is launched in parallel with the execution of the process. Markers called check points are added to the rules process code, and they are also translated and added to the execution code.

In our paper, the exception handling is launched on two steps:

First, is in manual exceptions handling step at the modeling time, the modeler mark the process parts which may lead to an exceptions.

For this, we propose to use a special attribute in the CECAPENETE rule to mark the process. It is called execution check. This attribute can take the values as examples: deadlock, live lock, service deny, any… We use this attribute to allow the modeler to mark the exceptions identified by him. For example, R9 is marked in execution check attribute by the value service deny (Figure 8).

This may be detected at run time if there is lot of successive logins failed. But, at exception handling step, it can't detect this. For business process performance requirements, the modeler

Figure 8. Rules marked

R2	
CONCERN	Security
ON	Receive Msg
IF	True
DO	Execute: CompCustLogin
CHECK	CompCustLogin ()=true
POINT	Livelock
NB	3
ELSE	RejectOrder
TRIGGER	Executed
EVENT	Send Message

R9	
CONCERN	Security
ON	RPB executed
IF	True
DO	Execute: CustBanklogin
CHECK	CustBanklogin=true
POINT	Service Deny
NB	3
ELSE	RejectOrder
TRIGGER	Executed
EVENT	Send Message

can help to mark login rules which represent the most risk of service deny.

Second, in automatic exceptions handling step at run time, the recognition exception marks the process parts, which will likely lead to exceptions with the appropriate value in the execution check attribute. If both manual and automatic exception handling mark the same part of the process, so the same rule, which mark will be mentioned? Or, are all marks be mentioned? In what order the marks will be processed? This discussion is not scope of this paper. In a simplified way, the mark mentioned by the automatic exceptions handling overwrite the mark mentioned by the manual one.

RELATED WORK

Bertino (2006) believes that it is important to couple WS-BPEL with a model for expressing authorization policies and constraints, and a mechanism to enforce them. They see that it is important that such an authorization model be high-level and expressed in terms of entities that are relevant from the organizational perspective. They propose an extension of WS-BPEL syntax with an authorization model that also supports the specification of a large number of different types of constraints.

Sun (2009) proposed a flexible access control policiy through the use of three classes of restraint rules in active cooperation: authorization rules, assignment rules and activation rules. A restraint rule consists of prerequisite conditions and a consequence. Each condition is in form of one or more weighted atomic conditions combined through logic operation connectors.

To enable a dynamic business process management, the authorization policies in Cao (2009) are expressed in an SQL-like language which can be rewritten into query sentences for execution. The framework proposed supports dynamic integration and execution of multiple access control polices from disparate enterprise resources.

In order to support the authorization policy development, Bartsch (2008) introduce a simple and readable authorization rules language implemented in a Ruby on Rails (http://www.rubyon-rails.org) authorization plug-in that is employed in workflow application. Ruby on Rails is a Web development framework that supports agile development and draws from the meta-programming features of the programming language Ruby.

CONCLUSION AND FUTURE WORK

In this paper, we present a multi concern rules business process modeling. We are proposed a new ECA based rule to govern the business rules in multi-concerns. The approach is thoroughly illustrated using an order purchase example. For consolidating this promising and practical approach for dynamically and non-intrusively adapting software intensive applications at the high level, we may experiment it with more complex case-studies from the E-commerce world (e.g., an E-shopping application).

For operational formalization, we aim to transform this service architectural modeling for security concern to rewriting logic and its efficient MAUDE language.

REFERENCES

Ahn, G. J., Sandhu, R., Kang, M., & Park, J. (2000). Injecting RBAC to secure a web-based workflow system. In *Proceedings of the 5th ACM Workshop on Role-Based Access Control* (pp. 1-10).

Alonso, G., Casati, F., Kuno, H., & Machiraju, V. (2004). *Web services*. Berlin, Germany: Springer-Verlag.

Aoumeur, N., Barkaoui, K., & Saake, G. (2009). A multi-dimensional architectural approach to behavior-intensive adaptive pervasive applications. In *Proceedings of the 4th International Conference on Wireless Pervasive Computing* (pp. 1-8).

Bartsch, S., Sohr, K., & Bormann, K. (2008, November 13-16). Supporting agile development of authorization rules for SME applications. In *Proceedings of the 4th International Conference on Collaborative Computing: Networking, Applications and Worksharing*, Orlando, FL.

Bertino, E., Crampton, J., & Paci, F. (2006). Access control and authorization constraints for WS-BPEL. In *Proceedings of the IEEE International Conference on Web Services* (pp. 275-284).

Boukhebouze, M., Amghar, Y., Benharkat, A., & Maamar, Z. (2010). Rule-based approach to model and verify flexible business processes. *International Journal of Business Process Integration and Management.*

Business Rules Group. (2005). *Defining business rules - What are they really?* Retrieved from http://www.businessrulesgroup.org

Cao, J., Chen, J., Zhao, H., & Li, M. (2009). A policy-based authorization model for workflow-enabled dynamic process management. *Journal of Network and Computer Applications, 32*(2), 412–422. doi:10.1016/j.jnca.2008.02.021

Kazhamiakin, R., Benbernou, S., Baresi, L., Plebani, P. M., & Barai, O. (2010). Adaptation of service-based systems service research challenges and solutions for the future internet. In Papazoglou, M., Pohl, K., Parkin, M., & Metzger, A. (Eds.), *Service research challenges and solutions for the future internet: S-cube - towards engineering, managing and adapting service-based systems.* Berlin, Germany: Springer-Verlag.

Papazoglou, M. P. (2007). *Web service: Principle and technology.* Upper Saddle River, NJ: Prentice Hall.

Papazoglou, M. P., Traverso, P., Dustdar, S., & Leymann, F. (2008). Service-oriented computing: A research roadmap. *International Journal of Cooperative Information Systems, 17*(2), 223–255. doi:10.1142/S0218843008001816

Sun, Y., Gong, B., Meng, X., Lin, Z., & Bertino, E. (2009). Specification and enforcement of flexible security policy for active cooperation. *Information Sciences: An International Journal, 179*(15), 2629–2642.

Wan-Kadir, W. M. N., & Loucopoulos, P. (2003). Relating evolving business rules to software design. *Journal of Systems Architecture, 50*(7).

This work was previously published in the International Journal of Information Technology and Web Engineering (IJITWE), Volume 6, Issue 2, edited by Ghazi I. Alkhatib and Ernesto Damiani, pp. 57-67, copyright 2011 by IGI Publishing (an imprint of IGI Global).

Chapter 12

An Experimental Study for the Effect of Stop Words Elimination for Arabic Text Classification Algorithms

Bassam Al-Shargabi
Isra University, Jordan

Fekry Olayah
Isra University, Jordan

Waseem AL Romimah
University of Science and Technology, Yemen

ABSTRACT

In this paper, an experimental study was conducted on three techniques for Arabic text classification. These techniques are Support Vector Machine (SVM) with Sequential Minimal Optimization (SMO), Naïve Bayesian (NB), and J48. The paper assesses the accuracy for each classifier and determines which classifier is more accurate for Arabic text classification based on stop words elimination. The accuracy for each classifier is measured by Percentage split method (holdout), and K-fold cross validation methods, along with the time needed to classify Arabic text. The results show that the SMO classifier achieves the highest accuracy and the lowest error rate, and shows that the time needed to build the SMO model is much lower compared to other classification techniques.

INTRODUCTION

Text classification (TC) is the process of classifying documents into a predefined set of categories based on the content of documents. Arabic is a greatly inflectional and derivational language which makes text and web mining a difficult task. The organization of text in categories allow the user to limit the target of a search submitted to information retrieval systems, to explore the collection and to find relevant information they need with poor knowledge about the keywords

DOI: 10.4018/978-1-4666-2157-2.ch012

of a theme (Al-Harbi, Almuhareb, Al-Thubaity, Khorsheed, & Al-Rajeh, 2008).

The aim of the classification techniques is to minimize information loss while maximizing reduction in dimensionality. The set of documents to be categorized must transformed into a set of feature vectors in a relatively low dimensional feature space. The set of reduced feature vectors is then fed to the text classifier as input. The SMO and NB classifier must be trained before it can be used for text categorization. The neural network is used to train classifier using the back propagation learning rule based on supervised learning. A set of training documents along with a set of pre-defined categories that documents belong to are required.

However, in Arabic language there is a very limited work in automatic classification. Classifying Arabic text is different than classifying English language because Arabic is a highly inflectional and derivational language which makes monophonical analysis a very complex task (Al-Shalabi, Kanaan, Jaam, Hasnah, & Hilat, 2004; Sawaf, Zaplo, & Ney, 2001).

Few researches tackled the area of Arabic text classification. A statistical method called maximum entropy is used to classify Arabic News articles (El Kourdi, Bensaid, & Rachidi, 2004). Another statistical classifier based on NB used to categorize Arabic web documents using the root based stemmer to extract the roots of the words (Al-Shalabi, Kanaan, Jaam, Hasnah, & Hilat, 2004). Although in Gharib and Badieh (2009) they used SVM to classify Arabic text and compared result with K-Nearest Neighbor classifier.

In this paper we compared the accuracy of three classifiers along with studying the effects of elimination of stop word for Arabic text. The first classifier is support vector machine (SMO) with sequential minimal optimization (SMO), Naïve Bayesian (NV), and J48. A standard Arabic data set was used to test the above techniques.

The rest of the paper organized as follows: First we discuss preprocessing of Arabic text document and introduce proposed comparative process for the three classifying techniques used in this paper. Next, we present Experimental results and discussions, and finally conclusion is presented.

PREPROCESSING AND CLASSIFICATION PROCESS

The preprocessing of data set deals with the elimination of non-meaningful words which do not indicate semantic content of the document. Some words appear in the sentences and don't have any meaning or indications about the content such as (بالنسبة for, تأكيدا confirmation, بالإشارة with, لذلك so) or appearing frequently in the document like pronouns such as (هو he, هي she, هم they). Although the prepositions like (من from, إلى to, في in, عن about) or demonstratives like (هذا this, هؤلاء these, there أولئك) or interrogatives like (أين where, أي which, من who). These words may have a bad effect on statistical information and co-occurrence of the words as stated in Abo Alkhair (2006) and Said, Wanas, Darwish, and Hegazy (2009).

Also the numbers and symbols like (@, #, &, %, *) and some words that indicates a sequence of the sentences like (أولا firstly, ثانيا secondly, ثالثا thirdly), these words will be considered as an Arabic stop words. Some Arabic documents may contain foreign words, especially science documents, these words are alo considered as stop words as in Al-Shalabi, Kanaan, Jaam, Hasnah, and Hilat (2004) and El-Kourdi, Bensaid and Rachidi (2004).

In fact, a word which occurs in 80% of the documents in the collection is useless for purposes of retrieval. Such words are frequently referred to as stop words and are normally filtered out as potential index terms. Articles, prepositions, and conjunctions are natural candidates for a list of stop words. Elimination of stop words has an additional important benefit. It reduces the size of the indexing structure considerably. In fact, it is typical to obtain a compression in the size of the indexing structure of 40% or more solely with the elimination of stop words. Despite these benefit, elimination of stop words might reduce recall (Al-Shalabi, Kanaan, Jaam, Hasnah, & Hilat, 2004; El-Kourdi, Bensaid, & Rachidi, 2004). For instance, consider a user who is looking for documents containing the phrase 'من فيها ما فيها و الاسرار' Elimination of stop words might leave only the term 'الاسرار' making It almost impossible to properly recognize the documents which contain the phrase specified.

The next step as illustrated in Figure 1 is to match the words in each sentence to a predefined database contains about 1,040 stop words, if there is a match, the word will be deleted, if no match is found the word will stay in the sentence and moved to the next step. After removing all the above types of stop words, we have pure sentences with meaningful words and from these sentences the system will extract candidate keywords.

The approach as presented in Figure 1 is to teach classifier algorithm which document contents are associated to a category, By extracting the keywords that represent the syntactic of a document by feature of vector space techniques, then training the SMO, NB using back propagation feed forward using training set. The DF,TF_

IDF,CF is used to get the keyword document frequency which is equal to number of documents that the keyword appear in it. TF-IDF is used to get the keyword term frequency which is equal to number of term that appear in one documents and inverse document frequency for all terms of document. CF used is to get the keyword category frequency which is equal to number of category that the keyword appears in it for all terms of each category. The more challenging component that is responsible for feature reduction is the keywords extractor, which is used to prepare the training set and testing set that will enter to each classifier (Mitchell, 1997; Rogati, & Yang, 2002). To classify a new document; the feed-forward classifier algorithm is used (Mena, Zaki, & Tarek, 2006; John, 1998; Evegniy, & Shaul, 2004) as shown in Figure 1.

EXPERMINTAL RESULTS AND DISCUSION

The Arabic data set contains 2,363 documents divided into six categories Sport, Economic, Medicine, Politic, Religion, and Science. All document already pre-classified collection of short articles.

Figure 1. Preprocessing and Arabic text classification approach

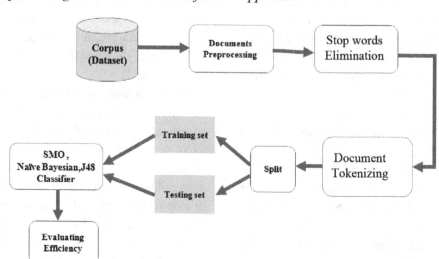

Each category among the six categories is treated as a binary classification task to evaluate the classifiers for each category separately as shown in Table 1. The experiments were conducted using Wakaito Environment for Knowledge Acquisition (WEKA) (Witten & Frank, 2005), where J48, NB, and SMO are already implemented.

The dataset was tested using percentage split method (holdout), where 60% of the data were used as training and the remaining 40% were used as testing.

K-fold cross validation methods. The data set divided into 10 fold, each fold is used as testing and the remaining folds are used as training set. The results of accuracy and error rate for the three classifiers: SMO (SVM) (John, 1998), NB and J48 as before the elimination of stop word as shown in Table 2.

Accuracy and Error rate using percentage split method for SMO (SVM) classifier achieves the highest accuracy (94.8%) and the lowest error rate (5.2%) using percentage split. On the other hand the accuracy for J48 classifier is (89.42%), and error rate (10.85). However, the NB classifier achieves the lowest accuracy (85.07%) and the highest error rate (14.92%) as illustrated in Figure 2.

Although, the Accuracy and Error rate using 10-folds cross validation: SMO classifiers achieve the highest accuracy (96.61%) compared to J48

Table 1. Documents per category in dataset

Category Name	Number of Documents
رياضة (Sport)	466
اقتصاد (Economic)	93
صحة (Medicine)	42
سياسة (Politic)	1040
دين (Religion)	324
علوم (Science)	391

Table 2. Accuracy and error rate before stop word elimination

	Accuracy			Error Rate		
	SMO	**NB**	**J48**	**SMO**	**NB**	**J48**
Percentage Split 60%	94.8	85.07	89.42	5.2	14.93	10.85
10 Folds CV	96.4	83.87	91.37	3.6	16.12	8.62

Figure 2. Accuracy and error rate using percentage split method

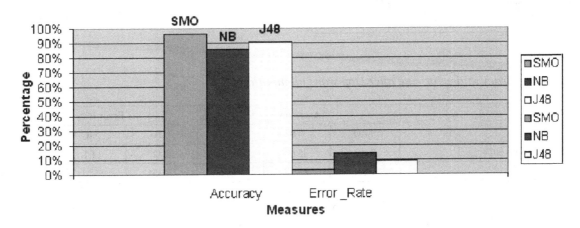

Figure 3. Accuracy and error rate using 10-folds cross validation

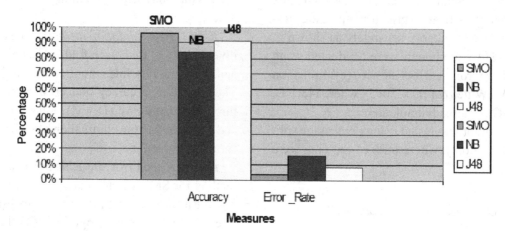

(91.37%), and NB achieves the lowest accuracy with (83.87%). While SMO achieved the lowest error rate (3.6%) compared to J48 (8.62%), and NB (16.12%) as illustrated in Figure 3.

Another measure used in this paper is the amount of time taken to build the models which used for testing the accuracy of the classifiers before stop words eliminations. As shown in Table 3, SMO and NB classifiers require a small amount of time to build the needed model for testing the accuracy of the classifier. On the other hand the J48 requires a more of time than SMO and NB.

Table 3. Time needed to build the models in seconds

	SMO	NB	J48
Percentage Split 60%	7.94	15.25	261.81
10 Folds CV	7.52	20.98	263.61

Accuracy and Error rate after stop word elimination: The results of accuracy and error rate measures obtained for the classifiers are as seen in Table 4. Time measure after stop words elimination used to measure is the amount of time taken to build the models, which used for testing the accuracy of the classifiers as shown in Table 5. The results for all classifiers were improved after the elimination of stop words, and SMO outperforms all classifiers with 5.2 seconds as training and Cross validation with 4.97 seconds

Finally, measuring the accuracy for all classification techniques used in this paper before and after removing stop words using precision and recall measures as illustrated in Figures 4 and 5. The recall and precision is improved after eliminating stop word for all document categories.

Table 4. Accuracy and error rate after stop word elimination

	Accuracy			Error Rate		
	SMO	**NB**	**J48**	**SMO**	**NB**	**J48**
Percentage Split 60%	96.08	85.60	90.48	3.42	14.4	9.52
10 Folds CV	96.64	83.79	90.9	3.35	16.21	9.1

Table 5. Time needed to build the models in seconds

	SMO	NB	J48
Percentage Split 60%	5.2	12.0	291.72
10 Folds CV	4.97	17.08	286.81

CONCLUSION

Several algorithms have been implemented to solve the problem of text categorization. Most of the work in this area was performing for the English text, while very few researches have been performing for the Arabic text. The study compares between three classification techniques for Arabic text. The results show that there are differences between the classifiers from three aspects (the accuracy, error rate, and time taken to build the classification model). The results show that SMO classifier achieves the highest accuracy and the lowest error rate. The second part of the results shows that the time needed to build the SMO model is smaller compared to the other techniques.

Figure 4. Effects on recall before and after stop word elimination

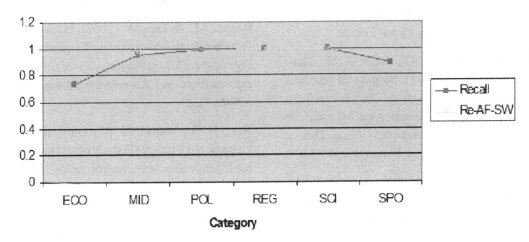

Figure 5. Effects on precision before and after stop word elimination

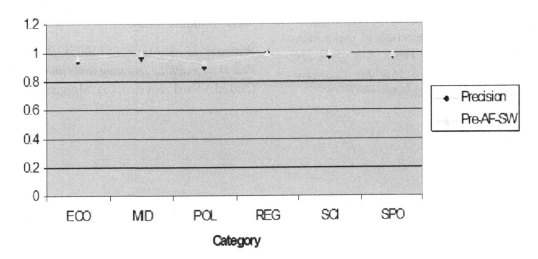

ACKNOWLEDGMENT

I would like to thank everyone who contributed to the completion of this work.

REFERENCES

Abo Alkhair, A. (2006). Effect of stop words removing for Arabic information retrieval. *International Journal of Computing &. Information Science, 4*(3).

Al-Harbi, S., Almuhareb, A., Al-Thubaity, A., Khorsheed, M. S., & Al-Rajeh, A. (2008). Automatic Arabic text classification. In *Proceedings of the 9th International Conference on the Statistical Analysis of Textual Data*, Lyon, France.

Al-Shalabi, R., Kanaan, G., Jaam, J. M., Hasnah, A., & Hilat, E. (2004). Stop-word removal algorithm for Arabic language. In *Proceedings of 1st International Conference on Information & Communication Technologies: From Theory to Applications*, Damascus, Syria (pp. 545-550).

El-Kourdi, M., Bensaid, A., & Rachidi, T. (2004). Automatic Arabic document categorization based on the Naïve Bayes algorithm. In *Proceedings of the 20th International Conference on Computational Linguistics*, Geneva, Switzerland.

Evegniy, G., & Shaul, M. (2004, July 4-8). Text classification with many redundant features: Using aggressive feature selection to make svms competitive with C4.5. In *Proceeding of the 21st International Conference Machine Learning*, Banff, AB, Canada (p. 41).

Gharib, T. F., & Badieh, H. M. (2009). Arabic text classification using support vector machines. *International Journal of Computers and their Applications, 16*(4), 192-199.

Mena, B. H., Zaki, T. F., & Tarek, F. G. (2006). A hybrid feature selection approach for Arabic documents classification. *Egyptian Computer Science Journal, 28*(4), 1–7.

Mitchell, T. (1997). *Machine learning.* New York, NY: McGraw-Hill.

Platt, J. C. (1998). *Sequential minimal optimization: A fast algorithm for training support vector machine* (Tech. Rep. No. MST-TR-98-14). Cambridge, UK: Microsoft Research.

Rogati, M., & Yang, Y. (2002). High-performing feature selection for text classification. In *Proceedings of the Eleventh International Conference on Information and Knowledge Management* (pp. 659-661).

Said, D. A., Wanas, N. M., Darwish, N. M., & Hegazy, N. H. (2009). A study of text preprocessing tools for Arabic text categorization. In *Proceedings of the Second International Conference on Arabic Language* (pp. 230-236).

Sawaf, H., Zaplo, J., & Ney, H. (2001). Statistical classification methods for Arabic news articles. In *Proceedings of the ACL/EACL Workshop on Arabic Language Processing: Status and Prospects*, Toulouse, France.

Witten, I. H., & Frank, E. (2005). *Data mining: Practical machine learning tools and techniques* (2nd ed.). San Francisco, CA: Morgan Kaufmann.

This work was previously published in the International Journal of Information Technology and Web Engineering (IJITWE), Volume 6, Issue 2, edited by Ghazi I. Alkhatib and Ernesto Damiani, pp. 68-75, copyright 2011 by IGI Publishing (an imprint of IGI Global).

Chapter 13
Productivity Evaluation of Self–Adaptive Software Model Driven Architecture

Basel Magableh
Trinity College Dublin, Ireland

Stephen Barrett
Trinity College Dublin, Ireland

ABSTRACT

Anticipating context changes using a model-based approach requires a formal procedure for analysing and modelling context-dependent functionality and stable description of the architecture which supports dynamic decision-making and architecture evolution. This article demonstrates the capabilities of the context-oriented component-based application model-driven architecture (COCA-MDA) to support the development of self-adaptive applications; the authors describe a state-of-the-art case study and evaluate the development effort involved in adopting the COCA-MDA in constructing the application. An intensive analysis of the application requirements simplified the process of modelling the application's behavioural model; therefore, instead of modelling several variation models, the developers modelled an extra-functionality model. COCA-MDA reduces the development effort because it maintains a clear separation of concerns and employs a decomposition mechanism to produce a context-oriented component model which decouples the applications' core functionality from the context-dependent functionality. Estimating the MDA approach's productivity can help the software developers select the best MDA-based methodology from the available solutions. Thus, counting the source line of code is not adequate for evaluating the development effort of the MDA-based methodology. Quantifying the maintenance adjustment factor of the new, adapted, and reused code is a better estimate of the development effort of the MDA approaches.

DOI: 10.4018/978-1-4666-2157-2.ch013

INTRODUCTION

Mobile computing environments are heterogeneous and dynamic. Everything from the devices used and resources available to network bandwidths and user context can change drastically at runtime (Belaramani, Wang, & Lau, 2003). This presents the software developers with the challenge of tailoring behavioural variations both to each specific user need and to the context information. Context-dependent behavioural variations can be seen as a collaboration of individual features expressed in requirements, design, and implementation. Before encapsulating the crosscutting context-dependent behaviours into a software module, the developers must first identify them both in the requirements document and in the software model. This is difficult to achieve because, by their nature, context-dependent behaviours are entangled with other behaviours, and are likely to be included in multiple parts (scattered) of the software modules. Using intuition or even domain knowledge is not necessarily sufficient for identifying the behavioural variations; instead, it requires a formal analysis procedure for the software requirements and a separation of their individual concerns. Moreover, a formal procedure for modelling these variations is needed. This kind of analysis and modelling procedure can reduce the complexity in modelling self-adaptive applications and encapsulate the context-dependent part of the distinct architecture module (component).

In this sense, a context oriented component model (COCA-component) (Magableh & Barrett, 2009) is used to encapsulate behavioural variations and decouple them from the application's core functionality. In this way, dynamic component composition is achieved. Additionally, from the software developer's perspective, it is vital to know the productivity of the development paradigm which might be used in constructing the self-adaptive application. Productivity evaluation of model-driven approaches can assist the developers in selecting among the proposed methodologies in

the literature which approach dynamic behavioural variations of self-adaptive software. Context-oriented component-based application-model-driven architecture (COCA-MDA) emerged as a development paradigm which facilitates the development of self-adaptive context-oriented software (Magableh & Barrett, 2011b, 2011c).

This article evaluates the development effort involved in adopting COCA-MDA when constructing a self-adaptive application for an indoor wayfinding application (IWayfinder) targeting individuals with cognitive impairments. The development effort of COCA-MDA is compared to other model-driven approaches proposed in the literature.

The remainder of the article is structured as follows. The next section provides a comparative analysis of related studies. A case study of a self-adaptive application is then demonstrated. The COCA-MDA phases are also described. The following section provides a COCA-MDA evaluation using constructive cost model II (COCOMO II). The last section summarizes the research findings and describes directions for future work.

RELATED WORK

In the literature, there are several MDA approaches which target the development of self-adaptive applications for mobile computing environments which produce component-based applications; this study borrows from the following methodologies: MUSIC, proposed by Wagner, Reichle, Khan, and Geihs (2011); U-MUSIC (Khan, 2010); and Paspallis MDA (Paspallis, 2009).

The MUSIC development methodology (Wagner et al., 2011) adopts a model-driven approach to constructing the application variability model. The applications are built as a component framework with component types as variation points. Middleware is used to resolve the variation points, which involves the election of a concrete component as a realization of the component type. Using this method, a number of application variants can automatically be derived.

The U-MUSIC methodology, proposed by Khan (2010), adopts the model-driven approach to constructing self-adaptive applications and enabling dynamic unanticipated adaptation based on a component model. The U-MUSIC system enables the developers to specify the application variability model, context elements, and data structure. The developers are able to model the component functionalities and quality of service (QoS) properties using an abstract, platform-independent model (PIM).

Paspallis (2009) proposes another MDA-based methodology which considers the context providers for the application. For each context provider, a plug-in is proposed during the design phase. At runtime, a utility function is used to consider the context state and perform decision-making. Once the plug-in is selected (to be load into the application), middleware support performs dynamic runtime loading of the plug-in. However, it is impossible to consider all the context providers which might produce context information at runtime.

In MUSIC, U-MUSIC, and Paspallis approaches, dynamic decision making is supported by a utility function. The utility function is defined as the weighted sum of the different objectives based on user preferences and QoS. However, this approach suffers from a number of drawbacks. First, it is well known that correct identification of the weight of each goal is a major difficulty. Second, the approach hides conflicts among multiple goals in a single, aggregate objective function, rather than exposing the conflicts and reasoning about them. At runtime, a utility function is used to select the best application variant; this is the so-called 'adaptation plan'. Potentially, it is impossible for the developer to predict all possible variations of the application when unanticipated conditions arise. In addition, mobile computing devices have limited resources for evaluating the many application variations at runtime and can

consume significant amounts of device resources. As an outcome, the benefit gained from the adaptation is negated by the overhead required to achieve the adaptation. Because of the above issue, it is impossible to use MUSIC to provide unanticipated adaptation in a self-adaptive application. Moreover, modelling the application using U-MUSIC, MUSIC, and Paspallis's MDA produces an architecture with a tight coupling between the architecture and the target platform.

Lewis and Wrage (2005) have evaluated the impact of MDA on the development effort and the learning curve of the MDA-based development tools based on their own experiences. The authors concluded that the real potential behind MDA is not completely supported either by current tools or by the proposed MDA approaches in the literature. In addition, the developers have to modify the generated code such that it is suitable for the target platform. The degree to which the generated code needs modification is affected by the MDA tools used. In the same way, the developer's understanding of the MDA tasks and familiarity with the target platform have direct impacts on MDA productivity. Constructive cost model II (COCOMO II) (Boehm et al., 2000) emerged as a software cost estimation model which considers the development methodology productivity. The productivity evaluates the quality of benefits derived from using the development methodology, in terms of its impact on the development time, complexity of implementation, code quality, and cost effectiveness (Calic, Dascalu, & Egbert, 2008). COCOMO II allows estimation of the effort, time, and cost required for software development. The main advantage of this model is that COCOMO II is an open model with various parameters which affect the estimation of the development effort. Moreover, the COCOMO II model allows estimation of the software application development effort in both person-months (PM) and time to develop (TDEV). A set of inputs such as software scale factors (SFs) and 17 effort multipliers is needed. A full description of these parameters can be found in Boehm et al. (2000). An example of an evaluation of MDA approaches with (COCOMO II) can be found in Achilleos (2010).

Self-Adaptive Indoor Wayfinding Application for Individuals with Cognitive Impairments

IWayFinder provides distributed cognition support for indoor navigation to persons with cognitive disabilities. RFID tags and QR-codes are placed at decision points such as hallway intersections, exits, elevators, and entrances to stairways. After reading the encoded URL in the QR-codes, the Cisco engine provides the required navigation information and instructs the user. The proposed self-adaptive application uses an augmented reality browser (ARB) to display the navigation directions. The browser displays the directions on the physical display of the tool's camera. The application is able to provide the user with time-based events such as the opening hours of the building, lunch time, closing hours of the offices, location access rights which control the entrance of users to certain locations, and any real-time alarm events. Moreover, the infrastructure support allows several persons to monitor and collaborate with the user en route. The IWayFinder application and the COCA-MDA development methodology were fully described in our previous work (Magableh & Barrett, 2011b, 2011c). This article focuses on describing an evaluation of the cost effectiveness when adopting the COCA-MDA (among other MDA approaches) in developing the IWayFinder application. Assuming that the context information is delivered by the Cisco infrastructure, we propose the following anticipation scenarios:

A1: Self-Tuning

The application must track the user's path inside the building. When decision points (DPs) are reached, the application places a marker for each DP the user passed. If the user is unable to locate

a decision point in the building, the application must be able to guide the user towards a safe exit. The route directions can be delivered to the user in several output formats: video, still images, and voice commands. The application should change the direction output while also considering the device resources and the level of cognitive impairment of the individual.

A2: Self-Recovering

Assuming that the user is trapped in a lift with no GPRS connection (or in the case of a fire), the fire alarm is raised, the application is notified, and the application adopts the shortest path to the nearest fire exit. In both cases, the application submits the user's current coordinates and an emergency help message to the emergency number, parents, career team, and security staff. The communication is achieved using the available connection, regardless of the resource cost, to alert any nearby devices to the emergent need for help. If no connection is made, the device emits an alarm sound and increases the device volume to maximum. The security staff or fire fighters receive the emergency message and can view the CCTV video to identify the floor on which the user is trapped. When the CCTV system locates the user, full information about the user is displayed, including a personal and health profile. At the same time, the application guides the user to a safe exit using a preloaded path (in case the CCTV camera is disabled and the services engine is off). Fire fighters can use the received message to locate the user in the building.

COCA-MDA Development Approach

The COCA-MDA follows the principles of the object management group (OMG) model-driven architecture. The design of a context-aware application according to the COCA-MDA approach generally involves the six phases shown in Figure 1. Modelling IWayfinder using COCA-MDA can

Figure 1. Context-oriented component-based application model-driven architecture (COCA-MDA)

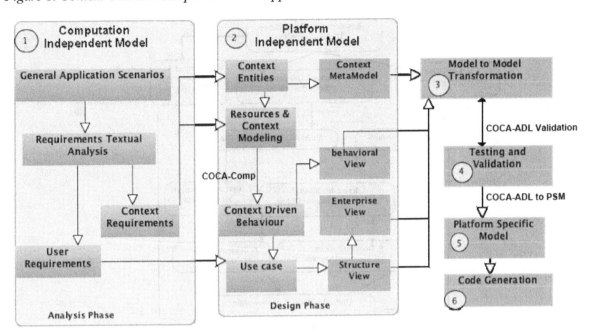

be summarised as shown in Figure 2. The figure summarizes the modelling tasks using the associated UML diagrams. The developer can start the analysis of an application scenario to capture the requirements.

Analysis. The requirements of the system are modelled in a computation-independent model (CIM), thus describing the situation in which the application will be used and predicting the exact behaviour of the application as a result of runtime context changes. This phase is accomplished by performing the following tasks.

Task 1: Requirement capturing by textual analysis. In this task, the developer identifies the candidate requirements for the illustration scenario using a textual analysis of the application scenario. It is recommended that the developer identify the candidate actors, use-cases, classes, and activities. This can be achieved by creating a table which lists the results of the analysis.

Task 2: Identifying the extra-functional requirements and relating them to the middleware functionality. The requirement is classified in the requirements' diagram, based on its type and whether it comes from a context provider or a consumer. The next level of requirements classification is to classify the requirements based on their anticipation level: foreseeable, foreseen, or unforeseen. This classification allows the developer to model the application behaviour as much as possible and to plan for the adaptation actions. However, to facilitate this classification framework, a UML profile is designed to support the requirements analysis and to be used by the software designer, as shown in Figure 3. For example, displaying the direction output in the camera browser is a functional requirement which drives the extra-functional requirement number 4, 'utilise the resources', which requires a middleware functionality to manage the context changes

Figure 2. Modelling tasks

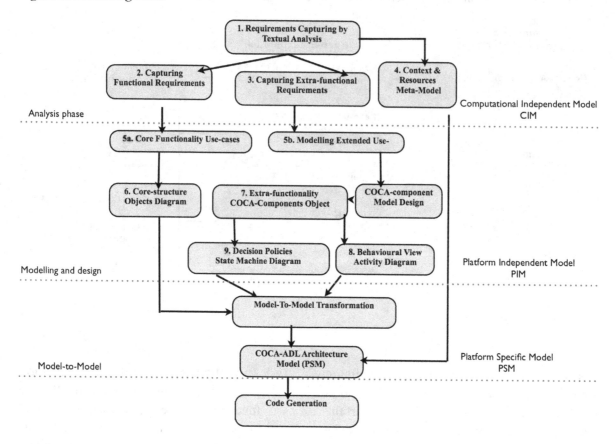

Figure 3. Requirements UML profile

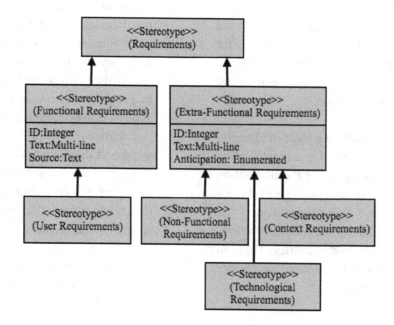

and take the adaptation actions which satisfy it. This requirement is classified as the foreseeable anticipation level.

Task 3: Capturing user requirements. This task is combined with the previous requirements diagram. This task focuses on capturing the user's requirements as a subset of the functional requirements, as shown in the UML profile in Figure 3 and Figure 4. This task allows the developers to analyse the main functions of the application which achieve specific goals or objectives. Normally, this kind of requirement is expressed by "The user must be able to do..."

    ○   **Modelling and Design:** COCA-MDA has adopted the component collaboration architecture (CCA) (OMG, 2004) at the PIV phase by partitioning the software into two views: the structure view and the behaviour view. The structure view focuses on the core components of the self-adaptive application and hides the context-driven components. The behaviour viewpoint focuses on modelling the context-driven behaviour of the component, which may be invoked in the application execution at

runtime. To achieve this function, the following tasks are performed.

Task 4: Resources and context entity model. Resources and context model refers to a generic overview of the underlying device's resources, sensors, and logical context providers. This diagram models the engagement between the resources and the application under development. It facilitates the developer in understanding the relationship between the context providers and their dependency.

Task 5: Use cases. In this phase, the requirements diagram is combined into a use-case model. The use-cases describe the interactions between the software system and the actor. The system-dependent and environment-dependent behaviours are modelled as extensions of the functional use-cases. The functional use-cases are modelled in a class diagram describing the application core functions. The extended use-cases are modelled as another object diagram which describes the application's behavioural view. For example, the 'adapt the direction output' use-case is a contextually driven use-case which extends the application functionality to utilise the devices' resources so as to provide a route to the nearest fire exit.

Figure 4. Partial requirements diagram

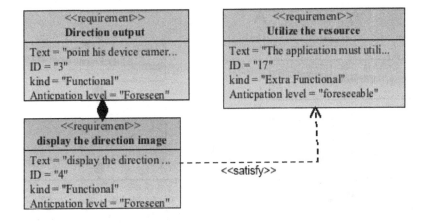

Task 6: Modelling the application core structure. In this task, a classical class diagram models the components which provide the application's core functions. These functions are identified in the use-case diagram in the previous task. However, the class diagram is modelled independently of the variations in the context information. In this scenario, some classes, such as "Displaying POIs," "Route-Planning UI, CameraUI, MapUI, and User Interface," are classified to be in the application core. These classes provide the core functions for the user during his tour of Petra. Figure 5 shows the core-structure class model without any interaction with the context environment or the middleware.

Task 7: Identifying application variant behaviour (behaviour view). The use-case diagram is split into two distinct object diagrams. The first diagram describes the basic application components which are executed regardless of the execution context. The core structure

is integrated with the extra-functional class model in the final architecture model. The extra-functionality class diagram provides a detailed view of the application COCA-component and the COCA-middleware. In addition, these diagrams model the desired behaviour, which can be used to anticipate context changes. Figure 6 shows a COCA-component modelled to anticipate the 'direction output'. The COCA-component implements delegate objects and sub layers; each layer implements a specific context-dependent function. The COCA-middleware (Magableh & Barrett, 2009, 2011a), uses this delegate object to redirect the execution among the sub layers based on the context condition.

The application behavioural model is used to demonstrate the decision points in the execution which might be reached whenever internal or external variables are found. This decision point

Figure 5. IWayFinder core-classes structure

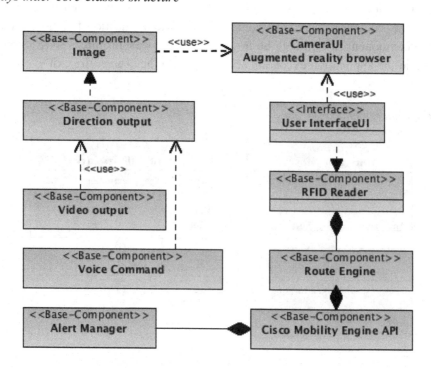

Figure 6. Direction output context oriented component

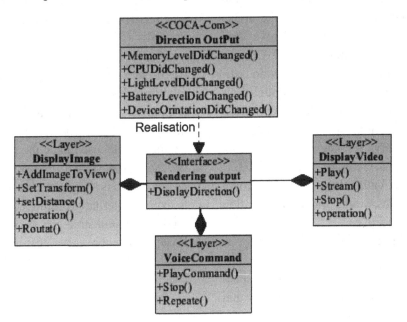

requires several parameter inputs to make the correct choice at this critical time. Using the activity diagram, the developers can extract numerous decision polices. Each policy must be modelled in a state diagram: textbfPolicy: Direction output. This policy is attached to the 'direction output' COCA-component in Figure 6. The policy syntax can be described by the code shown in Box 1.

The variant behaviour model is supported by a state-machine model which describes the application decision polices. The three models of the application are used as input for the next phase, model-to-model transformation.

• **Model-to-Model Transformation:** The platform-independent model and behavioural model are translated into architecture description language (COCA-ADL). This phase includes model-to-model transformation and model verification for the application's structure and behaviour views. The COCA-ADL is implemented by extending the xADL schema (an extensible XML language). ArchStudio is an environment of integrated tools for modelling, visualizing, analysing, and implementing software and systems architectures. The

Box 1. Decision policy 2

```
If (direction is Provided && Available memory >= 50
&& CPU throughput <= 89 && light level >= 50
&& BatteryLevel >= 50) then fPlayVideo(); displayImage(); VoiceCommand();g
Else If (BatteryLevel < 50 jj memory level < 50 jj CPU >92)
then fdisplayImage(); VoiceCommand();g
else If(BatteryLevel < 20)
then VoiceCommand();
```

ArchStudio provides Archipelago as the graphical editor used to model the architecture. Archipelago was used to extend the xADL by implementing the COCA-ADL meta-model. The ArchStudio editor enables the developer to model their application using three distinct models: structure, state machine, and activity diagram (Dashofy, Asuncion, Hendrickson, Suryanarayana, Georgas, & Taylor, 2007).

- **Testing and Validating:** Tests the model and verifies its fitness for the application goals and objectives.
- **Platform-Specific Model:** The platform-specific model produced by the transformation is a model of the same system specified by the PIM (it also specifies how that system makes use of the chosen platform). A PSM may provide more or fewer details, depending on its purpose. A PSM will be an implementation if it provides all the information needed to construct a system and to put it into operation. Alternatively, it may act as a PIM used to further refine the PSM so that it can be directly implemented.
- **Code Generation:** Model-to-text includes model-to-text transformation deployment and execution verification. The COCA-ADL XMI code is transformed into the implementation language.

EVALUATING COCA-MDA WITH COCOMO II

The IWayFinder application has been selected to determine the development effort using COCA-MDA compared with that using three MDA approaches proposed in the literature: U-MUSIC-MDA proposed by Khan (2010), Paspallis's MDA proposed by Paspallis (2009), and MUSIC-MDA proposed by Wagner et al. (2011). The enterprise architecture tool (EA) (Sparx Systems, 2010) was

used to develop the IWayFinder application using the four MDAs (COCA, MUSIC, U-MUSIC, and Paspallis's). Each MDA phase was carried out separately. COCOMO II (Boehm et al., 2000) was used to find the development effort in person-months for each MDA. There are two COCOMO II models, i.e., the post-architecture and early design models. The post-architecture model is a detailed model used once the project is ready to develop and sustain a fielded system. The early design model is a high-level model which is used to explore alternative architectures or incremental development strategies (Boehm et al., 2000). Based on the above, the post-architecture model has been selected to evaluate the four MDAs: COCA, MUSIC, U-MUSIC, and Paspallis's.

Based on the COCOMO II model, the sizing of new and reused code can be estimated via three major methods, as described in Boehm et al. (2000). These methods are counting SLOC; counting UFP; and aggregating new, adapted, and reused code, i.e., ASLOC. This type of reused code is estimated using the automatically translated code factor; this is considered to be a separate activity from development.

With regard to counting SLOC, the code generated from the MDA tool (EA) is excluded from the estimation. The effort for modelling the architecture can be captured using UFP. In such cases, COCOMO II is capable of relating UFP to SLOC in the implementation language. Starting from the fact that a UML is used to draw the model, the UML is classified on the same scale as a fourth-generation language. The relating process provides greater accuracy during the estimation than is obtained by estimating the generated lines of code using the MDA tool. Based on the above, the final SLOC for a module = the final application SLOC - the generated SLOC. This increases the accuracy of estimating the development effort.

COCOMO II is not only capable of estimating the cost and schedule for a development starting from 'scratch', it is also able to estimate the cost and schedule for products which are built upon already existing code, i.e., reused code. However, the third sizing measure, which aggregates new, adapted, and reused code, is suitable for MDA-based approaches. Starting from this fact, code taken from another source used in another product under development also contributes to the product's effective size.

Pre-existing code which is treated as a white-box and is modified for use with a product is called adapted code. The effective size of reused and adapted code is adjusted to be its equivalent in new code. The adjustment on the additional effort it takes to modify the code for inclusion in the product. This method allows us to estimate the development effort during the transformation and deployment phases, phases which all MDA approaches have. When the developer transforms the application from a PIM into a PSM, specific configurations are needed and this can be captured by the percentage of code modified and the percentage of integration modified.

The following equations describe the effort PM and the TDEV, taking into consideration the aforementioned inputs, as shown in Equation 1. The primary equation in 1 denotes the effort in person-months derived from the software size defined in thousands of lines of code (KLOC). The exponent E defines the sum of the scale factors (SF), i.e., the Cartesian product of the effort multipliers (EM) and the constant value A,

A value was calibrated from several software projects surveyed in Boehm et al. (2000). The second equation in Equation 2 depicts the time required to develop a software, derived from the nominal effort (PM), the sum of SFs, and the constant values calibrated from several software projects evaluated in COCOMO II. The rating scale factors and the effort multipliers used in this work to derive the effort and the time required to develop the IWayFinder application using COCA-MDA.

$$PM = A \times (Size)^E \times \overset{17}{\underset{i=1}{Y}} EM_i$$
$$where\ E = B + (0.01 \times \overset{17}{\underset{i=1}{X}} SF_i), \quad (1)$$
$$A = 2.95,\ B = 0.91$$

$$TDEV = C \times (PM)^F,$$
$$where\ F = D + 0.2 \times (E - B),$$
$$C = 3.67,\ D = 0.28 (COCOMOII.2000)$$
$$(2)$$

Thus, counting the SLOC is not adequate for evaluating the development effort in MDA-based methodology. Sizing software maintenance is better for MDA because, after the code is generated, the developer has to maintain the code and add the target platform configuration. This is required in the PSM phase and in the deployment and transformation phases. So, Equation 3 is used to calculate the sizing of code maintenance (Boehm et al., 2000). The initial maintenance size estimate is adjusted with a maintenance adjustment factor (MAF). This relationship can estimate the level of effort, using the Full Time Equivalent Software Personnel F SP_M, given T_M as in annual maintenance estimates, as shown in Equation 4, where T_M=12 months, or, given a fixed maintenance staff level, F SP_M, determine the necessary time, T_M, to complete the effort (Boehm et al., 2000). To estimate the adapted code, the COCOMO II model uses an additional set of equations to calculate the final count for source instructions and related costs and schedule. The equations in 3, 4, and 5 use the following values as parameters.

- **ASLOC:** The number of source lines of code adapted from existing software used in developing the new product.
- **Percentage of Design Modification (DM):** The percentage of the adapted software's design which received modifications to fulfil the objectives and environment of the new product.

- **Percentage of Code Modification (CM):** The percentage of the adapted software's code which receives modifications to fulfil the objectives and environment of the new product.

- **Percentage of Integration Required for Modified Software (IM):** The percentage of effort needed for integrating and testing of the adapted software in order to combine it into the new product.

- **Percentage of Reuse Effort Resulting from Software Understanding (SU):** Percentage of reuse effort resulting from assessment and assimilation (AA); programmer unfamiliarity with software domain (UNFM). Boehm et al. (2000) provides a rating scale for programmer unfamiliarity (UNFM) is shown in Figure 7.

$$MAF = 1 + \frac{SU}{100} \times UNFM,$$

$SU : Software\ Unders\tan ding$

(zero if DM=0 and CM=0), (3)

DM: percentage of design modified,

CM: percentage of code modified,

UNFM=0.4

$$PM_M = T_M = FSP_M,$$
$where\ T = 12\ months$ (4)

$$PM = AX(Size)^B + \frac{^\&ASLOC\left(\frac{AT}{100}\right)}{ATPROD} \quad (5)$$

In general, MDA-based approaches must apply CIM, PIM, PSM, transformation, deployment, and code generation. For each phase in the MDA a sizing method was adapted for estimating the development effort as shown in Table 1. However, the code which is directly generated from the MDA tool (EA) is excluded from the development effort, but is used as an input to measure the software maintenance effort. In addition, the middleware code has to be adapted and maintained, or even configured, to suit the new application platform.

COCOMO II Evaluation Results

The COCOMO II tool was used to estimate COCOA-MDA, U-MUSIC, MUSIC, and Paspallis's MDA. The evaluations produced the following results for COCA-MDA and the alternative methodologies.

Figures 8 and 9 provide the estimated efforts for the four MDAs. It also shows the total size (SLOC) for the IWayFinder application after it has been developed in each MDA. The figures show that COCA-MDA requires less effort in PM, despite the fact that the total SLOC is greater than for Paspallis's MDA. In Paspallis's MDA,

Figure 7. Rating scale for programmer unfamiliarity (UNFM)

UNFM Increment	Level of Unfamiliarity
0.0	Completely familiar
0.2	Mostly familiar
0.4	Somewhat familiar
0.6	Considerably familiar
0.8	Mostly unfamiliar
1.0	Completely unfamiliar

Table 1. MDA phases and size factors

Phase	Sizing Method	Results
CIM	Counting Unadjusted Function Points (UFP)	Relating UFP into SLOC
PIM	UFP	UFP into SLOC
PSM	Quantifying the Maintenance Adjustment Factor (MAF)	(Size) PM
Transformation	Quantifying the Maintenance Change Factor (MCF)	(Size) PM
Final code	Source Line of Code	SLOC = Final SLOC - Generated SLOC
Deployment integration	Quantifying the Maintenance Change Factor (MCF)	SLOC

Figure 8. Total effort for each MDA approach

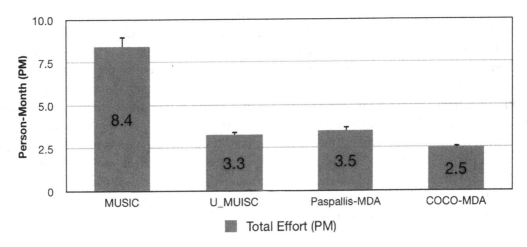

Figure 9. Total source lines of code

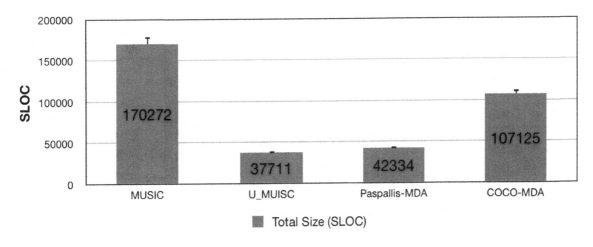

each context provider requires a separate plug-in architecture, which requires new software engineering to build the plug-in. The MDA tool does not generate the required code for the plug-in, but leaves the required code to be composed and configured in the deployment stage. This requires more effort to configure and maintain the plug-in architecture. This effort is captured using the UFP analysis, so the total effort for Paspallis's MDA is one of the highest because the ratio of the maintenance adjustment factor is very high. Such facts demonstrate the accuracy obtained using COCOMO II in estimating self-adaptive software development methodology. In addition, the figures show that the effort in MUSIC is the greatest; the reason for this is a lower ratio of adaptive and reused code in MUSIC compared to that in its extensions U-MUSIC and Paspallis's MDA.

Figure 10 provides more information for each MDA in terms of the estimated cost per MDA phase. As shown in the figure, the cost of performing the PIM was large for all MDAs. The reason for this is that all MDAs focus more on modelling the application variation model through the PIM. The cost of adapting the PIM in MUSIC is the largest because of the complexity of adapting the MUSIC PIM tasks; this requires the developer to produce more UML models than in the others.

For the same stage, Paspallis's MDA comes with less cost. In Paspallis's MDA, the time spent by the developers in building the context-provider plug-ins is greater than the effort required to build the architecture itself. This is why Paspallis's MDA comes second, after U-MUSIC, when evaluating the PSM phase.

Figure 11 provides the cumulative cost in PM for each MDA phase. As shown in the figure, the cost of performing the PIM was large for all MDAs. COCA-MDA reduced the effort required to generate the PSM during deployment, as shown in Figure 11. On the other hand, Paspallis's MDA increased the effort required for software maintenance in the transformation and deployment phases. Specifically, COCA-MDA and U-MUSIC reduce the effort needed to implement new or reused context provider, i.e., integrating a new sensor in the platform. This result reflects the benefits gained from employing the COCA-ADL for architecture deployment in several platforms. It is worth mentioning here that the 'labour rate per month' has been given the same value for all the MDAs throughout the evaluation.

In order to provide more information about each MDA approach, we have analysed the effort per phase for each MDA. Figure 12 shows the estimated effort for each phase for the MUSIC

Figure 10. Estimated cost per phase

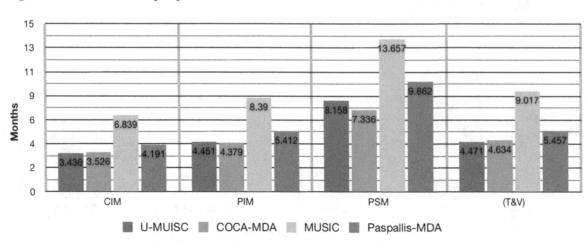

Figure 11. MDA cumulative effort in person-months

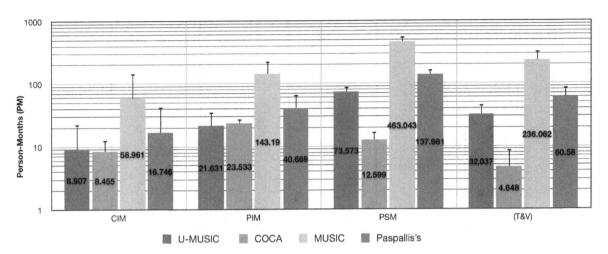

Figure 12. MUSIC effort (PM) per phase

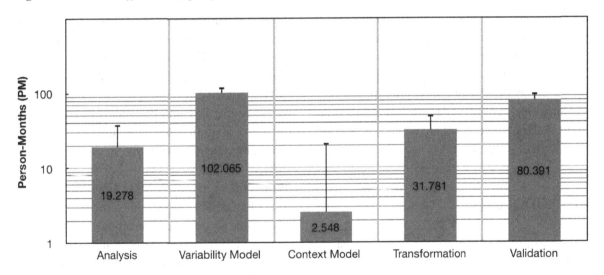

methodology. In this case, the design of variability models and validation require more effort than in the others, but modelling the context model require less effort. This figure demonstrate that MUSIC requires more effort and provides no cost effectiveness in developing the IWayFinder application.

In the same way, the U-MUSIC evaluation is illustrated in Figure 13. The domain model proposed by U-MUSIC MDA requires more effort than the variability model does. In U-MUSIC, the domain model requires the developer to split the context model into four models: functionality ontology, service ontology, context and resource model, and context provider. These models require more effort than building a simple context model like MUSIC. These models are collaborated into architecture constraints in the variability model, which uses them as inputs for the utility functions. Such an effort in domain modelling can increase

Figure 13. U-music effort (pm) per phase

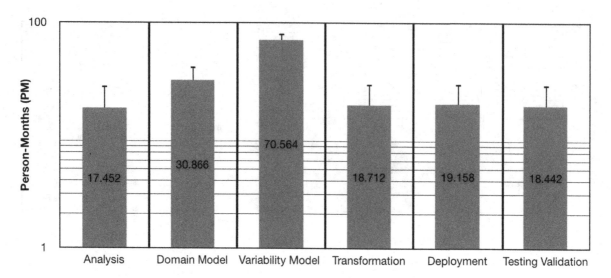

the developers' understanding of the application domain, but it does not really enable them to enhance the architecture design. In our experience, the results from the domain model are not reflected in the architecture variability model; the domain model is only used to obtain information on the architecture constraints which are used as input for the utility function.

METHODOLOGY

The development of context providers and analysis are the phases which require most effort by the developers. The effort in the deployment and maintenance phases are very high compared to those in the others. Thus, a planning-based adaptation requires more effort in the requirements and the proposed methodology requires more effort in developing the required plug-ins which fit the planned adaptation. Although this methodology does not suit self-adaptive applications when unanticipated conditions are in place, it does increase the development and maintenance efforts.

Figure 14 shows the estimated effort for each phase for the COCA-MDA methodology. The

figure illustrates that less effort is required to construct the application through the COCA-MDA phases. For example, to model the PIM of the architecture, 21 PM are required in COCA-MDA, but MUSIC requires 102 PM, U-MUSIC requires 70.5 PM, and Paspallis's MDA requires 40.4 PM, assuming that the context providers are not changed at runtime with respect to Paspallis's MDA. The intensive analysis of the application requirements in COCA-MDA simplified the process of modelling the variability model. Instead of modelling several variation models, as in MUSIC and U-MUSIC, the developers' model one extra-functionality model and another core structure model. In addition, the methodology modularizes each context-dependent functionality in a separate component model instead of designing a new plug-in from scratch and then configuring it, as in Paspallis's MDA.

Figure 15 shows the estimated effort for each phase in Paspallis's MDA. Finally, Figure 16 shows the required staff per phase in each methodology. The MUSIC methodology requires the most staff to develop the I WayFinder application, and COCA-MDA requires the least. Next to MUSIC comes Paspallis's MDA and then U-

Figure 14. COCA Effort (PM) per phase

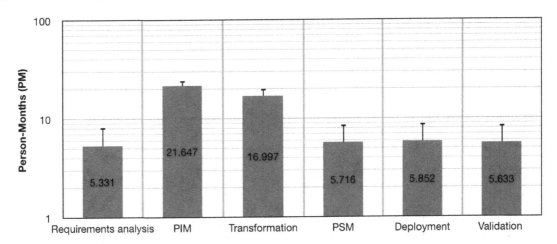

MUSIC. This analysis reflects the effort required in 12 months with respect to the ratio of code maintenance and deployment plus the required effort to model the architecture.

LESSONS LEARNED

COCA-MDA provides the following benefits:

- Intensive analysis of the application requirements simplified the process of modelling the application's behavioural model, so, instead of modelling several variation models as in MUSIC and U-MUSIC, the developer models one behavioural model.

- It enables the architecture to anticipate several behavioural variations, based on the context and the specific needs of individuals with cognitive impairments.

- It enables the application to proactively anticipate or reactively address unforeseen changes through the support of a dynamic decision-making and policy framework.

Figure 15. Paspallis's MDA effort (PM) per phase

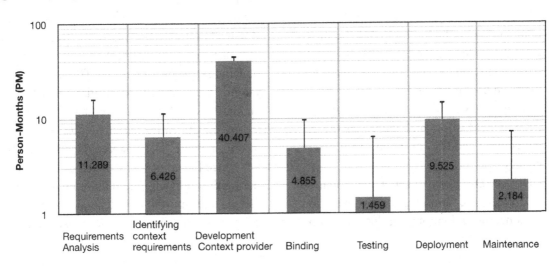

Figure 16. Project personnel for each phase for each MDA approach

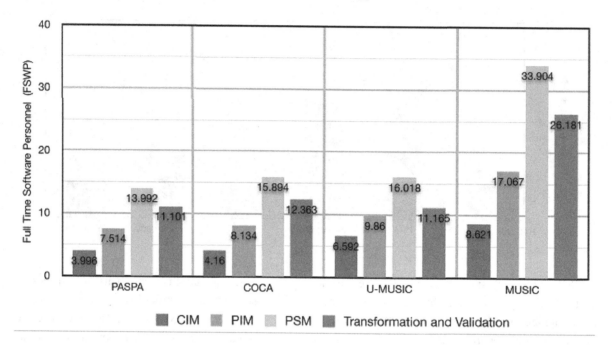

The policy framework is based on a stable description of software models and proprieties.

- It can decompose the application into several architectural units to allow developers to decide which part of the architecture should be notified when a specific context condition occurs.

- Counting the SLOC is not adequate for evaluating the development effort in MDA-based methodology. Sizing software maintenance is better for MDA because, after the code is generated, the developer has to maintain the code and add the target platform configuration.

- Clearly, COCA-MDA has reduced the development effort and increased the architecture's ability to adapt to context changes.

- COCA-MDA decreases the development effort because it uses a clear separation of concerns and employs a decomposition

mechanism to produce a context-oriented component model. Using these techniques reduces the modelling tasks and combines the MDA phases in a simple way.

CONCLUSION AND FUTURE WORK

Self-adaptability requirement, modelling, architecture, implementation, and assurance approaches require a systematic solution which inter-relates all aspects on a single platform. Requirements analysis can provide a great deal of information about the extra-functionalities of the self-adaptive system. In the same way, requirements analysis can facilitate and simplify architecture reflection by providing the information required by the software to manage itself. Moreover, COCA-MDA can reduce the complexity of self-adaptive engineering through mapping requirements to actor-, system-, and environment-dependent behaviours. This study shows how COCA-MDA reduces the required development effort compared to other MDAs. It also demonstrates how COCA-MDA reduces the software maintenance ratio through the architecture deployment and transformation.

The COCA-MDA requires improvement before it can support requirements reflection and modelling requirements as runtime entities. The requirements reflection mechanism requires support at the modelling level and architecture level. Requirements reflection can be used to anticipate the evolution of both functional and non-functional requirements.

REFERENCES

Achilleos, A. (2010). *Model-driven petri net based framework for pervasive service creation.* Unpublished doctoral dissertation, University of Essex, UK.

Belaramani, N. M., Wang, C.-L., & Lau, F. C. M. (2003, May). Dynamic component composition for functionality adaptation in pervasive environments. In *Proceedings of the 9th IEEE Workshop on Future Trends of Distributed Computing Systems,* San Juan, Puerto Rico (pp. 226–232).

Boehm, B. W., Abts, C., Brown, A. W., Chulani, S., Clark, B. K., & Horowitz, E. (2000). *Software cost estimation with COCOMO II* (1st ed.). Upper Saddle River, NJ: Prentice Hall.

Calic, T., Dascalu, S., & Egbert, D. (2008). Tools for MDA software development: Evaluation criteria and set of desirable features. In *Proceedings of the 5th International Conference on Information Technology,* Istanbul, Turkey (pp. 44–50).

Dashofy, E., Asuncion, H., Hendrickson, S., Suryanarayana, G., Georgas, J., & Taylor, R. (2007). Archstudio 4: An architecture-based meta-modeling environment. In *Proceedings of the 29th International Conference on Software Engineering* (pp. 67–68).

Khan, M. U. (2010). *Unanticipated dynamic adaptation of mobile applications.* Unpublished doctoral dissertation, University of Kassel, Kassel, Germany.

Lewis, G., & Wrage, L. (2005). *Model problems in technologies for interoperability: Model-driven architecture (Tech. Rep.).* Pittsburgh, PA: Software Engineering Institute.

Magableh, B., & Barrett, S. (2009). Pcoms: A component model for building context-dependent applications. In *Proceedings of the 1st International Conference on Adaptive and Self-adaptive Systems and Applications,* Athens, Greece (pp. 44–48).

Magableh, B., & Barrett, S. (2011a, September). Adaptive context oriented component-based application middleware (coca-middleware). In *Proceedings of the 8th International Conference on Ubiquitous Intelligence and Computing (UIC 2011),* Banff, AB, Canada (LNCS 6905, pp. 137-151).

Magableh, B., & Barrett, S. (2011b, May). Objective-cop: Objective context oriented programming. In *Proceedings of the 1st International Conference on Information and Communication Systems,* Irbid, Jordan (pp. 45–49).

Magableh, B., & Barrett, S. (2011c, June). Self-adaptive application for indoor wayfinding for individuals with cognitive impairments. In *Proceedings of the 24th International Symposium on Computer-based Medical Systems,* Bristol, UK (pp. 1 -6).

Object Management Group (OMG). (2004). *Enterprise collaboration architecture (ECA) specification*. Retrieved from http://www.omg.org/

Paspallis, N. (2009). *Middleware-based development of context-aware applications with reusable components*. Unpublished doctoral dissertation, University of Cyprus, Nicosia, Cyprus.

Sparx Systems. (2010). *Enterprise architect 8*. Retrieved December 1, 2010, from http://www.sparxsystems.com.au/

Wagner, M., Reichle, R., Khan, M. U., & Geihs, K. (2011). *Software development method for adaptive applications in ubiquitous computing environments* (Tech. Rep.).

Chapter 14

Design and Operation of a Cell Phone–Based Community Hazard Information Sharing System

Mayayuki Shinohara
Kanagawa Institute of Technology, Japan

Hiroshi Tanaka
Kanagawa Institute of Technology, Japan

Akira Hattori
Kanagawa Institute of Technology, Japan

Haruo Hayami
Kanagawa Institute of Technology, Japan

Shigenori Ioroi
Kanagawa Institute of Technology, Japan

Hidekazu Fujioka
Morinosato 4-Chrome Association in Atsugi City, Japan

Yuichi Harada
Morinosato 4-Chrome Association in Atsugi City, Japan

ABSTRACT

This paper presents a hazard/crime incident information sharing system using cell phones. Cell phone penetration is nearly 100% among adults in Japan, and they function as a telecommunication tool as well as a Global Positioning System (GPS) and camera. Open source software (Apache, Postfix, and MySQL) is installed on a system server, and together with the information service provided by Google Maps, are used to satisfy system requirements for the local community. Conventional systems deliver information to all people registered in the same block, even if an incident occurred far from their house. The key feature of the proposed system is that the distribution range of the hazard notification e-mail messages is determined by the geometrical distance from the incident location to the residence of each registered member. The proposed system applies not only to conventional cell phones but also smart phones, which are rapidly becoming popular in Japan. The new system functionality has been confirmed by a trial using members of the local community. System operation began after the successful trial and a training meeting for the local residents. System design, verification results, and operating status are described in this paper.

DOI: 10.4018/978-1-4666-2157-2.ch014

INTRODUCTION

Being informed about crime in one's community is the first step to preventing future occurrences, so public agencies provide various kinds of map-based incident information. For example, in San Diego, the community uses http://mapping.arjis.org/. As well as such formal information produced by public agencies, it is also important to have local information from local residents. Such information represents personal and experiential location-based knowledge. Thus, a number of map-based systems to share local knowledge have been developed on the web (Rantanen, 2007; Waters & Evans, 2003; Hattori, Goto, & Hayami, 2008). In these systems, users can enter local safety/hazard incident information on a map. The system that Hattori, Goto, and Hayami (2008) proposed is based on an open source content management system (Xoops), and citizens can manage and develop it to adapt it to the needs of the community. However, in this system, citizens do not use cell phones or location information obtained by GPS. Consequently, it is quite difficult to share information about incidents in real time or even within a short time. Moreover, it is impossible to send location information if the user does not know the address where the incident has occurred.

Terashima, Sekizuka, and Sasaki (2008) and Nagasaka (2006) have developed town map systems for disaster or crime prevention in Japan. In their systems, users can use a cell phone to send image data of locations with security problems, together with the location data obtained from a GPS and appropriate comments, for inclusion in a map which is available on the web. With these systems, residents, neighborhood associations and citizen groups can share information about hazards or incidents in the area. Stevens and D'hondt (2010) presented a crowdsourcing approach for measuring and mapping urban pollution and nuisance. Furtado, Ayres, Oliveira, Filho, Caminha, D'orleans, and Belchior (2010) developed the

WikiCrimes system that makes it possible for the general public to share information about the occurrence of criminal acts in a particular location. San Francisco Crimespotting (http://sanfrancisco.crimespotting.org/) is an interactive crime map with an associated timeline in San Francisco. Ganapati (2010) uses OpenStreetMap to produce the interactive crime map. OpenStreetMap is a free map of the world that can be edited by anyone with an Internet connection. Although users can monitor all information relating to the area using a web browser, the information required is different for each person. The necessary information seems to be mainly information near a person's house or their nearest station, etc.

In the geographic information field, it is now common for individuals with little or no training in geographic concepts to use online mapping services and GPS-enabled mobile devices to create, edit, and update spatial data relating to features or events of personal interest. This new mode of producing and using spatial data through mass participation and collaboration is referred to as volunteered geographic information (VGI). Goodchild (2007) described the technologies that make VGI possible, its concepts and issues. He pointed out that the most important value of VGI may lie in the reports about local activities that go unreported by the world media and thus about life at a local level. Hall, Chipeniuk, Feick, Leahy, and Deparday (2010) have developed the MapChat tool to facilitate web-based interaction among members of the general public interested in discussing geographic issues of local relevance. The tool was initially introduced to residents of a small and cohesive community through a series of small scale workshops. Depending on the nature of the chat, the tool needs a web browser.

Twitter, which is a popular microblogging service, has received much attention in recent years. One of the most important characteristics of Twitter is its real-time nature. Sakaki, Okazaki, and Matsuo (2010) consider each Twitter user as a sensor, and they seek to solve the problem of detecting an event based on sensory observations. They use location estimation methods such as Kalman filtering and particle filtering on an event. One application they developed was an earthquake reporting system. The system shows the tweets relating to an earthquake on a map. White and Roth developed TwitterHitter, which gathers and analyzes VGI from Twitter (2010). Their system is a desktop application, but it can report collected tweets using a linked map-timeline view that plots the tweets of a single individual or group of individuals. They described how TwitterHitter could support the functions of crime analysis to demonstrate their system's potential. These systems are appropriate for real-time use, but they seem to be insufficient for use as an information sharing system for registered members since they cannot send detailed information due to the limitation of using words and other data typed in by users. Consequently, a Twitter-based system is not necessarily the best basis for constructing a hazard/incident information sharing system.

Since we started our investigation, there has been no report of an information sharing system that gathers information from cell phones using GPS and which sends the information in real time to regional inhabitants based on their residential address. We have constructed such a system, considering the requirements of a local community, and conducted a trial to confirm its function and usability as a precursor to full-scale operation. This paper presents a summary of the system requirements, system configuration, and sequence of operation. In addition, the results of a trial with regional inhabitants to verify the system functions and operation are described in a forthcoming section.

SYSTEM CONCEPT AND SYSTEM DESIGN

System Concept and Basic Requirements

The main purpose of our proposed system is gathering information from a small area and sharing this information among the local residents. Information relating to larger areas or serious incidents is reported by mass media such as television news or newspapers. But there is no media that reports such information for local areas, and therefore such information cannot be shared appropriately among residents. The aim of the proposed system is information sharing to enhance security among the local residents. The basic concept may be described as follows.

1. Sharing information relating to crime prevention and hazards in normal circumstances and the status of damage in a disaster situation.
2. Operation by a self-governing neighborhood body, not a commercial service.

Information in a small residential area about incidents such as a sneak thief and attempted kidnapping should be made available to all residents. In addition, the current situation in local streets, etc., should be available in a timely manner, especially when a natural disaster occurs.

Although these kinds of information seem to be quite important and should be made available to all residents, commercial or local government services do not meet this need. It seems to be difficult to allocate funds for the development cost of such a system. Thus, we have tried to create a system for sharing local hazard/incident information at minimal cost using open source software (OSS).

The system requirements for information sharing in a local area are summarized in Table 1. Basic schemes used to satisfy these requirements

Table 1. Requirements for proposed system

Requirement	Applied scheme
Location information	Cell phone GPS Input of address information
Hazard information	Item category selection Free text input
Image information	Cell phone camera
Map information	Use of GoogleMaps service

are also shown in this table. An indispensable function is linking a location with information about incidents occurring at that location. The location is one of the most important items of information, and it is clear that information about the area in the vicinity of a resident's house is the most important and necessary information. For this reason, acquisition of location information is required. There are two methods for obtaining location information. One method is using a cell phone's GPS function. The government recommends that Japanese cell phone carriers embed a GPS function so location information can be sent automatically in an emergency call. An alternative method is to enter an address manually. The cell phone is used as the basic equipment for sending and receiving information, since almost everyone always carries one.

Information category selection is necessary for quick and easy information input. A free text input function is required for detailed information. These items need to be determined based on the requirements of the user.

Image information that can be obtained using a cell phone camera seems to be quite effective in conveying the situation at the location. For example, the status of roads in an area stricken by an earthquake or the water level of a river can be easily understood by means of an image. The situation can be displayed on a map by combining image information and location information. The location information obtained by GPS, that is, latitude and longitude, does not help a human

user understand the significance of a location. The proposed system takes map information via the Google Maps API from the Google server, and the location of the incident is plotted on the map.

Database Schema

Two tables (an information table and a user management table) are prepared in the database management system. The schema of the user management table depends on the user's intentions. The information table is explained in a forthcoming section.

The information table schema is shown in Table 2. Each information field is identified and managed by an information ID. The database fields are prepared based on the system requirements. Two kinds of information are used to show the location of the incident. One is a method using latitude and longitude, and the other is address information. The former information is obtained from a GPS embedded cell phone and is converted to address information by using a function provided by the Google server via the Google Maps application programming interface (API) (http://code.google.com/intl/ja/apis/maps/documentation/javascript/babasi.html). Address information is entered manually in a cell phone without a GPS function, and this information can be converted to latitude and longitude by the Google server. The location information, that is, latitude and longitude information from a GPS, is used to indicate the location on the map, while

Table 2. Information table

Field	Contents	Example
id	information id	89
lat	latitude of location	35.4485352
lon	longitude of location	139.3089152
address	address of location	Morinosato 4-7-5
time	time that information was posted	2010/11/8 18:32
category	type of information	Person
detail	explanation of information	Middle-aged person with mask took pictures of empty houses etc.
img_id	image data id	1110
img_name	image data name	2010-11-8-18-32.gif

the address information can indicate its location without a map.

The category is introduced to make it quicker and easier to post information by selecting the information type. Additional text information is added for details. If necessary, image information can be sent using a cell phone's camera. A camera is considered to be highly useful, especially in the case of a disaster.

System Configuration and Sequence

Figure 1 shows the system configuration. The specification of the system server is CPU Intel Core2Duo 2.93 GHz, memory 2 GB, HDD 500 GB. The installed OS is Ubuntu 9.04. Apache and Postfix are used as the web server and mail server, respectively. The database management system is MySQL and the development language is PHP, which is used for making dynamic web pages. All the software used is OSS, so the only expense is for the server machine.

The system operation sequence is shown in Figure 2. The sequence of information gathering and sharing (posting and receiving) is as follows.

1. Registration to the system is required for access. For registration and for further system access as in step (2), the system uses the subscriber ID passed on by the mobile service provider for a conventional cell phone, or it requires a user login ID and password for a smart phone. The necessary user information, including his/her house location, is stored in the database.

2. The user accesses the web server from his/her cell phone when he/she posts information about an incident.

3. The cell phone gets the location information if the phone has GPS. This information is converted to address information. When the user enters address information because his/her phone does not have GPS, the web server gets the location information from the Google Maps server.

4. The user sends the information category and a text explanation as supplementary information. A photograph from a cell phone camera can also be sent to the system server.

5. Immediately after the web server has received information, it sends it to the database as hazard/incident information.

6. The web server gets user information from the database and requests the mail server to send the incident information in an e-mail to those members registered in advance.

Figure 1. System configuration

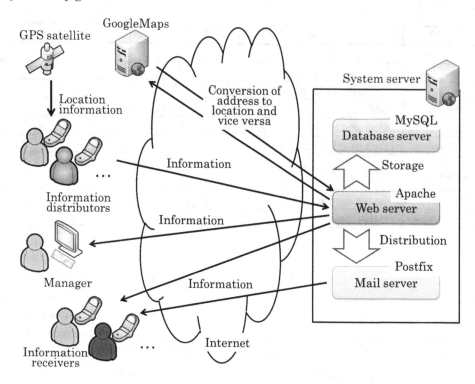

Figure 2. System sequence

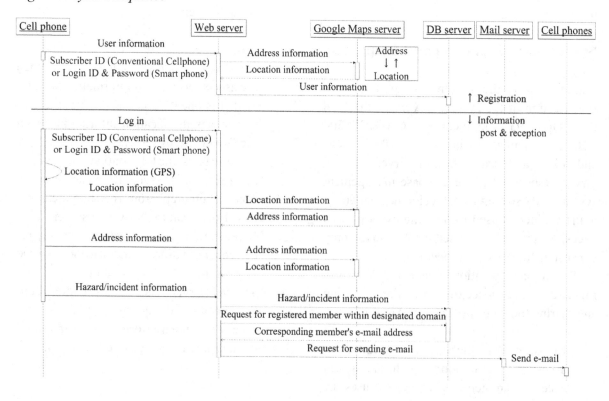

Information about the local area can be shared by this scheme with very little time delay. A link to a map in which the location information is posted is included in this e-mail, so recipients can easily visualize the location.

COLLABORATIVE TRIAL WITH A LOCAL COMMUNITY

System Customization

The director of the local neighborhood of Morinosato (4th block district in the city of Atsugi) proposed that they try out our system to enhance the safety and security awareness of those living in the district. The location of Morinosato 4th block is shown in Figure 3. Atsugi is located in the center of Kanagawa Prefecture, next to the Tokyo metropolitan area, and has a total population of about 400,000. The self-governing Morinosato district is divided into 5 parts or blocks: 1st block to 5th block. There are 573 households and about 2000 people in Morinosato 4th block. We investigated how to customize the proposed system to meet the needs of the local community.

The requirements of the local residents are summarized in Table 3. Operation, including server access from a cell phone for posting incident information, must be as simple as possible. Authentication without needing a user ID and password was required for easy access to the system server. The subscriber number given by each mobile service provider (for a standard cell phone) was used to identify a registered member in this trial. This number was used in place of a user ID and password for authentication, and can be sent automatically to the system server via a provider server.

The basic functions for normal users are to post information about hazards/incidents and to receive e-mails posted by other members. However, the following administration functions were required for an official of the city hall or the director of a local community to use the system.

1. Management of registered users. An administrator must be able to amend incorrect items in the user table information and to delete a user who posts inappropriate information.
2. Monitoring of all information and deletion of inappropriate posted information. This

Figure 3. Location of the Morinosato self-governing community

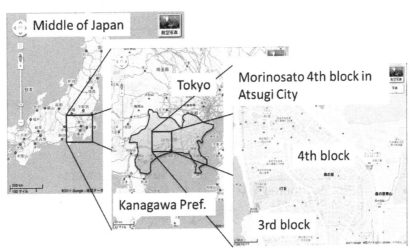

Table 3. Requirements of local residents

Requirement	Content
Simplified server access	Automatic or one click authentication
Functions for system manager	Confirmation and deletion of registered user information Monitoring of all posted information Multicast to all registered users
Distribution area of e-mails	Distribution range : Near inhabitant's house >>Radius of distribution area : 300m from posted incident location

function is very important for maintaining a trustworthy system. Inappropriate information should be deleted to avoid rumor and confusion. The viable information gathered should be sent to a city official for use, for example, in selecting police patrol areas.

3. Multicasting to all registered users. Although this requirement is not crucial in the proposed system, it is desirable to have a function to send notices to all members, independent of the location of their house.

The most significant and unique point of this system is the restriction of the e-mail distribution region. For general members, the only essential information is that relating to incidents occurring near their house. In a conventional system, each member receives all incidents which occur in the same block, even if an incident occurred far from their house, as shown in Figure 4. There are two problems with this scheme.

Figure 4. Conventional area for information distribution

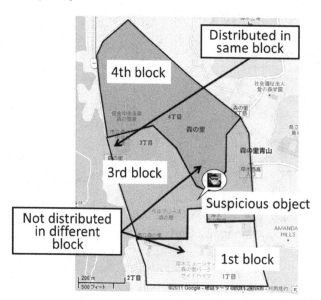

1. If a resident's residential block is different from that of information posted, he/she will not receive information even if he/she lives near the place where the information was posted.
2. If a resident's residential block is the same as that for which the information was posted, he/she receives information even if he/she lives far from the place where the information was posted. This results in unnecessary mail.

The method we applied to solve these problems is shown in Figure 5. The e-mail is sent to residents whose house is within a predetermined range of the incident: for example, 300 m from the spot where the information was posted. The cell phone's GPS sends the latitude and longitude when posting, or these values are obtained from the address information, then the system server calculates the distribution range and sends an e-mail to members based on the location of their house. This scheme helps to avoid unnecessary

e-mail transmission and ensures that only information of value is sent.

The user management table contains the user names, house addresses, e-mail addresses, etc. The contents of the user management table are shown in Table 4. The ID to access the system server is different between a conventional cell phone subscriber ID and a smart phone (login ID and password). The ID for a conventional cell phone is supplied by each cell phone service provider. When information is posted via a cell phone, this ID is added automatically by service provider and is sent to the system server. Authentication is successful if this identification and the registered identification in the table match. This makes it easy to post the information to the system. On the other hand, a smart phone is not provided with a subscriber ID during communication, so a login ID and password are necessary in the same way as when accessing personal computers.

A resident's house location is required to determine the appropriate e-mail distribution. Latitude and longitude can be obtained from address

Figure 5. Proposed area for information distribution

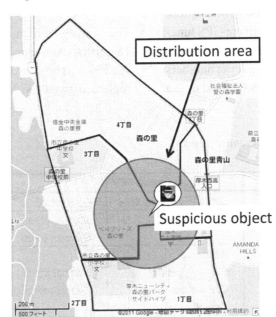

Table 4. User management table

Field	Contents	Example
Conventional Cell phone		
subscriber_id	subscriber_ID given by provider	02XXXCT
Smart phone		
login_id	login ID	fujioka2011
login_pwd	login password	12345678
Common items		
usr_id	user ID	10
surname	surname	Fujioka
first_name	first name	Masayuki
house_address	address of resident	Morinosato 4-26-2
house_lon	longitude of residence	139.305646
house_lat	latitude of residence	35.4523929
mail_address	e-mail address of cell phone	ht09XXXXX@docomo.ne.jp
distribution_range	range from posted location (m)	300

information of their house. The distribution range is also set and stored in this table.

The items shown in Table 5 were defined as input information after discussion with the director of the community of Morinosato 4th block, (i) location information, (ii) the type of suspicious object category, here, person, car with/without person, etc., and (iii) supplementary information. The item (i) is obtained either from the GPS function or from the address information, which is input using a selection menu of building numbers (when the GPS satellite signal is blocked or the user has a cell phone without GPS). Similarly, item (ii) can be input by menu selection for quick and easy operation. Supplementary information via text input is not compulsory because some elderly people are not accustomed to using cell phones.

System Verification Trial

The system verification trial was carried out by 18 participants - the group leaders in Morinosato 4th block. The person who noticed the incident reports it from the incident location, using his/

Table 5. Items that local residents must input

Item	Contents	Applied scheme
Location information	Latitude and longitude	GPS function
	Address	Manual input (Menu selection of building number, etc.)
Category of suspicious object	Person Car with person Car without person Others	Manual input (Menu selection)
Detailed information	Explanation of object	Manual input

her cell phone to send information to the system server. Figure 6(a) shows the input display of a cell phone. The hazard/incident information was sent using GPS positioning results as shown in the system sequence in Figure 2. If the user's phone did not have GPS, address information was entered in the blank fields. The category of suspicious object, that is, a person, or a car with/without person, etc., was selected as a second input item, and supplementary information added as free text as shown in Figure 6(b).

Figure 7(a) shows a received e-mail, in which the time of posting, the address, the category of suspicious object, and any supplementary information, are included as details. The posted incident location is indicated in the map, as shown in Figure 7(b). It is easy to comprehend the location and distance from a user's house. This kind of

Figure 6. Input display of cell phone

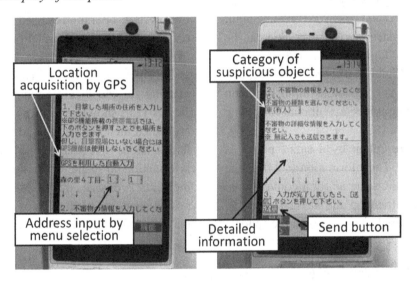

Figure 7. Information reception by e-mail

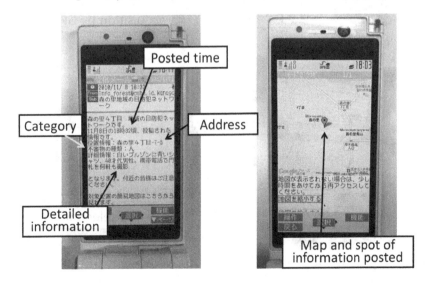

information sharing enhances local community safety awareness. As a result, the existence of this kind of system is also considered to discourage thieves from moving into a local community.

Smart phone penetration has increased rapidly in Japan; the ratio was over 20% at the end of 2011. The example confirmation has been done with a smart phone. Figure 8 shows the login and address input page of the smart phone. Figure 7(b) corresponds to Figure 6(a) for a conventional cell phone. As the subscriber ID is not given to a smart phone by the mobile service provider, a login ID and password must be input and sent to the system server. A cookie can be used for automatic login after the first login. The upper button in Figure 8(b) is for GPS use, and the lower button is for address input by menu selection - the same as for conventional cell phone shown in Figure 6(a).

Information reception by a smart phone is shown in Figure 9. The information sent from the system server is the same as for a conventional cell phone. Magnification and navigation in the map is easy compared to a conventional cell phone.

An overview of the information gathered in this trial is shown in Figure 10. Police officers or local government officials of the city and/or town, as well as the director of the local community, should be notified of all incident information. The data gathered from each local community can be reflected in policies concerning municipal administration.

System in Operation for Local Residents

Full system operation started for all the local residents after the completion of the system verification trial carried out by group leaders of Morinosato 4th block. The system training meeting for the local community was held in July 2011 as shown in Figure 11. There were 53 registered members at the end of January 2012, that is, about 10% of the households. The posted information on suspicious people, cars and other incidents is described in Table 6. Although the posted incidents seem to be of minor concern, it may indicate safety in this local area. At the same

Figure 8. Login and input display of smart phone

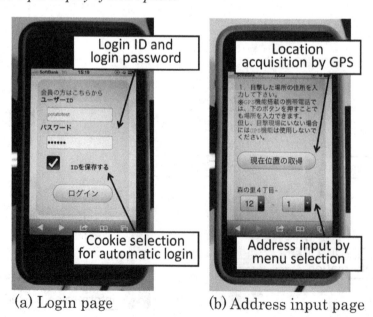

(a) Login page   (b) Address input page

Figure 9. Information received by e-mail

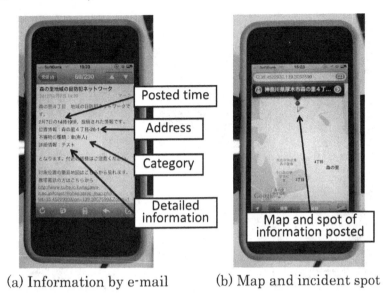

(a) Information by e-mail　　(b) Map and incident spot

Figure 10. All posted information from registered members in trial stage

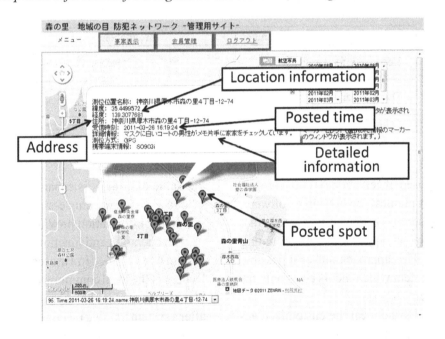

time, the existence of this system is considered not only to share hazard information but also to enhance safety consciousness. The existence of this system helps deter local crimes.

CONCLUSION

This paper has proposed a regional hazard information sharing system in which information is posted by local community members. The system requirements were investigated, and the resulting

Figure 11. Training meeting for the local community

Table 6. Incident information posted by the local residents

Item	Number	Information
Location information	2	Illegally parked car Car driven recklessly
Dubious car	2	Man with cotton mask took pictures of houses when unoccupied.
Others	4	Appearance of troop of wild monkeys

system is composed of cell phones (both conventional and smart phones), open source software, and a network service provided by Google that can be used via an application programming interface (API). This approach makes it possible to construct a system which incurs costs only for server hardware.

The proposed system can be customized according to the requirements of the members of a local community. The distribution of e-mails conveying hazard/incident information is determined by the distance of residents' houses from the posted location of the incident. This reduces irrelevant or unnecessary e-mails, and as a result, the value of e-mails is enhanced and the people who receive the warning e-mails pay more attention to the information provided.

The operation and function of the constructed system were verified in a trial carried out by group leaders of the local community of Morinosato 4th block. The system has been put into operation after a system training meeting for members of the local community. Some incident information has been posted since the system has started operating. The developed system contributes to information sharing and enhances safety consciousness among the local community.

REFERENCES

Furtado, V., Ayres, L., Oliveira, M. D., Filho, E. V., Caminha, C., D'orleans, J., & Belchior, M. (2010). Collective intelligence in law enforcement: The WikiCrimes system. *Information Sciences*, *180*(1), 4–17. doi:10.1016/j.ins.2009.08.004

Ganapati, S. (2010). *Using Geographic Information Systems to Increase Citizen Engagement*. Washington, DC: IBM Center for the Business of Government.

Goodchild, M. F. (2007). Citizens as sensors: the world of volunteered geography. *GeoJournal*, *69*(4), 211–221. doi:10.1007/s10708-007-9111-y

Hall, G. B., Chipeniuk, R., Feick, R. D., Leahy, M. G., & Deparday, V. (2010). Community-based production of geographic information using open source software and Web 2.0. *International Journal of Geographical Information Science*, *24*(5), 761–781. doi:10.1080/13658810903213288

Hattori, A., Goto, M., & Hayami, H. (2008). A Local Safety Knowledge Sharing System for Proactive Management by Citizens. *Journal of Convergence Information Technology*, *3*(4), 26–34.

Nagasaka, T. (2006). New Mode of Risk Governance Enhanced by an E-community Platform. In *A Better Integrated Management of Disaster Risks toward Resilient Society to Emerging Disaster Risks in Mega-Cities* (pp. 89-107).

Rantanen, H. (2007). Mapping and managing local knowledge in urban planning. In *Proceedings of the International Conference on Sustainable Urban Areas (ENHR 2007)*. Retrieved from http://www.enhr2007rotterdam.nl/documents/W21_paper_Rantanen.pdf

Sakaki, T., Okazaki, M., & Matsuo, Y. (2010). Earthquake shakes Twitter users: real-time event detection by social sensors. In *Proceedings of the 19th International Conference on the World Wide Web* (pp. 851-860).

Stevens, M., & D'hondt, E. (2010). Crowd-sourcing of Pollution Data using Smartphones. In *Proceedings of the Workshop on Ubiquitous Crowdsourcing*. Retrieved from http://soft.vub.ac.be/Publications/2010/vub-tr-soft-10-15.pdf

Terashima, T., Sekizuka, H., & Sasaki, T. (2008). Developing a Collaborative Map Creation Support System by Multi-modal Information-gathering. In *Proceedings of 4th International Conference on Information and Automation for Sustainability* (pp. 179-183).

Waters, T., & Evans, A. J. (2003). Tools for web-based GIS mapping of a "fuzzy" vernacular geography. In *Proceedings of the 7th International Conference on GeoComputation*.

White, J. J. D., & Roth, R. E. (2010). TwitterHitter: Geovisual Analytics for Harvesting Insight from Volunteered Geographic Information. In *Proceedings of the GIScience 2010 Doctoral Colloquium*. Retrieved from http://www.giscience2010.org/pdfs/paper_239.pdf

This work was previously published in the International Journal of Information Technology and Web Engineering (IJITWE), Volume 6, Issue 4, edited by Ghazi I. Alkhatib and Ernesto Damiani, pp. 35-50, copyright 2011 by IGI Publishing (an imprint of IGI Global).

Section 4
Web Engineering Network and Communication Platforms

Chapter 15
Improved Algorithm for Error Correction

Wael Toghuj
Isra University, Jordan

Ghazi Alkhatib
Princess Sumaya University for Technology, Jordan

ABSTRACT

Digital communication systems are an important part of modern society, and they rely on computers and networks to achieve critical tasks. Critical tasks require systems with a high level of reliability that can provide continuous correct operations. This paper presents a new algorithm for data encoding and decoding using a two-dimensional code that can be implemented in digital communication systems, electronic memories (DRAMs and SRAMs), and web engineering. The developed algorithms correct three errors in codeword and detect four, reaching an acceptable performance level. The program that is based on these algorithms enables the modeling of error detection and correction processes, optimizes the redundancy of the code, monitors the decoding procedures, and defines the speed of execution. The performance of the derived code improves error detection and correction over the classical code and with less complexity. Several extensible applications of the algorithms are also given.

INTRODUCTION AND RELATED WORK

From browsing the Web to launching a space rocket, today we are relying heavily on digital communication systems. A primary objective of any digital communication system is to transmit information at the maximum possible rate and receive it at the other end with minimum errors. Receiving information without errors becomes a critical task. As a result, finding good codes with practical decoders turns out to be the main challenge in achieving reliable transmission at rates close to the channel capacity (Bajcsy, Chong, Garr, Hunziker, & Kobayashi, 2001).

On the other hand, another application of digital communication techniques is storage systems. In this case the objective is not transmission "from here to there" but rather "from now to then." These media have unique impairments, different

DOI: 10.4018/978-1-4666-2157-2.ch015

from those in transmission media, but many of the same basic techniques apply (Barry, Lee, & Messerschmitt, 2004).

One of the most intractable sources of failures in computer has been the soft memory error: a random event that corrupts the value stored in a memory cell without damaging the cell itself.

Initially, the soft error problem gained widespread attention in the late 1970s as a memory data corruption issue, when DRAMs began to show signs of apparently random failures. Although the phenomenon was first noticed in DRAMs, SRAM memories and SRAM-based programmable logic devices are also subject to the same effects.

At ground level, cosmic radiation is about 95% neutrons and 5% protons. These particles can cause soft errors directly; they can also interact with atomic nuclei to produce troublesome short-range heavy ions. Cosmic rays cannot be eliminated at the source, and effective shielding would require meters of concrete or rocks. Soft Error Rates (SERs) are 5 times as high at 2600 feet as at sea level, and 10 times as high in Denver (5280 feet) as at sea level. "SRAM tested at 10,000 feet above sea level will record SERs that are 14 times the rate tested at sea level (Graham, 2002).

Changes in technology have significant impacts on error rates, but not always in predictable ways. For example, DRAM error rates were widely expected to increase as devices became smaller, while small scale DRAMs demonstrate a much better error resistance. One reason for this is that their smaller size allows less charge collection (Ziegler, 2000); another reason is that cell size has scaled faster than storage capacitance (Johnston, 2000a), so the capacitance ratio has actually increased (Johnston, 2000b). On the other hand, SOI (Silicon on Insulator) technology was expected to resist errors (Johnston, 2000a); however, it

demonstrates an unexpected tendency toward large charge collection, which may dramatically increase error rates (Dodd, 2001).

To eliminate the soft memory errors that are induced by cosmic rays, memory manufacturers must either produce designs that can resist cosmic ray effects or else invent mechanisms to detect and correct the errors.

In mathematics, computer science and information theory, error correction and detection has great practical importance in maintaining data (information) integrity across noisy channels and storage media. Error correcting codes (ECC) are traditionally used in communications to deal with the corruption of transmitted data by channel noise. Extra information is added to the original data to enable the reconstruction of the original data transmitted. The encoded data, or codewords, are sent through the channel and decoded at the receiving end. During decoding the errors are detected and corrected if the amount of error is within the allowed, correctable range. This range depends on the extra information, i.e. parity bits, which were added during encoding.

In computer memories, saving data corresponds to sending it by noisy channel. Figure 1 shows the usage of ECC to correct errors in a memory system.

Traditionally, ECC has been used to correct soft errors caused by α-ray during operation. Due to the random distribution of the error in memory, parity code (parity check) and Hamming code were most commonly used. The algorithms of Hamming code can correct single-bit errors and detect double-bit errors, while parity code can only detect errors.

Taking into account the above-stated theme this work introduces an algorithm that corrects three-bit errors and detects four-bit errors in codeword.

Figure 1. Data flow in ECC added memory

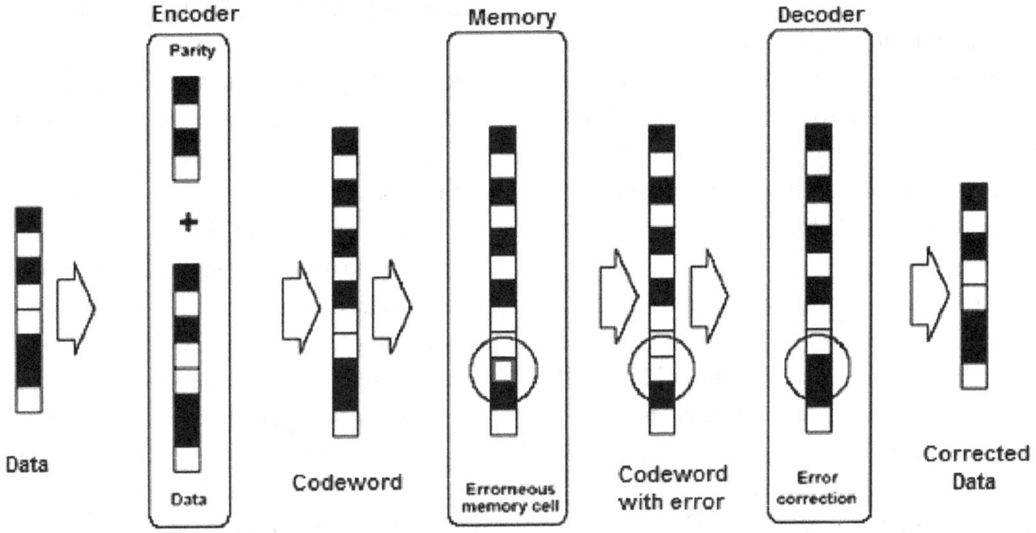

Encoder   Memory   Decoder

Data   Data   Codeword   Errorneous memory cell   Codeword with error   Error correction   Corrected Data

Parity   +   Data

CORRECTING THREE-BIT ERRORS ALGORITHM

This research developed algorithms using a two-dimensional iterated code (IC) and created a program for modeling the processes of detection and correction of errors.

The main concept of the two-dimensional iterated code is the following. The set collection of data bits is represented in a table form consisting of q of rows and m of columns as shown in Figure 2. Thus, check bits are added to row and columns so that rows and columns become words of some code.

Recently, the interest in algorithms with low complexity has been revived in relationship to the problem of decoding iterated (concatenated) coding schemes. Concatenated coding schemes were first proposed by G.D. Forney as a means of achieving large coding gains by combining two or more relatively simple codes (Benedetto, Divsalar, Montorsi, & Pollarab, 1996).

This research expands on the basic two-dimensional iterated code by using combinations of different codes for building the two-dimensional iterated code and compares their results. Some of the results show that an IC with minimum code distance higher than 8 may correct five errors and even more, but it also show that they have higher complexity (In information theory, the minimum code distance (or code distance) between two strings of equal length is the number of positions

Figure 2. The structure of a two-dimensional iterated code using odd parity check

$A = 1101\ 1001\ 0011\ 1011$

$M = m \cdot q$

Example: $\beta_1 = 1 \oplus 1 \oplus 0 \oplus 1 = 1$

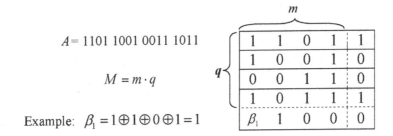

at which the corresponding symbols are different). The research proved that IC with a combination of the extended Hamming code and parity-check code is the optimal solution for data protection from multiple errors. The offered two-dimensional IC is characterized with code distance $d=8$ and, therefore, allows to correct three errors regardless of their location in the table and the appearance reasons.

The process of encoding consists of two levels: a) encoding all of the data words using extended Hamming code; in this case, $2+[\log_2 m]$ bits will be added per every data word, and b) all of the columns will be encoded using parity check (XOR operator), formatting the check row.

Encoding function is set as $E=E_2 \circ E_1$. Thus E_1 (where $E_1 = E_{11}E_{12}...E_{1q}$) is the operation of coding of all data words m_1, m_2,...,m_q by extended Hamming code, and E_2 is the operation of table columns encoding by modulo-2-adder (XOR).

Figure 3 shows a detailed description of the developed encoding algorithm that implements two-dimensional IC.

Reading from Memory or Receiving from Communication Channel Data

The decoding process starts by checking the values of the syndrome and parity check. If both of values are equal zero, then it is assumed that the original data does not contain any errors and is used.

On the other hand, if an error (or errors) is detected, the following steps should be executed: The values of the other syndromes and parity check of the original data within the segment will be evaluated. If their values equal zero, this mean that one or three errors are exist in data word. To get the real number and the locations of the errors, all of the rows within the segment will be encoded together with the check row using XOR operator and the result will be saved in the check row. Finally, according to the received results of the analysis concerning the data word which crosses the columns that contain errors location, the bits values will be inverted. Thus, symbols will be corrected.

This algorithm may correct three errors in a data word even if the other words consist not more than one bit error. In this case, after detecting that an error exist in the data word, the values of the other syndromes and parity check within the data segment will be evaluated, and whenever an error is detected, it will be corrected using Hamming

Figure 3. Encoding algorithm using two-dimensional iterated code with d=8

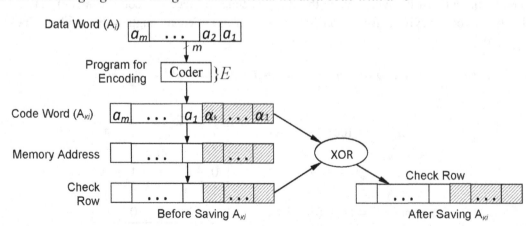

decoder. Finally, depending on the bits in the check row that refer to errors location in the data word, the correction process will be performed.

Figure 4 shows a detailed description of the developed decoding algorithm that implements two-dimensional IC.

On the basis of the derived algorithms, a program is created that models the process of detec-

tion and correction of multiple errors (Toghuj, 2007). The program performs the following operations:

- Calculates the optimal q value for given M.
- Defines the speed of events execution.
- Calculates redundancy of different code distances.

Figure 4. Decoding algorithm using two-dimensional iterated code with d=8

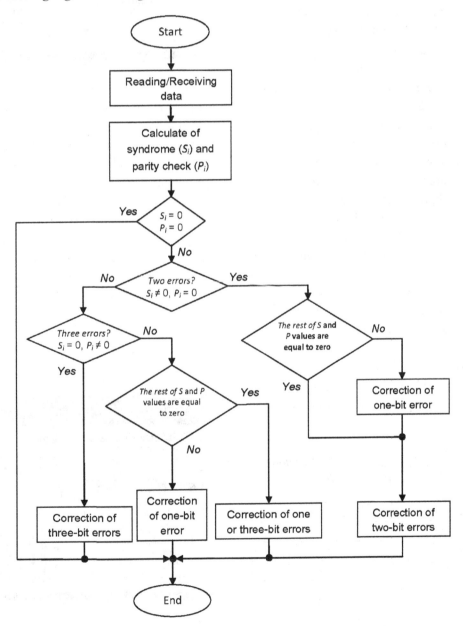

- Makes calculation of probability of errors occurrence in a data word depending on different factors.
- Checks up step by step of all stages of algorithm.

The following paragraphs explain the above operations in detail.

One subprogram solved the task of redundancy minimization of the code for effective data transmission. To achieve the stated optimization task, it would require the following two input parameters: the number of data bits and Hamming inequality. The developed subprogram finds the minimum values of q for M=16, 32, 64 and 128. The q Values which define the minimum redundancy at M=8, 16, 32, 64 and 128 bits of data for realization IC with code distance 8 are shown in Table 1.

For example the results stated in the table suggests that for M = 32 bits the segment table should have three rows and ten columns.

Another subprogram computes data decoding speed, as shown in Figure 5. The subprogram calculates the needed pulses depending on segment size M, as well as the amount of time to read the codeword from memory depending on the speed of the central microprocessor. Other factors that affect speed of execution may include compiler type, and the operating system mode in which the program is executed.

The next operation includes two subprograms for modeling IC redundancy. The first subprogram calculus redundancy factor (R) using the input

Figure 5. Interface of subprogram data decoding speed

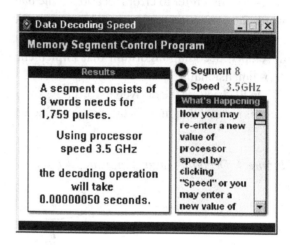

parameters and corresponding calculations, as shown in Figure 6.

The second subprogram compares redundancy factors with a constant M and variable q. For example, the relationship scheme of redundancy R depending on code distance d (d=6 and d=8), in 32-bit data word (M) protected by a two-dimensional IC is presented in Figure 7. The figure shows that the optimal redundancy (R) with a d=8 is achieved at q=3. Other input parameters would yield different output values.

Figure 6. Interface of subprogram redundancy model

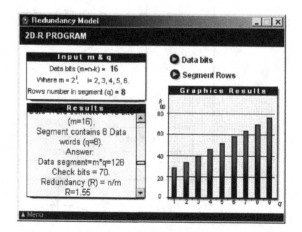

Table 1. Values q, defining minimum redundancy for a data word consisting of M bits

M	q
16	2.2
32	2.9
64	3.8
128	5.0

Figure 7. The relationship scheme of redundancy R depending on code distances where d=6 (dotted line) and d=8 (continuous line), in 32-bit data word protected by a two-dimensional IC

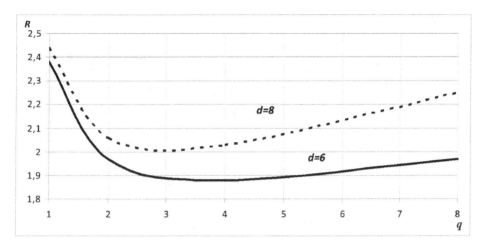

The next operation is performed by a program that includes a set of instructions related to four different characteristics, as shown in Figure 8. These include Linear Energy Transfer (LET) which is a measure of the energy transferred to material as an ionizing particle travels through it. Typically, this measure is used to quantify the effects of ionizing radiation on biological specimens or electronic devices, transmission fre-

Figure 8. The interface of subprogram simulating process of errors occurrence (Note: MeV-cm²: million electron volt per square cintmeter)

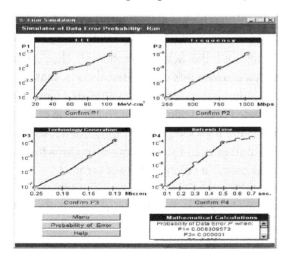

quency, memory generations, and refreshing time of memory elements. This program calculates probability of errors occurrence in a data word of one mega byte, depending on different factors, such as LET, transmission frequency, memory generations, and refreshing time of memory elements.

In P1, the improvement of the probability of error started becoming insignificant higher than 40 McV-cm², while in P4 the improvement of the probability of error started leveling off after 0.5 second. Conversely, P2 and P3 expound a negative relationship with memory generation and positive relationship with refreshing time of memory elements, respectably.

For the last operation, an error correction simulation subprogram allows checking up step by step of all stages of coding and decoding algorithms, and as well as detection and correction of errors. In Figure 9 we see that three bits in error are detected and localized, which will be corrected on a following step. In this case, three errors appear in the fifth row in $a_{5,5}$, $a_{5,9}$, and $a_{5,14}$. In the process of decoding the subprogram "2Dcode" forms values of syndrome S_5 corresponding to the fifth row and checks the parity P_5 of that row, as a result, $S_5 \neq 0$ and $P_5 \neq 0$.

Figure 9. A window of subprogram error correction simulation, modeling the algorithm that corrects three-bit errors

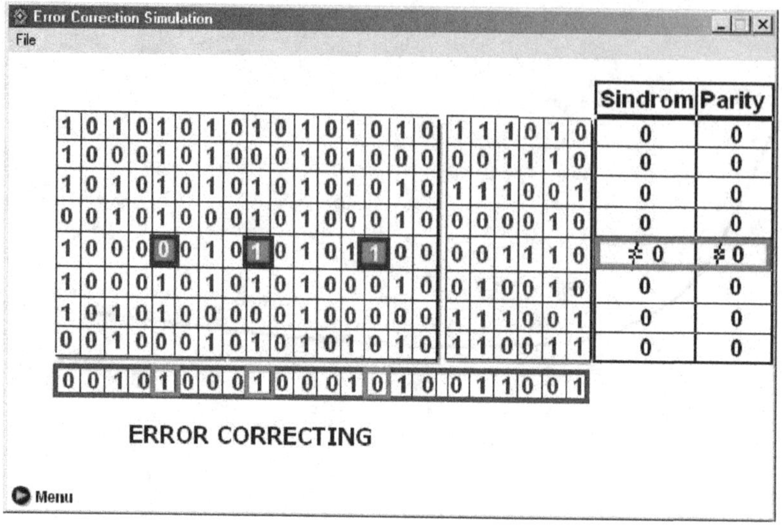

Then, depending on analyzing of the results of check row, the subprogram gives out a signal pointing on columns 5, 9 and 14 where errors exist. Finally, according to the received results of the analysis concerning the fifth row which crosses the columns that contain errors, the values of memory elements (bits) in $a_{5,5}$, $a_{5,9}$, and $a_{5,14}$ will be inverted. Thus, symbols will be corrected.

COMPARATIVE ANALYSIS

The comparison will be done using classical code (26,16) vs. the derived two-dimensional iterative code on the basis of redundancy, efficiency of coding and possibilities of correcting errors. The code parameters (26,16) refer to 26 bits of codeword and 16 data bits, which means that 10 extra bits is added to the original data.

The efficiency of coding *EF* is defined as the relation of number of data bits m to number of check bits k. For derived two-dimensional IC efficiency of coding can be found from the following expression:

$$EF_{IC} = \frac{m \cdot q}{(1 + [\log_2 m])(q + 1) + m} \quad (1)$$

Suppose that $q=16$, hence, the quantity of data bits in one data segment in memory is equal to 16 multiplies m. Using Equation 1, we observe the following, while volume of the saved bits is increasing, EF_{IC} increases too. In this case,

$$EF_{classical.C} = \frac{m}{k}$$

Comparative estimations of EF_{IC} and $EF_{classical.C}$ are shown in Figure 10. Notice that finding out the actual number of check bits (added or extra bits) for classical code, that corresponds to the demanded value of Hamming distance (code distance) at a fixed value of data bits, using for example Hamming bound, should be supplemented by modeling of code behavior on all possible combinations of errors.

At the same time, finding out the actual number of check bits for the developed code may

Figure 10. Efficiency of coding (EF) for two-dimensional IC (2D IC) and classical code (26,16) with q=16

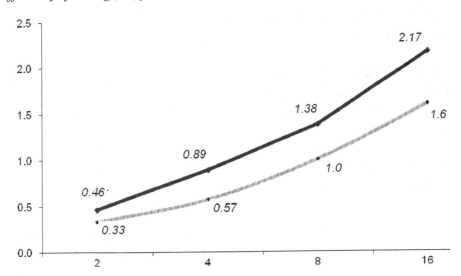

simply be calculated using the following expression:

$$(1 + [\log_2 m])(q + 1) + m$$

The performances of the two codes are compared on the basis of correctable range. Suppose that errors range is $1 \leq d_e \geq 4$. As it is known, finding out and correcting possibilities of a code can be done by using its code distance d. The generated program that realizes the algorithm of classical code (26,16), is characterized with code distance d=5. This means that the given code corrects up to two errors in data word consisting of 16 bits of information. In a case of occurrence of three or four errors, the decoding algorithm of classical code (26,16) brings additional number of errors in a word, carrying out false decoding.

The developed code consisting of an extended Hamming code and parity check is characterized with code distance d=8 and, hence, allows to detect up to 4 and to correct up to 3 errors within the data word.

In Table 2 the comparison of parameters of a two-dimensional iterative code and classical code (26,16) is presented. The computation complexity

of the decoding algorithm has also been evaluated using Equation 4.

A binary (n,m) code is a linear block code described by a sparse (k,n) parity-check matrix H. A bipartite graph with k check nodes in one class and n symbol nodes in the other can be created using H as its incidence matrix (Chen et al., 2005). This graph has two kinds of nodes: n symbols nodes, corresponding to each bit in the codeword, and k check nodes, corresponding to the parity checks. Each symbol node is con-

Table 2. Correcting possibilities and parameters of classical code (26,16) and the developed two-dimensional iterative code

N°	Parameters	Classical Code (26,16)	Two-Dimensional Iterative Code
1	Code Distance *(d)*	5	8
2	Number of Correctable Errors	2	3
3	Number of Detectable Errors	2	4
4	Redundancy R where $m=q=16$	1.625	1.47
5	Efficiency of Coding EF where $m=q=16$	1.6	2.14

nected to the check nodes it participates in, and each check node is connected to the symbol nodes it checks (Eleftheriou, Mittelholzar, & Dholakia, 2001).

The complexity of decoding scheme depends on the selected (n,m) code and the number of errors that should be corrected. While the computation complexity of syndrome values depends on how many ones exist in matrix H of (n,m) code.

The scheme of computing k-bits syndrome is based on the number of soft-XORs that can be found using:

$$L_{Syndrome} \geq m(d-1) \qquad (2)$$

where d= code distance, m= number of data bits.

The complexity of decoding depends on the selected code (n,m) and the number of correctable errors d_u. Thus, we used the classical code (19,8) that obtain the same capabilities of errors correction and the same value of m.

The outputs number of the decoder is equal to

$$\sum_{i=0}^{d_*} C_m^i$$

In this case every output is built using AND logic element with k-inputs. On the other hand, the inputs of the decoder will be connected to k logic elements of type NOT. Thus, the complexity of the decoder may be found using the following formula:

$$L_{DECODER} = (n-m-1)\sum_{i=0}^{d_u} C_m^i + (n-m) \qquad (3)$$

Then the general computation complexity of decoding is defined as:

$$L \geq L_{Syndrome} + L_{DECODER}$$
$$= m(d-1) + (n-m-1)\sum_{i=0}^{d_u} C_m^i + (n-m) \qquad (4)$$

The result of comparison between the classical code (19,8) and derived code allows to make the conclusion that the offered code possesses much lower computation complexity of decoding ($L=102$) comparing with the classical code (19,8) that corrects also three errors. Correcting possibilities and parameters of classical code (19,8) and the two-dimensional iterated code with $d=8$ and $q=2$ are shown in Table 3.

CONCLUSION

This research suggested concrete and practical solutions and guidelines which allow carrying out parallel methods of noise-immunity of data coding with a minimum of computational burden. The results of research can be used to design and manufacture parallel information processing systems which demand more operation reliability.

Table 3. Correcting possibilities and parameters of classical code (26,16) and the developed two-dimensional iterative code with d=8 and q=2

N°	Code	Hamming Distance d	Number of Correctable Errors	Number of Detectable Errors	Bits Redundancy R	Efficiency of Coding EF	Complexity of Decoding L
1	(19,8)	7	3	3	2,38	0,73	989
2	(24,8)	8	3	4	3	0,5	102

Program modeling of algorithms of data coding-decoding has passed expertise and is registered at the Russian Federal Agency for Intellectual Property, Patents and Trademarks (Toghuj, 2006). The program allows essentially improving efficiency of the algorithm, optimizing redundancy of the code, defining events execution speed, computing the probability of errors occurrence in a data word depending on different factors and checking up step by step of all stages of algorithm.

With code distance equal eight the derived code can detect four and correct three errors. It is proved that frequency rate of corrected errors essentially increases in following cases: 1) odd number of errors rate are concentrated within one row or a column, 2) any odd number of errors in one row, and each of other rows contains no more than one error.

The computation complexity of decoding is 9.7 times simpler than classical code (19,8), which means that the decoding algorithm can greatly reduce the computational complexity.

The algorithms can be used as a building block to decode continuously transmitted sequences obtained by parallel concatenated codes. It can be used in the third and fourth generations of technology for mobile networking in order to enhance the reliability of communication system.

Today the increased accuracy, bandwidth, flexibility, and speed of fiber optic cables make them perfect candidates for Internet communications and computer networking. Our study proved that the developed code can be recommended to be used in fiber optic cables especially in long-distance communications where the majority of errors rate under operating conditions are distributed between one error (66%) and two-three errors (23%).

Extensible applications for the theme of the paper are given below. As to extending the application domain to Web engineering, one of the developed solutions for higher reliable information is API client-side data deduplication. The algorithm in this paper may be applied at the backup process and at the end of a restore, if all of the data was restored through the API, and the object was deduplicated by the client, an end-to-end digest is calculated and compared to the value calculated at backup time. If those values do not match, error is returned. If an application receives this error, the data is corrupt. In addition, Web engineering is concerned with the debugging and error correction both at the server side of the application as well as the client. The server must verify that the data is well formed and correct. On the client side, it should be simple to debug errors in the response. In the case of XML, is relatively easy to verify that the data sent to the client, correctly formed and correct. You can use the schema for your data, and apply it to verify the data. On the client side it is hard to detect errors. For XML browser will not be able to convert it into response XML. When small amounts of JSON-data (JSON: JavaScript Object Notation) you can use the extension FireBug for debugging and error correction. But with larger amounts of data, it becomes more difficult to correlate the error message with a specific place in the code.

Such solutions may be also used in improving the basic watermarking method of encryption. The authors are currently developing a research framework for using the algorithm presented in this paper in enhancing the level of reliability of data transmission in cloud computing deployment models, whether it is public, community, hybrid, or private. Specifically, the framework will apply to storage-as-a-service type of cloud computing services.

The presented algorithm in this paper can be applied to the representation of XML data model instances providing rapid feedback and error correction. The derived algorithm enables to identify a section in which format errors can be located and to recover the undistorted section from the erroneous one. To support for error correction, an XML format has to interface with common channel coding algorithms. For interfacing the format shall allow partitioning of the representation according to the importance of the represented information to support unequal error protection based on the importance of the information.

Finally, the offered algorithm may be used in Differential Global Positioning System (DGPS) which is an enhancement to Global Positioning System (GPS) that uses a network of fixed, ground-based reference stations. These stations broadcast the difference between the measured satellite pseudoranges and actual pseudoranges, and receiver stations may correct their pseudoranges by the same amount. The correction signal is typically broadcast over UHF radio modem. DGPS reference stations transmit GPS error corrections in real time. The derived algorithm can be used to improve the reliability of the DGPS signal.

REFERENCES

Bajcsy, J., Chong, C., Garr, D., Hunziker, J., & Kobayashi, H. (2001). On iterative decoding in some existing systems. *IEEE Journal on Selected Areas in Communications, 19*(5), 883–890. doi:10.1109/49.924872

Barry, J., Lee, E., & Messerschmitt, D. (2004). *Digital Communication*. Dordrecht, The Netherlands: Kluwer Academic.

Benedetto, S., Divsalar, D., Montorsi, G., & Pollarab, F. (1996). Soft-output decoding algorithms in iterative decoding of turbo codes. *TDA Progress Report, 42*(124), 63–87.

Chen, J., Dholakia, A., Eleftheriou, E., Fossorier, M., & Hu, X. (2005). Reduced-complexity decoding of LDPC codes. *IEEE Transactions on Communications, 53*(8), 1288–1299. doi:10.1109/TCOMM.2005.852852

Dodd, P. E. (2001). *Epi, Thinned, and SOI Substrates*. Retrieved from http://parts.jpl.nasa.gov/mrqw/mrqw_presentations/S4_dodd.ppt

Eleftheriou, E., Mittelholzar, T., & Dholakia, A. (2001). Reduced-complexity decoding algorithm for low-density parity-check codes. *Electronics Letters Online, 37*(2), 102–104. doi:10.1049/el:20010077

Graham, J. (2002). *Soft errors a problem as SRAM geometries shrink*. Retrieved from http://www.ebnews.com/story/OEG20020128S0079

Johnston, A. (2000a). *Recent work on radiation effects in microelectronics at JPL*. Retrieved from http://rd49.web.cern.ch/RD49/RD49News/Allan_Johnston.pdf

Johnston, A. (2000b). *Scaling and technology issues for soft error rates*. Retrieved from http://nepp.nasa.gov/docuploads/40D7D6C9-D5AA-40FC-829DC2F6A71B02E9/Scal-00.pdf

Toghuj, W. (2006). *Software program and algorithm for correcting multi-error using two dimensional iterated code*. Moscow, Russia: Russian Federal Agency for Intellectual Property, Patents and Trademarks.

Toghuj, W. (2007). Program for modeling the detection and correction processes of multiple error using two dimensional iterated code. In *Proceedings of the 2nd International Conference on Modeling of Sustainable Regional Development* (Vol. 3, pp. 116-123). Nalchik, Russia: Russian Academy of Sciences.

Ziegler, J. F. (2000). *Review of accelerated testing of SRAMs*. Retrieved from http://www.srim.org/SER/SERTrends.htm

This work was previously published in the International Journal of Information Technology and Web Engineering (IJITWE), Volume 6, Issue 1, edited by Ghazi I. Alkhatib and Ernesto Damiani, pp. 1-12, copyright 2011 by IGI Publishing (an imprint of IGI Global).

Chapter 16
PECA:
Power Efficient Clustering Algorithm for Wireless Sensor Networks

Maytham Safar
Kuwait University, Kuwait

Hasan Al-Hamadi
Kuwait National Petroleum Company, Kuwait

Dariush Ebrahimi
Kuwait University, Kuwait

ABSTRACT

Wireless sensor networks (WSN) have emerged in many applications as a platform to collect data and monitor a specified area with minimal human intervention. The initial deployment of WSN sensors forms a network that consists of randomly distributed devices/nodes in a known space. Advancements have been made in low-power micro-electronic circuits, which have allowed WSN to be a feasible platform for many applications. However, there are two major concerns that govern the efficiency, availability, and functionality of the network—power consumption and fault tolerance. This paper introduces a new algorithm called Power Efficient Cluster Algorithm (PECA). The proposed algorithm reduces the power consumption required to setup the network. This is accomplished by effectively reducing the total number of radio transmission required in the network setup (deployment) phase. As a fault tolerance approach, the algorithm stores information about each node for easier recovery of the network should any node fail. The proposed algorithm is compared with the Self Organizing Sensor (SOS) algorithm; results show that PECA consumes significantly less power than SOS.

DOI: 10.4018/978-1-4666-2157-2.ch016

1. INTRODUCTION AND RELATED WORK

A wireless sensor network (WSN) is a form of network that consists of randomly distributed devices/nodes in a known space. Each node is typically equipped with radio transceiver, power source (usually a battery), processor, memory and/or other wireless communication device such as GPS receiver. WSN was originally developed for military purposes in the battle field. For example in a rescue operation these sensors that can be dropped by an airplane prior the actual operation, can reduce the risk of the operations by having the rescue crew aware of the overall situation (Akkaya, 2005). However, the development of such networks has encouraged the healthcare, industrial, environmental and other industries to utilize this technology. The size of each sensor node varies from 1 foot squared box to the size of a golf ball.

There are few challenges that faces the routing protocols, and hence the network formation in WSN. 1) Although in some applications the nodes' locations in Wireless Sensor Networks (WSN) are known and prefixed, however, the majority uses random distribution of nodes, which makes it difficult since the locations of the nodes are unknown. 2) The data flow from multiple nodes to a central base station. 3) Data redundancy, since many nodes could sense the same phenomena and hence producing redundant data. 4) Last and most important of all, is the power constraint and the limitation of radio transmission and communications among the WSN nodes (Akkaya, 2005).

According to Akkaya (2005) power consumption in WSN is closely related to its architectural issues, that is 1) Network dynamics, 2) Network deployment, 3) Energy consideration 4) Data delivery model 5) Node capabilities, and 6) Data aggregation. The WSN formation and setup has a great influence on power consumption and hence the network life time.

The main contribution of this paper is a new algorithm that significantly reduces the power consumption during the setup of a wireless sensor network, and hence prolongs the network life.

This solution relies on GPS technology to locate each node in the network. According to Sivaradje (2006) this may be a limitation especially in the urban areas were GPS signals are estimated to be around 15-40% less accurate due to magnetic disturbances, masking, unfavorable error propagation and other line of sight limitations. On the other hand WSN is normally applied in areas where human intervention is not probable; therefore the urban areas limitation is considered a major limitation.

Normally WSN nodes are distributed in an environment in which usual maintenance of the node is very difficult or highly undesirable, therefore the power source within the node is only and most valuable resource since it cannot be replaced. Hence keeping the network alive by using minimum resources is a big challenge (Pemmaraju, 2006). The transmission of data between WSN nodes consumes most of the node's power. One way to reduce this consumption is by grouping nodes into small groups within the transmission range of each node (cluster). Each cluster has a cluster-head that is usually at the center of the cluster radius and has the largest number of nodes within its transmission range (Guru, 2004). Figure 1 illustrates clustering in WSN.

The cluster approach normally puts a large constraint on the cluster head since it is the communication center, and hence loses its battery power rapidly (Shin, 2006). The cluster algorithms in WSN aim to build the network in a way in which data can be transferred between the network and base station with minimum radio transmission to reduce power consumption, on the other hand good algorithms must also build the network with maximum fault tolerance rate possible, which is another challenge beside power consumption (Kumar, 2006).

Figure 1. Example of WSN

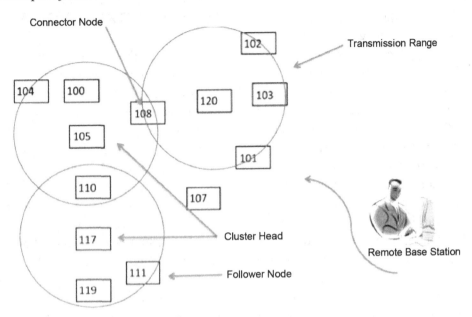

There are two main types of routing protocols in WSN, 1) the Data-Centric, and 2) the Clustering-Based approaches. The Data-Centric approach is reliable and robust solution to WSN, however despite many attempts to reduce the power consumption it is still power hungry approach, also due to its design it suffers relative delay in relaying the collected data to the base station. The clustering based approach on the other hand is more energy aware protocol, where many of the radio transmissions required in the data-centric approach is waved and compromised by a dedicated cluster node that forwards the collected data to another cluster node till the base station is reached (Akyildiz, 2002).

Many algorithms were introduced in the literature for the clustering of WSN (Shin, 2006), for example, Low- Energy Adaptive Clustering Hierarchy (LEACH). This protocol is self-organizing, that uses the clustering techniques to form the network. The principle idea behind this protocol is the random rotating of cluster heads in the network, which is divided into two phases, namely, the setup and the transmission phases. The idea is to reduce the power consumption and

prolong the lifetime of the network by reducing the load on the cluster heads that normally drain the power due to the overwhelming radio transmission (Heinzelman, 2000).

Centralized Low-Energy Adaptive Clustering Hierarchy (LEACH-C) is very similar to the LEACH protocol except that the decision of the next round of cluster heads is instructed by the base station rather than the self re-organizing technique in LEACH. During the initial setup of the network the information regarding the location and power level of each node is sent to the base station. Unlike LEACH, the base station is in a position to form much more effective clusters since it has the advantage of the global knowledge of the network. For example the cluster heads in each round are optimal, whereas in LEACH varies from round to another because it does not have the global knowledge of the network (Muruganathan, 2005).

Power Efficient Gathering in Sensor Information Systems (PEGASIS) protocol reduces the power consumption of WSN by forming "local collaboration" between sensor nodes. This protocol organizes the sensor nodes in a chain format where only one neighbor of the cluster is used to transmit the collected data. The next round, this neighbor is changed to the next in the chain, and so on. This will reduce energy by reducing the radio communication between the cluster heads and the neighbors (Muruganathan, 2005).

Based Station Controlled Dynamic Clustering Protocol (BCDCP) is similar to LEACH and LEACH-C in the sense that cluster heads function is rotated among nodes and the base station is going to take a big portion of the rotating operations to reduce power consumption. Further, the cluster selection is performed by the level of power in each node. The nodes are grouped and sorted based on power level and then, the cluster head operation is given to the node with high power level. The remaining nodes (those were not selected as cluster heads) are passed through a simple algorithm of splitting mechanism to obtain the number of neighbors for each cluster head. This was proven to be more efficient than LEACH, LEACH-C and PEGASIS (Muruganathan, 2005).

Algorithm for Cluster Establishment (ACE) uses a random function to select "candidate" nodes, further it depends on a manually adjusted parameters to control the creation of a new cluster (Sivaradje, 2006).

Shin et al. (2006) introduced Self-Organizing Sensor (SOS) networks. This algorithm aims to reduce power consumption by minimization the number of cluster heads. Unlike ACE, SOS does not use manually adjusted parameters, the results of both algorithms were compared and SOS proven to be more efficient in terms of network formation. SOS does not consider problems such as fast dying clusters heads.

This paper introduces a new clustering algorithm that is using less radio transmission to form the clustering network than SOS, and hence the proposed Power Efficient Cluster Algorithm (PECA) will create a more power efficient WSN than SOS if both were applied to the same network.

2. POWER EFFICIENT CLUSTERING ALGORITHM

In order to define the research problem we need to establish few facts regarding WSN. First, WSN nodes are normally (as mentioned earlier) distributed in areas where human intervention is not probable.

Second, each node operates using a battery as the only source of power and therefore energy is precious. Third, the nodes are randomly scattered, therefore it is imperative to organize the communication between these nodes for the network to deliver its purpose. Forth, radio transmission is energy hungry process. Fifth, the initialization and setting up the network is the stage were power is significantly consumed. The challenge is to form a cluster network between these nodes with minimum radio transmissions in order to preserve energy and hence prolong the lifetime and efficiency of the WSN.

This algorithm aims to reduce the power consumed to setup a WSN, it accomplishes this by attempting to lower the total number of radio transmission transactions between the nodes at this stage. The contribution of this algorithm does not include the data transmission and routing protocols; it merely covers the power consumption during the very beginning of setting up the network and just before the actual data transmission.

2.1. PECA Algorithm

The algorithm assumes the following:

- The sensors are distributed randomly in a known sized field.
- The nodes are of the same type in terms of radio transmission and battery power.
- Each node has a built-in GPS receiver.
- Each node has a unique numerical ID.

In this section the proposed algorithm is illustrated using in Table 1. What follows is a description of each column:

- **Step No.:** This shows the sequence order as the algorithm executes.
- **Step Details:** This illustrates single process details of the algorithm.
- **Step Result:** This explains the output of the process just executed.
- **Process Type:** This determines if the process is using the radio transmission or not.

Considering Figure 1 as an example of WSN distribution, Table 2 illustrates an example of the table created in node 105, the number between the {} represents the step number in Table 1. Note that the location parameters are just for illustration and are not real figures.

The table in each node (as illustrated in Table 2) has two sections: the self and neighbors' infor-

mation. The node ID is hard-coded and known to the node before deployment into the network. All other information are gathered and stored in the node's memory as the network gets formed.

In case of a connector node such as node 110, its table would show that it has 2 cluster head nodes in its transmission range i.e. 105, and 117; therefore, it changes its status to connector. This scenario would determine all cluster heads, followers and connectors in the network, and each node would have enough information to transmit data across the network to the base station.

As indicated earlier each node (in PECA) has a unique absolute integer, this number is hard-coded into its memory. This unique ID serves two major purposes. One, it uniquely identifies a node among other nodes in the network. And two, it is used to decide which node gets to be the cluster head if two nodes have the same number of followers in their transmission ranges. In this case two nodes on the network have the same neighbors

Table 1. Steps of PECA

Step No	Step Details	Step Result	Process Type
1	Using the GPS receiver each node identifies its current position in the network	Each node stores its GPS format location in its own memory	Communication
2	Each node broadcasts its ID and GPS location to every node in its transmission range	Each node will have a table of IDs and locations of each node in its transmission range.	Communication
3	Each node calculates the number of its neighbors using the table created in step 1	The number of neighbors for each node is known and recorded in the node parameters	Processing
4	Each node broadcasts the number of its neighbors to every node in its transmission range	The table created in step 1 will have the number of neighbors of each node in its transmission range.	Communication
5	Each node Look-up the table (updated in step 3) and finds the largest number of neighbors for each node, if the node ID matches the largest number then it make itself as Cluster Head, otherwise it is a follower.	Each node will know if it is a cluster head or a follower.	Processing
6	Broadcast those collected information	The network is formed; each node status is updated accordingly. And the table is updated with the status of each node.	Communication
7	Look-up the table and see if there are 2 cluster heads in the table or more if yes change the status to a connector	The connectors are identified	Processing
8	Broadcast the new status to all its neighbors	The network is complete.	Communication

Table 2. Example of a table created in each node in PECA network

Node Parameters			
ID 105		**Location {1}** E 208.456.88, N 048.56.87	
Status {5} Cluster Head		**Neighbors {3}** 4	
Neighbors Parameters			
ID {2}	**Location {2}**	**Neighbors {4}**	**Status {6}, {8}**
108	E 208.456.89, N 048.56.88	3	Connector
110	E 208.456.90, N 048.56.89	3	Connector
100	E 208.456.91, N 048.56.90	3	Follower
117	E 208.456.92, N 048.56.91	2	Cluster Head

and consequently the same number of followers, therefore both nodes are a legitimate candidate to be the cluster head of the group. PECA, then checks to see the two nodes numeric unique IDs and promotes the higher ID node to be the cluster of that group. For example if the two nodes have the IDs 10, and 20, the node with ID 20 will be assigned to be the cluster head in that case.

2.2. Power Consumption in WSN

This section aims to study the average power consumption of the Mica2 sensors that are usually powered by two AA batteries. The specifications of any sensor include: range, transmit, receive and sleep current draw. Range is usually specified in meters and communication range is usually larger than the sensing range. Manufacturers usually specify how much current is drawn in every operation.

For example, for Mica2 - Transmit operation consumes 27 mA, Receive operation consumes 10 mA, and Sleep operation consumes 1 microA.

On average, 8 mA in active mode and 15 microA in sleep mode. Now, let us assume that the sensor is always in active mode; how long would it last operating?

Each battery has a capacity that is measured in Wh (Watt hour) or Ah (Ampere hour) (1 Watt=1 Joul/Second)

Watt = V(volt)* A(current)

Hence, Wh =Ah * V

Usually an AA battery has a capacity of 2100 to 2900 mAh (average of 2500 mAh) and is operating at 1.5 volt. This means that if we draw a constant current of 2500 mA (at a constant voltage of 1.5 V) from the battery it would die after one hour. However, if we consume a constant current of 1250 mA the battery would last for 2 hours.

Now since Mica2 is using one 1.5 v battery, this means that it would have a capacity of 2500 mAh (2500 mA→ 1 hour) Now if we assume that we need to receive data all the time (receive current draw= 10 mA) this implies that the batteries would last for 2500/10*1 hour= 250 hours.

3. COMPARING SOS WITH PECA

As illustrated in Section 2, PECA stores a table in each node that holds information about all the nodes in its transmission range. SOS on the other hand does not, and this poses a dilemma in case of a crash. Hence, SOS would require establishing the network from scratch, which requires many radio transmissions that are power hungry. Moreover not having a table such as PECA would eliminate the possibility of programming for each node individually.

PECA assumes that each node has a GPS receiver built-in; this is used to locate each node in the network, once they are disbursed in the field. This assumption was based on the fact that GPS technology is now available and feasible to be installed on the WSN nodes. The idea is that each node would broadcast its GPS location and knowing the transmission radius of each node it is easier to identify the neighbors for each node and determine the cluster heads and connectors accordingly.

In PECA the number of radio transmissions to build the network is significantly less compared to those of SOS, nevertheless the number of cluster heads, connectors, and followers are the same. Moreover in SOS topology, it is required to do a number of iterations to find the cluster head to be accurate. As number of iteration increases, accuracy will increase.

To obtain accurate results when analyzing WSN algorithms, three major factors needs to be tested, namely 1) the number of nodes in the network, 2) the size of the area where the nodes to be disbursed, and 3) the transmission radius that each node is capable of communicating within. PECA was tested against SOS using these three factors as variables to study the impact of changing these values on the overall consumption of power. As mentioned earlier the radio transmission operation is the function that consumes most of the WSN nodes' power, hence we will use the total number of messages sent and received in each scenario to determine which algorithm is power efficient.

For example Table 3 shows the results of the test where the number of nodes in the network is variable i.e. 50,100 and 150, and the area and the transmission radius are constants. The "Total Send" and "Total Rcvd" parameters represent

Table 3. PECA and SOS comparison where number of nodes is variable

		Constants: Area = 2000 * 2000, Radius = 200							
No	Nodes	SOS				PECA			
1	50	Total Send	203	AVG Send	4.06	Total Send	58	AVG Send	1.16
		Total Rcvd	129	AVG Rcvd	2.58	Total Rcvd	28	AVG Rcvd	0.56
		CH	42	%CH	85.2	CH	42	%CH	84.4
		FN	6	%FN	12.6	FN	7	%FN	15
		CN	1	%CN	2.2	CN	0	%CN	0.6
2	100	Total Send	391	AVG Send	3.91	Total Send	134	AVG Send	1.34
		Total Rcvd	313	AVG Rcvd	3.13	Total Rcvd	131	AVG Rcvd	1.31
		CH	73	%CH	73.1	CH	69	%CH	69.5
		FN	21	%FN	21.4	FN	28	%FN	28.5
		CN	5	%CN	5.5	CN	2	%CN	2
3	150	Total Send	573	AVG Send	3.82	Total Send	223	AVG Send	1.486
		Total Rcvd	550	AVG Rcvd	3.666	Total Rcvd	286	AVG Rcvd	1.906
		CH	95	%CH	63.4	CH	89	%CH	59.6
		FN	43	%FN	29.066	FN	53	%FN	35.666
		CN	11	%CN	7.53	CN	7	%CN	4.733
		CH	158	%CH	35.311	CH	143	%CH	31.911
		FN	177	%FN	39.422	FN	205	%FN	45.711
		CN	113	%CN	25.266	CN	100	%CN	22.377

the total number of radio transmissions sent or received respectively in a given network by all nodes. The "AVG Send" and "AVG Rcvd" indicate the average radio transmissions sent or received for each node in a given network. And finally CH, CN and FN are the number of cluster heads, connector nodes and follower nodes respectively after the network is created and the algorithm is terminated in a given network.

Based on the fact that radio transmission in a WSN is power hungry, the more radio transmission is required to setup a WSN, the more power is consumed. Hence, the tests that are carried out focus on the total number of radio transmissions sent and received from and to each node in the network in order to have a fully functional (ready for communication) WSN using both PECA and SOS algorithms. In this test PECA uses a significant less amount of power to construct the network than SOS. Nevertheless the more nodes in the network, the more power is required from both algorithms, which is inevitable due to the complexity of the network as the number of nodes increases. The conclusion is then drawn to determine which algorithm is more power efficient in terms of setting-up a WSN based on the total number of radio transmission calculated upon the termination of each algorithm.

Another test was carried out where 200 nodes (constant value) are disbursed randomly in variable sized fields. The square areas of 500, 1000, 1500, and 2000 where used to examine the impact of area size upon the radio transmissions required and hence the power consumption. As the area increases both SOS and PECA consume less power, however, on average, PECA consume 50% less power than SOS in this test. Unlike PECA the average radio messages sent in SOS algorithm decreases as the number of nodes increases in the network, which is efficient. However the total number of radio transmissions is significantly less in PECA than SOS. This concludes that PECA consumes less power than SOS regardless of the number of nodes in the network.

The third important factor of determining power consumption within WSN is the transmission radius of each node in the network. Hence a third test was conducted where the transmission radius of each node varies from 25 to 100 divided on 4 tests. SOS algorithm consumes less power as the transmission radius of the node increases; on the other hand PECA consumes more power as the transmission rate of each node increases. However, the overall number of radio transmissions required to setup the network is significantly less in PECA than SOS. That was evidenced even with the largest radio transmission radius tested. Therefore this test concludes that PECA is more power efficient. Moreover it is very unlikely to have a node in the WSN that has a very large transmission radius that would make a significant difference in the obtained results.

Table 4 summarizes the comparison results between SOS and PECA algorithms in terms of power consumption. The rate was calculated using the total number of radio transmission (sent and received) required for each scenario. For example, SOS would require 5 times the power required for PECA to establish a WSN where the area= 2000*2000, transmission radius= 200, and there

Table 4. Power efficiency rate between SOS and PECA

Test Description	Variable Value	SOS:PECA
Variable Number of Nodes Constants: Area = 2000 * 2000, Radius = 200	50	5:1
	100	3:1
	150	2:1
Variable Transmission Radius Constants: Area = 2000*2000, Nodes = 200	25	5:1
	50	4:1
	75	3:1
	100	2:1
Variable Size of Network Area Constants: Radius = 200, Nodes = 200	500*500	7:1
	1000*1000	10:1
	1500*1500	2:1
	2000*2000	2:1

are 50 nodes in the network. As illustrated in the table, PECA power efficiency rate varies from 2 to 10 which is a significant deference where power is precious. In general SOS tends to gain efficiency as the number of nodes, transmission radius, or the network area increases. However in its best case scenario (according to the tests conducted in this paper) SOS consumes twice as much of energy to setup the network.

As mentioned earlier, if 2 nodes have the same number of followers within their transmission range, PECA would promote the node with the higher ID to be a CH, and demote the other to be FN. During the development of this scenario, few tests were conducted and the results were compared to those of SOS, and the results were indeed interesting.

Although PECA required more radio transmissions (compared to the tests above) to overcome this dilemma, it was evidenced that PECA is more reliable than SOS. The empirical results showed that PECA generated more clusters yet more connector nodes and hence higher availability rate of the network.

We believe that the late experiment is a great opportunity for future and further research of PECA algorithm. In this paper the main concern was to reduce the power consumption (as illustrated in details above), however the above results could be used so PECA could have a high level of fault tolerance as well as being power conservative.

4. CONCLUSION

This paper introduces a new cluster algorithm that aims to reduce the power consumption in WSN. The results of the proposed algorithm (PECA) were compared to those of SOS and the following were concluded. First, PECA incorporates the GPS technology (which is feasible nowadays) to locate a node in the network and saves significant amount of radio transmission used to form the network if compared to SOS algorithm. Second, the distance between cluster heads in PECA are not maximized; hence less energy is required than SOS to communicate between cluster heads. Third, in order to achieve its goal of having the least number of cluster heads in the network, SOS algorithm minimized the distance between CH, which results in less connector nodes between clusters and consequently less reliable network. PECA on the other hand does not minimize the distance between cluster heads, yet they have slightly the same number of CH, and consequently more connectors in the network.

The table formed and stored in each node in PECA opens a great opportunity to enhance the routing protocol in WSN. This is planned to be the future research of this paper.

Relying on GPS receivers to locate the node in the network poses a limitation, that is, all nodes in the network must have clear eyesight to the sky, and hence PECA algorithm would not operate in closed environment applications.

ACKNOWLEDGMENT

This research was funded by Research Administration at Kuwait University (Project No EO 09/06).

REFERENCES

Akkaya, K., & Younis, M. (2005). A survey on routing protocols for wireless sensor networks. *Ad Hoc Networks*, *3*(3), 325–349. doi:10.1016/j.adhoc.2003.09.010

Akyildiz, I. F., Su, W., Sankarasubramaniam, Y., & Cayirci, E. (2002). Wireless sensor networks: a survey. *Computer Networks*, *38*(4), 393–422. doi:10.1016/S1389-1286(01)00302-4

Baryshnikov, Y. M., Coffman, E. G., & Kwak, K. J. (2008). High performance sleep-wake sensor systems based on cyclic cellular automata. In *Proceedings of the 7th International Conference on Information Processing in Sensor Networks* (pp. 517-526).

Chan, H., & Perrig, A. (2004). ACE: An emergent algorithm for highly uniform cluster formation. In *Proceedings of the European Workshop on Sensor Networks* (pp. 154-171).

Gfeller, B., & Vicari, E. (2007). A randomized distributed algorithm for the maximal independent set problem in growth-bounded graphs. In *Proceedings of the 26th Annual ACM Symposium on Principles of Distributed Computing.*

Guru, S. M., Hsu, A., Halgamuge, S., & Fernando, S. (2004). Clustering sensor networks using growing self-organising map. In *Proceedings of Intelligent Sensors, Sensor Networks and Information Processing Conference* (pp. 91-96).

Heinzelman, W. R., Chandrakasan, A. P., & Balakrishnan, H. (2000). Energy-efficient communication protocol for wireless microsensor networks. In *Proceedings of the 33rd Annual Hawaii International Conference* (pp. 3005-3014).

Kumar, S. (2006). *Foundations of Coverage in Wireless Sensor Networks.* Unpublished doctoral dissertation, The Ohio State University, Columbus, OH.

Kwak, K. J., Baryshnikov, Y. M., & Coffman, E. G. (2008). Cyclic cellular automata: a tool for self-organizing sleep scheduling in sensor networks. In *Proceedings of the 7th International Conference on Information Processing in Sensor Networks* (pp. 535-536).

Kwak, K. J., Baryshnikov, Y. M., & Coffman, E. G. (2008). Self-assembling sweep-and-sleep sensor systems. *ACM SIGMETRICS Performance Evaluation Review, 36*(2), 131–133. doi:10.1145/1453175.1453207

Muruganathan, S. D., Ma, D. C., Bhasin, R. I., & Fapojuwo, A. O. (2005). A centralized energy-efficient routing protocol for wireless sensor networks. *IEEE Communications Magazine, 43*(3), S8–S13. doi:10.1109/MCOM.2005.1404592

Pemmaraju, S. V., & Pirwani, I. A. (2006). Energy conservation in wireless sensor networks via domatic partitions. In *Proceedings of the 7th ACM International Symposium on Mobile Ad hoc Networking and Computing.*

Shin, K., Abraham, A., & Han, S. Y. (2006). Self-organizing sensors by minimization of cluster heads using intelligent clustering. In *Proceedings of the Computational Science and Its Applications (ICCSA) Conference, Workshop on Ubiquitous Web Systems and Intelligence* (LNCS 3983, pp. 40-49).

Sivaradje, G., Nakkeeran, R., & Dananjayan, P. (2006). A Prediction-Based Flexible channel Assignment in Wireless Networks Using Road Topology Information. *Journal of Information Technology and Web Engineering, 1*(4), 37–48. doi:10.4018/jitwe.2006100103

This work was previously published in the International Journal of Information Technology and Web Engineering (IJITWE), Volume 6, Issue 1, edited by Ghazi I. Alkhatib and Ernesto Damiani, pp. 49-58, copyright 2011 by IGI Publishing (an imprint of IGI Global).

Chapter 17
Relay Selection in Distributed Transmission Based on the Golden Code Using ML and Sphere Decoding in Wireless Networks

Lu Ge
Loughborough University, UK

Gaojie J. Chen
Loughborough University, UK

Jonathon. A. Chambers
Loughborough University, UK

ABSTRACT

The implementation of cooperative diversity with relays has advantages over point-to-point multiple-input multiple-output (MIMO) systems, in particular, overcoming correlated paths due to small inter-element spacing. A simple transmitter with one antenna may exploit cooperative diversity or space time coding gain through distributed relays. In this paper, similar distributed transmission is considered with the golden code, and the authors propose a new strategy for relay selection, called the maximum-mean selection policy, for distributed transmission with the full maximum likelihood (ML) decoding and sphere decoding (SD) based on a wireless relay network. This strategy performs a channel strength tradeoff at every relay node to select the best two relays for transmission. It improves on the established one-sided selection strategy of maximum-minimum policy. Simulation results comparing the bit error rate (BER) based on different detectors and a scheme without relay selection, with the maximum-minimum and maximum-mean selection schemes confirm the performance advantage of relay selection. The proposed strategy yields the best performance of the three methods.

DOI: 10.4018/978-1-4666-2157-2.ch017

1. INTRODUCTION

In a wireless network, independent paths between the source and destination exist when multiple users act as relays for each other (Jing & Jafarkhani, 2006). Such cooperative diversity has been shown to be an effective technique to enable single-antenna users to share their antennas to create a virtual MIMO system (Li, 2009). Cooperative diversity has potential application in mobile wireless ad hoc networks. Better system performance gains can be achieved by exploiting relays due to pathloss gains as well as diversity and multiplexing gains. In traditional direct link communication systems, it is difficult to achieve high quality of service (QoS) for users, but with the exploitation of relays higher quality and cost effective transmission can be obtained (Dohler & Li, 2010). In recent years there has been considerable effort in the development of cooperative diversity schemes. A variety of cooperative schemes has been proposed. Among these strategies, perhaps the most important are amplify-and-forward (AF) and decode-and-forward (DF) approaches. For AF schemes, every relay cooperates and just retransmits its received signal scaled by its own transmitted power. For most DF schemes, every relay decodes the transmitted information before retransmitting it using its transmit power (Jing & Jafarkhani, 2009). However, using all the relays may not obtain the optimal performance of the relay network, and present practical problems such as asynchronism (Li & Xia, 2007) between the relays. Improved performance can be potentially achieved by selecting the cooperating relays to employ. In particular, selection can aim to find the best relay for solving the problem of multiple relay transmissions by requesting only a single relay or a subset of relays forwards the information from the source (Uysal, 2010). Best relay selection must be repeated as the channel conditions can change for each symbol block.

On the other hand, space-time coding is also used to exploit spatial diversity in traditional point-to-point MIMO systems and in recent years such encoding has been adopted in distributed cooperative networks (Jafarkhani, 2005). While space-time codes for MIMO systems can achieve full spatial diversity, a new full-rate and full-diversity linear dispersion algebraic space time code based on the golden number was proposed in Belfiore, Rekaya, and Viterbo (2005). It is best matched to a 2×2 coherent MIMO system. The minimum determinant of the golden code matrix does not depend on the size of the signal constellation and it achieves the diversity-multiplexing tradeoff (DMT) (Yao & Wornell, 2003; Goldsmith, 2005), which for the single-antenna N-relay NAF channel can be characterized by Azarian, Gamal, and Schniter (2005).

$$d_{NAF}\left(r\right) = \left(1-r\right) + N(1-2r)^{+} \tag{1}$$

where $(x)^{+}$ means the max$\{x,0\}$, r is the multiplexing gain and d is the diversity gain, which are given by

$$\lim_{SNR \to \infty} \frac{R(SNR)}{\log(SNR)} = r$$

and

$$\lim_{SNR \to \infty} \frac{\log P_{e}(SNR)}{\log(SNR)} = -d \tag{2}$$

where SNR is the signal-to-noise ratio, *R(SNR)* is the data rate measured by bits per channel usage and *Pe(SNR)* is the average error probability using the maximum likelihood (ML) decoder. The construction of the golden code allows application of spatial multiplexing so that it has higher bit rates. Meanwhile, the spatial diversity can improve the bit error performance (Mietzner, Schober, Lampe, Gerstacker, & Hoeher, 2009). These features of the golden code should therefore be exploited in distributed transmission in order to improve link performance. A multiple-input multiple-output (MIMO) system using space-time (ST) coding techniques can potentially achieve a huge capacity increase over a single wireless link. In such processing, the received signal is given by a nonlinear or a linear combination of the data symbols with additive noise. As the best detection method, maximum-likelihood (ML) depends on searching all of the transmitted signals possibilities in the constellations and chooses the closest to the received signals as the estimated transmitted signal (Choi, Negi, & Cioffi, 2000), but it has high complexity. On the other hand, due to redundant information which can make the ST system orthogonal, the linear decoder can approach approximate ML performance with lower complexity (Tarokh, Jafarkhani, & Calderbank, 1999). For overcoming the weaknesses of ML detection, the sphere decoder was proposed by Pohst (1981).

In this paper, we therefore focus on multiple relay selection in distributed transmission based on the golden code. In Section 2, we first review the construction of the golden code, and build and analyze the basic fixed relay selection scheme using full maximum-likelihood and a sphere decoder for detection. Section 3 elaborates two different relay selection strategies. In this section, based on previous relay selection strategies of optimal-SNR (signal-to-noise ratio) and maximum-minimum selection, we propose a new approach for distributed golden code transmission which we call maximum-mean selection. The SNR-maximizing multiple relay selection can be achieved over all relays (Jing & Jafarkhani, 2009). However, it is not appropriate for our relay network model and its complexity is exponential in the numbers of relays in the networks. Computer simulation results are presented in Section 4 which show the

new strategy proposed in this paper has advantage for a distributed golden code in wireless networks.

Throughout this paper, we use respectively bold upper and lower case letters to denote matrices and vectors; $|| \cdot ||$ denotes the Euclidean norm operator; $\overline{(\cdot)}$ is the conjugate operator; $(\cdot)^*$ denotes the Hermitian operator; $\lceil \cdot \rceil$ and $\lfloor \cdot \rfloor$ are respectively rounded up and rounded down; $(\cdot)^T$ denotes the transpose operator, and $i \triangleq \sqrt{-1}$.

2. OVERVIEW ON GOLDEN CODE AND INTRODUCTION OF SYSTEM MODEL

2.1. Golden Code

The golden code is a full rate and full diversity 2×2 linear dispersion algebraic space-time code for two transmit antennas and two or more receive antennas MIMO system (Belfiore, Rekaya, & Viterbo, 2005). The essence of the code is the golden number:

$$\theta = \frac{1 + \sqrt{5}}{2}$$

which is used to generate the best performance (Belfiore, Rekaya, & Viterbo, 2005). The codeword is of the form

$$\mathbf{C} = \frac{1}{\sqrt{5}} \begin{bmatrix} \alpha(a + b\theta) & \alpha(c + d\theta) \\ \gamma\overline{\alpha}(c + d\overline{\theta}) & \overline{\alpha}(a + b\overline{\theta}) \end{bmatrix} = \frac{1}{\sqrt{5}} \begin{bmatrix} s_1 & s_2 \\ s_3 & s_4 \end{bmatrix} \quad (3)$$

where a, b, c, d are drawn from the information symbol constellation.

$$\theta = \frac{1+\sqrt{5}}{2}$$

$$\bar{\theta} = \frac{1-\sqrt{5}}{2}$$

$$\alpha = 1 + i(1-\theta)$$

$$\bar{\alpha} = 1 + i(1-\bar{\theta})$$

To avoid vanishing determinants, the factor $|\gamma|$ is set as unity, which guarantees that the same average power is transmitted from each antenna at each channel use (Belfiore, Rekaya, & Viterbo, 2005). For the golden code, the elements of the codeword matrix are from the information symbol constellation. The constellation of the golden code is a rotated regular quadrature amplitude modulation (QAM) constellation. The golden code integer lattice structure provides efficient constellation shaping, so it can lead to the information lossless property (Viterbo & Hong, 2007). The diversity multiplexing tradeoff is an essential tradeoff between the error probability and the data rate of a system. The golden code can achieve optimal diversity-multiplexing tradeoff for a 2×2 MIMO system (Belfiore, Rekaya, & Viterbo, 2005). Due

to obtaining simultaneously both diversity and multiplexing gain, the golden code scheme is "Perfect." Several decoding strategies for golden codes have been studied, such as full maximum-likelihood and sphere decoding (Damen, Chkeif, & Belfiore, 2000). In this paper, we adopt these two methods to decode the golden code at the destination as we assume 4-QAM transmission.

2.2. Fixed Relay Scheme with Golden Code

For satisfying the basic environment of a 2×2 MIMO channel when transmitting a golden code, our fixed relay scheme adopts the model shown in Figure 1. It is composed of one source, two relays and one destination. There are respectively two antennas at the source and the destination, but only one antenna at each relay. Each node is half-duplex. The information symbols are coded with the golden code in the source rather than in the relays. We assume that the channels are quasi-static Rayleigh flat fading with coefficients h_{ij} and g_{ji} which are independent identically distributed (i.i.d.) complex Gaussian random variables with zero-mean and unit-variance, subscript i represents the i-th antenna at the source and the destination, and j denotes the j-th relay.

Figure 1. The two-input two-output relay network transmission structure for the golden code

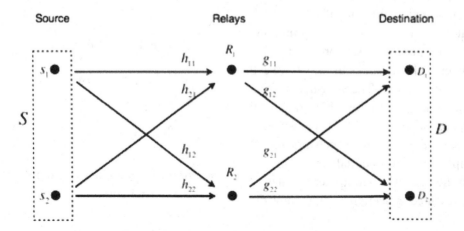

There are two transmission phases in the model. In step one, from Equation 3, s_1 and s_2 are broadcasted respectively by the source to the destination through relays R_1 and R_2, and then the source broadcasts s_3 and s_4 in the second symbol period. Mathematically, the signal received by the j-th relay can be expressed as

$$r_j^k = \sqrt{P_t}\left(s_{2k-1}h_{1j} + s_{2k}h_{2j}\right) + n_{rj}^k \qquad (4)$$

where P_t denotes the average transmit power of the source, and $k \in (1,2)$ is the symbol index; n_{rj}^k is the additive white Gaussian noise (AWGN) at the j-th relay. The signal received by the i-th antenna of the destination, during the relaying phase, can be expressed as

$$y_i^k = \sum_{j=1}^{2}\sqrt{P_r}\, r_j^k g_{ji} + n_{di}^k \qquad (5)$$

where P_r represents the average transmit power of the relay node, n_{di}^k is the additive white Gaussian noise (AWGN) at the i-th antenna of the destination. The power of every transmitting antenna in the source and relays is given by

$$P_t = P_r = \frac{P}{2A} \qquad (6)$$

where P is the total transmit power of the system (Jing & Jafarkhani, 2007), and A denotes the number of relays used. The vector of symbols received at the destination across the two antennas is denoted as y. Thus, the received signal can be written as

$$y = HS + n \qquad (7)$$

where y is the vector

$$[\,y_1^1 \quad y_2^1 \quad y_1^2 \quad y_2^2\,]^T$$

and s is the source vector

$$[\,s_1 \quad s_2 \quad s_3 \quad s_4\,]^T.$$

H is a 4×4 block diagonal matrix of effective transmission channels which is given by

$$\mathbf{H} = \begin{bmatrix} \mathbf{M} & 0 \\ 0 & \mathbf{M} \end{bmatrix} \qquad (8)$$

where

$$\mathbf{M} = \begin{bmatrix} h_{11}g_{11} + h_{12}g_{21} & h_{21}g_{11} + h_{22}g_{21} \\ h_{11}g_{12} + h_{12}g_{22} & h_{21}g_{12} + h_{22}g_{22} \end{bmatrix} \qquad (9)$$

and $\mathbf{0}$ represents a 2×2 full zero matrix. The total noise $\mathbf{n}$ is the vector

$$[\,n_1^1 \quad n_2^1 \quad n_1^2 \quad n_2^2\,]^T.$$

The elements of $\mathbf{n}$ can be written as

$$n_i^k = \sum_{j=1}^{2}\sqrt{P_r}\, n_{rj}^k g_{ji} + n_{di}^k \qquad (10)$$

2.3. Maximum-Likelihood Decoding

First, we adopt full maximum-likelihood (ML) for decoding the golden code:

$$\hat{s} = \arg\min_{s \in S_c}\left\{\| y - Hs \|^2\right\} \qquad (11)$$

where S_c denotes the collection of all member of the symbol constellation. The principle of ML detection is to compare all possible values of the received signals and transmitted one by one, and then to take the closest one to be the estimated signal (Alamouti, 1998). In the AWGN channel environment, in the sense of obtaining the minimum bit error rate (BER) for every antenna, this decoding approach has the best performance. From Equation 11, when calculating one $\hat{s}$, it has to compare one by one all the possible signals transmitted to determine the estimated signals. Therefore, with the increasing number of transmitted antennas and modulation levels, the complexity of maximum-likelihood detection increases exponentially. It causes so large a calculation that it would be very difficult to realize. For overcoming this computational complexing weakness of ML, lower complexity sphere decoding (SD) is applied.

2.4. Sphere Decoding

All possible received signals can be represented in a lattice structure, therefore, the SD algorithm is easily used for decoding the MIMO system (El-Khamy, Vikalo, Hassibi, & McEliece, 2009). The principle of the SD algorithm is to search the closest lattice points to the received signal within a radius c of sphere centred at the particular received signal value (Viterbo & Boutros, 1999). The choice of c is crucial to the speed of the algorithm. Decreasing the radius r, the number of searching signal points can be reduced and the speed of calculation will rise (Damen, Gamal, & Caire, 2003), however the performance of the decoding may be affected.

2.5. Initial Radius

As for the basic maximum-likelihood (ML) algorithm (Equation 11), the sphere decoder of the golden code searches over only a radius c centred around the received signal vector, i.e. (Zhang, Li, Yuan, Zhang, & Yang, 2007):

$$\| \mathbf{y} - \mathbf{Hs} \|^2 \le c^2$$

From Equation 3, we can get the channel matrix $\mathbf{A}$:

$$\mathbf{A} = \frac{1}{\sqrt{5}} \begin{bmatrix} \alpha & \alpha\theta \\ \alpha & \alpha\theta \end{bmatrix} \tag{12}$$

Therefore, the initial radius can be defined as

$$c^2 = \| \mathbf{y} - \mathbf{As}_{zf} \|^2 \tag{13}$$

where $\mathbf{s}_{zf}$ denotes the initial estimate, which is the Zero-Forcing (ZF) detection solution. Therefore,

$$\mathbf{s}_{zf} = \mathbf{A}^+ \mathbf{y} \tag{14}$$

where $\mathbf{A}^+$ denotes the pseudo-inverse of $\mathbf{A}$

$$\mathbf{A}^+ = (\mathbf{A}^T \mathbf{A})^{-1} \mathbf{A}^T \tag{15}$$

2.6. Derivation

Assuming the channel is known at the receiver and taking the QR factorization of the channel matrix $\mathbf{A}$ (Equation 12):

$$\mathbf{A} = \mathbf{Q} \begin{bmatrix} \mathbf{R} \\ 0 \end{bmatrix} \tag{16}$$

where $\mathbf{R}$ is an upper triangular matrix with positive diagonal elements, $\mathbf{0}$ is a null matrix, and $\mathbf{Q} = [\mathbf{Q}_1, \mathbf{Q}_2]$ is an unitary matrix. Therefore, we can get:

$$c^2 \geq \mathbf{y} - \begin{bmatrix} \mathbf{Q}_1 & \mathbf{Q}_2 \end{bmatrix} \begin{bmatrix} \mathbf{R} \\ 0 \end{bmatrix} \mathbf{s}^2$$
$$= \mathbf{Q}_1^* \mathbf{y} - \mathbf{R}\mathbf{s}^2 + \mathbf{Q}_2^* \mathbf{y}^2$$

where $(\cdot)^*$ denotes Hermitian matrix transposition. We also easily obtain

$$c'^2 - \| \mathbf{Q}_2^* \mathbf{y} \|^2 \geq \| \mathbf{Q}_1^* \mathbf{y} - \mathbf{R}\mathbf{s} \|^2 \qquad (17)$$

Setting

$$y' = \mathbf{Q}_1^* \mathbf{y} \text{ and } r'^2 = r^2 - \left| \mathbf{Q}_2^* \right|^2 ,$$

we can rewrite Equation 17 as

$$c'^2 \geq \sum_{i=1}^{m} (y_i - \sum_{j=i}^{m} r_{i,j} s_j)^2 \qquad (18)$$

where $r_{i,j}$ denotes the (i,j) entry of $\mathbf{R}$. Expanding Equation 18 yields

$$c' \geq \left(\mathrm{y}_m - \mathrm{r}_{m,m} \mathrm{s}_m \right)^2$$
$$+ \left(\mathrm{y}_{m-1} - \mathrm{r}_{m-1,m} \mathrm{s}_m - \mathrm{r}_{m-1,m-1} \mathrm{s}_{m-1} \right)^2 + \cdots \qquad (19)$$

From Equation 19, the first term depends only on s_m, the second term depends on $\{s_m, s_{m-1}\}$ and so on. Therefore, a necessary condition

$$r'^2 \geq (y_m - r_{m,m} s_m)^2$$

leads to

$$\left\lceil \frac{-r' + y_m}{r_{m,m}} \right\rceil \leq s_m \leq \left\lfloor \frac{r' + y_m}{r_{m,m}} \right\rfloor \qquad (20)$$

where $\lceil \cdot \rceil$ and $\lfloor \cdot \rfloor$ denote rounded up and rounded down. For every s_m satisfying Equation 20, we can obtain s_{m-1} in Equation 19. According to the iteration, we can also easily get s_{m-2}. After searching the entire collection

$$\left\{ s_m, s_{m-1}, \cdots, s_2, s_1 \right\},$$

we compare the distance c_1 between point s_1 and the centre of sphere with the initial radius c. If $c_1 < c$, the initial radius is changed to c_2. If not, the process has to return to the last step to continue to calculate until the entire set

$$\left\{ s_m, s_{m-1}, \cdots, s_2, s_1 \right\}$$

is found. If the entire collection cannot be found, the value of the initial radius needs to be increased. In the simulation section of this paper, the simulation results of the golden code with maximum-likelihood detection and sphere detection will be given.

3. SELECTIVE RELAY SCHEME WITH THE GOLDEN CODE

In this section, we propose a multi-relay selection strategy with the golden code in wireless networks as represented in Figure 2, which shows the scheme of relay selection with the golden code in wireless networks. In the model, the channel from the source to the i-th relay is denoted as h_i and from the i-th relay to the destination as g_i. All assumptions are the same as those for the system model of Figure 1. Firstly, we adopt the maximum-minimum selection method in the model. Then, the new selection scheme which finds the mean of the maximum values among the channels is presented. Our aim is to select the best two relays

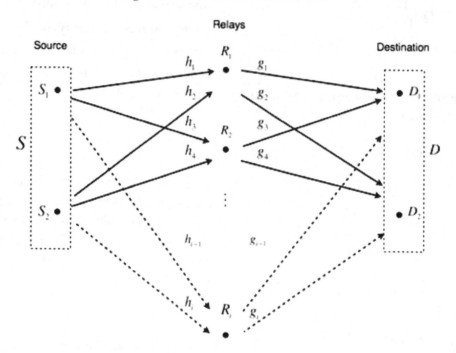

Figure 2. Relay selection with the golden code in a wireless network

from i relays for transmission in a cooperative network.

3.1. Maximum-Minimum Selection

This strategy of relay selection was presented in Bletsas, Khisti, Reed, and Lippman (2006); however, there is a significant difference in our model. To form the basic 2×2 MIMO transmission channels, every relay node has four channels attached to it, rather than two. Two channels from the source to the relay denoted by h_{2i-1} and h_{2i}, meanwhile g_{2i-1} and g_{2i} depict the other two channels from the relay to the destination. Relay selection in this context therefore becomes choosing the best relay and the second best from i relays to yield the most effective transmission. Using the notation of Figure 2, the worst channel of the i-th relay is given by:

$$
\begin{aligned}
&L_{min}^{(i)} \\
&= min\left\{ \left|h_{2i-1}\right|^2, \left|h_{2i}\right|^2, \left|g_{2i-1}\right|^2, \left|g_{2i}\right|^2 \right\}
\end{aligned}
\tag{21}
$$

These values are then calculated for all of the relays and stored in the vector $\boldsymbol{L}_{min}$. The relay corresponding to the maximum of these minima is selected, together with the relay which has the maximum of the remaining minima.

3.2. Maximum-Means Selection

Our second selection approach is based on calculating the mean of the strengths of the channels connected to each relay. The mean of these four channels for the i-th relay is obtained as

$$
\begin{aligned}
&L_{mean}^{(i)} \\
&= \frac{\left|h_{2i-1}\right|^2 + \left|h_{2i}\right|^2 + \left|g_{2i-1}\right|^2 + \left|g_{2i}\right|^2}{4}
\end{aligned}
\tag{22}
$$

This mean value is then calculated for all relays and stored in the vector L_{mean}. The relay with the maximum value of these minima is selected as the relay with the maximum of the remaining means. Comparing with maximum-minimum selection, this method can better balance the level among the channels, since the maximum-minimum selection just depends on the minimum value of one channel, rather than an overall performance measure. Therefore, the maximum-mean selection can be better for relay selection. In the next section, the performance of these schemes is evaluated.

4. SIMULATION RESULTS

In the simulation results, first we use the full diversity and full rate golden code and the modulation is 4-QAM in the point-to-point MIMO system and the distributed MIMO system. The transmitted number of symbols is 10^6. The numbers of transmit antennas N_t and the receive antennas N_r are two, and the number of relays is two. The assumptions are that the channel is quasi-static flat fading and perfectly known at the receiver. Figure 3 and Figure 4 show the bit error rate (BER) performances with the increased signal-noise-ratio (SNR).

Figure 3 is the comparison of the performances of the golden code in the point-to-point MIMO system with the maximum likelihood (ML) detection and the sphere detection (SD) with the radius 1. Clearly, from 0dB to 12dB of SNR, the performance of SD is worse than the ML. When the SNR is approximately 0dB, almost every symbol is decoded in error when using SD. However, the slope of the SD curve decreases rapidly. Therefore, when the SNR equals to approximately 12dB, the meeting point with these two curves occurs, and after that, the performance of SD can reach the performance of ML.

Figure 3. Comparison of the performances of the golden code in the MIMO system with the maximum-likelihood detection and the sphere detection

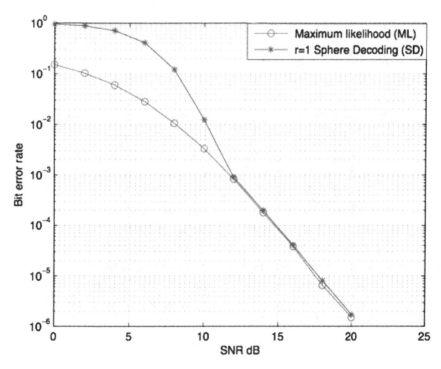

Figure 4. Comparison of the performances of the golden code in the distributed MIMO system with the different radii of the sphere decoding

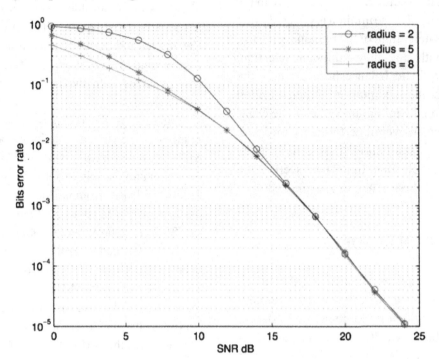

Figure 4 shows the comparison of the performances of the golden code in the distributed MIMO system with the different radii of the sphere decoding. The simulation is based on the radius respectively equal to 2, 5, and 8. Therefore, it is easy to show that the bit error rate of the system decreased with increasing the value of SNR. When the radius is equal to 5 and 8, the performances of the system are nearly the same at 10dB of SNR, after that these two are always the same. When the radius is 2, the system performance approaches to the performance of the system with radii 5 and 8 at 16dB SNR. Therefore, for high SNR, based on the different radii of sphere detection the performance of the system is nearly the same. Secondly, we show the simulated performance of the relay selection with distributed transmission based on the golden code in wireless networks. The performance is shown by bit error rate (BER) using quadrature phase-shift keying (QPSK) symbols as well. The total transmission power of the system is

fixed as P and the additive noise variance at each receiving node is unity. We consider the selection of 2 relays from a total of 4, 6, and 8 relays for the above two different selection strategies.

In Figure 5, the BER performance compares the fixed relay and maximum-minimum relay selection scheme. The BER performance of the fixed relay is clearly worse than the maximum-minimum relay selection. For example, to obtain BER performance of 10^{-3} with four participated relays, the maximum-minimum relay selection scheme needs essentially 13dB total power, P, but the fixed relay system requires almost 14dB. The figure also shows a small improvement in performance as the total number of relays is increased.

Figure 6 is the simulation results of BER performance of the maximum-mean relay selection and the fixed relay scheme. Obviously, the BER performance of the maximum-mean relay selection outperforms the fixed relay scheme. For example, the selection case requires approxi-

Figure 5. Performances of no selection and maximum-minimum relay selection within the golden code two stage network

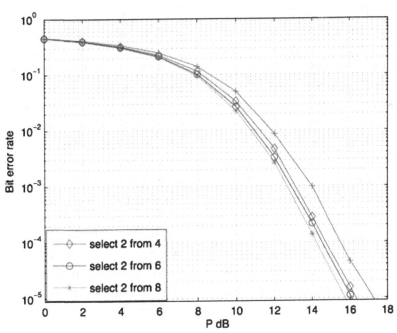

Figure 6. Performances of no selection and maximum-mean relay selection within the golden code two stage network

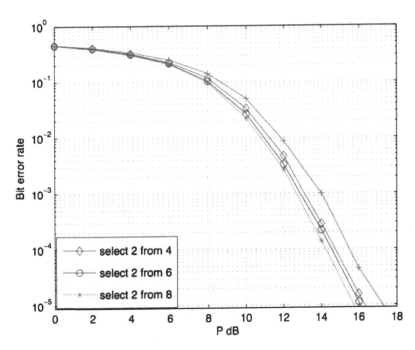

mately 12dB of total power, P, and the power of the no selection case is 14dB at BER 10^{-3}. Moreover, with increasing the total number of relays, the BER performances can be improved, i.e., when BER=10^{-3}, the total transmission powers of the 4, 6, and 8 relay cases respectively needs approximately 13.5dB, 12.5dB, and 12dB.

Figure 7 shows a direct comparison of performances of maximum-minimum strategy and maximum-mean strategy. The dashed curves represent the performances of maximum-minimum selection, and the solid curves show the performances of maximum-minimum selection. Clearly, the maximum-mean scheme shows a small advantage. Generally, when the number of selected relays equals to 4, 6, and 8, the maximum of means selection always has approximately 1dB superiority. That is because the maximum-mean selection can better balance the channel qualities.

5. CONCLUSION

We have realized transmission using the golden code in wireless relay networks and proposed a new multiple relay selection strategy. Through bit error rate simulations, the maximum of the channel parameter means selection achieves the best performance. The improvement is because this approach performs an overall channel strength tradeoff at every relay node to select the best two relays. Therefore, this new maximum-mean policy appears valuable for cooperative diversity systems based on the golden code.

Moreover, we used both full ML and sphere detection for decoding the golden code. The speed of calculation of sphere decoding is faster than the ML approach. In simulation on a dual core PC under Windows 7 and MATLAB 7.1, the simulations presented in Figure 3 would take more than

Figure 7. Comparison of performances of maximum-minimum strategy and maximum-mean strategy

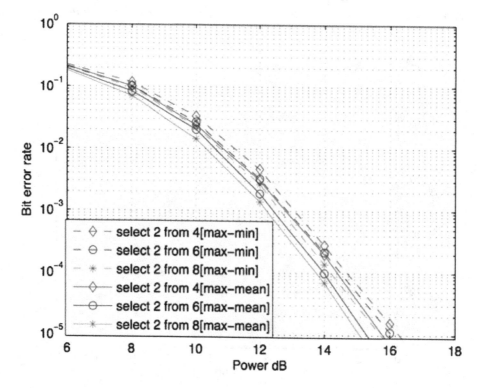

6 hours with full ML whereas this time is halved with SD. The weakness of sphere detection is that the performance can be worse than the maximum-likelihood at low SNR if the radius is chosen to be too small. For future work, further analysis of the relay selection scheme is being considered, such as outage probability and capacity measures.

ACKNOWLEDGMENT

Part of this paper was presented as a conference work at NGMAST 2011.

REFERENCES

Alamouti, S. M. (1998). A simple transmit diversity technique for wireless communications. *IEEE Journal on Selected Areas in Communications*, *16*(8), 1451–1458. doi:10.1109/49.730453

Azarian, K., Gamal, H. E., & Schniter, P. (2005). On the achievable diversity multiplexing tradeoff in half-duplex cooperative channel. *IEEE Transactions on Information Theory*, *51*(12), 4152–4172. doi:10.1109/TIT.2005.858920

Belfiore, J.-C., Rekaya, G., & Viterbo, E. (2005). The golden code: a 2×2 full-rate space-time code with nonvanishing determinants. *IEEE Transactions on Information Theory*, *51*(4), 1432–1436. doi:10.1109/TIT.2005.844069

Bletsas, A., Khisti, A., Reed, D. P., & Lippman, A. (2006). A simple cooperative diversity method based on network path selection. *IEEE Journal on Selected Areas in Communications*, *24*(3), 659–672. doi:10.1109/JSAC.2005.862417

Choi, W. J., Negi, R., & Cioffi, J. M. (2000). Combined ML and DEF decoding for the V-BLAST system. In *Proceedings of the IEEE International Conference on Communications* (Vol. 3, pp. 1243–1248).

Damen, M. O., Chkeif, A., & Belfiore, J.-C. (2000). Lattice code decoder for space-time codes. *IEEE Communications Letters*, *4*(5), 161–163. doi:10.1109/4234.846498

Damen, M. O., Gamal, H. E., & Caire, G. (2003). On maximum-likelihood detection and the search for the closest lattice point. *IEEE Transactions on Information Theory*, *49*(10), 2389–2402. doi:10.1109/TIT.2003.817444

Dohler, M., & Li, Y. H. (2010). *Cooperative communications hardware, channel & PHY*. Hoboken, NJ: Wiley.

El-Khamy, M., Vikalo, H., Hassibi, B., & McEliece, R. J. (2009). Performance of sphere decoding of block codes. *IEEE Transactions on Communications*, *57*(10), 2940–2950. doi:10.1109/TCOMM.2009.10.080402

Fitzek, F. H. P., & Katz, M. D. (Eds.). (2006). *Cooperation in Wireless Networks: Principles and Applications – Real Egoistic Behavior is to Cooperate*. Berlin, Germany: Springer. doi:10.1007/1-4020-4711-8

Goldsmith, A. (2005). *Wireless Communications*. Cambridge, UK: Cambridge University Press.

Jafarkhani, H. (2005). *Space-Time Coding – Theory and Practice*. Cambridge, UK: Cambridge University Press. doi:10.1017/CBO9780511536779

Jing, Y., & Jafarkhani, H. (2006). Distributed space-time coding in wireless relay networks. *IEEE Transactions on Wireless Communications*, *5*(12), 3524–3536. doi:10.1109/TWC.2006.256975

Jing, Y., & Jafarkhani, H. (2007). Using orthogonal and quasi-orthogonal designs in wireless relay networks. *IEEE Transactions on Information Theory*, *53*(11), 4106–4118. doi:10.1109/TIT.2007.907516

Jing, Y., & Jafarkhani, H. (2009). Single and multiple relay selection schemes and their achievable diversity orders. *IEEE Transactions on Wireless Communications*, 8(3), 1414–1423. doi:10.1109/TWC.2008.080109

Li, Y. (2009). Distributed coding for cooperative wireless networks: An overview and recent advances. *IEEE Communications Magazine*, 47(8), 71–77. doi:10.1109/MCOM.2009.5181895

Li, Z., & Xia, X. G. (2007). A simple Alamouti space–time transmission scheme for asynchronous cooperative systems. *IEEE Signal Processing Letters*, 14(11), 804–807. doi:10.1109/LSP.2007.900224

Mietzner, J., Schober, R., Lampe, L., Gerstacker, W. H., & Hoeher, P. A. (2009). Multiple-antenna techniques for wireless communications - a comprehensive literature survey. *IEEE Communications Surveys and Tutorials*, 11(2), 87–103. doi:10.1109/SURV.2009.090207

Pohst, M. (1981). On the computation of lattice vectors of minimal length, successive minima and reduced basis with applications. *ACM SIGSAM Bulletin*, 15(1), 37–44. doi:10.1145/1089242.1089247

Tarokh, V., Jafarkhani, H., & Calderbank, A. R. (1999). Space-time block codes from orthogonal designs. *IEEE Transactions on Information Theory*, 45(5), 1456–1467. doi:10.1109/18.771146

Uysal, M. (Ed.). (2010). *Cooperative communications for improved wireless network transmission: Framework for virtual antenna array applications*. Hershey, PA: Information Science Reference.

Viterbo, E., & Boutros, J. (1999). A universal Lattice Code decoder for fading channel. *IEEE Transactions on Information Theory*, 45(5), 1639–1642. doi:10.1109/18.771234

Viterbo, E., & Hong, Y. (2007). Applications of the Golden Code. In *Proceedings of the Information Theory and Applications Workshop* (pp. 393–400).

Yao, H., & Wornell, G. W. (2003). Achieving the full MIMO diversity multiplexing frontier with ratation-based space-time codes. In *Proceedings of the Allerton Conference on Communication, Control, and Computing* (pp. 400–409).

Zhang, L., Li, B. J., Yuan, T. T., Zhang, X., & Yang, D. C. (2007, September). Golden Code with low complexity sphere decoder. In *Proceedings of the IEEE International Symposium on Personal, Indoor and Mobile Radio Communications* (pp. 1–5).

This work was previously published in the International Journal of Information Technology and Web Engineering (IJITWE), Volume 6, Issue 4, edited by Ghazi I. Alkhatib and Ernesto Damiani, pp. 63-75, copyright 2011 by IGI Publishing (an imprint of IGI Global).

Chapter 18
Convergence Aspects of Autonomic Cooperative Networks

Michał Wódczak
Telcordia Technologies, Poland

ABSTRACT

The current efforts across industry and academia are to develop new paradigms that enable ubiquitous on-demand service provision. This aim may be achievable because of the envisaged deployment of cutting-edge technologies such as cooperative transmission. However, a real advancement is only attainable when autonomic system design principles are taken into account. Looking at the concept of the Relay Enhanced Cell, one may come across commonalities with Mobile Ad-hoc Networks. Especially in Local Area scenarios, Base Stations seem to resemble advanced Access Points, while fixed and movable Relay Nodes might be replaced by powerful mobile User Terminals. On top of it, Generic Autonomic Network Architecture would help accommodate the fact that network devices may expose autonomic cooperative behaviors, allowing them to play certain roles. Finally, such a network must interact with Operations Support System deployed by the network operator for uninterrupted, continued operation.

INTRODUCTION

The most recent trends in research, industry and academia domains aim to develop new networking paradigms that would enable ubiquitous service delivery upon request. In fact, the end user mobile devices are envisaged to be equipped with the most advanced technologies, such as cooperative transmission (Doppler, Osseiran, Wódczak, & Rost, 2007). However, a real advancement will only be attainable, when the ground for convergence among different concepts supporting cooperative mobile networking has been accurately established. This will undoubtedly result in even further increased complexity as compared to the current solutions, however, the changes seem imminent. Looking at the concept of the Relay Enhanced Cell (REC), one can come across some commonalities with Mobile Ad-hoc Networks (Wódczak, 2007). Especially, for Local

DOI: 10.4018/978-1-4666-2157-2.ch018

Area scenarios, the Base Station (BS) might be very generally perceived as an advanced Access Point (AP) and the fixed and/or movable Relay Nodes (RN) might be replaced by movable and/or mobile User Terminals (UTs). Going further, the resulting networked system needs to be designed to accommodate the fact that the UTs can expose certain dose of autonomic behaviors, allowing them to auto-discover and choose to play certain roles, such as cooperation. In this context and with the use of autonomic system design principles, cooperative transmission can be translated into autonomic cooperative networking. From the business perspective, such a system needs to be managed accordingly and, therefore; the Generic Autonomic Network Architecture would be incorporated into the global picture to enable the interactions with Operations Support System (OSS) (Jain, Hayward, & Kumar, 2003). Consequently, one can expect that in the nearest future, network operators might be able to exploit the possibility of cooperation among the devices belonging to the end users to extend the capabilities of their networks and to facilitate Quality of Service (QoS) provision. Obviously, certain issues need to be tackled by the business models, such as the necessity for the incorporation of special incentive mechanisms, so the end users would be more willing to agree to trade quicker drainage of their batteries for additional bandwidth or other benefits. This paper discusses the selected aspects of the current advancements in the area of autonomic cooperative networking and outlines the way forward in terms of progressing the convergence among the aforementioned technologies to allow the instantiation of cooperative behaviors for the benefit of mobile network operators, service providers and of course the end users.

COOPERATIVE MOBILE NETWORKS

Current Deployments

Cooperative relaying emerged as a very promising method for improving the process of transmission in wireless mobile networks (Herhold, Zimmermann, & Fettweis, 2004; Pabst et al., 2004). This approach is based on spatio-temporal processing and this work assumes the use of space-time block coding, while different techniques are applicable depending on specific requirements (Alamouti, 1998; Tarokh, Jafarkhani, & Calderbank, 1999). In general, cooperative transmission is performed by groups of nodes forming Virtual Antenna Arrays (VAA), and so making use of transmission diversity. This helps improve the quality of the radio links between the source and destination nodes. Such a process may also take place over multiple hops where multiple tiers of nodes cooperatively apply distributed space-time block coding (Laneman & Wornell, 2003) to process the transmitted signal in both the spatial and temporal domains (Dohler, Gkelias, & Aghvami, 2004). This will be further discussed in the section describing the convergence aspects related to the incorporation of network layer routines provided by the Optimized Link State Routing Protocol. Such an approach is beneficial because usually it not obvious which nodes should be assigned to different VAAs (Wódczak, 2007).

As it was already mentioned, the currently investigated Local Area Relay Enhanced Cells tend to expose common aspects with Mobile Ad-hoc Network set-ups. Yet still, even if the Base Station were to be replaced with an Access Point and Fixed Relay Nodes substituted by mobile User Terminals, the system would behave in way more specific for cellular networks. This is well illustrated by the scenario of interest, depicted in Figure 1, where the REC comprises one floor of the height of 3 m located in a building. The floor is organized into two corridors of the dimensions

Figure 1. Relay enhanced cell

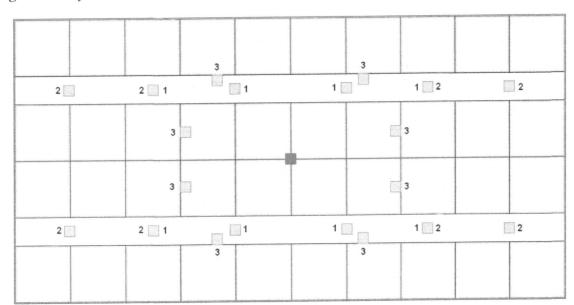

5 m x 100 m, as well as 40 rooms of the dimensions 10 m x 10 m. In the reference case the area is operated by the Base Station (BS) only, positioned in the centre. The scenario is very specific because the signal transmitted by the BS is significantly attenuated by numerous walls, crossing its way towards the UT(s). However, the fact that this scenario is composed of rooms of office type means that it is quite straightforward to assume that there will be many pluggable end user devices and sockets all over around. Consequently, the battery constraints are not so strict here and it seems feasible to employ for example also laptops as RNs.

System Parameters

Not only does the described system follow the general assumptions for the indoor environment (Abaii et al., 2006), but it also takes into account the specific parameters outlined in Table 1. In particular, it uses fixed modulation and coding scheme based on Quadrature Phase Shift Keying (QPSK) modulation and the (4, 5, 7) convolutional code. Additive White Gaussian Noise (AWGN)

radio channel is employed and the Line-of-Sight (LOS) or Non Line-of-Sight (NLOS) radio propagation models (A1) (Abaii et al., 2006) are used interchangeably, depending on the presence of walls between the BS, RNs and UTs. The LOS model is defined by the following formula:

$$PL_{LOS}=18.7\log(d)+46.8+\sigma[dB] \quad (1)$$

where d denotes the distance in meters between the transmitter and the receiver and σ represents the standard deviation of the shadow fading, here equal to 3 dB. In turn, the NLOS propagation model is given by:

$$PL_{NLOS}=20.0\log(d)+46.4+5n_w+\sigma[dB] \quad (2)$$

where n_w denotes the number of walls between the transmitter (either BS or RN) and the receiver (either RN or UT), while σ=6 dB, i.e., for all walls to be of the same, light type.

More specifically, the average interference power level of -125 dBm per subcarrier is assumed, while no outdoor users are explicitly taken into account. Orthogonal Frequency Division Multiple

Table 1. System parameters

Parameter	Value	Information
Carrier frequency	5.0 GHz	TDD mode
Channel bandwidth	100 MHz	OFDMA
Spatial processing	Distributed STBC	RN-RN cooperation
BS antennas	1	Omnidirectional
RN antennas	1	Omnidirectional
UT antennas	1	Omnidirectional
BS transmit power	21 dBm	14 dBi antenna gain
RN transmit power	21 dBm	7 dBi antenna gain
UT transmit power	21 dBm	0 dBi antenna gain
Channel modeling	AWGN channel	A1 NLOS Room-Room model for BS-RN and RN-UT links (also Room-Corridor)
Link adaptation	Fixed code and modulation scheme	QPSK and (4, 5, 7) convolutional code
Mobility	Yes	User terminals
Resource scheduling	Fixed	Each user is assigned 1 chunk (8 subcarriers and 15 OFDM symbols)
RAP selection	Signal power	According to Algorithm 1
Traffic model	CBR	Constant bit rate

Access (OFDMA) is employed and time division duplex (TDD) mode is used at the carrier frequency of 5.0 GHz with the channel bandwidth of 100 MHz. The transmission power for BS, RN and UT is at the same level of 21 dBm, whereas the antenna gains are different and equal to 14 dBi, 7 dBi and 0 dBi, respectively. The noise figure at the receiver is amounts to 7 dB and the noise power spectral density equals -174 dBm/Hz. Each UT may be assigned at least one chunk of radio resources of the size of 8 subcarriers by 15 OFDM symbols. The relative user throughput is the evaluation parameter defined as the ratio between the number of bits transmitted successfully and the total number of transmitted bits (Doppler, Redana, Wódczak, Rost, & Wichman, 2007).

Performance Challenges

A series of different set-ups were evaluated and three example configurations are discussed below (Dottling, Irmer, Kalliojarvi, & Rouquette-Leveil,

2009). For each of them, the three dimensional relative throughput figures are presented and additionally, all of them are compared in terms of the Cumulative Distribution Function (CDF) in reference to the results obtained for the BS only reference scenario, where transmission is not assisted by RN(s) but directed immediately to UT(s). In particular, the nodes are assigned to cooperating pairs denoted as VAAs according to Algorithm 1, initially applied to ad-hoc setups (Wódczak, 2007) and then also to autonomic cooperative sensor networks (Wódczak, 2011). The notation is purposely kept conceptually close to MANETs to highlight the importance of the aforementioned convergence aspects.

In Algorithm 1, x denotes the BS as the scenario is centralized; however, in general the transmissions between two different UTs belonging to the same REC would not need to be operated by a BS at all. Instead, the option of direct peer-to-peer transmissions can be admitted equally well. Following, n denotes the one-hop

Algorithm 1. Selection of cooperating stations

for each $n^2 \in N^2(x)$ do

  if neighbour(n, n^2) then

    $i = \text{size}\left[\text{VAA}(x, n^2) \right] - 1$

    while $(i \geq 0$ and $P^{n^2}_{\text{VAA}(x,n^2)[i]} < P^{n^2}_n)$ do

      $\text{VAA}(x, n^2)[i+1] \leftarrow \text{VAA}(x, n^2)[i]$

      $i = i - 1$

    end while

    $\text{VAA}(x, n^2)[i+1] \leftarrow n$

  end if

end for

neighbor of the source node x, while n^2 is its two-hop neighbor, respectively. On this basis $N^2(x)$ is defined as the set of two-hop neighbors of the node x and VAA(x,n^2) denotes a Virtual Antenna Array selected to assist in the transmission between

x and n^2. In other words, VAAs are composed of nodes belonging to the set $N^2(x)$, i.e., the RNs. The assignment of Relay Nodes, in a given deployment, to a specific VAA(x,n^2) is performed on the basis of the power of the signal received from them by UTs belonging to $N^2(x)$, i.e., nodes denoted as n^2. In general such an approach is advantageous (Wódczak, 2007). However, in the very case of the analyzed Local Area REC scenario, numerous walls deteriorate the signal received by the RNs from the BS despite the availability of additional antenna gains. For this reason, selected relay positioning schemes are investigated below as previously outlined in Figure 2, so the RNs marked with 1 form the Scenario 1, the ones marked with 2 form the scenario 2 and the ones marked with 3 form the Scenario 3.

In the case of the evaluation results for the first scenario, as presented in Figure 2, all the cooperative RNs were located in the corridors at

Figure 2. Relative throughput for scenario 1

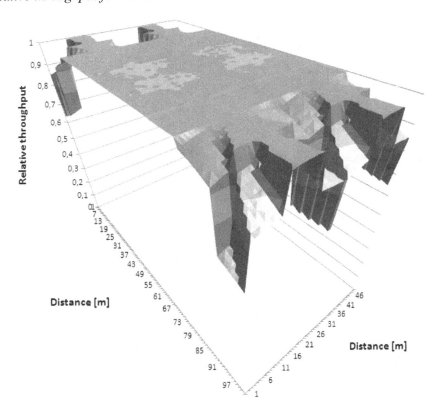

not so distant positions from the BS. It is visible that the relative throughput was dropping in the farther corners by about 30 percent. This situation is clearly a result of the existence of numerous walls altogether posing a serious obstacle to radio signal propagation (Figure 3). Also the obtained CDF shown in Figure 5 proves that such a system tends to behave better compared to a Base Station only scenario; however, there appear some low relative throughput values not observable in the reference case.

Moving RNs farther from the center (Figure 1) to potentially increase the coverage in the distant corners proves that the influence of walls is really significant. This is clearly visible in Figure 4 where the results are even worse than for the reference scenario without RNs, pointing out the extent to which the average relative throughput might drop. Not only is a bigger area

affected by low throughput values, but also the drop exceeds 40 per cent when compared to Scenario 1. The penalty in CDF is also clearly noticeable in Figure 5.

Finally, an attempt was made to position the cooperating RNs in a circular manner, again closer to the BS, as outlined by Scenario 3 (Figure 4). The performance looks improved yet again but the first investigated case, i.e., Scenario 1, still seems to offer better throughput. This observation is again proved by the CDF presented in Figure 5.

In general, the results confirm explicitly that system performance in terms of throughput is highly dependent on the way the cooperating RNs are deployed. This conclusion justifies the need for convergence between similar technologies so the resulting network can behave in a more autonomic way and adapt to the environment

Figure 3. Relative throughput for scenario 2

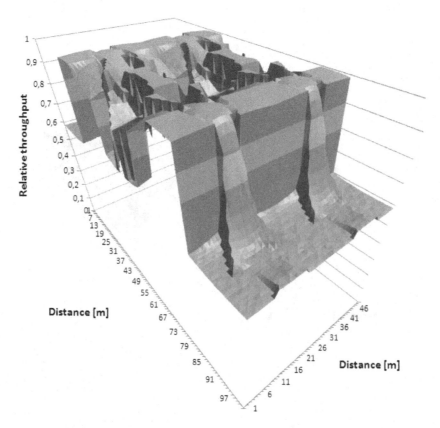

Figure 4. Relative throughput for scenario 3

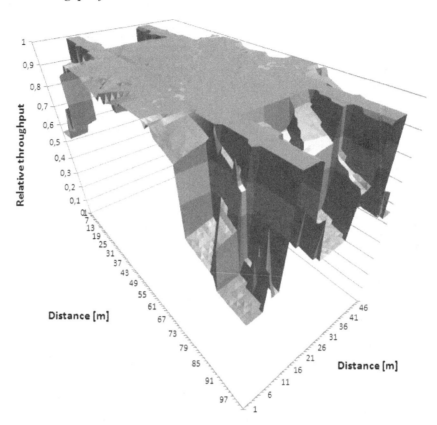

TOWARDS CONVERGENCE

Cross-Layer Design

and requirements through self-organization. In other words, the similarities between the REC and MANETs can be exploited for the purposes of introducing a cross-layer approach where routines resembling the network layer protocol would be used to orchestrate cooperative transmission. Such a design can be enhanced with the flavor of autonomic behaviors so the UTs would be able to self-configure without any specific external triggers.

This might be achieved by the incorporation the relevant entities of the Generic Autonomic Network Architecture. Going further, GANA could also form the interface with Operations Support System to efficiently integrate REC into the global landscape as viewed by the network operator. Different aspects of such a convergent approach are discussed in the following section.

For the discussed networked systems, the issue of proper selection of the cooperating RNs may become substantial and, surprisingly, fluctuations in network topology may be even advantageous. In particular, specific existing network layer mechanisms become of interest for the purposes of making use of the topology information readily available within the repositories of a routing protocol. In particular the Optimized Link State Routing (OLSR) protocol (Clausen & Jacquet, 2003) seems very appropriate here as it belongs to the proactive protocol class and is tailored accordingly to the specifics of MANET environments. Obvious pros of this protocol include its ability

Figure 5. Cumulative distribution function

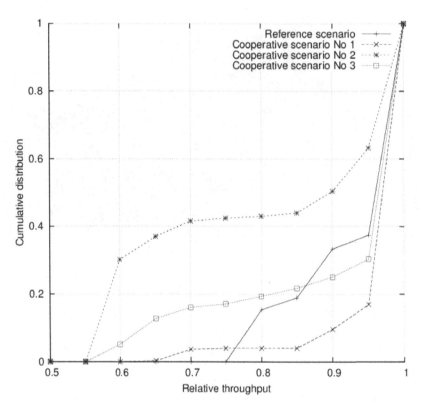

to discover the network topology regularly with optimized control overhead. Its built-in optimized broadcasting mechanism is known as the Multi-Point Relay (MPR) station selection heuristic (Jacquet, Muhlethaler, Clausen, Laouiti, Qayyum, & Viennot, 2001). In fact the cross-layer design described in Wódczak (2006, 2007) proves that additional information readily available at the network layer can help in employing the MPR station selection heuristic for the optimization of the performance through the inclusion of Virtual Antenna Arrays in joint operation mode.

The rationale behind such a joint approach to Multi-Point Relay selection heuristic and Virtual Antenna Arrays is outlined in Figure 6. Yet again one comes across a convergence aspect as both these concepts overlap in the sense that MPR stations can take the role of RNs and cooperatively constitute VAAs. What is important here is that the concept can be implemented on top of the

Figure 6. Multi-point relays and virtual antenna arrays

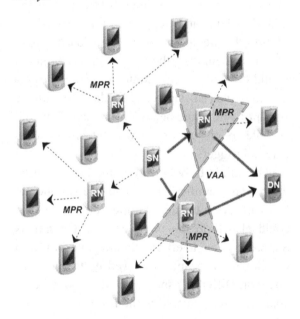

REC to allow the end UTs play the role of mobile/ movable RNs. The reason for this is that, on the one hand, the system needs to be scalable so it is able to use numerous Relay Nodes, and on the other hand, it needs to be ready for the inclusion of the paradigm of autonomic system design on top.

Autonomic Networking

Autonomic networking has emerged as one of the most promising approaches towards the instantiation of the self-organizing future networked systems (Chaparadza et al., 2009). The notion of being autonomic seems rather capacious but it does not mean the system becomes either more cognitive or autonomous. The primary role of autonomics is the support for self-configuration without any need for explicit external intervention over most of the time of system operation (Liakopoulos, Zafeiropoulos, Polyrakis, Grammatikou, Gonzalez, Wódczak, & Chaparadza, 2008). In other words, an autonomic network should behave like a living organism so the centralized network management entities located in the Base Station or Access Point, only monitor the overall network status but refrain themselves from any

substantial interference unless ultimately needed. To map such a concept onto a networked system one needs to apply specific network engineering mechanisms. Such mechanisms are currently introduced into standardization (Wódczak et al., 2011). In particular, the idea of control loops is applicable to such systems, where Decision Elements (DEs) are controlling Managed Entities (MEs) based on closed loop information flows. Such a control process needs to be obviously supported with external monitoring and policies related data. Control loops are presented in Figure 7 where the integration between GANA and OSS is further explained.

For the investigated case of REC, the decision element would steer the cooperation protocol, which in that very case would translate to the cross-layer approach outlined above. Generally, one should note that not only distinct nodes should express autonomic behaviors but the network should be autonomic as a whole. It means that the network should monitor itself all the time so it is able to align its operation with the requirements arising from monitoring data and/or from the policies imposed by the network operator. Distinct nodes should then express autonomic behaviors

Figure 7. OSS, GANA and REC

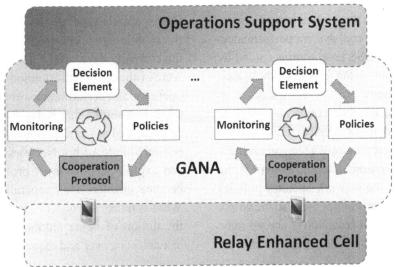

but in specific cases the final decisions might need to be taken at the network level. This means there are hierarchical interdependencies among DEs so that the lower level DE may take the role of ME. Such an approach would be very advantageous from the REC perspective as it would aid the above-mentioned cross-layer design with the ability of network nodes to express autonomic behaviors.

Network Management Perspective

Operations Support Systems (OSS) need to be able to manage a diverse set of network devices offering different capabilities and behaving in various ways (Jain, Hayward, & Kumar, 2003). In particular, some of the devices might be equipped with capabilities allowing for certain cooperative behaviors, such as the ones translating into cooperative VAA-aided networking. Currently developed next generation networks often assume the possibility for the devices to have the ability of routing data in a cooperative manner, to enhance the provided QoS. Such devices are preliminarily to be deployed by network operators as fixed, and only later as movable or even mobile ones. As such deployments develop, certain requirements will be put on the networked system to facilitate the discovery of the capabilities of distinct devices and then use the acquired information efficiently for the purposes of exploiting these behaviors whenever beneficiary for the overall system performance. This involves other OSS level routines aided by software components in the form of GANA Decision Elements (Figure 7).

This way an autonomic cooperative mobile network deployed in Local Area REC can be brought into a bigger picture of a telecommunications system. Operations Support System is the place from where the network operator policies can be fed into distinct control loops so the whole system can modify its behavior(s) accordingly. Cooperative behaviors can be beneficial from the

system performance perspective; however, they will come at a certain cost. The cost may result from the fact that additional network devices may need to be deployed so they can be automatically configured to expose cooperative behaviors when there is a need. As it is advocated for in this paper, this equipment may be the end user devices but in that case users might want to trade what they can offer for some other privileges and/or benefits. The reason is that the end user mobile devices such as smartphones are power constrained and if they agree to forward packets to and from some other users they might drain their batteries much quicker, not to mention the security issues. Potentially, the end users might be likely to accept such a situation but the likelihood would be much higher if they were offered some incentives such as for example free of charge access to the Internet, either at the very moment or later in the future. This is a very vital question to be tackled also from the business model perspective. Nonetheless, the autonomic approach seems to be the only reasonable way for managing such diverse environments characterized by so many degrees of freedom in terms of network configurations and service provision requirements.

CONCLUSION

In this paper the aspects of convergence in cooperative mobile networks were presented. In particular the currently developed relay enhanced designs were evaluated and the methods to improve their operation and performance were outlined. First of all, it was shown that Relay Enhanced Cell can be perceived as overlapping with some concepts behind Mobile Ad-hoc Networks. Such a network can exploit network layer protocols which can become enablers for cooperative transmission. What is more, the system can be enhanced with the notion of being autonomic so the devices can auto-discover and expose certain behaviors, including the cooperative ones. Being driven by the paradigm behind autonomic networking, such a cooperative networked system would need to deploy Decision Elements and control loops. This would result in a logic forming an overlay ready to be integrated with Network Management and Operations Support Systems. Eventually, one would ends up with an autonomic cooperative mobile network able to instantiate cooperative transmission through cooperative behaviors exposed by autonomic cooperative nodes of REC. The latter would be able to auto-configure and auto-discover and the additional transmission gains could be rewarded to the users with certain incentives such as additional bandwidth or smaller latency. All these elements add together and create a complete and vital picture of an autonomic networked relay enhanced system exposing self-manageability.

ACKNOWLEDGMENT

This paper has been prepared on the basis of the work on cooperative transmission the author initially performed in EU FP6 projects WINNER I and II at Poznan University of Technology and which was then extended with the part on autonomic networking performed in EU FP7 project EFIPSANS at Telcordia Technologies.

REFERENCES

Abaii, M., Auer, G., Cho, Y., Cosovic, I., Döttling, M., George, K., Hamm, L., et al. (2006). *IST-4-027756 WINNER II D6.13.7. Test Scenarios and Calibration Cases Issue 2*. Munich, Germany: EU FP6 WINNER II Project.

Alamouti, S. (1998). A simple transmit diversity technique for wireless communications. *IEEE Journal on Selected Areas in Communications, 16*(8), 1451–1458. doi:10.1109/49.730453

Chaparadza, R., Papavassiliou, S., Kastrinogiannis, T., Vigoureux, M., Dotaro, E., & Davy, K. A. (2009). Creating a viable evolution path towards self-managing future internet via a standardizable reference model for autonomic network engineering. In Tselentis, G., Domingue, J., Galis, A., Gavras, A., Hausheer, D., & Krco, S., et al. (Eds.), *Towards the Future Internet – A European Research Perspective* (pp. 136–147). Amsterdam, The Netherlands: IOS Press.

Clausen, T., & Jacquet, P. (2003). *Optimised Link State Routing Protocol (OLSR) (RFC No. 3626)*. Internet Engineering Task Force.

Dohler, M., Gkelias, A., & Aghvami, H. (2004). A resource allocation strategy for distributed MIMO multi-hop communication systems. *IEEE Communications Letters, 8*(2), 99–101. doi:10.1109/LCOMM.2004.823425

Doppler, K., Redana, S., Wódczak, M., Rost, P., & Wichman, R. (2007). Dynamic resource assignment and cooperative relaying in cellular networks: Concept and performance assessment. *EURASIP Journal on Wireless Communications and Networking*.

Doppler, L., Osseiran, A., Wódczak, M., & Rost, P. (2007, July). On the Integration of Cooperative Relaying into the WINNER System Concept. Paper presented at the 16th IST Mobile & Wireless Communications Summit, Budapest, Hungary.

Dottling, M., Irmer, R., Kalliojarvi, K., & Rouquette-Leveil, S. (2009). System Model, Test Scenarios, and Performance Evaluation. In Dottling, M., Mohr, W., & Osseiran, A. (Eds.), *Radio Technologies and Concepts for IMT-Advanced*. Hoboken, NJ: Wiley. doi:10.1002/9780470748077.ch13

Herhold, P., Zimmermann, E., & Fettweis, G. (2004, June) *Relaying and Cooperation - A System Perspective*. Paper presented at the 13th IST Mobile & Wireless Communications Summit, Lyon, France.

Jacquet, P., Muhlethaler, P., Clausen, T., Laouiti, A., Qayyum, A., & Viennot, L. (2001, December). Optimised link state routing protocol for ad hoc networks. In *Proceedings of the IEEE International Multi Topic Conference* (pp. 62–68).

Jain, S., Hayward, M., & Kumar, S. (2003). *The Ultimate Guide to Building and Delivering OSS/BSS*. Dordrecht, The Netherlands: Kluwer Academic Publishers.

Laneman, J. N., & Wornell, G. W. (2003). Distributed space-time-coded protocols for exploiting cooperative diversity in wireless networks. *IEEE Transactions on Information Theory, 49*(10), 2415–2425. doi:10.1109/TIT.2003.817829

Liakopoulos, A., Zafeiropoulos, A., Polyrakis, A., Grammatikou, M., Gonzalez, J. M., Wódczak, M., & Chaparadza, R. (2008). *Monitoring Issues for Autonomic Networks: The EFIPSANS Vision*. Paper presented at European Workshop on Mechanisms for the Future Internet.

Pabst, R., Walke, B., Schultz, D. C., Herhold, P., Yanikomeroglu, H., & Mukherjee, S. (2004). Relay-Based Deployment Concepts for Wireless and Mobile Broadband Radio. *IEEE Communications Magazine, 42*(9), 80–89. doi:10.1109/MCOM.2004.1336724

Tarokh, V., Jafarkhani, H., & Calderbank, A. R. (1999). Space-time block coding for wireless communications: Performance results. *IEEE Journal on Selected Areas in Communications, 17*(3), 451–460. doi:10.1109/49.753730

Wódczak, M. (2006). *On Routing information Enhanced Algorithm for space-time coded Cooperative Transmission in wireless mobile networks*. Unpublished doctoral dissertation, Poznań University of Technology, Poznań, Poland.

Wódczak, M. (2007, July). *Extended REACT – Routing information Enhanced Algorithm for Cooperative Transmission*. Paper presented at the 16th IST Mobile & Wireless Communications Summit, Budapest, Hungary.

Wódczak, M. (2011). Autonomic cooperative networking for wireless green sensor systems. *International Journal of Sensor Networks, 10*(1-2), 83–93. doi:10.1504/IJSNET.2011.040906

Wódczak, M., Meriem, T. B., Chaparadza, R., Quinn, K., Lee, B., & Ciavaglia, L. (2011). Standardising a Reference Model and Autonomic Network Architectures for the Self-managing Future Internet. *IEEE Network Magazine, 25*(6), 50–56. doi:10.1109/MNET.2011.6085642

This work was previously published in the International Journal of Information Technology and Web Engineering (IJITWE), Volume 6, Issue 4, edited by Ghazi I. Alkhatib and Ernesto Damiani, pp. 51-62, copyright 2011 by IGI Publishing (an imprint of IGI Global).

Chapter 19
Development of a Novel Compressed Index–Query Web Search Engine Model

Hussein Al-Bahadili
Petra University, Jordan

Saif Al-Saab
University of Banking & Financial Sciences, Jordan

ABSTRACT

In this paper, the authors present a description of a new Web search engine model, the compressed index-query (CIQ) Web search engine model. This model incorporates two bit-level compression layers implemented at the back-end processor (server) side, one layer resides after the indexer acting as a second compression layer to generate a double compressed index (index compressor), and the second layer resides after the query parser for query compression (query compressor) to enable bit-level compressed index-query search. The data compression algorithm used in this model is the Hamming codes-based data compression (HCDC) algorithm, which is an asymmetric, lossless, bit-level algorithm permits CIQ search. The different components of the new Web model are implemented in a prototype CIQ test tool (CIQTT), which is used as a test bench to validate the accuracy and integrity of the retrieved data and evaluate the performance of the proposed model. The test results demonstrate that the proposed CIQ model reduces disk space requirements and searching time by more than 24%, and attains a 100% agreement when compared with an uncompressed model.

INTRODUCTION

A Web search engine is an information retrieval system designed to help finding information stored on the Web (Levene, 2005). It allows us to search the Web storage media for a certain content in a form of text meeting specific criteria (typically those containing a given word or phrase) and retrieving a list of files that match those criteria (Brin & Page, 1998). Web search engine consists of three main components: Web crawler, document analyzer and indexer, and search processor (Calishain, 2004).

DOI: 10.4018/978-1-4666-2157-2.ch019

Due to the rapid growth in the size of the Web, Web search engines face enormous performance challenges, in terms of: storage requirement, data retrieval rate, query processing time, and communication overhead. Large search engines, in particular, have to be able to process tens of thousands of queries per second on tens of billions of documents, making query throughput a critical issue (Fagni, Perego, & Silvestri, 2006). To satisfy this heavy workload, Web search engines use a variety of performance optimizations including succinct data structure (Ferragina et al., 2005; Gonzalez & Navarro, 2006), compressed text indexing (Ferragina & Manzini, 2006; Ferragina et al., 2009), query optimization (Chen, Gehrke, & Korn, 2001; Long & Suel, 2003), high-speed processing and communication systems (Badue et al., 2002), and efficient search engine architectural design (Zobel & Moffat, 2006).

Compressed text indexing has become a popular alternative to cope with the problem of giving indexed access to large text collections without using up too much space. Reducing space is important because it gives the chance of maintaining the whole collection of data in main memory. The current trend in compressed indexing is full-text compressed self-indexes (Ferragina et al., 2007). Such a self-index replaces the text by providing fast access to arbitrary text substrings, and, in addition, gives indexed access to the text by supporting fast search for the occurrences of arbitrary patterns. It is believed that the performance of current search engine models that base on compressed text indexing techniques only, is still short from meeting users and applications needs.

In this work, we present a description of a novel Web search engine model that utilizes the concept of compressed index-query search; therefore, it is referred to as the CIQ Web search engine model. The new model incorporates two bit-level compression layers implemented at the server side, one after the indexer acting as a second compression layer to generate a double compressed index (index compressor), and the other one after the query parser for query compression (query compressor) to enable bit-level compressed index-query search. The main features of the new model are it requires less index storage requirement and I/O overheads, which result in cost reduction and higher data retrieval rate or performance. Furthermore, the compression layers can be used to compress the any index regardless of indexing technique.

The data compression algorithm that will be used in this model is the novel Hamming codes-based data compression (HCDC) algorithm (Al-Bahadili, 2008), which is a lossless bit-level data compression algorithm. The main reason for using this algorithm is that its internal structure allows compressed data search. Moreover, recent investigations on using this algorithm for text compression showed that the algorithm can provide an excellent performance in comparison with many widely-used data compression algorithms and state-of-the-art tools (Al-Bahadili & Rababa'a, 2010).

The different components of the new Web model are implemented and integrated to build a prototype CIQ Web search engine, which also used as a test bench to validate the accuracy and evaluate and compare the performance of the CIQ model, namely, the CIQ test tool (CIQTT) (Al-Saab, 2011). The CIQTT was used to collect a test corpus of 104000 documents from 30 well-known Websites; process and analyze the test corpus; generate five inverted indexes of different sizes (1000, 10000, 25000, 50000, and 75000 documents), compress the indexes and measure the compression ratio and the storage reduction factor; search the indexes for 29 different keywords in both compressed and uncompressed forms; and finally, compare the outcomes of the different search processes and estimate the speedup factor and the time reduction factor.

The test results demonstrate that the HCDC algorithm achieves a compression ratio of more than 1.3, which reduces the storage requirement by more than 24%. The searching processes can be performed faster on compressed index-query providing speed up factor of more than 1.3 (i.e., reducing processing time by more than 24%) in comparison with equivalent uncompressed search. Furthermore, CIQTT achieves a 100% agreement between the compressed and uncompressed search processes.

LITERATURE REVIEW

In this section, we present a review on the most recent work related to Web search engine. Al-Bahadili and Al-Saab (2010) proposed and investigated the performance of a Web search engine model based on index-query bit-level compression. The model incorporates two compression layers both implemented at the server side, one layer resides after the indexer acting as a second compression layer to generate a double compressed index, and the second layer be located after the query parser for query compression to enable bit-level compressed index-query search. The data compression scheme used in this model is the adaptive character wordlength (ACW) scheme (Al-Bahadili & Hussein, 2010; Al-Bahadili & Hussain, 2008), which is an asymmetric, lossless, bit-level scheme. Results investigating the performance of the ACW scheme is presented and discussed.

De Moura, Navarro, and Ziviani (1997) presented a technique to build an index based on suffix arrays for compressed texts. They proposed a compression scheme for textual databases based on generating a compression code that preserves the lexicographical ordering of the text words. As a consequence it permits the sorting of the compressed strings to generate the suffix array without decompressing. Their results demonstrated that the size of the compressed text is 30% less than the original text. The suffix array builds up time on compressed text is 50% less than that on the original text. The compressed text plus index is 55-60% of the size of the original text. In addition,

the technique reduced the index and search times to approximately half the time.

Varadarajan and Chiueh (1997) described a text search engine called shrink and search engine (SASE), which operates in the compressed domain. SASE provides an exact search mechanism using an inverted index and an approximate search mechanism using a vantage point tree. The SASE allows a flexible trade-off between search time and storage space required to maintain the search indices. The experimental results showed that the compression efficiency is within 7-17% of GZIP. The sum of the compressed file size and the inverted indices is only between 55-76% of the original database, while the search performance is comparable to a fully inverted index.

Anh and Moffat (2004) described a scheme for compressing lists of integers as sequences of fixed binary codewords that had the twin benefits of being both effective and efficient. Because Web search engines index large quantities of text, the static costs associated with storing the index can be traded against dynamic costs associated with using it during query evaluation. The approach resulted in a reduction in index storage costs compared to their previous word-aligned version, with no cost in terms of query throughput.

Gonzalez and Navarro (2007a) introduced a compression scheme for suffix arrays which permits locating the occurrences extremely fast, while still being much smaller than classical indexes. The index permits a very efficient secondary memory implementation, where compression permits reducing the amount of I/O needed to answer queries. Gonzalez and Navarro (2007b) later improved their work by introducing a practical compressed text index that, when the text is compressible, takes little more than the plain text size. It provides very good I/O times for searching, which in particular improve when the text is compressible. They analyzed the index and showed that it is extremely competitive on compressible texts.

Moffat and Culpepper (2007) showed that a relatively simple combination of techniques allows fast calculation of Boolean conjunctions within a surprisingly small amount of data transferred. This approach exploits the observation that queries tend to contain common words, and that representing common words via a bitvector allows random access testing of candidates, and, if necessary, fast intersection operations prior to the list of candidates being developed. By using bitvectors for a very small number of terms that (in both documents and in queries) occur frequently, and byte coded inverted lists for the balance can reduce both querying time and also query time data-transfer volumes. The techniques described by Moffat and Culpepper (2007) are not applicable to other powerful forms of querying. For example, index structures that support phrase and proximity queries have a much more complex structure, and are not amenable to storage (in their full form) using bitvectors.

Ferragina et al. (2009) presented an article to fill the gap between implementations and focused comparisons of compressed indexes. They presented the existing implementations of compressed indexes from a practitioner's point of view; introduced the *Pizza&Chili* site, which offers tuned implementations and a standardized API for the most successful compressed full-text self-indexes, together with effective test-beds and scripts for their automatic validation and test; and they showed the results of extensive experiments on a number of codes with the aim of demonstrating the practical relevance of this technology.

Yan, Ding, and Suel (2009) studied index compression and query processing techniques optimized reordered indexes. They performed an extensive study of compression techniques for document IDs and presented new optimizations of existing techniques which can achieve significant improvement in both compression and decompression performances. They also proposed and evaluated techniques for compressing frequency values. In addition, they studied the effect of their

approach on query processing performance. Their experiments showed very significant improvements in index size and query processing speed on the TREC GOV2 collection of 25.2 million Web pages.

Zhang, Long, and Suel (2008) provided an updated discussion and evaluation of inverted index compression and index caching, which play a crucial rule in Web search engines as well as other high-performance information retrieval systems, to show how to select the best set of approaches and settings depending on parameter such as disk speed and main memory cache size. They compared and evaluated several compression algorithms including new variants of existing algorithms, evaluate different inverted list caching policies on large query traces, and studied the possible performance benefits of combining compression and caching.

SEARCH ENGINE MODEL

Standard Web search engine consists of the following main components: Web crawler, document analyzer and indexer, and searching process (Brin & Page, 1998; Calishaun, 2004). Figure 1 outlines the architecture and main components of a standard search engine model. Next, we provide a brief description for each of the above components.

Web Crawler

A Web crawler is a computer program that browses the Web in a methodical, automated manner. Other terms for Web crawlers are ants, automatic indexers, bots, and worms or Web spider. Each spider has its own agenda as it indexes a site. Some utilize META tag keywords; another may use the beta description of a site, and some use the first sentence or paragraph on the sites homepage. In other words, a page that ranks well on one search engine may not rank as well on another. Given a set of "seed" URLs, the crawler repeatedly removes

Figure 1. Main components of standard search engine model

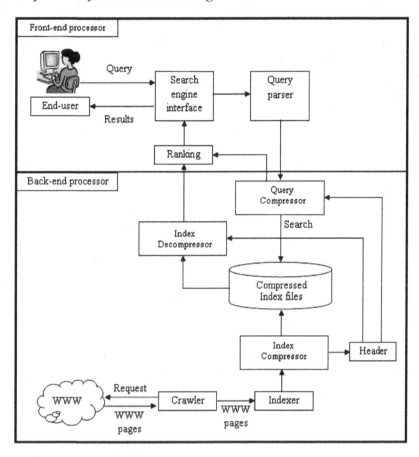

one URL from the seeds, downloads the corresponding page, extracts all the URLs contained in it, and adds any previously unknown URLs to the seeds (Levene, 2005).

Web search engines work by storing information about many Web pages, which they retrieve from the Web itself. These pages are retrieved by a spider - sophisticated Web browser which follows every link extracted or stored in its database. The contents of each page are then analyzed to determine how it should be indexed, for example, words are extracted from the titles, headings, or special fields called Meta tags.

Document Analyzer and Indexer

Indexing is the process of creating an index that is a specialized file containing a compiled version of documents retrieved by the spider (Levene, 2005). Indexing process collects, parses, and stores data to facilitate fast and accurate information retrieval. Index design incorporates interdisciplinary concepts from linguistics, mathematics, informatics, physics and computer science (Zobel & Moffat, 2006).

The purpose of storing an index is to optimize speed and performance in finding relevant documents for a search query. Without an index, the Web search engine would scan every (possible) document on the Internet, which would require considerable time and computing power (impossible with the current Internet size); e.g., while an index of 10^4 documents can be queried within milliseconds, a sequential scan of every word in the documents could take hours. The additional computer storage required to store the index, as well as the considerable increase in the time required for an update to take place, are traded off for the time saved during information retrieval (Brin & Page, 1998).

Index Design Factors

Major factors in designing a Web search engine's architecture include the following (Levene, 2005; Calishain, 2004):

- **Merge Factors:** How data enters the index, or how words or subject features are added to the index during text corpus traversal, and whether multiple indexers can work asynchronously. The indexer must first check whether it is updating old content or adding new content. Traversal typically correlates to the data collection policy. Search engine index merging is similar in concept to the SQL Merge command and other merge algorithms.
- **Storage Techniques:** How to store the index data, i.e., whether information should be data compressed or filtered.
- **Index Size:** How much storage is required to support the index.
- **Lookup Speed:** How quickly a word can be found in the index. The speed of finding an entry in a data structure, compared with how quickly it can be updated or removed, is a central focus of computer science.
- **Maintenance:** How the index is maintained over time.
- **Fault Tolerance:** How important it is for the service to be reliable. Issues include dealing with index corruption, determining whether bad data can be treated in isolation, dealing with bad hardware, partitioning, and schemes such as hash-based or composite partitioning, as well as replication.

Index Data Structures

Search engine architectures vary in the way indexing is performed and in methods of index storage to meet the various design factors. There are many architectural designs for the indexes and the most widely-used one is inverted index (Badue et al., 2002; Zobel & Moffat, 2006). Inverted index stores a list of occurrences of each atomic search criterion, typically in the form of a hash table or binary tree.

The inverted index structure is widely used in the modern super fast search engines like Google, Yahoo, Lucene and other major search engines. Through the indexing, there are several processes take place; here the processes that related to our work will be discussed. The use of these processes depends on the search engine configuration (Melnik et al., 2000).

- **Extract URLs:** A process of extracting all URLs from the document being indexed, it used to guide crawling the website, do link checking, build a site map, and build a table of internal and external links from the page.
- **Code Striping:** A process of removing HTML tags, scripts, and styles, and decoding HTML character references and entities used to embed special characters.
- **Language Recognition:** A process by which a computer program attempts to automatically identify, or categorize, the language or languages of a document.
- **Document Tokenization:** A process of detecting the encoding used for the page; determining the language of the content (some pages use multiple languages); finding word, sentence and paragraph bound-

aries; combining multiple adjacent-words into one phrase; and changing the case of text.

- **Document Parsing or Syntactic Analysis:** The process of analyzing a sequence of tokens (for example, words) to determine their grammatical structure with respect to a given (more or less) formal grammar.
- **Lemmatization/Stemming:** The process for reducing inflected (or sometimes derived) words to their stem, base or root form – generally a written word form, this stage can be done in indexing and/or searching stage. The stems need not be identical to the morphological root of the word; it is usually sufficient that related words map to the same stem, even if this stem is not in itself a valid root. The process is useful in search engines for query expansion or indexing and other natural language processing problems.
- **Normalization:** The process by which text is transformed in some way to make it consistent in a way which it might not have been before. Text normalization is often performed before text is processed in some way, such as generating synthesized speech, automated language translation, storage in a database, or comparison.

Searching Process

When the index is ready the searching process can be performed through query interface, a user enters a query into a Web search engine (typically by using keywords), the engine examines its index and provides a listing of best matched Web pages according to its criteria, usually with a short summary containing the document's title and sometimes parts of the text. At this stage, the results ranked, where ranking is a relationship between a set of items such that, for any two items, the first is either "ranked higher than", "ranked lower than" or "ranked equal" to the second. In

mathematics, this is known as a weak order or total pre-order of objects. It is not necessarily a total order of documents because two different documents can have the same ranking. Ranking is done according to document relevancy to the query, freshness and popularity (Calishain, 2004).

THE NOVEL CIQ MODEL

In this section, a description of the proposed Web search engine model is presented. The new model incorporates two bit-level data compression layers, both installed at the back-end processor (server side), one for index compression (index compressor) and one for query compression (query compressor or keyword compressor), so that the search process can be performed at the compressed index-query level and avoid any decompression activities, therefore, this model is referred to as the compressed index-query (CIQ) Web search engine model or simply the CIQ model. In order to be able to perform the search process at the compressed index-query level, we use the HCDC algorithm (Al-Bahadili, 2008). Figure 2 outlines the main components of the new CIQ model and where the compression layers are located.

The CIQ model works as follows: At the back-end processor, after the indexer generates the index, and before sending it to the index storage device it compresses the index using the HCDC algorithm, and then sends the compressed index to the storage device. The HCDC algorithm creates a compressed-file header (compression header) to store some parameters that are needed by the compression/decompression processes. This header should be stored separately to be accessed by the query compression layer (query compressor) and the index decompressor.

On the other hand, instead of passing the query to the index to start the searching process, it is compressed at the query compressor. In order to produce similar binary pattern for the similar compressed characters from the index and the query,

Figure 2. Main components of the CIQ Web search engine model

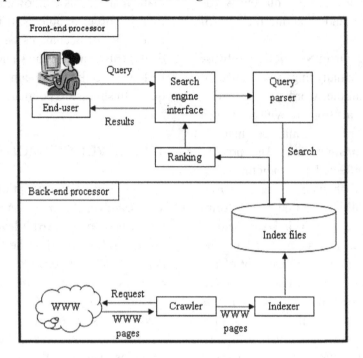

the character-to-binary codes used in converting the index file are passed to be used at the query compressor. Then the compressed query is passed to the index to start the searching process. If a match is found the retrieved data is decompressed, using the index decompressor, and passed through the ranker and the Web search engine interface to the end-user.

The CIQ Test Tool (CIQTT)

This section describes the implementation of a CIQ-based test tool (CIQTT), which can be considered as a prototype CIQ Web search engine (Al-Saab, 2011). CIQTT is developed to:

- Validate the accuracy and integrity of the retrieved data to ensure the same data sets can be retrieved by the new model.
- Evaluate the performance of the CIQ model in terms of the parameters, which will be discussed in the next section.

The CIQTT consists of six main procedures; these are:

1. **COLCOR:** Collect the test corpus (documents).
2. **PROCOR:** Process and analyze the test corpus (documents).
3. **INVINX:** Build the inverted index.
4. **COMINX:** Compress the inverted index.
5. **SRHINX:** Search the index (inverted or inverted/compressed index) for a certain keyword or phrase.
6. **COMRES:** Compare the outcomes of the different search processes.

In what follows, we shall provide a brief description for each of the above procedures.

COLCOR: Collect the Testing Corpus

In this procedure, the Nutch crawler (Nutch, 2011) is used to collect the targeted corpus. Nutch is an open-source search technology initially developed by Douglas Reed Cutting who is an advocate and creator of open-source search technology. He originated Lucene and, with Mike Cafarella, Nutch, both open-source search technology projects which are now managed through the Apache Software Foundation (ASF). Nutch builds on Lucene (2011) and Solr (2011). The main features of the Nutch crawler:

- Fetching, parsing and indexation in parallel and/or distributed clusters.
- Support many formats, such as: plaintext, HTML, XML, ZIP, OpenDocument, Microsoft Office (Word, Excel, Access, PowerPoint), PDF, JavaScript, RSS, RTF, MP3, etc.
- It has a highly modular architecture, allowing developers to create plug-ins for media-type parsing, data retrieval, querying and clustering.
- It supports ontology or Web archiving, which is the process of collecting portions of the Web and ensuring the collection is preserved in an archive, such as an archive site, for future researchers, historians, and the public. Due to the massive size of the Web, Web archivists typically employ Web crawlers for automated collection. The largest Web archiving organization based on a crawling approach is the Internet Archive which strives to maintain an archive of the entire Web.
- It is based on MapReduce (Wikipedia, 2011), which is a patented software framework introduced by Google to support distributed computing on large data sets on clusters of computers. The framework is inspired by the "map" and "reduce" functions commonly used in functional programming, although their purpose in the MapReduce framework is not the same as their original forms. MapReduce libraries have been written in C++, C#, Erlang,

Java, Ocaml, Perl, Python, Ruby, F#, R and other programming languages.

- It supports a distributed file system (via Hadoop) (Hadoop, 2011), which a software framework that supports data-intensive distributed applications under a free license. It enables applications to work with thousands of nodes and petabytes of data. Hadoop was inspired by Google's MapReduce and Google File System (GFS) papers. It uses the Java programming language. Yahoo! uses Hadoop extensively across its businesses. Hadoop was created by Doug Cutting to support distribution for the Nutch search engine project.
- It utilizes Windows NT LAN Manager (NTLM) authentication (Ashton, 2011), which is a suite of Microsoft security protocols that provides authentication, integrity, and confidentiality to users. NTLM is the successor to the authentication protocol in Microsoft LAN Manager (LANMAN), an older Microsoft product, and attempts to provide backwards compatibility with LANMAN. NTLM version two (NTLMv2), which was introduced in Windows NT 4.0 SP4 (and natively supported in Windows 2000), enhances NTLM security by hardening the protocol against many spoofing attacks, and adding the ability for a server to authenticate to the client.

Nutch crawler has some advantages over a simple fetcher, such as:

- Highly scalable and relatively feature-rich crawler.
- Obey robots.txt rules.
- Robust and scalable. It can run on a cluster of 100 machines.
- High quality, as it can bias the crawling to fetch "important" pages first.

- Support clustering of the retrieved data.
- Access a link-graph database.

PROCOR: Process and Analyze Testing Corpus

This procedure processes and analyzes the corpus, which goes through several stages; these are:

- **Language Filtering:** In this stage all non-English documents are filtered-out to get an English index only.
- **Content Extracting and Code Striping:** In this stage the content is extracted and isolated from the site menus, navigators, copyright notes and any other non-related text. Also remove and strip the HTML, tags, styles and any scripting code.
- **Special Characters Removal:** In this stage all the special characters are removed.
- **Stop-Word Removal:** Removing the stop-words is a well-known practice in Web search engine technology, specially, when uses the inverted indexes.
- **Converting Characters to Lower-Case Format:** In this stage all characters are converted to a lower-case format.

INVINX: Build the Inverted Index and Indexing

Before indexing process take place, all the crawled documents must be renamed (numbered) with a new and unique ID (sequence number). There are many numbering methods that can be adopted to assign these IDs; all of them are based on assigning a unique m-digit ID to each crawled document, where these digits are selected from a certain character set. The character sets are either numeric set, or letters set, or a combination of numeric and letters set. The total number of documents that can be numbered per index (T) depends on the total number of characters in the adopted character set (D), and the number of digits allocated to the document ID (m); such that $T=D^m$. The IDs can be assigned sequentially or assigned randomly subject to a condition that each document should have a unique m-digit ID.

The character frequencies of the index file may change significantly depending on the adopted characters set, and the size of the generated index. This issue should be carefully considered as it significantly affects the algorithm data compression ratio. However, we must emphasize that at this stage we have given little attention to this issue, and in the current CIQTT, we choose a simple inverted index architecture that contains the keyword and only 6-digit numeric ID, which enable us to index up to 10^6 documents. A unique 6-digits random numbers list is generated, and every document is renamed with a number from this list. To generate the inverted index, we scan and list all the keywords occur in all documents that were crawled, and then sort these keywords with the ID of the documents containing that keyword. Two special characters before and after every keyword are added to differentiate them from the documents ID; these special characters are: the characters '^' and '|', which are added before and after the keyword, respectively.

The procedure INVINX is implemented in a number of stages to provide high flexibility and to enable straightforward evolution. These stages can be summarized as follows:

- Select the character set.
- Select the length of the documents IDs (m).
- Select the index generation method (sequential or random).
- Scan and list all the keywords occur in all the documents that are crawled.
- Construct and store the index.

COMINX: Compressing the Inverted Index

In this procedure, the data compression algorithm is implemented. It includes the following sub-procedures:

- Read the index file.
- Compress the index file using the index compressor.
- Store the compressed index.
- Store the compression header to be accessed by the query compressor and the extracted data decompressor.

The main requirements for a data compression algorithm to be used by COMINX are:

- Lossless data compression algorithm.
- Allows compressed index-query search.
- Provides adequate performance; such as: high compression ratio, fast decompression time, small memory requirement, and small-size compressed file header. Nevertheless, it is not necessary for the algorithm to have symmetric processing time.

SRHINX: Searching the Index File

This procedure searches the index file (inverted or inverted/compressed index) as follows:

- Read the query and identify the list of keywords or phrases to be searched for.
- Compress each keyword/phrase separately using the query compressor and the compression header created by the index compressor.
- Perform the searching process to extract the documents IDs that matched all or some keywords/phrases.

- Decompress the extracted data using the index decompressor and the compression header.
- Store the decompressed data to be accessed by COMRES for performance comparison.
- Measure and record the processing times to be accessed by COMRES for performance comparison.

COMRES: Compare the Outcomes of Different Search Processes

To validate the accuracy of the new model both the number of extracted documents and their IDs must be similar to those extracted by an uncompressed model. In this procedure, the outcomes of different search processes for the same keywords on uncompressed/compressed index-query models are compared.

Implementation of the HCDC Algorithm in CIQTT

The HCDC algorithm (Al-Bahadili, 2008; Al-Bahadili & Rababa'a, 2010) is implemented in three different sub-procedures. Two of them for compression, in particular for index and query compression, and one for retrieved data decompression as shown in Figure 2. These sub-procedures can be explained as:

- **Index Compressor (INXCOM):** It reads the index file, finds the character frequencies, converts characters to binary sequence using the characters ASCII code, creates and stores the compression header, compresses the binary sequence, and converts the compressed binary sequence to characters and stores them in a compressed index.
- **Query Compressor (QRYCOM):** It reads the keywords, converts characters to bi-

nary sequence using the characters ASCII code, reads the compression header created by INXCOM, compresses the binary sequence, converts the compressed binary sequence back to characters, and finally stores the compressed index.

- **Index Decompressor (INXDEC):** It reads part of the compressed index file that match the search keyword, converts characters in that particular part to binary sequence using the characters ASCII codes, reads the compression header created by INXCOM, decompresses the binary sequence, and converts the decompressed binary sequence to characters so that it can process by the query ranker and other procedures at the front-end processor.

PERFORMANCE MEASURES

In order to evaluate and compare the performance of the CIQ model, a number of performance measures are considered; these are:

1. **Compression Ratio (C):** It is the ratio between the sizes of the index before and after compression, and it is expressed as:

$$C = \frac{S_o}{S_c} \qquad (1)$$

where S_o and S_c are the sizes of the uncompressed and compressed indexes.

2. **Storage Reduction Factor (R_s):** It represents the percentage reduction in storage requirement. It is calculated by dividing the difference between S_o and S_c by S_o; and it expressed as:

$$R_S = \left(\frac{S_o - S_c}{S_o}\right) \times 100 \left(1 - \frac{S_c}{S_o}\right) \times 100 \qquad (2)$$

3. **Speedup Factor (S_f):** It is the ratio between the time required for searching the uncompressed and compressed indexes for a certain word or phrase, and it is calculated as:

$$S_f = \frac{T_o}{T_c} \qquad (3)$$

where T_o and T_c are the times required for searching the uncompressed and compressed index for a certain word or phrase, respectively.

4. **Time Reduction Factor (R_t):** It represents the percentage reduction in processing (searching) time. It is calculated by dividing the difference between T_o and T_c by T_o:

$$R_t = \left(\frac{T_o - T_c}{T_o}\right) \times 100 = \left(1 - \frac{T_C}{T_o}\right) \times 100 \qquad (4)$$

The accuracy is validated by comparing the total number of documents found while searching compressed and uncompressed indexes for a certain keyword (N_c and N_o respectively), and the IDs of the matched documents.

TEST PROCEDURES AND DISCUSSION

In this paper, a number of search processes (test procedures) are performed to evaluate the performance and validate the accuracy of the new CIQ model using the CIQTT test bench. For each search process, the following parameters S_o, S_c, T_o, and T_c are recorded and used to calculate C, R_s, S_f, and R_t. The accuracy is validated by comparing N_c and N_o for a certain keyword, and the IDs of the matched documents.

Determination of C and R_s

In this work, first, a corpus is collected from 30 well-known Websites (include sub-domains) using the procedure COLCOR. A list of these websites is given in Table 1. The total number of documents collected is 104000 documents; all of them are in English and in HTML format. Other formats like PDF, PS, DOC, etc. are excluded.

Five inverted indexes of different sizes are generated from the collected documents. These indexes contain 1000, 10000, 25000, 50000, and 75000 documents. The sizes of these indexes are given in Table 2. The index files generated in the previous step is compressed using the HCDC algorithm. In particular in this step, we call the INXCOM procedure, which is especially developed for index compression. It reads the index file, finds the character frequencies, converts characters to binary sequence using the characters ASCII codes, creates and stores the compression header, compresses the binary sequence, and converts the compressed binary sequence to characters and stores them in a compressed index file. Table 2 summarizes the values of S_o, S_c, C, and R_s, for each index file.

It can be seen from Table 2 that the storage requirement are reduced by more than 24%, which

Table 1. List of visited websites

#	Website	#	Website
1	http://www.aljazeera.net/	16	http://www.azzaman.com/
2	http://www.bbc.co.uk/	17	http://www.en.wna-news.com/
3	http://www.tradearabia.com/	18	http://www.visitabudhabi.ae/
4	http://www.krg.org/	19	http://interactive.aljazeera.net/
5	http://www.iranpressnews.com/	20	http://bbcworld.mh.bbc.co.uk/
6	http://blogs.bbc.co.uk/	21	http://bahrainnews.net/
7	http://labs.aljazeera.net/	22	http://www.khilafah.com/
8	http://www.terrorism-info.org.il/	23	http://conference.khilafah.com/
9	http://www.live.bbc.co.uk/	24	http://electroniciraq.net/
10	http://evideo.alarabiya.net/	25	http://www.alarabiya.net/
11	http://www.electroniciraq.net/	26	http://blogs.aljazeera.net/
12	http://www.alsumaria.tv/	27	http://bbcworld.mh.bbc.co.uk/
13	http://www.pukmedia.com/	28	http://terrorism-info.org.il/
14	http://alhurriatv.com/	29	http://www.ameinfo.com/
15	http://www.tacme.com/	30	http://grievance.khilafah.com/

Table 2. Values of C and R_s for the different five indexes

Index	S_o (Byte)	S_c (Byte)	C	R_s (%)
1000	1 937 277	1 464 222	1.323	24.42
10000	16 439 380	12 003 725	1.370	26.98
25000	24 540 706	17 842 316	1.375	27.30
50000	52 437 195	37 948 720	1.382	27.63
75000	65 823 202	47 579 010	1.384	27.72

enables larger indexes to be stored. In real world the main cost of search engine comes from the data centers which store huge indexes. Thus, reducing the index size by nearly 24% means reduces the cost of data centers in a close percentage.

For the HCDC algorithm, the block size (n) is 7 and the number of parity bits (p) is 3, thus the maximum compression ratio (C_{max}) that can be achieved by the algorithm is 1.4 (Al-Bahadili, 2008). This demonstrates that the compression efficiency ($E=C/C_{max}$) of the HCDC algorithm is around 95%.

Determination of S_f and R_t

To determine S_f and R_t, a list of 29 keywords are chosen from diverse interest and character combination to search for within the different indexes, the keywords are listed in Table 3.

Second, we perform the search processes within both compressed and uncompressed indexes. For each search process, we take a record of the CPU time required to search for each keyword, and the number of documents that contains each keyword (search results), i.e., T_o, T_c, N_o, and N_c. Third, Equations 3 and 4 are used to calculate S_f and R_t, respectively, and the results obtained are given in Table 4.

Table 3. List of keywords

24am	jail	problem	worth
appeared	leader	reached	young
business	mail	science	years
charms	met	success	zoo
children	microwave	time	zero
environmental	modeling	unions	
estimated	numbers	victim	
government	people	white	

Determination of N_o and N_c

In order to validate the accuracy of the CIQ model, we determine and compare the values of N_o and N_c. In addition, we compare the actual IDs of the retrieved documents. The values of N_o and N_c are given in Table 5 for all searched keywords on the different searched indexes. Table 5 demonstrates that N_o and N_c are equal for all searched keywords in all index files.

Furthermore, an internal comparison processes were carried-out to ensure that the documents IDs retrieved by both the compressed and the uncompressed models are similar. The test results demonstrate a 100% agreement between the two models, which means despite the compressed level search, the new model achieved 100% accuracy. The final results are outlined in the CIQ performance triangle in Figure 3.

CONCLUSION

This paper presents a description and performance evaluation of a novel compressed index-query (CIQ) Web search engine model. The model incorporates two compression layers both implemented at the back-end processor side, one after the indexer (index compressor) acting as a second compression layer to generate a double compressed index, and the other one after the query parser for query compression (query compressor) to enable compressed index-query search. So that less disk space is required storing the index file, reducing disk I/O overheads, and consequently it can achieve higher retrieval rate. The data compression algorithm used is the HCDC algorithm. In order to validate the accuracy and integrity of the retrieved data, and to evaluate the performance of the CIQ model, a test procedure was performed using the CIQTT. Based on the test results, the new CIQ

Table 4. S_f and R_t for different search processes

Keyword	S_f					R_t				
	1000	10000	25000	50000	75000	1000	10000	25000	50000	75000
24am	1.323	1.369	1.579	1.792	1.384	24.44	26.96	36.68	44.19	27.76
appeared	1.335	1.353	1.356	1.377	1.750	25.09	26.10	26.23	27.36	42.85
business	1.233	1.347	1.331	1.346	1.338	18.89	25.78	24.87	25.69	25.24
charms	1.290	1.356	1.338	1.343	1.357	22.50	26.28	25.25	25.51	26.30
children	1.264	1.003	1.327	1.577	1.345	20.89	0.32	24.66	36.57	25.67
environmental	1.294	1.357	1.392	1.084	1.073	22.70	26.29	28.16	7.77	6.79
estimated	1.316	1.363	1.554	1.359	1.374	24.03	26.61	35.64	26.40	27.23
government	1.294	1.299	1.326	1.322	1.314	22.72	23.03	24.58	24.36	23.89
jail	1.303	1.200	1.345	1.343	1.336	23.23	16.69	25.65	25.56	25.12
leader	1.279	1.478	1.285	1.327	1.263	21.82	32.32	22.17	24.66	20.80
mail	1.290	1.389	1.329	1.279	2.586	22.47	28.03	24.76	21.79	61.33
met	1.309	1.366	1.286	1.032	1.753	23.61	26.80	22.26	3.13	42.95
microwave	1.312	1.026	1.350	1.678	1.332	23.76	2.49	25.94	40.41	24.91
modeling	1.451	1.356	1.347	1.836	1.349	31.10	26.25	25.74	45.54	25.88
numbers	1.667	1.583	1.361	1.544	1.057	40.02	36.84	26.51	35.22	5.39
people	1.392	1.311	1.351	1.874	3.191	28.15	23.69	25.97	46.63	68.67
problem	1.351	1.350	1.054	1.769	4.011	25.96	25.91	5.12	43.48	75.07
reached	1.279	1.350	1.803	1.360	1.271	21.79	25.93	44.54	26.46	21.29
science	1.314	1.355	1.351	1.348	1.332	23.92	26.19	25.99	25.82	24.90
success	1.328	1.297	1.573	1.369	1.833	24.73	22.89	36.41	26.93	45.44
time	1.318	1.360	1.331	1.328	1.340	24.15	26.45	24.88	24.69	25.39
unions	1.329	1.315	1.297	1.331	1.367	24.74	23.94	22.92	24.87	26.85
victim	1.310	1.321	1.305	1.396	1.348	23.68	24.29	23.35	28.36	25.82
white	1.303	1.336	1.330	1.303	1.310	23.23	25.14	24.79	23.25	23.64
worth	1.328	1.352	1.354	2.105	2.387	24.70	26.06	26.17	52.49	58.10
young	1.329	1.340	1.329	1.353	1.333	24.76	25.37	24.76	26.08	24.96
years	1.317	1.323	1.338	1.748	1.330	24.09	24.44	25.24	42.79	24.79
zoo	1.317	1.356	1.420	1.710	1.518	24.07	26.23	29.56	41.51	34.12
zero	1.316	1.288	1.335	1.351	1.398	24.00	22.36	25.07	25.96	28.46
Average	**1.327**	**1.328**	**1.352**	**1.468**	**1.606**	**24.46**	**24.13**	**26.34**	**30.12**	**31.71**

Table 5. $N_o = N_c$ for different search processes on the different five indexes

Keyword	1000	10000	25000	50000	75000
24am	8	72	107	245	292
appeared	47	395	574	1281	1631
business	263	2651	3854	8354	10769
charms	1	18	12	20	45
children	146	1582	2435	5134	6397
environmental	29	216	319	783	957
estimated	45	353	538	1075	1376
government	300	3219	4926	10555	13374
jail	39	405	568	1260	1553
leader	108	1111	1775	3756	4777
mail	148	1437	2323	4897	6243
met	59	653	884	2058	2521
microwave	3	22	43	89	95
modeling	1	9	7	22	25
numbers	59	621	969	2034	2666
people	505	5254	8008	16967	21599
problem	145	1385	2183	4811	6096
reached	59	416	686	1461	1782
science	107	1050	1666	3540	4514
success	77	712	1150	2462	3156
time	423	4424	6834	14553	18398
unions	14	157	252	537	651
victim	19	230	302	690	894
white	78	790	1196	2648	3290
worth	77	790	1202	2615	3333
young	108	1206	1850	3906	4996
years	346	3752	5764	12259	15583
zoo	5	30	52	105	136
zero	1	2	3	5	12
Total Match	**3220**	**32962**	**50482**	**108122**	**137161**

Figure 3. CIQ performance triangle

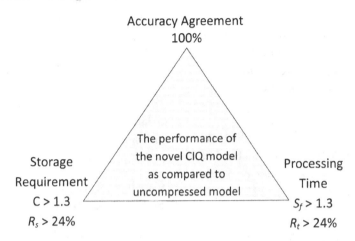

model demonstrated an excellent performance as compared to uncompressed model, as such:

- It demonstrated a tremendous accuracy with 100% agreement between the results retrieved by the CIQ and the uncompressed models.
- The new model demands less disk space as the HCDC algorithm achieves a compression ratio over 1.3. This implies a reduction in storage requirement over 24%.
- The new CIQ model performs faster than the uncompressed model. It achieved a speed up factor over 1.3 providing a reduction in processing time of over 24%.

It is believed that the CIQ model has opened an interesting research area aiming to develop more efficient Web search engine model by utilizing the concept of compressed index-query search. Thus, there are a number of recommendations for future work, however, in what follow, we shall emphasize what we believe main issues that need to be considered soon. These are:

- Perform further studies to optimize the statistics of the inverted index file to achieve maximum possible performance in terms

of compression ratio and minimum processing time.
- Cluster documents according to their characters frequencies to ensure higher compression ratio.
- Evaluate and compare the performance of the CIQ model against uncompressed model by considering the following test scenarios:
  ○ Larger index files.
  ○ Index files of different structure; for example, add more meta-data such as keyword position, near keyword, and other information to the index structure.
  ○ Index files that support incremental updates whereby documents can be added without re-indexing.
  ○ Mixed language index files.
  ○ Implement the enhanced HCDC (E-HCDC) algorithm.
  ○ Implement different character sets in naming or numbering crawled documents.
  ○ Perform further investigation using different list of Website and keywords.

REFERENCES

Al-Bahadili, H. (2008). A novel data compression scheme based on the error correcting Hamming code. *Journal of Computers & Mathematics with Applications, 56*(1), 143–150. doi:10.1016/j.camwa.2007.11.043

Al-Bahadili, H., & Hussain, S. M. (2008). An adaptive character wordlength algorithm for data compression. *Journal of Computers & Mathematics with Applications, 55*(6), 1250–1256. doi:10.1016/j.camwa.2007.05.014

Al-Bahadili, H., & Hussein, S. M. (2010). A bit-level text compression scheme based on ACW algorithm. *International Journal of Automation and Computing, 7*(1), 128–136. doi:10.1007/s11633-010-0123-6

Al-Bahadili, H., & Rababa'a, A. (2010). A bit-level text compression scheme based on the HCDC algorithm. *International Journal of Computers and Applications, 32*(3). doi:10.2316/Journal.202.2010.3.202-2914

Al-Bahadili, S., & Al-Saab, S. (2010). A compressed index-query web search engine model. *International Journal of Computer Information Systems, 1*(4), 73–79.

Al-Saab, S. (2011). *A novel search engine model based on index-query bit-level compression* (Unpublished doctoral dissertation). University of Banking & Financial Sciences, Faculty of Information Technology and Systems, Amman, Jordan.

Anh, V. N., & Moffat, A. (2004, January). Index compression using fixed binary codewords. In *Proceedings of the 15th Australasian Database Conference*, Dunedin, New Zealand.

Ashton, P. (2011). *Windows NT NTML Auto-Authentication*. Retrieved from http://insecure.org/sploits/NT.NTLM.auto-authentication.html

Badue, C., Baeza-Yates, R., Ribeiro-Neto, B., & Ziviani, N. (2002, September). Distributed query processing using partitioned inverted files. In *Proceedings of the 9th String Processing and Information Retrieval Symposium*.

Brin, S., & Page, L. (1998). The anatomy of a large-scale hypertextual Web search engine. *Journal of Computer Networks and ISDN Systems, 30*(1-7), 107-117.

Calishain, T. (2004). *Web search garage*. Upper Saddle River, NJ: Prentice Hall.

Chen, Z., Gehrke, J., & Korn, F. (2001, May 21-24). Query optimization in compressed database systems. In *Proceedings of the ACM Conference on Special Interest on Management of Data*, Santa Barbara, CA (pp. 271-282).

de Moura, E. S., Navarro, G., & Ziviani, N. (1997). Indexing compressed text. In *Proceedings of the 4th South American Workshop on String Processing*, Ottawa, ON, Canada (Vol. 8, pp. 95-111).

Fagni, T., Perego, R., Silvestri, F., & Orlando, S. (2006). Boosting the performance of Web search engines: Caching and prefetching query results by exploiting historical usage data. *ACM Transactions on Information Systems, 24*(1), 51–78. doi:10.1145/1125857.1125859

Ferragina, P., Gonzalez, R., Navarro, G., & Venturini, R. (2009). Compressed text indexes: From theory to practice. *Journal of Experimental Algorithmics, 13*(1), 12.

Ferragina, P., Luccio, F., Manzini, G., & Muthukrishnan, S. (2005). Structuring labeled trees for optimal succinctness, and beyond. In *Proceedings of the IEEE Symposium on Foundations of Computer Science* (pp. 184-193).

Ferragina, P., & Manzini, G. (2005). Indexing compressed texts. *Journal of the ACM, 52*(4), 552–581. doi:10.1145/1082036.1082039

Ferragina, P., Manzini, G., Makinen, V., & Navarro, G. (2007). Compressed representation of sequences and full-text indexes. *ACM Transactions on Algorithms, 3*(2).

Gonzalez, R., & Navarro, G. (2006, July 5-7). Statistical encoding of succinct data structures. In *Proceedings of the 17th Annual Conference on Combinatorial Pattern Matching*, Barcelona, Spain (pp. 295-306).

Gonzalez, R., & Navarro, G. (2007a, July 9-11). Compressed text indexes with fast locate. In *Proceedings of the 18th Annual Symposium on Combinatorial Pattern Matching*, London, ON, Canada (pp. 216-227).

Gonzalez, R., & Navarro, G. (2007b). A compressed text index on secondary memory. In *Proceedings of the 18th International Workshop on Combinatorial Algorithms* (pp. 80-91).

Hadoop. (2011). *What is Hadoop?* Retrieved from http://hadoop.apache.org/#What+Is+Hadoop%3F

Levene, M. (2005). *An introduction to search engine and navigation.* Upper Saddle River, NJ: Pearson Education.

Long, X., & Suel, T. (2003, September 9-12). Optimized query execution in large search engines with global page ordering. In *Proceedings of the 29th International Conference on Very Large Databases*, Berlin, Germany (Vol. 29).

Lucene. (2011). *What is Apache Lucene?* Retrieved from http://lucene.apache.org/#What+Is+Apache+Lucene%3F

Melnik, S., Raghavan, S., Yang, B., & Garcia-Molina, H. (2000, May 2-5). Building a distributed full-text index for the Web. In *Proceedings of the 10th International World Wide Web Conference*, Hong-Kong.

Moffat, A., & Culpepper, J. S. (2007, December). Hybrid bitvector index compression. In *Proceedings of the 12th Australasian Document Computing Symposium*, Melbourne, Australia (pp. 25-31).

Nutch. (2011). *About Nutch.* Retrieved from http://nutch.apache.org/about.html

Solr. (2011). *What is Solr?* Retrieved from http://lucene.apache.org/solr/#intro

Varadarajan, S., & Chiueh, T. C. (1997). SASE: Implementation of a compressed text search engine. In *Proceedings of the USENIX Symposium on Internet Technologies and Systems on USENIX Symposium on Internet Technologies and Systems* (p. 23).

Wikipedia. (2011). *MapReduce.* Retrieved from http://en.wikipedia.org/wiki/MapReduce

Yan, H., Ding, S., & Suel, T. (2009, April 20-24). Inverted index compression and query processing with optimized document ordering. In *Proceedings of the 18th International Conference on World Wide Web*, Madrid, Spain.

Zhang, J., Long, X., & Suel, T. (2008, April 21-25). Performance of compressed inverted list caching in search engines. In *Proceeding of the 17th International Conference on the World Wide Web*, Beijing, China.

Zobel, J., & Moffat, A. (2006). Inverted files for text search engines. *ACM Computing Surveys, 38*(2), 1–56. doi:10.1145/1132956.1132959

This work was previously published in the International Journal of Information Technology and Web Engineering (IJITWE), Volume 6, Issue 3, edited by Ghazi I. Alkhatib and Ernesto Damiani, pp. 39-56, copyright 2011 by IGI Publishing (an imprint of IGI Global).

Compilation of References

Abaii, M., Auer, G., Cho, Y., Cosovic, I., Döttling, M., George, K., Hamm, L., et al. (2006). *IST-4-027756 WINNER II D6.13.7. Test Scenarios and Calibration Cases Issue 2*. Munich, Germany: EU FP6 WINNER II Project.

Aberer, K., Hauswirth, M., & Salehi, A. (2007). Infrastructure for data processing in large-scale interconnected sensor networks. In *Proceedings of the 8th International Conference on Mobile Data Management* (pp. 198–205).

Abo Alkhair, A. (2006). Effect of stop words removing for Arabic information retrieval. *International Journal of Computing &. Information Science, 4*(3).

Achilleos, A. (2010). *Model-driven petri net based framework for pervasive service creation.* Unpublished doctoral dissertation, University of Essex, UK.

Adida, B., & Birbeck, M. (2008). *RDF a primer – bridging the human and data webs.* Retrieved from http://www.w3.org/TR/xhtml-rdfa-primer/

Agarwal, V., Dasgupta, K., Karnik, N., Kumar, A., Kundu, A., Mittal, S., & Srivastava, B. (2005). A service creation environment based on end to end composition of web services. In *Proceedings of the 14th International World Wide Web Conference*, Japan (pp. 128-137). New York, NY: ACM.

Ahn, G. J., Sandhu, R., Kang, M., & Park, J. (2000). Injecting RBAC to secure a web-based workflow system. In *Proceedings of the 5th ACM Workshop on Role-Based Access Control* (pp. 1-10).

Akilandeswari, J., & Gopalan, N. P. (2008). An Architectural Framework of a Crawler for Locating Deep Web Repositories Using Learning Multi-Agent Systems. In *Proceedings of the 2008 3rd International Conference on Internet & Web Applications and Services* (pp. 558-562).

Akkaya, K., & Younis, M. (2005). A survey on routing protocols for wireless sensor networks. *Ad Hoc Networks, 3*(3), 325–349. doi:10.1016/j.adhoc.2003.09.010

Akkiraju, R., Flaxer, D., Chang, H., Chao, T., Zhang, L. J., Wu, F., & Jeng, J. J. (2001). A framework for facilitating dynamic e-business via web services. In *Proceedings of the OOPSLA Workshop on Object-Oriented Web Services*, Tampa, FL.

Akrich, M. (1992). The description of technical objects. In Bijker, W. E., & Law, J. (Eds.), *Shaping technology/building society: Studies in sociotechnical change* (pp. 205–224). Cambridge, MA: MIT Press.

Aksenov, P., Luyten, K., & Coninx, K. (2009). Coping with variability of location sensing in large-scale ubicomp environments. In *Proceedings of the International Workshop on Sensing and Acting in Ubiquitous Environments* (pp. 1–5).

Akyildiz, I. F., Su, W., Sankarasubramaniam, Y., & Cayirci, E. (2002). Wireless sensor networks: a survey. *Computer Networks, 38*(4), 393–422. doi:10.1016/S1389-1286(01)00302-4

Al-Ali, R. J., Rana, O. F., Walker, D. W., Jha, S., & Sohail, S. (2002). G-QoSM: Grid service discovery using QoS properties. *Computing and Informatics Journal, 21*, 363–382.

Alamouti, S. M. (1998). A simple transmit diversity technique for wireless communications. *IEEE Journal on Selected Areas in Communications, 16*(8), 1451–1458. doi:10.1109/49.730453

Al-Bahadili, H. (2008). A novel data compression scheme based on the error correcting Hamming code. *Journal of Computers & Mathematics with Applications, 56*(1), 143–150. doi:10.1016/j.camwa.2007.11.043

Al-Bahadili, H., & Hussain, S. M. (2008). An adaptive character wordlength algorithm for data compression. *Journal of Computers & Mathematics with Applications, 55*(6), 1250–1256. doi:10.1016/j.camwa.2007.05.014

Al-Bahadili, H., & Hussein, S. M. (2010). A bit-level text compression scheme based on ACW algorithm. *International Journal of Automation and Computing, 7*(1), 128–136. doi:10.1007/s11633-010-0123-6

Al-Bahadili, S., & Al-Saab, S. (2010). A compressed index-query web search engine model. *International Journal of Computer Information Systems, 1*(4), 73–79.

Al-Harbi, S., Almuhareb, A., Al-Thubaity, A., Khorsheed, M. S., & Al-Rajeh, A. (2008). Automatic Arabic text classification. In *Proceedings of the 9th International Conference on the Statistical Analysis of Textual Data*, Lyon, France.

Al-Masri, E., & Qusay, H. (2007). QoS-based discovery and ranking of web services. In *Proceedings of the 16th International Conference on Computer Communications and Networks* (pp. 529-534).

Alonso, G., Casati, F., Kuno, H., & Machiraju, V. (2004). *Web services*. Berlin, Germany: Springer-Verlag.

Al-Saab, S. (2011). *A novel search engine model based on index-query bit-level compression* (Unpublished doctoral dissertation). University of Banking & Financial Sciences, Faculty of Information Technology and Systems, Amman, Jordan.

Al-Shalabi, R., Kanaan, G., Jaam, J. M., Hasnah, A., & Hilat, E. (2004). Stop-word removal algorithm for Arabic language. In *Proceedings of 1st International Conference on Information & Communication Technologies: From Theory to Applications*, Damascus, Syria (pp. 545-550).

Al-Shargabi, B., El Shiekh, A., & Sabri, A. (2010). Web service composition survey: State of the art review. *Recent Patent on Computer science Journal, 3*(2), 91-107.

Al-Tahan Al-Nu'aimi, A. S., & Qahwaji, R. S. (2006). Digital coloured images watermarking Using YIQ colour format in discrete transform domain. In *Proceedings of the Fourth Saudi Technical Conference and Exhibition*, Riyadh, Saudi Arabia (pp. 383-388).

Alvarez, M., Raposo, J., Cacheda, F., & Pan, A. (2006). *A Task-specific Approach for Crawling the Deep Web*. Retrieved from http://www.engineeringletters.com/issues_v13/issue_2/EL_13_2_19.pdf

Alvarez, M., Raposo, J., Pan, A., Cacheda, F., Bellas, F., & Carneiro, V. (2007). A Focused Crawler for Accessing Hidden Web Content. In *Proceedings of DEECS2007* (pp. 18–25). San Diego, CA: DeepBot.

Anbazhagan, M., & Arun, N. (2002). *Understanding quality of service for Web services*. Retrieved from http://www.ibm.com/developerworks/webservices/library/ws-quality/index.html

Anderson, R. J., & Petitcolas, F. A. (1998). On the limits of steganography. *Journal of Selected Area in Communications, 16*(4), 474–481. doi:10.1109/49.668971

Anh, V. N., & Moffat, A. (2004, January). Index compression using fixed binary codewords. In *Proceedings of the 15th Australasian Database Conference*, Dunedin, New Zealand.

Aoumeur, N., Barkaoui, K., & Saake, G. (2009). A multi-dimensional architectural approach to behavior-intensive adaptive pervasive applications. In *Proceedings of the 4th International Conference on Wireless Pervasive Computing* (pp. 1-8).

Aschoff, F., Schmalhofer, F., & van Elst, L. (2004). Knowledge mediation: A procedure for the cooperative construction of domain ontologies. In *Proceedings of the ECAI Workshop on Agent-Mediated Knowledge Management*, Valencia, Spain (pp. 29-38).

Ashton, P. (2011). *Windows NT NTML Auto-Authentication*. Retrieved from http://insecure.org/sploits/NT.NTLM.auto-authentication.html

Azarian, K., Gamal, H. E., & Schniter, P. (2005). On the achievable diversity multiplexing tradeoff in half-duplex cooperative channel. *IEEE Transactions on Information Theory, 51*(12), 4152–4172. doi:10.1109/TIT.2005.858920

Badue, C., Baeza-Yates, R., Ribeiro-Neto, B., & Ziviani, N. (2002, September). Distributed query processing using partitioned inverted files. In *Proceedings of the 9ᵗʰ String Processing and Information Retrieval Symposium*.

Bajcsy, J., Chong, C., Garr, D., Hunziker, J., & Kobayashi, H. (2001). On iterative decoding in some existing systems. *IEEE Journal on Selected Areas in Communications*, *19*(5), 883–890. doi:10.1109/49.924872

Banerjee, N., Agarwal, S., Bahl, P., Chandra, R., Wolman, A., & Corner, M. (2010). Virtual Compass: relative positioning to sense mobile social interactions. In *Proceedings of the 8th International Conference on Pervasive Computing* (pp. 1–21).

Banett, R., & Sytems, S. (1999). Digitl watermarking: Applications, techniques and challenges. *Electronics & Communications Engineering Journal*, *11*(4), 173–183. doi:10.1049/ecej:19990401

Barbosa, L., & Freire, J. (2005). Searching for Hidden-Web Databases. In. *Proceedings of WebDB*, *05*, 1–6.

Barry, J., Lee, E., & Messerschmitt, D. (2004). *Digital Communication*. Dordrecht, The Netherlands: Kluwer Academic.

Bartsch, S., Sohr, K., & Bormann, K. (2008, November 13-16). Supporting agile development of authorization rules for SME applications. In *Proceedings of the 4ᵗʰ International Conference on Collaborative Computing: Networking, Applications and Worksharing*, Orlando, FL.

Baryshnikov, Y. M., Coffman, E. G., & Kwak, K. J. (2008). High performance sleep-wake sensor systems based on cyclic cellular automata. In *Proceedings of the 7th International Conference on Information Processing in Sensor Networks* (pp. 517-526).

Baus, J., & Kray, C. (2002). Frames of reference, positional information and navigational assistance. In S. M. Haller & G. Simmons (Eds.), *Proceedings of the 15th International Florida Artificial Intelligence Research Society Conference* (pp. 461–465). AAAI Press.

Beckett, D., & McBride, B. (2004). *RDF/XML syntax specification (revised)*. Retrieved from http://www.w3.org/TR/rdf-syntax-grammar/

Belaramani, N. M., Wang, C.-L., & Lau, F. C. M. (2003, May). Dynamic component composition for functionality adaptation in pervasive environments. In *Proceedings of the 9th IEEE Workshop on Future Trends of Distributed Computing Systems*, San Juan, Puerto Rico (pp. 226–232).

Belfiore, J.-C., Rekaya, G., & Viterbo, E. (2005). The golden code: a 2 × 2 full-rate space-time code with nonvanishing determinants. *IEEE Transactions on Information Theory*, *51*(4), 1432–1436. doi:10.1109/TIT.2005.844069

Belton, V., & Stewart, T. (2002). *Multi criteria decision analysis – An integrated approach* (pp. 151–159). Boston, MA: Kluwer Academic.

Benedetto, S., Divsalar, D., Montorsi, G., & Pollarab, F. (1996). Soft-output decoding algorithms in iterative decoding of turbo codes. *TDA Progress Report*, *42*(124), 63–87.

Benford, S., Crabtree, A., Flintham, M., Drozd, A., Anastasi, R., & Paxton, M. (2006). Can you see me now? *ACM Transactions on Human-Computer Interaction*, *13*(1), 100–133. doi:10.1145/1143518.1143522

Bennett, S., McRobb, S., & Farmer, R. (2006). *Object-oriented systems analysis and design using UML* (3rd ed.). Berkshire, UK: McGraw-Hill.

Bequet, H., Kunnumpurath, M. M., Rhody, S., & Tost, A. (2002). *Beginning Java web services*. Birmingham, UK: Wrox Press.

Bergman, M. K. (2001). The Deep Web: Surfacing Hidden Value. *Journal of Electronic Publishing*, *7*(1). Retrieved from http://www.press.umich.edu/jep/07-01/bergman.html. doi:10.3998/3336451.0007.104

Berners-Lee, T., Hendler, J., & Lassila, O. (2001). The semantic web. *Scientific American*, *284*(5), 28–37. doi:10.1038/scientificamerican0501-34

Bertino, E., Crampton, J., & Paci, F. (2006). Access control and authorization constraints for WS-BPEL. In *Proceedings of the IEEE International Conference on Web Services* (pp. 275-284).

Bhagdev, R., Chapman, S., Ciravegna, F., Lanfranchi, V., & Petrelli, D. (2008). Hybrid search: Effectively combining keywords and semantic searches. In *Proceedings of the 5th European Semantic Web Conference on The Semantic Web: Research and Applications* (pp. 554-568).

Bhatti, N., Bouch, A., & Kuchinsky, A. (2000). Integrating user-perceived quality into web server design. *Computer Networks, 33,* 1–16. doi:10.1016/S1389-1286(00)00087-6

Bikakis, N., Giannopoulos, G., Dalamagas, T., & Sellis, T. (2010). Integrating keywords and semantics on document annotation and search. In *Proceedings of the International Conference On the Move to Meaningful Internet Systems: Part II* (pp. 921-938).

Blei, D. M., Ng, A. Y., & Jordan, M. I. (2003). Latent dirichlet allocation. *Journal of Machine Learning Research, 3*(1), 993–1022. doi:10.1162/jmlr.2003.3.4-5.993

Bletsas, A., Khisti, A., Reed, D. P., & Lippman, A. (2006). A simple cooperative diversity method based on network path selection. *IEEE Journal on Selected Areas in Communications, 24*(3), 659–672. doi:10.1109/JSAC.2005.862417

Blum, A. (2004). UDDI as an extended web services registry: Versioning, quality of service, and more. *SOA World Magazine, 4*(6).

Boehm, B. W., Abts, C., Brown, A. W., Chulani, S., Clark, B. K., & Horowitz, E. (2000). *Software cost estimation with COCOMO II* (1st ed.). Upper Saddle River, NJ: Prentice Hall.

Booth, D., Hass, H., Mccabe, F., Newcomer, E., Champion, M., Ferris, C., & Orchard, D. (2005). *Web services architecture.* Retrieved from http://www.w3.org/TR/ws-arch/

Bouamrane, M.-M., Luz, S., & Masoodian, M. (2008). Ontologies in interactive systems. In *Proceedings of the 1st International Workshop on Ontologies in Interactive Systems* (pp. 3–6).

Boukhebouze, M., Amghar, Y., Benharkat, A., & Maamar, Z. (2010). Rule-based approach to model and verify flexible business processes. *International Journal of Business Process Integration and Management.*

Brickley, D., & Guha, R. (2004). *RDF vocabulary description language 1.0: RDF schema.* Retrieved from http://www.w3.org/TR/rdf-schema/

Brin, S., & Page, L. (1998). The anatomy of a large-scale hypertextual Web search engine. *Journal of Computer Networks and ISDN Systems, 30*(1-7), 107-117.

Brown, A., Johnston, S., & Kelly, K. (2002). *Using service-oriented architecture and component-based development to build web service applications.* Retrieved from http://citeseerx.ist.psu.edu/viewdoc/download?doi=10.1.1.86.510&rep=rep1&type=pdf

Buchanan, R. (1985). Declaration by design: Rhetoric, argument and demonstration in design practice. *Design Issues, 2*(1), 4–22. doi:10.2307/1511524

Bulterman, D., Grassel, G., Jansen, J., Koivisto, A., Layaida, N., & Michel, T. …Zucker, D. (2005). *Synchronized Multimedia Integration Language (SMIL 2.1).* Retrieved from http://www.w3.org/TR/SMIL/

Burigat, S., & Chittaro, L. (2011). Pedestrian navigation with degraded GPS signal: investigating the effects of visualizing position uncertainty. In *Proceedings of the 13th International Conference on Human Computer Interaction with Mobile Devices and Services* (pp. 221–230).

Business Rules Group. (2005). *Defining business rules - What are they really?* Retrieved from http://www.businessrulesgroup.org

Calic, T., Dascalu, S., & Egbert, D. (2008). Tools for MDA software development: Evaluation criteria and set of desirable features. In *Proceedings of the 5th International Conference on Information Technology,* Istanbul, Turkey (pp. 44–50).

Calishain, T. (2004). *Web search garage.* Upper Saddle River, NJ: Prentice Hall.

Callahan, E. (2005). Cultural similarities and differences in the design of University Websites. *Journal of Computer-Mediated Communication, 11*(1), 239–273. doi:10.1111/j.1083-6101.2006.tb00312.x

Cao, J., Chen, J., Zhao, H., & Li, M. (2009). A policy-based authorization model for workflow-enabled dynamic process management. *Journal of Network and Computer Applications, 32*(2), 412–422. doi:10.1016/j.jnca.2008.02.021

Cardellini, V., Casalicchio, E., Colajanni, M., & Mambelli, M. (2001). Web switch support for differentiated services. *ACM SIGMETRICS Performance Evaluation Review, 29*(2), 14–19. doi:10.1145/572317.572320

Cardoso, J., Sheth, A., Miller, J., Arnold, J., & Kochut, K. (2004). Quality of service for workflows and web service processes. *Journal of Web Semantics*, *1*(3), 281–308. doi:10.1016/j.websem.2004.03.001

Castro, V. D., Marcos, E., & Vela, B. (2004). *Representing WSDL with Extended UML*. Retrieved from http://caribdis.unab.edu.co/pls/portal/url/ITEM/3F73657A-ABB5616CEO440003BA3D5405

Chan, H., & Perrig, A. (2004). ACE: An emergent algorithm for highly uniform cluster formation. In *Proceedings of the European Workshop on Sensor Networks* (pp. 154-171).

Chandrasekaran, S., Miller, J., Silver, G., Arpinar, B., & Sheth, A. (2003). Performance analysis and simulation of composite web services. *International Journal of Electron Commer Bus Media*, *13*(2), 18–30.

Chan, K., & Poernomo, I. (2007). QoS-aware model driven architecture through the UML and CIM. *Information Systems Frontiers*, *9*(2-3), 209–224. doi:10.1007/s10796-007-9033-8

Chaparadza, R., Papavassiliou, S., Kastrinogiannis, T., Vigoureux, M., Dotaro, E., & Davy, K. A. (2009). Creating a viable evolution path towards self-managing future internet via a standardizable reference model for autonomic network engineering. In Tselentis, G., Domingue, J., Galis, A., Gavras, A., Hausheer, D., & Krco, S., et al. (Eds.), *Towards the Future Internet – A European Research Perspective* (pp. 136–147). Amsterdam, The Netherlands: IOS Press.

Chappell, D., & Jewell, T. (2002). *Java web services*. Sebastopol, CA: O'Reilly Media.

Chen, Y., Tsai, F. S., & Chan, K. L. (2007). Blog search and mining in the business domain. In *DDDM '07: Proceedings of the 2007 International Workshop on Domain Driven Data Mining* (pp. 55-60).

Chen, Z., Chia, L. T., Silverajan, B., & Lee, B. S. (2003). UX- An architecture providing QoS - aware and federated support for UDDI. In *Proceedings of the First International Conference on Web Services* (pp. 1-6).

Chen, Z., Gehrke, J., & Korn, F. (2001, May 21-24). Query optimization in compressed database systems. In *Proceedings of the ACM Conference on Special Interest on Management of Data*, Santa Barbara, CA (pp. 271-282).

Cheng, Y.-C., Chawathe, Y., LaMarca, A., & Krumm, J. (2005). Accuracy characterization for metropolitan-scale Wi-Fi localization. In *Proceedings of the 3rd International Conference on Mobile Systems, Applications and Services* (pp. 233–245).

Chen, J., Dholakia, A., Eleftheriou, E., Fossorier, M., & Hu, X. (2005). Reduced-complexity decoding of LDPC codes. *IEEE Transactions on Communications*, *53*(8), 1288–1299. doi:10.1109/TCOMM.2005.852852

Chen, T. H., Horng, G., & Wang, S. H. (2003). A robust wavelet-based watermarking scheme using quantization and human visual system model. *Pakistan Journal of Information and Technology*, *2*(3), 213–230.

Chen, Y., Tsai, F. S., & Chan, K. L. (2008). Machine Learning Techniques for Business Blog Search and Mining. *Expert Systems with Applications*, *35*(3), 581–590. doi:10.1016/j.eswa.2007.07.015

Choi, W. J., Negi, R., & Cioffi, J. M. (2000). Combined ML and DEF decoding for the V-BLAST system. In *Proceedings of the IEEE International Conference on Communications* (Vol. 3, pp. 1243–1248).

Chung, J. Y., Lin, K. J., & Mathieu, R. G. (2003). Web services computing: Advancing software interoperability. *Computer*, *36*(10), 35–37. doi:10.1109/MC.2003.1236469

Clausen, T., & Jacquet, P. (2003). *Optimised Link State Routing Protocol (OLSR) (RFC No. 3626)*. Internet Engineering Task Force.

Cohn, D., & Hofmann, T. (2001). The missing link – a probabilistic model of document content and hypertext connectivity. *Advances in Neural Information Processing Systems*, *13*, 430–436.

Consolvo, S., Harrison, B., Smith, I., Chen, M., Everitt, K., Froelich, J., & Landay, J. (2007). Conducting in situ evaluations for and with ubiquitous computing technologies. *International Journal of Human-Computer Interaction*, *22*(1–2), 103–118.

Coronato, A., Esposito, M., & Pietro, G. (2009). A multimodal semantic location service for intelligent environments: an application for smart hospitals. *Personal and Ubiquitous Computing*, *13*(7), 527–538. doi:10.1007/s00779-009-0223-x

Cox, I., Kilian, F., Leighton, F., & Shamoon, T. (1997). Secure spread spectrum watermarking for multimedia. *IEEE Transactions on Image Processing*, *6*, 1673–1687. doi:10.1109/83.650120

Craven, M., & Kumlien, J. (1999). Constructing biological knowledge bases by extracting information from text sources. In *Proceedings of the 7th International Conference on Intelligent Systems for Molecular Biology* (pp. 77-86).

Curbera, F., Nagy, W. A., & Weerawarana, S. (2001). *Web services: Why and how*. Retrieved from http://nclab. kaist.ac.kr/lecture/cs744_2003_Spring/Webservices-whyandhow.pdf

D'Ambriogio, A., & Bocciarelli, P. (2007). A model-driven approach to describe and predict the performance of composite services. In *Proceedings of the 6th International Workshop on Software and Performance* (pp. 78-89). New York, NY: ACM.

D'Ambrogio, A. (2006). A model-driven WSDL extension for describing the QoS of web services. In *Proceedings of the IEEE International Conference on Web Services* (pp. 789-796). Washington, DC: IEEE Computer Society.

Damen, M. O., Chkeif, A., & Belfiore, J.-C. (2000). Lattice code decoder for space-time codes. *IEEE Communications Letters*, *4*(5), 161–163. doi:10.1109/4234.846498

Damen, M. O., Gamal, H. E., & Caire, G. (2003). On maximum-likelihood detection and the search for the closest lattice point. *IEEE Transactions on Information Theory*, *49*(10), 2389–2402. doi:10.1109/TIT.2003.817444

Dashofy, E., Asuncion, H., Hendrickson, S., Suryanarayana, G., Georgas, J., & Taylor, R. (2007). Archstudio 4: An architecture-based meta-modeling environment. In *Proceedings of the 29th International Conference on Software Engineering* (pp. 67–68).

Davies, J., Krohn, U., & Weeks, R. (2002). Quizrdf: Search technology for the semantic web. In *Proceedings of the 11th International WWW Conference Workshop on RDF and Semantic Web Applications*.

Day, J., & Deters, R. (2004). Selecting the best web service. In *Proceedings of the Conference of the Centre for Advanced Studies on Collaborative Research*, ON, Canada (pp. 293-307).

de Bruijn, J., Bussler, C., Domingue, J., Fensel, D., & Hepp, M. Kifer, et al. (2006). *Web service modeling ontology (WSMO)*. Retrieved from http://www.wsmo. org/TR/d2/v1.3/D2v1-3_20061021.pdf

de Moura, E. S., Navarro, G., & Ziviani, N. (1997). Indexing compressed text. In *Proceedings of the 4th South American Workshop on String Processing*, Ottawa, ON, Canada (Vol. 8, pp. 95-111).

Dearman, D., Varshavsky, A., de Lara, E., & Truong, K. N. (2007). An exploration of location error estimation. In *Proceedings of the 9th International Conference on Ubiquitous Computing* (pp. 181–198).

Decker, S., Melnik, S., van Harmelen, F., Fensel, D., Klein, M., & Broekstra, J. (2000). The semantic web: the roles of XML and RDF. *IEEE Internet Computing*, *15*(3), 63–73. doi:10.1109/4236.877487

Dey, A., Hightower, J., de Lara, E., & Davies, N. (2010). Location-based services. *IEEE Pervasive Computing / IEEE Computer Society [and] IEEE Communications Society*, *9*(1), 11–12. doi:10.1109/MPRV.2010.10

Dodd, P. E. (2001). *Epi, Thinned, and SOI Substrates*. Retrieved from http://parts.jpl.nasa.gov/mrqw/mrqw_presentations/S4_dodd.ppt

Dohler, M., Gkelias, A., & Aghvami, H. (2004). A resource allocation strategy for distributed MIMO multi-hop communication systems. *IEEE Communications Letters*, *8*(2), 99–101. doi:10.1109/LCOMM.2004.823425

Dohler, M., & Li, Y. H. (2010). *Cooperative communications hardware, channel & PHY*. Hoboken, NJ: Wiley.

Doppler, K., Redana, S., Wódczak, M., Rost, P., & Wichman, R. (2007). Dynamic resource assignment and cooperative relaying in cellular networks: Concept and performance assessment. *EURASIP Journal on Wireless Communications and Networking*.

Doppler, L., Osseiran, A., Wódczak, M., & Rost, P. (2007, July). On the Integration of Cooperative Relaying into the WINNER System Concept. Paper presented at the 16th IST Mobile & Wireless Communications Summit, Budapest, Hungary.

Dottling, M., Irmer, R., Kalliojarvi, K., & Rouquette-Leveil, S. (2009). System Model, Test Scenarios, and Performance Evaluation. In Dottling, M., Mohr, W., & Osseiran, A. (Eds.), *Radio Technologies and Concepts for IMT-Advanced*. Hoboken, NJ: Wiley. doi:10.1002/9780470748077.ch13

El Hadad, J., Manouvrier, M., & Rukoz, M. (2010). TQoS: Transactional and QoS-aware selection algorithm for automatic web service composition. *IEEE Transactions on Services Computing, 3*(1), 73–85. doi:10.1109/TSC.2010.5

Eleftheriou, E., Mittelholzar, T., & Dholakia, A. (2001). Reduced-complexity decoding algorithm for low-density parity-check codes. *Electronics Letters Online, 37*(2), 102–104. doi:10.1049/el:20010077

Eljinini, M.A. (2011). Health-related information structuring for the semantic web. In *Proceedings of the International Conference on Intelligent Semantic Web-Services and Applications* (p. 6).

Eljinini, M. A., & Sarhan, N. A. (2007). An ontology for extracting information from the World Wide Web. In *Proceedings of the Second Scientific Conference on Administrative and Strategic Thinking in Changing World*, Amman, Jordan.

Eljinini, M. A., Sarhan, N. A., & Carson, E. R. (2006). Towards the semantic web: Extracting common concepts from chronic disease - related websites. In *Proceedings of the International Medical Informatics and Biomedical Engineering Conference*, Amman, Jordan (pp. 118-123).

El-Khamy, M., Vikalo, H., Hassibi, B., & McEliece, R. J. (2009). Performance of sphere decoding of block codes. *IEEE Transactions on Communications, 57*(10), 2940–2950. doi:10.1109/TCOMM.2009.10.080402

El-Kourdi, M., Bensaid, A., & Rachidi, T. (2004). Automatic Arabic document categorization based on the Naïve Bayes algorithm. In *Proceedings of the 20th International Conference on Computational Linguistics*, Geneva, Switzerland.

Eriksson, H. E., & Penker, M. (1998). *UML toolkit*. Chichester, UK: John Wiley & Sons.

Erosheva, E., Fienberg, S., & Lafferty, J. (2004). Mixed-membership models of scientific publications. *Proceedings of the National Academy of Sciences of the United States of America, 101*, 5220–5227. doi:10.1073/pnas.0307760101

Evegniy, G., & Shaul, M. (2004, July 4-8). Text classification with many redundant features: Using aggressive feature selection to make svms competitive with C4.5. In *Proceeding of the 21st International Conference Machine Learning*, Banff, AB, Canada (p. 41).

Fagni, T., Perego, R., Silvestri, F., & Orlando, S. (2006). Boosting the performance of Web search engines: Caching and prefetching query results by exploiting historical usage data. *ACM Transactions on Information Systems, 24*(1), 51–78. doi:10.1145/1125857.1125859

Feng, X., & Yang, Y. (2005). A new watermarking method based on DWT. In Y. Hao, J. Liu, Y.-P. Wang, Y.-m. Cheung, H. Yin, L. Jiao et al. (Eds.), *Proceedings of the International Conference on Computational Intelligence and Security* (LNCS 3802, pp. 1122-1126).

Fenn, J. (2006). Managing citations and your bibliography with BibTeX. *The PracnTeX Journal, 4*. Retrieved from http://www.tug.org/pracjourn/2006-4/fenn/

Fensel, D. (2001). Ontologies: Dynamic networks of formally represented meaning. In *Proceedings of the 1st Semantic Web Working Symposium*, Stanford, CA.

Fensel, D., & Stollberg, M. (2005). *Ontology-based choreography and orchestration of WSMO services*. Retrieved from http://www.wsmo.org/TR/d14/v0.1/d14v01_20050301.pdf

Fensel, D., & Bussler, C. (2002). The web service modeling framework WSMF. *Electronic Commerce Research and Applications, 1*(2), 1–33. doi:10.1016/S1567-4223(02)00015-7

Ferragina, P., Luccio, F., Manzini, G., & Muthukrishnan, S. (2005). Structuring labeled trees for optimal succinctness, and beyond. In *Proceedings of the IEEE Symposium on Foundations of Computer Science* (pp. 184-193).

Ferragina, P., Manzini, G., Makinen, V., & Navarro, G. (2007). Compressed representation of sequences and full-text indexes. *ACM Transactions on Algorithms, 3*(2).

Ferragina, P., Gonzalez, R., Navarro, G., & Venturini, R. (2009). Compressed text indexes: From theory to practice. *Journal of Experimental Algorithmics, 13*(1), 12.

Ferragina, P., & Manzini, G. (2005). Indexing compressed texts. *Journal of the ACM, 52*(4), 552–581. doi:10.1145/1082036.1082039

Finin, T., & Ding, L. (2006). Search engines for semantic web knowledge. In *Proceedings of XTech: Building Web 2.0.*

Fitzek, F. H. P., & Katz, M. D. (Eds.). (2006). *Cooperation in Wireless Networks: Principles and Applications – Real Egoistic Behavior is to Cooperate.* Berlin, Germany: Springer. doi:10.1007/1-4020-4711-8

Ford, G., & Kotzé, P. (2005). Designing usable interfaces with cultural dimensions. In M. F. Costabile & F. Paternò (Eds.), *Proceedings of the IFIP TC13 International Conference on Human-Computer Interaction*, Rome, Italy (LNCS 3585, pp. 713-726).

Frkovic, F., Podobnik, V., Trzec, K., & Jezic, G. (2008). Agent-based user personalization using context-aware semantic reasoning. In I. Lovrek, R. J. Howlett, & L. C. Jain (Eds.), *Proceedings of the 12th International Conference on Knowledge-Based Intelligent Information and Engineering Systems* (LNCS 5177, pp. 166-173).

Fu, H., Gao, S., & Anyanwu, K. (2010). Disambiguating keyword queries on RDF databases using "deep" segmentation. In *Proceedings of the IEEE Fourth International Conference on Semantic Computing* (pp. 236-243).

Fukuda, K., Tsunoda, T., Tamura, A., & Takagi, T. (1998). Toward information extraction: Identifying protein names from biological papers. In *Proceedings of the Pacific Symposium on Biocomputing*, Maui, HI (pp. 707-718).

Fu, M. S., & Au, O. C. (2002). Data hiding watermarking for halftone images. *Transactions on Image Processing, 11*(4), 477–484. doi:10.1109/TIP.2002.999680

Fung, C. K., Hung, P. C. K., Linger, R. C., Wang, G., & Walton, G. H. (2006). A service-oriented composition framework with QoS management. *International Journal of Web Services Research, 3*(3), 108–132. doi:10.4018/jwsr.2006070105

Furtado, V., Ayres, L., Oliveira, M. D., Filho, E. V., Caminha, C., D'orleans, J., & Belchior, M. (2010). Collective intelligence in law enforcement: The WikiCrimes system. *Information Sciences, 180*(1), 4–17. doi:10.1016/j.ins.2009.08.004

Ganapati, S. (2010). *Using Geographic Information Systems to Increase Citizen Engagement.* Washington, DC: IBM Center for the Business of Government.

Ganic, E., & Eskicioglu, A. M. (2005). Robust embedding of visual watermarks using DWT-SVD. *Journal of Electronic Imaging, 14*(4), 4304. doi:10.1117/1.2137650

Geertz, C. (1973). *The interpretation of cultures.* New York, NY: Basic Books.

Gellersen, H., Lukowicz, P., Beigl, M., & Riedel, T. (2010). Cooperative relative positioning. *IEEE Pervasive Computing / IEEE Computer Society [and] IEEE Communications Society, 9*(4), 78–89. doi:10.1109/MPRV.2010.18

Gfeller, B., & Vicari, E. (2007). A randomized distributed algorithm for the maximal independent set problem in growth-bounded graphs. In *Proceedings of the 26th Annual ACM Symposium on Principles of Distributed Computing.*

Gharib, T. F., & Badieh, H. M. (2009). Arabic text classification using support vector machines. *International Journal of Computers and their Applications, 16*(4), 192-199.

Gilardoni, L., Biasuzzi, C., Ferraro, M., Fonti, R., & Slavazza, P. (2005). Lkms - a legal knowledge management system exploiting semantic web technologies. In *Proceedings of the International Semantic Web Conference* (pp. 872-886).

Girardin, F. (2007). Bridging the social-technical gap in location-aware computing. In *Proceedings of the 25th Conference on Human Factors in Computing Systems Extended Abstracts* (pp. 1653–1656).

Goldsmith, A. (2005). *Wireless Communications.* Cambridge, UK: Cambridge University Press.

Gonzalez, R., & Navarro, G. (2006, July 5-7). Statistical encoding of succinct data structures. In *Proceedings of the 17th Annual Conference on Combinatorial Pattern Matching*, Barcelona, Spain (pp. 295-306).

Gonzalez, R., & Navarro, G. (2007a, July 9-11). Compressed text indexes with fast locate. In *Proceedings of the 18th Annual Symposium on Combinatorial Pattern Matching*, London, ON, Canada (pp. 216-227).

Gonzalez, R., & Navarro, G. (2007). A compressed text index on secondary memory. In *Proceedings of the 18th International Workshop on Combinatorial Algorithms* (pp. 80-91).

Good, B. M., Tranfield, E. M., Tan, P. C., Sheata Singhera, G. K., Gosselik, J., Okon, E. B., & Wilkinson, M. D. (2006). Fast, cheap and out of control: A zero curation model for Ontology development. In *Proceedings of the Pacific Symposium on Biocomputing* (pp.128-139).

Goodchild, M. F. (2007). Citizens as sensors: the world of volunteered geography. *GeoJournal, 69*(4), 211–221. doi:10.1007/s10708-007-9111-y

Graham, J. (2002). *Soft errors a problem as SRAM geometries shrink.* Retrieved from http://www.ebnews.com/story/OEG20020128S0079

Gronmo, R., & Jaeger, M. C. (2005). Model-driven methodology for building QoS-optimised web service compositions. In L. Kutvonen & N. Alonistioti (Eds.), *Proceeding of the 5ᵗʰ IFIP International Conference on Distributed Applications and Interoperable Systems* (LNCS 3543, pp. 68-82).

Gronmo, R., Skogan, D., Solheim, I., & Oldevik, J. (2004, March 28-31). Model-driven Web services development. In *Proceedings of the IEEE International Conference on e-Technology, e-Commerce and e-Service* (pp. 42-45). Washington, DC: IEEE Computer Society.

Gruber, T. (2004). Every ontology is a treaty - a social agreement-among people with some common motive in sharing. *Official Bulletin of AIS Special Interest Group on Semantic Web and Information Systems, 1*(3).

Guha, R., McCool, R., & Miller, E. (2003). Semantic search. In *Proceedings of the 12ᵗʰ International Conference on World Wide Web* (pp. 700-709).

Gulstad, G., & Bruvold, K. (2003). *Digital image watermarking technique for copyright protection.* Retrieved from http://ucsb.edu/bruvold/ece178/report/repeam6report.html

Guo, Z., Zhu, S., Chi, Y., Zhang, Z., & Gong, Y. (2009). A latent topic model for linked documents. In *SIGIR '09: Proceedings of the 32nd International ACM SIGIR Conference on Research and Development in Information Retrieval* (pp. 720-721).

Guru, S. M., Hsu, A., Halgamuge, S., & Fernando, S. (2004). Clustering sensor networks using growing self-organising map. In *Proceedings of Intelligent Sensors, Sensor Networks and Information Processing Conference* (pp. 91-96).

Hadoop. (2011). *What is Hadoop?* Retrieved from http://hadoop.apache.org/#What+Is+Hadoop%3F

Hall, E., & Hall, M. R. (1990). *Understanding cultural differences.* Yarmouth, ME: Intercultural Press.

Hall, G. B., Chipeniuk, R., Feick, R. D., Leahy, M. G., & Deparday, V. (2010). Community-based production of geographic information using open source software and Web 2.0. *International Journal of Geographical Information Science, 24*(5), 761–781. doi:10.1080/13658810903213288

Hansen, R., Wind, R., Jensen, C. S., & Thomsen, B. (2009). Seamless indoor/outdoor positioning handover for location-based services in Streamspin. In *Proceedings of the 10th International Conference on Mobile Data Management* (pp. 267–272).

Hartung, F., & Girod, B. (1997). Copyright protection in video delivery networks by watermarking of pre-compressed video. In S. Fdida & M. Morganti (Eds.), *Proceedings of the Second European Conference on Multimedia Applications, Services and Techniques* (LNCS 1242, pp. 423-436).

Hattori, A., Goto, M., & Hayami, H. (2008). A Local Safety Knowledge Sharing System for Proactive Management by Citizens. *Journal of Convergence Information Technology, 3*(4), 26–34.

He, H. (2003). *What is service-oriented architecture.* Retrieved from http://www.xml.com/pub/a/ws/2003/09/30/soa.html

He, B., Patel, M., Zhang, Z., & Chang, K. C. (2007). Accessing the deep Web. *Communications of the ACM, 50*(5), 94–101. doi:10.1145/1230819.1241670

Heinzelman, W. R., Chandrakasan, A. P., & Balakrishnan, H. (2000). Energy-efficient communication protocol for wireless microsensor networks. In *Proceedings of the 33rd Annual Hawaii International Conference* (pp. 3005-3014).

Herhold, P., Zimmermann, E., & Fettweis, G. (2004, June) *Relaying and Cooperation - A System Perspective*. Paper presented at the 13th IST Mobile & Wireless Communications Summit, Lyon, France.

Herold, M. (2008). *WSMX documentation*. Retrieved from http://www.wsmx.org/papers/documentation/WSMXDocumentation.pdf

Herold, M. (2008). *Evaluation and advancement in context of a tourist information system*. Retrieved from http://www.fh-wedel.de/fileadmin/mitarbeiter/iw/Abschlussarbeiten/MasterarbeitHerold.pdf

Herzig, D. M. (2011). Hybrid search ranking for structured and unstructured data. In *Proceedings of the 8th Extended Semantic Web Conference on the Semantic Web: Research and Applications - Part II* (pp. 518-522).

Hofstede, G. (1991). *Cultures and organizations: Software of the mind*. New York, NY: McGraw-Hill.

Hofstede, G. (2003). *Culture's consequences: Comparing values, behaviours and organizations across nations*. Thousand Oaks, CA: Sage.

Horrocks, I., Patel-Schneider, P. F., & van Harmelen, F. (2003). From SHIQ and RDF to OWL: The making of a web ontology language. *Journal of Web Semantics, 1*(1), 7–26. doi:10.1016/j.websem.2003.07.001

Huang, F., & Guan, Z. H. (2004). A hybrid SVD-DCT watermarking method based on LPSNR. *Pattern Recognition Letters, 25*(15), 1769–1775. doi:10.1016/j.patrec.2004.07.003

Hyvarinen, A. (1999). Sparse code shrinkage: Denoising of nongaussian data by maximum likelihood estimation. *Neural Computation, 11*(7), 1739–1768. doi:10.1162/089976699300016214

Jacquet, P., Muhlethaler, P., Clausen, T., Laouiti, A., Qayyum, A., & Viennot, L. (2001, December). Optimised link state routing protocol for ad hoc networks. In *Proceedings of the IEEE International Multi Topic Conference* (pp. 62–68).

Jafarkhani, H. (2005). *Space-Time Coding – Theory and Practice*. Cambridge, UK: Cambridge University Press. doi:10.1017/CBO9780511536779

Jain, S., Hayward, M., & Kumar, S. (2003). *The Ultimate Guide to Building and Delivering OSS/BSS*. Dordrecht, The Netherlands: Kluwer Academic Publishers.

Jezequel, J. M., Hussmann, H., & Cook, S. (Eds.). (2002). *UML 2002 – The Unified Modeling Language: Model Engineering, Concept and Tools: 5th International Conference*. Berlin, Germany: Springer-Verlag.

Jiang, L., Wu, Z., Feng, Q., Liu, J., & Zheng, Q. (2010). Efficient Deep Web Crawling Using Reinforcement Learning. In *Advances in Knowledge Discovery and Data Mining* (LNCS 6118, pp. 428-439).

Jin, L. J., Machiraju, V., & Sahai, A. (2002). *Analysis on service level agreement of web services* (Tech. Rep.). Palo Alto, CA: Hewlett Packard Laboratory. Retrieved from http://athena.union.edu/~hemmendd/Gradseminar/hpl.pdf

Jing, Y., & Jafarkhani, H. (2006). Distributed space-time coding in wireless relay networks. *IEEE Transactions on Wireless Communications, 5*(12), 3524–3536. doi:10.1109/TWC.2006.256975

Jing, Y., & Jafarkhani, H. (2007). Using orthogonal and quasi-orthogonal designs in wireless relay networks. *IEEE Transactions on Information Theory, 53*(11), 4106–4118. doi:10.1109/TIT.2007.907516

Jing, Y., & Jafarkhani, H. (2009). Single and multiple relay selection schemes and their achievable diversity orders. *IEEE Transactions on Wireless Communications, 8*(3), 1414–1423. doi:10.1109/TWC.2008.080109

Johnston, A. (2000). *Recent work on radiation effects in microelectronics at JPL*. Retrieved from http://rd49.web.cern.ch/RD49/RD49News/Allan_Johnston.pdf

Johnston, A. (2000). *Scaling and technology issues for soft error rates*. Retrieved from http://nepp.nasa.gov/docuploads/40D7D6C9-D5AA-40FC-829-DC2F6A71B02E9/Scal-00.pdf

Joseph, J. K., Ruanaidh, O., & Pun, T. (1998). Rotation, scale and translation invarient digital image watermarking. *Signal Processing, 66*(3), 303–317. doi:10.1016/S0165-1684(98)00012-7

Karapiperis, S., & Apostolou, D. (2006). Consensus building in collaborative ontology engineering process. *Journal of Universal Knowledge Management, 1*(3), 199–216.

Kazhamiakin, R., Benbernou, S., Baresi, L., Plebani, P. M., & Barai, O. (2010). Adaptation of service-based systems service research challenges and solutions for the future internet. In Papazoglou, M., Pohl, K., Parkin, M., & Metzger, A. (Eds.), *Service research challenges and solutions for the future internet: S-cube - towards engineering, managing and adapting service-based systems*. Berlin, Germany: Springer-Verlag.

Kerrigan, M. (2005, June). The WSML editor plug-in to the web services modeling toolkit. In *Proceedings of the 2nd WSMO Implementation Workshop*, Innsbruck, Austria.

Kersten, G. E., Koszegi, S. T., & Vetschera, R. (2002). The effect of culture in anonymous negotiations: Experiment in four countries. In *Proceedings of the 35th Hawaii International Conference on System Sciences*.

Kersten, G. E., Kersten, M. A., & Rakowski, W. M. (2002). Software and culture: Beyond the internazionalization of the interface. *Journal of Global Information Management, 10*(4), 86–101. doi:10.4018/jgim.2002100105

Khan, M. U. (2010). *Unanticipated dynamic adaptation of mobile applications*. Unpublished doctoral dissertation, University of Kassel, Kassel, Germany.

Kiryakov, A., Popov, B., Terziev, I., Manov, D., & Ognyano, D. (2004). Semantic annotation, indexing, and retrieval. *Web Semantics: Science. Services and Agents on the World Wide Web, 2*(1), 49–79. doi:10.1016/j.websem.2004.07.005

Kolari, P., Finin, T., & Joshi, A. (2006). SVMs for the Blogosphere: Blog Identification and Splog Detection. In *Proceedings of the AAAI Spring Symposium on Computational Approaches to Analysing Weblogs.*

Kotis, K., Vouros, G. A., & Alonso, J. P. (2005). HCOME: A tool supported methodology for engineering living ontologies. In C. Bussler, V. Tannen, & I. Fundulaki (Eds.), *Proceedings of the Second International Workshop on Semantic Web and Databases* (LNCS 3372, pp. 155-166).

Krallinger, M., & Valencia, A. (2005). Text-mining and information-retrieval services for molecular biology. *Genome Biology, 6*(7), 224. doi:10.1186/gb-2005-6-7-224

Kratochvil, M., & McGibbon, B. (2003). *UML Xtra-Light: How to specify your software requirements*. Cambridge, UK: Cambridge University Press.

Ksalan, M., & Zionts, S. (2001). *Multiple criteria decision making in the new millennium*. Berlin, Germany: Springer-Verlag.

Kumar, S. (2006). *Foundations of Coverage in Wireless Sensor Networks*. Unpublished doctoral dissertation, The Ohio State University, Columbus, OH.

Kunder, D., & Hatzinakos, D. (2004). Toward robust logo watermarking using multiresolution image fusion principles. *IEEE Transactions on Multimedia, 6*(1), 185–198. doi:10.1109/TMM.2003.819747

Kutter, M., & Winkler, S. (2002). A vision-based masking model for spread-spectrum image watermarking. *IEEE Transactions on Image Processing, 11*(1), 16–25. doi:10.1109/83.977879

Kwak, K. J., Baryshnikov, Y. M., & Coffman, E. G. (2008). Cyclic cellular automata: a tool for self-organizing sleep scheduling in sensor networks. In *Proceedings of the 7th International Conference on Information Processing in Sensor Networks* (pp. 535-536).

Kwak, K. J., Baryshnikov, Y. M., & Coffman, E. G. (2008). Self-assembling sweep-and-sleep sensor systems. *ACM SIGMETRICS Performance Evaluation Review, 36*(2), 131–133. doi:10.1145/1453175.1453207

Kwee, A. T., Tsai, F. S., & Tang, W. (2009). Sentence-level Novelty Detection in English and Malay. In *Advances in Knowledge Discovery and Data Mining* (LNCS 5476, pp. 40-51).

Kwee, A. T., & Tsai, F. S. (2009). Mobile Novelty Mining. *International Journal of Advanced Pervasive and Ubiquitous Computing, 1*(4), 43–68. doi:10.4018/japuc.2009100104

LaMarca, A., Chawathe, Y., Consolvo, S., Hightower, J., Smith, I., Scott, J., et al. (2005). Place Lab: device positioning using radio beacons in the wild. In *Proceedings of the 3rd International Conference on Pervasive Computing* (pp. 116–133).

Laneman, J. N., & Wornell, G. W. (2003). Distributed space-time-coded protocols for exploiting cooperative diversity in wireless networks. *IEEE Transactions on Information Theory, 49*(10), 2415–2425. doi:10.1109/TIT.2003.817829

Lee, C. H., & Lee, Y. K. (1999). An adaptive digital image watermarking technique for copyright protection. *IEEE Transactions on Consumer Electronics, 45*(4), 1005–1015. doi:10.1109/30.809176

Lemelson, H., King, T., & Effelsberg, W. (2008). A study on user acceptance of error visualization techniques. In *Proceedings of the International Workshop on Human Control of Ubiquitous Systems*.

Lemelson, H., Kjærgaard, M. B., Hansen, R., & King, T. (2009). Error estimation for indoor 802.11 location fingerprinting. In *Proceedings of the 4th International Symposium on Location and Context Awareness* (pp. 138–155).

Levene, M. (2005). *An introduction to search engine and navigation*. Upper Saddle River, NJ: Pearson Education.

Lewis, G., Morris, E., O'Brien, L., Smith, D., & Wrage, L. (2005). *SMART: The service-oriented migration and reuse technique*. Retrieved from http://citeseerx.ist.psu.edu/viewdoc/download?doi=10.1.1.87.6762-&rep=rep1&type=pdf

Lewis, G., & Wrage, L. (2005). *Model problems in technologies for interoperability: Model-driven architecture (Tech. Rep.)*. Pittsburgh, PA: Software Engineering Institute.

Li, D., Finin, T., Joshi, A., Pan, R., Cost, R., Peng, Y., et al. (2004). Swoogle: A search and metadata engine for the semantic web. In *Proceedings of the Thirteenth ACM Conference on Information and Knowledge Management* (pp. 652-659).

Liakopoulos, A., Zafeiropoulos, A., Polyrakis, A., Grammatikou, M., Gonzalez, J. M., Wódczak, M., & Chaparadza, R. (2008). *Monitoring Issues for Autonomic Networks: The EFIPSANS Vision*. Paper presented at European Workshop on Mechanisms for the Future Internet.

Liang, H., Tsai, F. S., & Kwee, A. T. (2009). *Detecting Novel Business Blogs*. Paper presented at the 7th International Conference on Information, Communications, and Signal Processing (ICICS).

Lin, Y.-R., Sundaram, H., Chi, Y., Tatemura, J., & Tseng, B. L. (2007). Splog detection using self-similarity analysis on blog temporal dynamics. In *AIRWeb '07: Proceedings of the 3rd International Workshop on Adversarial Information Retrieval on the Web* (pp. 1-8).

Liu, J., Wu, Z., Jiang, L., Zheng, Q., & Liu, X. (2009). Crawling Deep Web Content through Query Forms. In *Proceedings of the 5th International Conference on Web Information Systems and Technologies*, Lisbon, Portugal (pp. 634-642).

Liu, Y., Niculescu-Mizil, A., & Gryc, W. (2009). Topic-link LDA: joint models of topic and author community. In *ICML '09: Proceedings of the 26th Annual International Conference on Machine Learning* (pp. 665-672).

Li, Y. (2009). Distributed coding for cooperative wireless networks: An overview and recent advances. *IEEE Communications Magazine, 47*(8), 71–77. doi:10.1109/MCOM.2009.5181895

Li, Z., & Xia, X. G. (2007). A simple Alamouti space–time transmission scheme for asynchronous cooperative systems. *IEEE Signal Processing Letters, 14*(11), 804–807. doi:10.1109/LSP.2007.900224

Long, X., & Suel, T. (2003, September 9-12). Optimized query execution in large search engines with global page ordering. In *Proceedings of the 29th International Conference on Very Large Databases*, Berlin, Germany (Vol. 29).

Looker, N., Munro, M., & Xu, J. (2004). Simulating errors in web services. *International Journal of Simulation, 5*(5), 29–37.

Lu, J., Wang, Y., Liang, J., Chen, J., & Liu, J. (2008). An Approach to Deep Web Crawling by Sampling. In *Proceedings of the IEEE/WIC/ACM Web Intelligence Conference*, Sydney, NSW, Australia (pp. 718-724).

Lu, C. S., & Liao, H. Y. (2001). Multipurpose watermarking for image authentication and protection. *IEEE Transactions on Image Processing, 10*(10), 1579–1592. doi:10.1109/83.951542

Lu, C. S., Liao, H. Y., & Kutter, M. (2002). Denoising and copy attacks resilient watermarking by exploiting prior knowledge at detector. *IEEE Transactions on Image Processing, 11*(3), 280–292. doi:10.1109/83.988961

Lucene. (2011). *What is Apache Lucene?* Retrieved from http://lucene.apache.org/#What+Is+Apache+Lucene%3F

Macdonald, C., Ounis, I., & Soboroff, I. (2007). Overview of the TREC-2007 Blog Track. In *Proceedings of the 16th Text Retrieval Conference (TREC 2007).*

Madaan, R., Dixit, A., Sharma, A. K., & Bhatia, K. K. (2010). A Framework for Incremental Hidden Web Crawler. *International Journal on Computer Science and Engineering, 2*(3), 753–758.

Madhavan, J., Ko, D., Kot, L., Ganapathy, V., Rasmussen, A., & Halevy, A. (2008). Google's Deep-Web Crawl. In *Proceedings of VLDB, 2008,* 1241–1252.

Magableh, B., & Barrett, S. (2009). Pcoms: A component model for building context-dependent applications. In *Proceedings of the 1st International Conference on Adaptive and Self-adaptive Systems and Applications,* Athens, Greece (pp. 44–48).

Magableh, B., & Barrett, S. (2011a, September). Adaptive context oriented component-based application middleware (coca-middleware). In *Proceedings of the 8th International Conference on Ubiquitous Intelligence and Computing (UIC 2011),* Banff, AB, Canada (LNCS 6905, pp. 137-151).

Magableh, B., & Barrett, S. (2011b, May). Objective-cop: Objective context oriented programming. In *Proceedings of the 1st International Conference on Information and Communication Systems,* Irbid, Jordan (pp. 45–49).

Magableh, B., & Barrett, S. (2011c, June). Self-adaptive application for indoor wayfinding for individuals with cognitive impairments. In *Proceedings of the 24th International Symposium on Computer-based Medical Systems,* Bristol, UK (pp. 1 -6).

Mahmood, Z. (2007). Service oriented architecture: Tools and technologies. In *Proceedings of the 11th WSEAS International Conference on Computers,* Crete Island, Greece.

Mani, A., & Nagarajan, A. (2002). *Understanding quality of services for web services.* India: IBM. Retrieved from http://www.ibm.com/developerworks/library/ws-quality.html

Manola, F., & Miller, E. (2004). *RDF primer.* Retrieved from http://www.w3.org/TR/rdf-primer/

Marcus, A., & Gould, E. W. (2000). Cultural dimensions and global Web user-interface design: What? So what? Now what? In *Proceedings of the 6th Conference on Human Factors and the Web,* Austin, TX (pp.1-15).

Martin, J., Arsanjani, A., Tarr, P., & Hailpern, B. (2003). Web services: Promises and compromises. *Queue, 1*(1), 48–58. doi:10.1145/637958.639315

Massink, M., & Faconti, G. (2002). A reference framework for continuous interaction. *Universal Access in the Information Society, 1*(4), 237–251. doi:10.1007/s10209-002-0027-5

Mathias, G., & Jean-Pierre, C. (2001). Toward a structured information retrieval system on the web: Automatic structure extraction of web pages. In *Proceedings of the International Workshop on Web Dynamics,* London, UK.

Mathijssen, S. (2005). A fair model for quality of web services. In *Proceedings of the 3rd Twente Student Conference on IT,* Twente, The Netherlands.

McGovern, J., Tyagi, S., Stevens, M. E., & Mathew, S. (2003). *Java web services architecture.* San Francisco, CA: Morgan Kaufmann.

McIlraith, S. A., Son, T. C., & Zeng, H. (2001). Semantic web services. *IEEE Intelligent Systems, 16*(2), 46–53. doi:10.1109/5254.920599

Medjahed, B., Bouguettaya, A., & Elmagarmid, A. K. (2003). Composing web services on the semantic web. *Very Large Data Bases Journal, 12*(4), 333–351. doi:10.1007/s00778-003-0101-5

Melnik, S., Raghavan, S., Yang, B., & Garcia-Molina, H. (2000, May 2-5). Building a distributed full-text index for the Web. In *Proceedings of the 10th International World Wide Web Conference,* Hong-Kong.

Mena, B. H., Zaki, T. F., & Tarek, F. G. (2006). A hybrid feature selection approach for Arabic documents classification. *Egyptian Computer Science Journal, 28*(4), 1–7.

Menasce, D. A., Ruan, H., & Gomaa, H. (2007). QoS management in service-oriented architectures. *Performance Evaluation, 64*(7-8), 646–663. doi:10.1016/j.peva.2006.10.001

Michael, C., Jaeger, G., Rojec, G., & Gero, M. (2004). QoS aggregation for web service composition using workflow patterns. In *Proceeding of the 8th International Enterprise Distributed Object Computing Conference* (pp. 149-159).

Mietzner, J., Schober, R., Lampe, L., Gerstacker, W. H., & Hoeher, P. A. (2009). Multiple-antenna techniques for wireless communications - a comprehensive literature survey. *IEEE Communications Surveys and Tutorials, 11*(2), 87–103. doi:10.1109/SURV.2009.090207

Miguel, M. A. (2003). General framework for the description of QoS in UML. In *Proceedings of the 6th IEEE International Symposium on Object-Oriented Real-Time Distributed Computing* (pp. 61-68). Washington, DC: IEEE Computer Society.

Milanovic, N., & Malek, M. (2004). Current solutions for web service composition. *IEEE Internet Computing, 8*(6), 51–59. doi:10.1109/MIC.2004.58

Mitchell, T. (1997). *Machine learning*. New York, NY: McGraw-Hill.

Moffat, A., & Culpepper, J. S. (2007, December). Hybrid bitvector index compression. In *Proceedings of the 12th Australasian Document Computing Symposium*, Melbourne, Australia (pp. 25-31).

Mohammad, A. A., Alhaj, A., & Shaltaf, S. (2008). An improved SVD-based watermarking scheme for protecting rightful ownership. *Signal Processing, 88*, 2158–2180. doi:10.1016/j.sigpro.2008.02.015

Moran, M., Zaremba, M., Mocan, A., & Bussler, C. (2004, September). Using wsmx to bind requester and provider at runtime when executing semantic web services. In *Proceedings of the 1st WSMO Implementation Workshop*, Frankfurt, Germany.

Muharemagic, E., & Furht, B. (2006). Survey of watermarking techniques and applications. *Multimedia Watermarking Techniques and Applications*, 91.

Müller, H. M., Kenny, E. E., & Sternberg, P. W. (2004). Textpresso: An ontology-based information retrieval and extraction system for biological literature. *Public Library of Science Biology, 2*(11), 309.

Muruganathan, S. D., Ma, D. C., Bhasin, R. I., & Fapojuwo, A. O. (2005). A centralized energy-efficient routing protocol for wireless sensor networks. *IEEE Communications Magazine, 43*(3), S8–S13. doi:10.1109/MCOM.2005.1404592

Myoung, J., Ouk-Kim, C., & Hyun, I. (2008). Quality-of-service oriented web service composition algorithm and planning. *Journal of Systems and Software, 81*(11), 2079–2090. doi:10.1016/j.jss.2008.04.044

Nagasaka, T. (2006). New Mode of Risk Governance Enhanced by an E-community Platform. In *A Better Integrated Management of Disaster Risks toward Resilient Society to Emerging Disaster Risks in Mega-Cities* (pp. 89-107).

Newcomer, E. (2002). *Understanding web services: XML, WSDL, SOAP, and UDDI*. Reading, MA: Addison-Wesley.

Ng, K. W., Tsai, F. S., & Goh, K. C. (2007). Novelty Detection for Text Documents Using Named Entity Recognition. In *Proceedings of the 2007 6th International Conference on Information, Communications and Signal Processing* (pp. 1-5).

Nisbett, R. E., Peng, K., Choi, I., & Norenzayan, A. (2001). Culture and systems of thought: Holistic versus analytic cognition. *Psychological Review, 108*(2), 291–309. doi:10.1037/0033-295X.108.2.291

Niu, W., & Kay, J. (2008). Location conflict resolution with an ontology. In *Proceedings of the 6th International Conference on Pervasive Computing* (pp. 162–179).

Novak, J., Cuel, R., Sarini, M., & Wurst, M. (2004). A tool for supporting knowledge creation and exchange in knowledge intensive organisations. In *Proceedings of the I-KNOW Conference*, Graz, Austria (pp. 311-319).

Ntoulas, A., Zerfos, P., & Cho, J. (2005). Downloading Textual Hidden Web Content through Keyword Queries. In *Proceedings of JCDL* (pp. 101-109).

Nutch. (2011). *About Nutch*. Retrieved from http://nutch.apache.org/about.html

O'Sullivan, J., Edmond, D., & Hofstede, A. T. (2002). What's in a service? *Distributed and Parallel Databases, 12*(23), 117–133. doi:10.1023/A:1016547000822

Object Management Group (OMG). (2004). *Enterprise collaboration architecture (ECA) specification.* Retrieved from http://www.omg.org/

OMG. (2004). *UML profile for modeling quality of service and fault tolerance characteristics and mechanisms* (Tech. Rep. No. ptc/04-09-012). Retrieved from http://www.omg.org/docs/ptc/04-09-01.pdf

OMG. (2006). *UML TM profile for modeling quality of service and fault tolerance characteristics and mechanisms, OMG available specification, version 1.0.* Retrieved from http://www.omg.org/docs/formal/06-05-02.pdf

OMG. (2008). *UMLTM profile for modeling quality of service and fault tolerance characteristics and mechanisms specification, version 1.1.* Retrieved from http://www.omg.org/docs/formal/08-04-08.pdf

OMG. (2009). *Unified modeling language.* Retrieved from http://www.uml.org/#UMLProfiles

Ong, C. L., Kwee, A. T., & Tsai, F. S. (2009). *Database Optimization for Novelty Detection.* Paper presented at the 7th International Conference on Information, Communications, and Signal Processing (ICICS).

Opperman, L., Broll, G., Capra, M., & Benford, S. (2006). Extending authorizing tools for location-aware applications with an infrastructure visualization layer. In *Proceedings of the 8th International Conference on Ubiquitous Computing* (pp. 52–68).

Ounis, I., de Rijke, M., Macdonald, C., Mishne, G. A., & Soboroff, I. (2006). Overview of the TREC-2006 Blog track. In *Proceedings of TREC 2006: Working Notes* (pp. 15-27).

Ouzzani, M. (2003). *Efficient delivery of web services* (Unpublished doctoral dissertation). Virginia Polytechnic Institute and State University, Blacksburg, VA. Retrieved August 26, 2008, from http://208.22.18.79/~mourad/mourad.ouzzani.pdf

Pabst, R., Walke, B., Schultz, D. C., Herhold, P., Yanikomeroglu, H., & Mukherjee, S. (2004). Relay-Based Deployment Concepts for Wireless and Mobile Broadband Radio. *IEEE Communications Magazine, 42*(9), 80–89. doi:10.1109/MCOM.2004.1336724

Pallickara, S., Fox, G., Aktas, M. S., Gadgil, H., Yildiz, B., & Oh, S. …Yemme, D. (2006). *A retrospective on the development of web service specifications.* Bloomington, IN: Community Grids Lab, Indiana University. Retrieved from http://www.naradabrokering.org/papers/CGL-WebServices-Chapter.pdf

Paolucci, M., Kawamura, T., Payne, T. R., & Sycara, K. P. (2002). Importing the semantic web in UDDI. *Revised Papers from the International Workshop on Web Services, E-Business, and the Semantic Web, 2512,* 225-236.

Papazoglou, M. P., & Kratz, B. (2006). A business-aware web services transaction model. In A. Dan & W. Lamersdorf (Eds.), *Proceedings of the 4th International Conference on Service-Oriented Computing* (LNCS 4294, pp. 352-364).

Papazoglou, M. P. (2008). *Web services: Principles and technology.* Upper Saddle River, NJ: Prentice Hall.

Papazoglou, M. P., Traverso, P., Dustdar, S., & Leymann, F. (2008). Service-oriented computing: A research roadmap. *International Journal of Cooperative Information Systems, 17*(2), 223–255. doi:10.1142/S0218843008001816

Paspallis, N. (2009). *Middleware-based development of context-aware applications with reusable components.* Unpublished doctoral dissertation, University of Cyprus, Nicosia, Cyprus.

Patashnik, O. (1988). *Bibtexing.* Retrieved from http://ftp.ntua.gr/mirror/ctan/biblio/bibtex/contrib/doc/btxdoc.pdf

Patel, S. N., Kientz, J. A., & Gupta, S. (2010). Studying the use and utility of an indoor location tracking system for non-experts. In *Proceedings of the 8th International Conference on Pervasive Computing* (pp. 228–245).

Peisu, X., Ke, T., & Qinzhen, H. (2008). A Framework of Deep Web Crawler. In *Proceedings of the 27th Chinese Control Conference,* Kunming, China.

Pemmaraju, S. V., & Pirwani, I. A. (2006). Energy conservation in wireless sensor networks via domatic partitions. In *Proceedings of the 7th ACM International Symposium on Mobile Ad hoc Networking and Computing.*

Perez, A. G., & Benjamins, V. R. (1999). Overview of knowledge sharing and reuse components: ontologies and problem solving methods. In *Proceedings of the IJCAI Workshop on Ontologies and Problem Solving Methods*, Stockholm, Sweden (pp. 1-15).

Pfeil, U., Zaphiris, P., & Ang, C. S. (2006). Cultural differences in collaborative authoring of Wikipedia. *Journal of Computer-Mediated Communication, 12*(1), 88–113. doi:10.1111/j.1083-6101.2006.00316.x

Pinto, H. S., Staab, S., & Tempich, C. (2004). DILIGENT: Towards a fine-grained methodology for distributed, loosely-controlled and evolving engineering of ontologies. In *Proceedings of the 16th European Conference on Artificial Intelligence*, Valencia, Spain (pp. 393-397).

Platt, J. C. (1998). *Sequential minimal optimization: A fast algorithm for training support vector machine* (Tech. Rep. No. MST-TR-98-14). Cambridge, UK: Microsoft Research.

Podilchuk, C. I., & Delp, E. J. (2001). Digital watermarking: Algorithms and applications. *Signal Processing Magazine, 18*(4), 33–46. doi:10.1109/79.939835

Pohst, M. (1981). On the computation of lattice vectors of minimal length, successive minima and reduced basis with applications. *ACM SIGSAM Bulletin, 15*(1), 37–44. doi:10.1145/1089242.1089247

Prud'hommeaux, E., & Seaborne, A. (2008). *SPARQL query language for RDF*. Retrieved from http://www.w3.org/TR/rdf-sparql-query/

Raghavan, S., & Garcia-Molina, H. (2001). Crawling the hidden Web. In *Proceedings of the 27th International Conference on Very Large Data Bases,* Rome, Italy.

Ranganathan, A., Al-Muhtadi, J., Chetan, S., Campbell, R., & Mickunas, M. D. (2004). MiddleWhere: a middleware for location-awareness in ubiquitous computing applications. In *Proceedings of the 5th International Conference on Middleware* (pp. 397–416).

Ran, S. (2003). A model for web services discovery with QoS. *ACM SIGecom Exchanges, 4*(1), 1–10. doi:10.1145/844357.844360

Rantanen, H. (2007). Mapping and managing local knowledge in urban planning. In *Proceedings of the International Conference on Sustainable Urban Areas (ENHR 2007)*. Retrieved from http://www.enhr2007rotterdam.nl/documents/W21_paper_Rantanen.pdf

Rebholz-Schuhmann, D., Arregui, M., Gaudan, S., Kirsch, H., & Jimeno, A. (2008). Text processing through Web services: Calling Whatizit. *Bioinformatics (Oxford, England), 24*(2), 296–298. doi:10.1093/bioinformatics/btm557

Rebholz-Schuhmann, D., Kirsch, H., Arregui, M., Gaudan, S., Riethoven, M., & Stoehr, P. (2007). EBIMed—text crunching to gather facts for proteins from Medline. *Bioinformatics (Oxford, England), 23*(2), 237–244. doi:10.1093/bioinformatics/btl302

Reilly, D., Dearman, D., Ha, V., Smith, I., & Inkpen, K. (2006). "Need to know": examining information need in location discourse. In *Proceedings of the 4th International Conference on Pervasive Computing* (pp. 33–49).

Rocha, C., Schwabe, D., & Aragao, M. P. (2004). A hybrid approach for searching in the semantic web. In *Proceedings of the 13th International Conference on World Wide Web* (pp. 374-383).

Rogati, M., & Yang, Y. (2002). High-performing feature selection for text classification. In *Proceedings of the Eleventh International Conference on Information and Knowledge Management* (pp. 659-661).

Romer, P. M. (1987). Growth based on increasing returns due to specialization. *American Economic Association, 77*(2), 56–62.

Rosen-Zvi, M., Griffiths, T., Steyvers, M., & Smyth, P. (2004). The author-topic model for authors and documents. In *AUAI '04: Proceedings of the 20th Conference on Uncertainty in Artificial Intelligence* (pp. 487-494).

Rumbaugh, J., Jacobson, I., & Booch, G. (2005). *The unified modeling language reference manual* (2nd ed.). Boston, MA: Pearson Education.

Rzhetsky, A., Iossifov, I., Koike, T., Krauthammer, M., Kra, P. B., & Morris, M. (2003). GeneWays: A system for extracting, analyzing, visualizing, and integrating molecular pathway data. *Journal of Biomedical Informatics*, *37*(1), 43–53. doi:10.1016/j.jbi.2003.10.001

Sahai, A., Machiraju, V., Sayal, M., Jin, L. J., & Casati, F. (2002). *Automated SLA monitoring for web services*. Palo Alto, CA: HP Laboratories. Retrieved from http://www.hwswworld.com/downloads/9_13_05_a_pdfs/HPL-2002-191.pdf

Said, D. A., Wanas, N. M., Darwish, N. M., & Hegazy, N. H. (2009). A study of text preprocessing tools for Arabic text categorization. In *Proceedings of the Second International Conference on Arabic Language* (pp. 230-236).

Sakaki, T., Okazaki, M., & Matsuo, Y. (2010). Earthquake shakes Twitter users: real-time event detection by social sensors. In *Proceedings of the 19th International Conference on the World Wide Web* (pp. 851-860).

Sawaf, H., Zaplo, J., & Ney, H. (2001). Statistical classification methods for Arabic news articles. In *Proceedings of the ACL/EACL Workshop on Arabic Language Processing: Status and Prospects*, Toulouse, France.

Schein, E. H. (1999). *The corporate culture survival guide: Sense and nonsense about culture*. San Francisco, CA: Jossey-Bass.

Schmit, B. A., & Dustdar, S. (2005). Model-driven development of web service transactions. *International Journal of Enterprise Modeling and Information Systems*, *1*(1), 46–60.

Seager, W., & Stanton Fraser, D. (2007). Comparing physical, automatic and manual map rotation for pedestrian navigation. In *Proceedings of the 25th Conference on Human Factors in Computing Systems* (pp. 767–776).

Sharma, D. K., & Sharma, A. K. (2009). Query Intensive Interface Information Extraction Protocol for Deep Web. In *Proceedings of the IEEE International Conference on Intelligent Agent & Multi-Agent Systems* (pp. 1-5).

Sharma, D. K., & Sharma, A. K. (2010). Deep Web Information Retrieval Process: A Technical Survey. *International Journal of Information Technology and Web Engineering*, *5*(1), 1–21. doi:10.4018/jitwe.2010010101

Sheng, Q. Z., & Benatallah, B. (2005). ContextUML: A UML-based modeling language for model driven development of context-aware web services. In *Proceedings of the International Conference on Mobile Business* (pp. 206-212). Washington, DC: IEEE Computer Society.

Sheth, A., Bertram, C., Avant, D., Hammond, B., Kochut, K., & Warke, Y. (2002). Managing semantic content for the web. *IEEE Internet Computing*, *6*(4), 80–87. doi:10.1109/MIC.2002.1020330

Shin, K., Abraham, A., & Han, S. Y. (2006). Self-organizing sensors by minimization of cluster heads using intelligent clustering. In *Proceedings of the Computational Science and Its Applications (ICCSA) Conference, Workshop on Ubiquitous Web Systems and Intelligence* (LNCS 3983, pp. 40-49).

Silver, G. A., Maduko, A., Jafri, R., Miller, J. A., & Sheth, A. P. (2003). Modeling and simulation of quality of service for composite web services. In *Proceedings of the 7th World Multiconference on Systemics* (pp. 420-425).

Sivaradje, G., Nakkeeran, R., & Dananjayan, P. (2006). A Prediction-Based Flexible channel Assignment in Wireless Networks Using Road Topology Information. *Journal of Information Technology and Web Engineering*, *1*(4), 37–48. doi:10.4018/jitwe.2006100103

Sivashanmugam, K., Miller, J. A., Sheth, A. P., & Verma, K. (2005). Framework for semantic web process composition. *International Journal of Electronic Commerce*, *9*(2), 71–106.

Soderland, S., Fisher, D., Aseltine, J., & Lehnert, W. (1995). CRYSTAL: Inducing a conceptual dictionary. In *Proceedings of the 14th International Joint Conference on Artificial Intelligence* (pp. 1314-1319).

Soderland, S. (1999). Learning information extraction rules for semi-structured and free text. *Machine Learning*, *34*, 233–272. doi:10.1023/A:1007562322031

Solachidis, V., & Pitas, I. (2001). Circularly symmetric watermark embedding in 2-D DFT domain. *IEEE Transactions on Image Processing*, *10*(11), 1741–1753. doi:10.1109/83.967401

Solachidis, V., & Pitas, I. (2004). Watermarking polygonal lines using fourier descriptors. *Computer Graphics and Applications*, *24*(3), 44–51. doi:10.1109/MCG.2004.1297010

Solr. (2011). *What is Solr?* Retrieved from http://lucene.apache.org/solr/#intro

Sparx Systems. (2010). *Enterprise architect 8.* Retrieved December 1, 2010, from http://www.sparxsystems.com.au/

Srirama, S. N., & Jarke, M. (2009). Mobile hosts in enterprise service integration. *International Journal of Web Engineering and Technology*, *5*(2), 187–213. doi:10.1504/IJWET.2009.028620

Stevens, M., & D'hondt, E. (2010). Crowdsourcing of Pollution Data using Smartphones. In *Proceedings of the Workshop on Ubiquitous Crowdsourcing.* Retrieved from http://soft.vub.ac.be/Publications/2010/vub-tr-soft-10-15.pdf

Stevenson, G., Ye, J., Dobson, S., & Nixon, P. (2010). LOC8: A location model and extensible framework for programming with location. *IEEE Pervasive Computing / IEEE Computer Society [and] IEEE Communications Society*, *9*(1), 28–37. doi:10.1109/MPRV.2009.90

Steyvers, M., Smyth, P., Rosen-Zvi, M., & Griffiths, T. (2004). Probabilistic author-topic models for information discovery. In *KDD '04: Proceedings of the 10th ACM SIGKDD International Conference on Knowledge Discovery and Data Mining* (pp. 306-315).

Stollberg, M., Shafiq, O., Domingue, J., & Cabral, L. (2006, September). Semantic web services: State of affairs. In *Proceedings of the First Asian Semantic Web Conference*, Beijing, China.

Strobbe, M., Van Laere, O., Ongenae, F., Dauwe, S., Dhoedt, B., & De Turck, F., Demeester, P., & Luyten, K (in press). Integrating location and context information for novel personalised applications. *IEEE Pervasive Computing / IEEE Computer Society [and] IEEE Communications Society*.

Sun, Y., Gong, B., Meng, X., Lin, Z., & Bertino, E. (2009). Specification and enforcement of flexible security policy for active cooperation. *Information Sciences: An International Journal*, *179*(15), 2629–2642.

Sycara, K., Paolucci, M., Ankolekar, A., & Srinivasan, N. (2003). Automated discovery, interaction and composition of semantic web services. *Web Semantics*, *1*(1), 27–46. doi:10.1016/j.websem.2003.07.002

Taher, L., Basha, R., & Khatib, H. E. (2005). Establishing association between QoS properties in service oriented architecture. In *Proceedings of the International Conference on Next Generation Web Services Practices* (pp. 6-11). Washington, DC: IEEE Computer Society.

Tang, W., & Tsai, F. S. (2009). Threshold Setting and Performance Monitoring for Novel Text Mining. In *Proceedings in Applied Mathematics: 9th SIAM International Conference on Data Mining 2009* (Vol. 3, pp. 1310-1319).

Tang, W., Tsai, F. S., & Chen, L. (2010). Blended Metrics for Novel Sentence Mining. *Expert Systems with Applications*, *37*(7), 5172–5177. doi:10.1016/j.eswa.2009.12.075

Tarokh, V., Jafarkhani, H., & Calderbank, A. R. (1999). Space-time block codes from orthogonal designs. *IEEE Transactions on Information Theory*, *45*(5), 1456–1467. doi:10.1109/18.771146

Terashima, T., Sekizuka, H., & Sasaki, T. (2008). Developing a Collaborative Map Creation Support System by Multi-modal Information-gathering. In *Proceedings of 4th International Conference on Information and Automation for Sustainability* (pp. 179-183).

Toghuj, W. (2007). Program for modeling the detection and correction processes of multiple error using two dimensional iterated code. In *Proceedings of the 2nd International Conference on Modeling of Sustainable Regional Development* (Vol. 3, pp. 116-123). Nalchik, Russia: Russian Academy of Sciences.

Toghuj, W. (2006). *Software program and algorithm for correcting multi-error using two dimensional iterated code.* Moscow, Russia: Russian Federal Agency for Intellectual Property, Patents and Trademarks.

Topley, K. (2003). *Java web services in a nutshell.* Sebastopol, CA: O'Reilly.

Toppano, E. (2010). A communication-based model of ontology design and (re)use. In *Proceedings of the Intelligent Semantic Web Services and Applications Conference* (pp. 38-44).

Toppano, E., Roberto, V., Giuffrida, R., & Buora, G. B. (2008). Ontology engineering: Reuse and integration. *International Journal of Metadata. Semantics and Ontologies, 3*(3), 233–247. doi:10.1504/IJMSO.2008.023571

Trompenaars, F., & Hampden-Turner, C. (1997). *Riding the waves of culture: Understanding cultural diversity in business.* London, UK: Nicholas Brealey Publishing.

Tsai, F. S., & Chan, K. L. (2007). Detecting cyber security threats in weblogs using probabilistic models. In *Intelligence and Security Informatics* (LNCS 4430, pp. 46-57).

Tsai, F. S., & Chan, K. L. (2009). Blog Data Mining for Cyber Security Threats. In *Data Mining for Business Applications* (pp. 169-182).

Tsai, F. S., Chen, Y., & Chan, K. L. (2007). Probabilistic techniques for corporate blog mining. In *Emerging Technologies in Knowledge Discovery and Data Mining* (LNCS 4819, pp. 35-44).

Tsai, F. S. (2009). Network intrusion detection using association rules. *International Journal of Recent Trends in Engineering, 2*(1), 202–204.

Tsai, F. S., & Chan, K. L. (2010). Redundancy and novelty mining in the business blogosphere. *The Learning Organization, 17*(6), 490–499. doi:10.1108/09696471011082358

Tsai, F. S., & Chan, K. L. (2011). An Intelligent System for Sentence Retrieval and Novelty Mining. *International Journal of Knowledge Engineering and Data Mining, 1*(3), 235–253. doi:10.1504/IJKEDM.2011.037645

Tsai, F. S., Etoh, M., Xie, X., Lee, W.-C., & Yang, Q. (2010). Introduction to Mobile Information Retrieval. *IEEE Intelligent Systems, 25*(1), 11–15. doi:10.1109/MIS.2010.22

Tsai, F. S., Han, W., Xu, J., & Chua, H. C. (2009). Design and Development of a Mobile Peer-to-peer Social Networking Application. *Expert Systems with Applications, 36*(8), 11077–11087. doi:10.1016/j.eswa.2009.02.093

Tsai, F. S., Kwee, A. T., Tang, W., & Chan, K. L. (2010). Adaptable Services for Novelty Mining. *International Journal of Systems and Service-Oriented Engineering, 1*(2), 69–85. doi:10.4018/jssoe.2010040105

Tsai, F. S., Tang, W., & Chan, K. L. (2010). Evaluation of Metrics for Sentence-level Novelty Mining. *Information Sciences, 180*(12), 2359–2374. doi:10.1016/j.ins.2010.02.020

Tsuruoka, Y., Tsujii, J., & Ananiadou, S. (2008). FACTA: A text search engine for finding associated biomedical concepts. *Bioinformatics (Oxford, England), 24*(21), 2559–2560. doi:10.1093/bioinformatics/btn469

Tzeng, J., Hwang, W. L., & Chern, I. L. (2002). Enhancing image watermarking methods with/without reference images by optimization on second-order statistics. *IEEE Transactions on Image Processing, 11*(7), 771–782. doi:10.1109/TIP.2002.800895

Uysal, M. (Ed.). (2010). *Cooperative communications for improved wireless network transmission: Framework for virtual antenna array applications.* Hershey, PA: Information Science Reference.

Vanderhulst, G., Luyten, K., & Coninx, K. (2007). Middleware for ubiquitous service-oriented spaces on the web. In *Proceedings of the 21st International Conference on Advanced Information Networking and Applications Workshops* (pp. 1001–1006).

Varadarajan, S., & Chiueh, T. C. (1997). SASE: Implementation of a compressed text search engine. In *Proceedings of the USENIX Symposium on Internet Technologies and Systems on USENIX Symposium on Internet Technologies and Systems* (p. 23).

Varshavsky, A., & Patel, S. (2009). Location in ubiquitous computing. In Krumm, J. (Ed.), *Ubiquitous computing fundamentals* (pp. 285–320). Boca Raton, FL: Chapman and Hall/CRC.

Verbeek, P. (2006). Materializing morality: Design ethics and technological mediation. *Science, Technology & Human Values, 31*(3), 361–380. doi:10.1177/0162243905285847

Viterbo, E., & Hong, Y. (2007). Applications of the Golden Code. In *Proceedings of the Information Theory and Applications Workshop* (pp. 393–400).

Viterbo, E., & Boutros, J. (1999). A universal Lattice Code decoder for fading channel. *IEEE Transactions on Information Theory, 45*(5), 1639–1642. doi:10.1109/18.771234

Wagner, M., Reichle, R., Khan, M. U., & Geihs, K. (2011). *Software development method for adaptive applications in ubiquitous computing environments* (Tech. Rep.).

WanAbRahman. W. N. (2010). *UML QoS profile exploration for the specifications of a generic QoS metamodel for designing and developing good quality web services* (Unpublished doctoral dissertation). School of Computing, Science and Engineering, University of Salford, Salford, UK.

Wang, G., Chen, A., Wang, C., Fung, C., & Uczekaj, S. (2004). Integrated quality of service management in service-oriented enterprise architectures. In *Proceedings of the 8th IEEE International Enterprise Distributed Object Computing Conference* (pp. 21-32). Washington, DC: IEEE Computer Society.

Wang, H., Tran, T., & Liu, C. (2008). CE2: towards a large scale hybrid search engine with integrated ranking support. In *Proceedings of the International Conference on Information and Knowledge Management* (pp. 1323-1324).

Wang, Y., Zuo, W., Peng, T., & He, F. (2008). Domain-Specific Deep Web Sources Discovery. In *Proceedings of the Fourth International Conference on Natural Computation.*

Wang, Z., Bovic, A., Sheikh, H., & Simoncelli, E. (2004). Image quality assessment: From error visibility to structural similarity. *IEEE Transactions on Image Processing, 13*(4), 600–612. doi:10.1109/TIP.2003.819861

Wan-Kadir, W. M. N., & Loucopoulos, P. (2003). Relating evolving business rules to software design. *Journal of Systems Architecture, 50*(7).

Waters, T., & Evans, A. J. (2003). Tools for web-based GIS mapping of a "fuzzy" vernacular geography. In *Proceedings of the 7th International Conference on GeoComputation.*

Weller, S. (2002). *Web services qualification: A recommendation system and feedback mechanism for web services.* Retrieved from http://www.ibm.com/developerworks/Webservices/library/ws-qual/

White, J. J. D., & Roth, R. E. (2010). TwitterHitter: Geovisual Analytics for Harvesting Insight from Volunteered Geographic Information. In *Proceedings of the GIScience 2010 Doctoral Colloquium.* Retrieved from http://www.giscience2010.org/pdfs/paper_239.pdf

Wikipedia. (2011). *MapReduce.* Retrieved from http://en.wikipedia.org/wiki/MapReduce

Witten, I. H., & Frank, E. (2005). *Data mining: Practical machine learning tools and techniques* (2nd ed.). San Francisco, CA: Morgan Kaufmann.

Wódczak, M. (2006). *On Routing information Enhanced Algorithm for space-time coded Cooperative Transmission in wireless mobile networks.* Unpublished doctoral dissertation, Poznań University of Technology, Poznań, Poland.

Wódczak, M. (2007, July). *Extended REACT – Routing information Enhanced Algorithm for Cooperative Transmission.* Paper presented at the 16th IST Mobile & Wireless Communications Summit, Budapest, Hungary.

Wódczak, M. (2011). Autonomic cooperative networking for wireless green sensor systems. *International Journal of Sensor Networks, 10*(1-2), 83–93. doi:10.1504/IJSNET.2011.040906

Wódczak, M., Meriem, T. B., Chaparadza, R., Quinn, K., Lee, B., & Ciavaglia, L. (2011). Standardising a Reference Model and Autonomic Network Architectures for the Self-managing Future Internet. *IEEE Network Magazine, 25*(6), 50–56. doi:10.1109/MNET.2011.6085642

Wurtz, E. (2005). A cross-cultural analysis of websites from high-context cultures and low context cultures. *Journal of Computer-Mediated Communication, 11*(1), 274–299. doi:10.1111/j.1083-6101.2006.tb00313.x

Yan, H., Ding, S., & Suel, T. (2009, April 20-24). Inverted index compression and query processing with optimized document ordering. In *Proceedings of the 18th International Conference on World Wide Web*, Madrid, Spain.

Yao, H., & Wornell, G. W. (2003). Achieving the full MIMO diversity multiplexing frontier with ratation-based space-time codes. In *Proceedings of the Allerton Conference on Communication, Control, and Computing* (pp. 400–409).

Yee, K. Y., Tiong, A. W., Tsai, F. S., & Kanagasabai, R. (2009). OntoMobiLe: A Generic Ontology-centric Service-Oriented Architecture for Mobile Learning. In *Proceedings of the 2009 10th International Conference on Mobile Data Management (MDM) Workshop on Mobile Media Retrieval (MMR)* (pp. 631-636).

Yu, Q., Liu, X., Bouguettaya, A., & Medjahed, B. (2008). Deploying and managing web services: Issues, solutions and directions. *The International Journal on Very Large Data Bases, 17*(3), 537–572. doi:10.1007/s00778-006-0020-3

Zeng, L., Benatallah, B., Dumas, M., Kalagnanam, J., & Sheng, Q. Z. (2003). Quality driven web services composition. In *Proceedings of the 12th International Conference on World Wide Web*, Budapest, Hungary (pp. 411-421). New York, NY: ACM.

Zeng, L., Benatallah, B., Ngu, A. H. H., Dumas, M., Kalagnanam, J., & Chang, H. (2004). QoS-aware middleware for web services composition. *IEEE Transactions on Software Engineering, 30*(5).

Zeng, W., & Lio, B. (1999). A statistical watermark detection technique without using original images for resolving rightful ownership of digital images. *IEEE Transactions on Image Processing, 8*, 1534–1548. doi:10.1109/83.799882

Zhang, J., Long, X., & Suel, T. (2008, April 21-25). Performance of compressed inverted list caching in search engines. In *Proceeding of the 17th International Conference on the World Wide Web*, Beijing, China.

Zhang, L., Li, B. J., Yuan, T. T., Zhang, X., & Yang, D. C. (2007, September). Golden Code with low complexity sphere decoder. In *Proceedings of the IEEE International Symposium on Personal, Indoor and Mobile Radio Communications* (pp. 1–5).

Zhang, Y., & Tsai, F. S. (2009). Chinese Novelty Mining. In *EMNLP '09: Proceedings of the Conference on Empirical Methods in Natural Language Processing* (pp. 1561-1570).

Zhang, Y., & Tsai, F. S. (2009). Combining Named Entities and Tags for Novel Sentence Detection. In *ESAIR '09: Proceedings of the WSDM '09 Workshop on Exploiting Semantic Annotations in Information Retrieval* (pp. 30-34).

Zhang, Y., Tsai, F. S., & Kwee, A. T. (in press). Multilingual Sentence Categorization and Novelty Mining. *Information Processing & Management*.

Zhao, H. (2010). Study of Deep Web Query Interface Determining Technology. In *Proceedings of CESCE 2010* (Vol. 1, pp. 546-548).

Zhao, Y. (2004). Combining RDF and OWL with SOAP for semantic web services. In *Proceedings of the 3rd Annual Nordic Conference on Web Services*, Linköping, Sweden.

Zhou, C., Chia, L., & Lee, B. S. (2004). QoS-aware and federated enhancement for UDDI. *International Journal of Web Services Research, 1*(2), 58–85. doi:10.4018/jwsr.2004040104

Ziegler, J. F. (2000). *Review of accelerated testing of SRAMs*. Retrieved from http://www.srim.org/SER/SERTrends.htm

Zimmermann, O., Tomlinson, M., & Peuser, S. (2003). *Perspectives on web services: Applying SOAP, WSDL and UDDI to real-world projects*. Berlin, Germany: Springer-Verlag Berlin.

Zobel, J., & Moffat, A. (2006). Inverted files for text search engines. *ACM Computing Surveys, 38*(2), 1–56. doi:10.1145/1132956.1132959

About the Contributors

Ghazi I. Alkhatib is an assistant professor of software engineering at the College of Computer Science and Information Technology, Applied Science University (Amman, Jordan). In 1984, he obtained his Doctor of Business Administration from Mississippi State University in information systems with minors in computer science and accounting. Since then, he has been engaged in teaching, consulting, training and research in the area of computer information systems in the US and gulf countries. In addition to his research interests in databases and systems analysis and design, he has published several articles and presented many papers in regional and international conferences on software processes, knowledge management, e-business, Web services and agent software, workflow and portal/grid computing integration with Web services.

* * *

Mariam Abed Mostafa Abed is a Muslim Egyptian graduate of the German University in Cairo. She was born in Cairo in 1990 and received her BSc in Business Informatics with Honors on July 2010. She helped as a junior teaching assistant at the GUC during studying, and currently working as a graduate part timer teaching assistant at the GUC.

Petr Aksenov obtained his MSc degree in Applied Mathematics from Saint-Petersburg State University, Russia, and MSc degree in Computer Science from the University of Joensuu (now the University of Eastern Finland), Finland, in 2004. After his graduation, Petr spent some time working as a research engineer at the LG Electronics' Digital Appliance Research Laboratory located in Seoul, South Korea, and then as a software test analyst at a software outsourcing company located in Saint-Petersburg, Russia. Currently, Petr is a doctoral candidate within the Human Computer Interaction group at the Expertise centre for Digital Media (EDM), a research institute of Hasselt University in Belgium. His research interest falls within the area of location-awareness in ubiquitous computing. In particular, he investigates the modelling and presentation aspects of the multifaceted variability and limitations of location sensing viewed from a frequently moving user's perspective.

Hussein Al-Bahadili is an associate professor at Petra University, Jordan. He received his B.Sc degree in Engineering from University of Baghdad in 1986. He received his MSc and PhD degrees in Engineering from University of London in 1988 and 1991, respectively. His field of study was parallel computers. He is a visiting researcher at the Wireless Networks and Communications Centre (WNCC) at University of Brunel, UK. He has published many papers and book chapters in different fields of science and engineering in numerous leading scholarly and practitioner journals, and presented at leading world-level scholarly conferences. His research interests include parallel and distributed computing, wireless communications, computer networks, Web search engine, cryptography and network security, data compression, image processing, and artificial intelligence and expert systems.

Waseem AL-Romimah is an instructor at The University of Science and Technology, Yemen. He received His M.Sc in Computer Information Systems from the University of Jordan (Jordan) in 2010. He received his BSc degree in Computer Information Systems from Zarqa private University (Jordan) in 2005. His current research interests are in Natural language processing, information retrieval.

Saif Al-Saab received his BS degree in Engineering from Al-Mustansiriyah University (Baghdad-Iraq) in 1999. He received his MSc and PhD degrees in Computer Information System from the Arab Academy for Banking and Financial Sciences (Amman-Jordan) in 2003 and 2010, respectively. He carried out his PhD research on the development of a new compressed index-query Web search engine model. He has published a number of papers in different journals and conferences. His research interests include search engine technology, data compression, artificial intelligence, and expert systems.

Bassam Al-Shargabi is an assistance professor at Al-Isra University, Jordan. He received His PhD and M.Sc in Computer Information Systems from the Arab Academy for Banking & Financial Sciences (Jordan) in 2009 and 2004, respectively. He received his BSc degree in Computer Science from Applied Science University (Jordan) in 2003. His current research interests are in Natural language processing, information retrieval, and Service Oriented architecture.

Abdallah Al-Tahan Al-Nu'aimi is an assistant professor of information technology. He got his B.Sc. and M.Sc. from Jordanian University of Science and Technology in Communications and Electronics Engineering and his Ph.D. from Bradford University in Electronic Imaging and Media Communications. He recently works in Isra University in Computer Multimedia Systems department. He has published several papers and articles in international conferences and journals. His research interests include, but not limited to, watermarking, steganography, cryptography, digital rights management, security, face recognition, digital image enhancement, electronic imaging and data mining. He was a reviewer and a TPC member of several international conferences.

Linda Anticoli received the Doctor degree in computer science from the University of Udine, Italy, in 2010. She is currently afferent at the Department of Electrical Engineering, Mechanical Engineering and Management of the University of Udine, Italy, for the development of a routing protocol based on open source code. Her main research interests are in the area of semantic web and cognitive psychology, artificial intelligence (in particular knowledge representation, ontologies and conceptual graphs) and design for experience. At present she is also interested in cultural/value-based web design and multimedia.

Stephen Barrett is currently a lecturer at Distributed Systems Group, Trinity College Dublin, Ireland. His research centers on middleware support for adaptive computing. (with particular focus on model driven paradigms) and on large scale applications research (particularly in the context of web search, trust computation and peer and cloud computing).

Khadhir Bekki received the engineer degree in Computer Science at University of Oran, Algeria in 1996. He received the Master degrees in Computer Science in 2007, respectively from the Abdelhamid Ibn Badis University in Mostaganem, Algeria. He is currently an Assistant Professor of computer Science at Ibn Khaldoune University in Tiaret, Algeria, and he is a PhD student at the Science and Technology University USTO in Oran. His current research interests include Web services, Business process, security and verification.

Hafida Belbachir received her PHD in Computer Science at University of Oran, Algeria in 1990. Currently, she is a professor at the Science and Technology University USTO in Oran, where she heads the Database System Group in the LSSD Laboratory. Her research interests include Advanced DataBases, DataMining and Data Grid.

Jonathon A. Chambers studied for his PhD degree in signal processing at Peterhouse Cambridge University, Cambridge, U.K., and the Imperial College of Science, Technology and Medicine (Imperial College London), London, U.K. From 1991 to 1994, he was a Research Scientist with Schlumberger Cambridge Research Centre, Cambridge, U.K. In 1994, he returned to Imperial College London, as a Lecturer in signal processing and was promoted as a Reader (Associate Professor) in 1998. From 2001 to 2004, he was the Director of the Centre for Digital Signal Processing. From 2004 to 2007, he was a Cardiff Professorial Research Fellow with the School of Engineering, Cardiff University, Wales, U.K. In 2007, he joined the Department of Electronic and Electrical Engineering, Loughborough University, Loughborough, U.K., where he heads the Advanced Signal Processing Group and serves as an Associate Dean within the School of Electronic, Electrical and Systems Engineering.

Gaojie Chen received his BEc degree and his BEng degree from Northwest University in China (2006). He received his M.Sc degree (distinction) from Loughborough University while obtaining the Best Project Award. He is a Ph.D student in the Advanced Signal Processing Group in Loughborough University. He currently works in the area of multi-relay selection for cognitive relay networks.

Karin Coninx received a PhD in Computer Science in 1997 following a study into Human-Computer Interaction in immersive virtual environments. She is full professor at Hasselt University (Belgium). As group leader of the human-computer interaction group of the Expertise Centre for Digital Media at the Hasselt University, she is responsible for guidance of (PhD) researchers and for various research projects relating to (multimodal) interaction in virtual environments, rehabilitation robotics, mobile and context-sensitive systems, interactive work spaces, user-centered software engineering and the model-based realization of user interfaces. She has coordinated several Flemish and international project consortia. Karin Coninx is co-author of more than 250 international publications (about 80 journal publications or book chapters), co-organizer of workshops and a member of several program committees. Besides leading the HCI group in EDM, Karin Coninx takes management responsibility, e.g., as Vice-Dean of the Faculty of Sciences in Hasselt University.

Mohammad Ali H. Eljinini earned his PhD in Health Informatics from City University, London, UK in 2006. Currently he is an assistant professor in the Department of Computer Information Systems, Isra University. His research interests include e-health, Web/Text Mining, Ontology, Knowledge Aquisition, and the Semantic Web.

Hidekazu Fujioka received the BS degree in human and culture from Tokai University, Japan in 1989. He joined a network system engineering company in 1989. He established a corporation "Compass" in 1997. He is now a president of Compass. He is a representative of Morinosato 4th Block Regional Community in Atsugi city, Kanagawa prefecture. He is also a member of Atsugi City Self Governing Conference, a special member of the Atsugi Young Men's Association (the 36th President), and a president of Parents Teacher Association of Morinosato elementary school. His current business area is digital contents development, business consulting and Web design by information technologies.

Lu Ge received the B.Tech degree in Communication Engineering from Chongqing University of Post and Telecommunications, Chongqing, China, in 2008, and received her M.Sc degree in Electronic and Electrical Engineering from Loughborough University, U.K. in 2010. She is currently a Ph.D student in the Advanced Signal Processing Group in Loughborough University. From 2009 to 2010, she researched quasi-orthogonal space-time block coding in distributed MIMO system. Now she is researching the application of the golden code and multi-relay selection for wireless relay networks.

Yuichi Harada received the BS, MS, and PhD degrees in Applied Electronics at Tokyo Institute of Technology (Tokyo Tech) in 1986, 1988, and 1991, respectively. He was the fellow researcher at the Japan Society for the Promotion of Science from 1991 to 1993 and the guest researcher at Chalmers University of Technology, Gothenburg, Sweden from 1992 to 1994, where he engaged in superconducting single electronics. Then, he joined NTT Basic Research Laboratories (NTT BRL) from 1994 until now. He worked as the managing-director of NTT Europe BRL located in England, UK from 2004 to 2007. He is currently engaged in spintronics research projects. For the academic engagements, he takes tasks as the adjunct professor at Tokyo Tech and Chuo University. He is a regular member of IEEE, APS, Institute of Electronics, Information and Communication Engineers of Japan, and the Japan Society of Applied Physics.

Akira Hattori received the BS degree from Aichi University of Education, Japan in 1997. He also received his MS and PhD degrees from Nagoya University, Japan in 2000 and 2005. His doctor thesis was on development of distributed database of urban information. He is an associate professor of the Department of Information Media at Kanagawa Institute of Technology. His specialty is socio informatics and study of information systems. His current researches are web and mobile applications and ICT support environment for non-profit organizations. Especially, he is interested in web-based map system to collect, manage and share local information on the web among local citizens.

Haruo Hayami is a professor in the Department of Information Media at Kanagawa Institute of Technology. He researches and educates database and groupware. He has published journal or international conference papers of 100 or more, and 14 books. He received his BS and MS in applied physics from Nagoya University, in 1970 and 1972, respectively. He received a Doctor's degree in computer engineering from Nagoya Institute of Technology in 1993. He worked at NTT laboratories from 1972 to 1998 and moved to Kanagawa Institute of Technology from NTT at 1998. He received IPSJ 40th Anniversary Paper Award in 2000, WfMC Marvin L. Manheim Award in 2002, WfMC Fellow Award in 2004 and IPSJ Fellow Award in 2006.

Shigenori Ioroi received the BS degree in applied mathematics from Tokyo University of Science, Japan in 1993. He joined PFU in 1993 until 1994. He received the MS and PhD degrees in Information Science from Japan Advanced Institute of Technology in 1999. He joined Kanagawa Institute of Technology, Japan in 1999. He is now an associate professor of the Department of Information and Computer Sciences. His current research interests software engineering. He also has interests on development of new input method. He is a member of Information and Communication Engineers of Japan, Japan Society for Software Science and Technology, and Association for Computing Machinery (ACM).

Kris Luyten received both a MS in Knowledge Engineering and Computer Science from the transnational University Limburg, a joint university of Hasselt University (BE) and Maastricht University (NL), in 2000. He has a PhD degree in computer science from Hasselt University, Belgium and is a professor there since 2006. His main research interests are situated in Context-Aware User Interfaces, User Interface Description Languages, Model-Based and User-Centered Interface Development, Multi-touch Interaction, Mobile Guides, Ubiquitous Computing and Social and Collaborative Software. Kris served as a co-chair for the CHI 2008 Work-in-Progress track, full paper co-chair for EICS 2011 and was program chair for TAMODIA 2006. He teaches courses on software engineering, mobile and pervasive computing and information visualization.

Basel Magableh received his MS degree in computer science from New York Institute of Technology, NY, USA, in 2004. He is currently a PhD candidate at Distributed Systems Group, Trinity College Dublin, Ireland. His research focuses in integrating Model Driven Architecture with a component-based system to construct self-adaptive and context-aware applications. He is a full-time lecturer in Grafton College of Management Science, Dublin, Ireland. He was member of staff in the National Digital Research Center of Ireland from 2008- 2011.

Fekry Olayah is an assistance professor at Al-Isra University, Jordan. He received His PhD and M.Sc in Computer Information Systems from the Arab Academy for Banking & Financial Sciences (Jordan) in 2010 and 2005, respectively. He received his BSc degree in Computer Science from Applied Science mustansiriyah University (Iraq) in 2000. His current research interests are in Natural language processing, information retrieval.

Dilip Kumar Sharma is B.Sc, B.E. (CSE), M.Tech. (IT), M.Tech. (CSE) and is pursuing a PhD in Computer Engineering from Shobhit University, Meerut, UP, India. He is life member of CSI, IETE, ISTE, ISCA, SSI and member of CSTA, USA. He has attended 21 short term courses/workshops/seminars organized by various esteemed originations. He has published 23 research papers in International Journals/Conferences of repute and participated in 18 International/National conferences. Presently he is working as Reader in Department of Computer Science, IET at GLA University, Mathura, U.P. since March 2003 and he is also CSI Student branch Coordinator. His research interests are deep Web information retrieval, Digital Watermarking and Software Engineering. He has guided various projects and seminars undertaken by the students of undergraduate/postgraduate.

Masayuki Shinohara received the BS degree in information and computer sciences from Kanagawa Institute of Technology, Japan in 2009. His graduate thesis was on Web system composed with a database management system and cell phones that is currently used as "Real time lecture support system by using cell phone" in actual lectures. He is now a master's degree student in Kanagawa Institute of Technology, Japan. His current interests are e-Learning system, Web based information system and motion recognition by acceleration sensors. He is a student member of Institute of Electronics, Information and Communication Engineers of Japan.

Hiroshi Tanaka received the BS, MS and PhD degrees in precision engineering from Hokkaido University, Japan in 1983, 1985 and 1994 respectively. He joined NTT (Nippon Telegraph and Telephone Corporation) in 1985. He had engaged in the research and development of satellite communication system. He worked at NASDA (National Space Development Agency of Japan, present JAXA) from 1994 to 1997 for developing satellite systems. After returning to NTT, he worked for mobile satellite communication systems and ubiquitous systems using RFID. He joined Kanagawa Institute of Technology, Japan in 2006. He is now a professor of the Department of Information and Computer Sciences. His current research interests include motion recognition, indoor positioning and its application. He also has interests on Web based information systems by mobile devices. He is a senior member of AIAA, Institute of Electronics, Information and Communication Engineers of Japan, Information Processing Society of Japan.

Elio Toppano received the Doctor degree in electronic engineering from the University of Trieste, Italy, in 1981. He is currently an Associate Professor of Computer Science at the Department of Computer Science of the University of Udine, Italy. His research interests are in the area of ontology engineering and include knowledge modelling and integration, model based reasoning, design methodologies with application in e-learning and semantic web services. Also, he has carried out research activity in the fields of multimedia, human computer interaction and user experience design.

Flora S. Tsai is currently with Nanyang Technological University (NTU), Singapore. Dr. Tsai is a graduate of MIT, Columbia University, and NTU with degrees in Electrical Engineering and Computer Science. Dr. Tsai's current research focuses on developing intelligent techniques for data mining in text and social media, which aims to balance the technical significance and business concerns to create techniques that are useful in real-world scenarios. In particular, Dr. Tsai has pioneered research in blog data mining, novelty mining, and mobile information retrieval. Other research interests include software engineering, mobile application development, cyber security, electronic healthcare, and machine learning techniques for bioinformatics. Dr. Tsai was a recipient of the 2005 IBM Faculty Award, 2007 IBM Real-time Innovation Award, 2010 IBM Faculty Innovation Award, and has published over 50 international journal and conference papers. She is a senior member of IEEE and member of ACM.

Michał Wódczak is a Senior Research Scientist, Program Manager at Telcordia Technologies, Inc. Applied Research Center in Poland. Michał Wódczak obtained MSc and BSc degrees in Telecommunications in 2001, and PhD degree in Wireless Communications Systems in 2006, all from Poznan University of Technology, Poland. Currently, Michał Wódczak is Senior Member of IEEE (Communications Society) and he is involved in standardization activities as a Vice Chairman of the ETSI Industry Specification Group on Autonomic network engineering for self-managing Future Internet (ETSI ISG AFI), Sophia-Antipolis, France. Most recently he has become a Rapporteur of ETSI ISG AFI on Autonomic Ad hoc, Mesh and Sensor Networks. Besides, he has been involved in the area of autonomic networking in EU FP7 INFSO-ICT-215549 project EFIPSANS, as well as in the field of emergency communications in EU FP7 SEC-242411 project E-SPONDER, where he has been also appointed as Innovation Manager. Prior to that, initially, he was with a telecommunications company, Teletra in Poznan, where he was responsible for the technology for optical fibre termination, and then, he became a Research Expert at Poznan University of Technology where he worked full-time in EU FP6 IST-2003-507581 WINNER and EU FP6 IST-4-027756 WINNER II projects on the topic of cooperative transmission in 4G systems. Michał Wódczak was also the Editor-in-Chief of the NEWCOM Newsletter in EU FP6 IST-2004-507325 Network of Excellence in Wireless Communications NEWCOM. He has published over 40 scientific publications in journal, magazine and conference papers, as well as in book chapters. Moreover, his interests include linguistics and so in 2009 he completed Postgraduate studies in Translation and Interpreting at Adam Mickiewicz University in Poznan, Poland. Now he additionally serves as Board Member of the Association of Polish Translators and Interpreters, Warsaw, Poland.

Index

A

Access Point (AP) 264
adaptive character wordlength (ACW) 277
additive white Gaussian noise (AWGN) 253, 265
Algorithm for Cluster Establishment (ACE) 242
amplify-and-forward (AF) 250
Analytical Hierarchy Process (AHP) 88
analytic thought 4, 8-10
anticipation 194
Apache Software Foundation (ASF) 283
application programming interface (API) 38, 214, 224
Arabic 184-186, 189-190
ArchStudio 199-200, 209
artefacts 5
aspect-oriented programming (AOP) 175
attribute-value pairs 22-23
augmented reality browser (ARB) 194
author-date-topic (ADT) model 98, 101
author-link-topic (ALT) model 97-99, 101
author search 143
author topic (AT) model 97
automatic exceptions recognition 180
automatic query generation 108
autonomic networking 263, 271, 273

B

Based Station Controlled Dynamic Clustering Protocol (BCDCP) 242
Base Station (BS) 264-265
BibTeX 142-157
binary bit string 132
bit error rate (BER) 249, 254, 257-258
blog 96, 99, 104
blog distillation 96
broker 74-76, 78, 80-90, 92
business process 176
business rules 176

C

cell phones 211, 220
Centralized Low-Energy Adaptive Clustering Hierarchy (LEACH-C) 241
certifier 74-76, 84, 86, 92
CIQ test tool 275-276, 282
classifier 108, 185, 187
cluster 240
cluster-based routing 241
cluster-head 240
cluster network 242
code generation 200, 202
code striping 280, 284
codeword 227-228, 232, 234-235, 251-252, 277, 292
collaboration 9
composite service 75-79, 83, 86, 89
composition history 76, 82-85, 88
compressed index query (CIQ) 276
compressed text indexing 276
computation complexity 235-237
computation-independent model (CIM) 195
concatenated coding scheme 229
concern 178
conjugate operator 251
constraints 77
constructive cost model II (COCOMO II) 192-193
context entity 197
context-oriented component-based application model-driven architecture (COCA-MDA) 191, 195
contextuality 3, 13
control-flow 53
control loop 271-273
crawl frontier 117, 119-120
cross-layer 269
culture 2
Cumulative Distribution Function (CDF) 266